BECOMING
A WOMAN

BECOMING A WOMAN

AND OTHER ESSAYS IN 19TH AND 20TH CENTURY FEMINIST HISTORY

SALLY ALEXANDER

NEW YORK UNIVERSITY PRESS
WASHINGTON SQUARE, NEW YORK

For Gareth and Raphael

NEW YORK UNIVERSITY PRESS
Washington Square, New York

Library of Congress Cataloging-in-Publication Data
Alexander, Sally.
Becoming a woman : and other essays in 19th and 20th century
feminist history / Sally Alexander.
p.   cm.
"First published by Virago Press, London, 1994."
Includes bibliographical references (p.   ) and index.
ISBN 0-8147-0635-5 (cloth.)—ISBN 0-8147-0636-3 (pbk.)
1. Women—Great Britain—Social conditions.   2. Feminism—Great
Britain—History.   I. Title.
HQ1593.A45   1995
305.42'0941—dc20   94-46873
CIP

New York University Press books are printed on acid-free paper, and
their binding materials are chosen for strength and durability.

Manufactured in the United States of America

10 9 8 7 6 5 4 3 2 1

CONTENTS

CONTENTS

ACKNOWLEDGEMENTS

The essays are the result of twenty years' research and writing history during which time I have incurred many debts. The Department of Cultural Studies of the University of East London provided one semester's paid leave to prepare the book for publication. My students at Uel will be familiar with some of this material, and will recognize their contributions and queries. Among many helpful librarians David Doughan of the Fawcett Library, has been a stimulating friend to me as to countless feminist researchers; Christine Coates of the TUC Library allowed me to read the Tuckwell collection in the original manuscripts. Rita Pankhurst (on the initiative of Mary Kennedy) enabled me to teach a class on 'Research and Resources in Feminist History' at the Fawcett Library. Eve Hostettler gave me access to the transcripts of the Island History Trust, a unique archive on the Isle of Dogs of which she is the founder.

The first essays arose out of the shared political curiosity of the Women's Liberation Movement. The editorial collectives of *Red Rag*, and the occasional *Shrew* provoked research and intellectual argument. I have changed my understanding of history while working closely with the editors of the *History Workshop Journal*. The adult education classes I taught for ten or twelve years literally made me a historian. Feminist history in Britain began in the WEA and Extra-Mural Departments. I was fortunate to meet Jim Fyrth – historian and teacher and friend – who introduced me into London's Extra-Mural Department. Sheila Rowbotham has talked history with me since we first met in the mid-sixties. Her writing was the inspiration for my generation of feminist historians. Barbara Caine, Mary Chamberlain, Anna Davin, Rosalind Delmar, Rick Gordon, Ron Grele, Alun Howkins, Michael Ignatieff, Cora Kaplan, Keith McClelland, Juliet Mitchell, Laura Mulvey, Luisa Passerini, Adam Phillips, Denise Riley, Bill Schwarz,

Carolyn Steedman, Deborah Sugg, Paul Thompson, Couse Venn, Tony Wailey, Jeffrey Weeks, and Jerry White have all given me insights, evidence or just listened. Jean McCrindle and Ursula Owen (who first persuaded me to write a book) – my fellow 'parfaits' of Dangerous Reputations – will detect the 'Lagrasse element' in some of these essays.

Catherine Hall's passionate love of history is an essential part of my life. Jacqueline Rose always gives her time and thought when I need it, and I have learned much from her brilliant applications of psychoanalysis. Barbara Taylor's intellectual daring has pushed me further in my thinking than I sometimes thought safe. The three of them have persuaded me into publication. But I would never have published without the calm but insistent presence of Ruth Petrie – an editor of integrity and tact.

In crucial ways history is about argument. In life I don't find argument difficult. In writing I do. Raphael Samuel has always given me plenty to argue about. He was also my first history tutor. To him and Gareth Stedman Jones I simply say, thank you. This book is for them.

I have too often tried to close my study door on Abigail Thaw and Daniel Jones, for thanks to be appropriate. I admit to the impossibility of shutting them out – ever. I learned to listen from having children – though *they* might say that in that respect I still have a lot to learn. Both have been loving in spite of my occasional manias and that has made all the difference. Daniel has played his record player below his tolerance level for several months. Ella and Lotte Butler have offered me tea and comfort often. I am very grateful.

'Women's Work in Nineteenth-Century London' was first published in eds. Juliet Mitchell, Ann Oakley, *The Rights and Wrongs of Women*, Penguin, 1976; 'Women's Factory Work in Western Europe' was the Introduction to Marianne Herzog, *Hand to Mouth*, Penguin, 1978; 'Women, Class and Sexual Difference in the 1830s and '40s', was first published in *History Workshop Journal*, Issue 17, Spring 1984; 'Victorian Feminism: The Emergence of the Women's Movement in The Mid-Nineteenth Century', was the Introduction to The Fawcett Library Feminist History Class, 1981–2, *Studies in the History of Feminism, 1850–1930*, London University, Dep. of Extra-Mural Studies, 1984; 'The Fabian Women's Group' was the Introduction to Maud Pember Reeves, *Round About a Pound a Week* (1913), Virago, 1979; 'Fabian Socialism and the Sex-Relation' was the Introduction to ed. Sally Alexander, *Fabian Women's Tracts*, RKP, 1987; 'Women's Voices: Civil War in Spain' was the Introduction to eds. Jim Fyrth with S. Alexander, *Women's Voices from the Spanish Civil War*, Lawrence and Wishart, 1991; 'I Have Always Been a Writer' was first published in ed. Mary Chamberlain, *Writing Lives; Conversations Between Women Writers*, Virago, 1988; 'Becoming a Woman', was first published in eds. G. S. Jones, David Feldman, *Metropolis: London, Histories and Representations since 1800*, RKP, 1989; 'Feminist History and Psychoanalysis', was first published in ed. Elizabeth Wright, *A Dictionary of Psychoanalysis and Feminism*, Basil Blackwell, 1991.

INTRODUCTION

'The ears of the historian are full of echoes, but since his own experience
is the most real to him, some sound more clearly than others.'

Eileen Power

'We study change because we are changeable. This gives us a direct
experience of change: what we call memory.'

Arnaldo Momigliano

'Radical Politics is only a declaration of war.'

Sarah Benton

The first essay in this collection was written in 1974, the last in 1993.
They tell several stories: of women's work in modern industry; of
subjectivity, phantasy and desire in democratic movements; of the
formation of the Victorian women's movement and the unstable identifications in both feminist political belief and the modern feminine self.
The telling has not been smooth. The first essay on women's work was
written against a secure historical landscape of industrial Britain in
which class relations and political affiliation seemed attached. The point
was to write women into the history of the working class. After some
struggle I understood the historical relationship between class and the
sexual division of labour as mediated by patriarchy (the law of the
father); and the structure and topography of the industrial revolution
itself changed when looked at through women's work. Some of the
steps in those discoveries are included in the essays on feminist history
and patriarchy in the appendix.[1] The essay – 'Memory, Generation and
History: Two Women's Lives in the Inter-War years' – considers how
twentieth-century British history might be recast through feminine
subjectivities after the First World War. A woman's metonymic memories of her mother's suicide and loss of language; the changing

experience of a woman's body bears witness to the shock of migration, ethnic division, new forms of poverty and women's changing reproductive cycle which underlined modernity in the metropolis after the First World War, prefiguring the fissures in social-democracy in the 1940s and '50s, the consequences of which we still inhabit.

The move the essays make from women's work in nineteenth-century manufactures to the emotional sources of a modern sensibility traverses several journeys only moments of which I will rehearse here. To anticipate what follows: in 1974 I was writing about women in British history within a narrative of historical materialism whose subject was class and whose determining relationships were those of production or property. Today we know that the temporalities of class and mode of production are only some of the many composite times which make up the present – and that history has no Subject. For me listening to women's speech – past and present – led to a concept of the subject divided by sex and driven by phantasy and the unconscious as well as by economic need: an understanding of subjectivity informed by psychoanalysis – which psychoanalysis has itself helped to produce. But so too has feminism. The history of the women's movement among other democratic movements in nineteenth and early twentieth century Britain remaps the progress of both liberal democracy and socialism in that period. 1848 remains a significant year for the failure of Chartism in Britain, for the echoes of revolutionary nationalism and liberalism in Europe. But 1918 marks the end of the propertied franchise in Britain, and 1928, universal suffrage. Women's suffrage has complicated the political narrative of modernity and feminist history is one way to explore those complications. In this introduction I want to suggest both how ideas took root within a political generation, and why some questions, not others, provoked my historical curiosity. If I am brief it is because I prefer to return to pasts other than my own.[2] Thirteen of the eighteen essays here have been published before. It was difficult to resist the temptation to rewrite them. Instead I have updated some of the reading in the footnotes to indicate the direction historical debate has taken. I have selected and ordered the essays in such a way that should the reader wish s/he may follow the uneven development of an argument.

The first essays have a firm location and origin in the political curiosity of the Women's Liberation Movement of the 1960s and early '70s – when to use the word 'woman' in intellectual work was radical in itself: what did it mean to be a woman, and what do women want? Critical feminist enquiry sprang from a sense of injustice spoken in consciousness-raising groups and made manifest in a politics of civil liberties, of direct action and of spectacle directed against the use of women's bodies as sex-objects, as objects of male violence and against women's status as the dependents of men.[3] The sense of injustice had its origins in a more familial grievance perhaps, prefigurative of a movement that was to re-align the personal and the public. Born between the late 1930s and early 1950s, we were the daughters of marriages chilled by six years' separation during the war, enraged by the fathers who turned us out of our mothers' beds. We were nevertheless – collectively – the heirs to our parents' dreams of 'good enough mothering', equal opportunities, and 'Never Again'.[4] Both the oedipal and the aspirant impulses of my feminism are rooted in the contradictions of the 1940s – (War-time and Attlee's Britain) – but its forcing ground was the political divide of the 1950s.[5] We grew up – as Sarah Benton recently recalled – with memories of movements for colonial liberation, but in the context of the Cold War.[6] For the radicals who came of age between 1956 and 1968 a sense of political right and wrong/good and bad was overdetermined by the divide between communism and the west.[7] One of the political effects of the 'liberation' movements of the late 1960s and the early 1970s was the damage they did to that ethical divide.[8] The essays written in the mid-1970s belong to that moment of polemical disturbance.

'Women's Work in Victorian London', the first essay in this collection, asked whether women have a different relationship to capital from men. This question was a deliberate challenge to economy-driven explanations of Britain's nineteenth-century industrial history, of which marxism was the most powerful in the 1960s and '70s.[9] These histories assumed a causal relation between production, social being and politics. The question implied too an impatience with Ivy Pinchbeck's conclusions that modern industry had improved the lives of married women by taking work out of the home, and of spinsters by offering them an independent wage. I wanted to know whether the industrial revolution changed when looked at through the experience of women's waged work – a question the economic historians Maxine Berg and Pat Hudson strive to place in the forefront of economic and demographic enquiry today.[10] One part of the argument – that competing pools of unskilled female (and male) labour in London sustained the slop and sweated trades, forms of manufacture as vital to modern industry as machinery and the factory owed as much to Henry Mayhew's study of London's casual labour markets as to Marx's detailed study of the labour process in the transition from manufacture to modern industry.[11] (The voices that Mayhew recorded on the streets of London in the 1850s speak clearly in my head still.) I wanted to demonstrate the material basis of female inequality and its political effects. I found that the political representations of women's labour and value in industrial capitalism were less heroic than men's.

The struggles over the wage among the very poor set men against women, fathers and sons against wives and daughters. The history of capitalism seemed as much the story of internal divisions among the poor as of class struggle; divisions transposed from the family to industry and back again, each transforming the other in the process – divisions overdetermined by sex and reproduced in male phantasy.[12] Working women's poverty and dependence – underlined by their formal exclusion from skill, by the ubiquity of domestic service, and haunted by the spectre of prostitution – could provoke antagonism between women and men in communities and in democratic movements. It also prompted a vocabulary of exclusion and lack among some feminist political economists and suffragists who from the mid-century, in likening women's work to 'slavery' or 'vice' exposed the apparent incompatibility between femininity and productive work. Because – in Sidney Webb the Fabian's throwaway phrase – women had something to sell other than their labour, women's wages fell below subsistence. They were cheap labour, and often used as scabs. Low wages and having something else to sell than their labour placed women in a different relation to labour, capital *and* the suffrage (which until 1918 had a property qualification) from men. A man's property was in his labour, a woman's in her person. Economic and political inequality between women and men was compounded by sexual difference. Skilled men throughout the nineteenth century derided women's work as an 'inferior' sort of work. A woman's place was in the home – as one furniture maker told Mayhew, whose wife didn't work – she just ran a corner shop.[13] This imaginative truth – what men wanted – ran through the aspirations of nineteenth-century democratic movements for shorter hours, co-operative workshops or the Charter, as did the family wage.[14] Founded on a disavowal it confirmed women's status in the political constitution as dependents, without political representation as women, and with limited rights over their own property and person. The Victorian women's movement (from the 1850s), the Women's Trade Union League (1870–1920) and the Fabian Women's Group (1908–1952) took up the woman question and the 'sex-relation' and tried to build a political movement of women which would render them visible to men by releasing them from a confining and private domestic world; which would replace the image of women in men's minds with the economic reality of women's lives and which would secure political and economic equality with men.

The nineteenth-century Women's Movement developed formidable political and propaganda skills, a literature of legal and constitutional argument, international and domestic organizations. If it often formed 'pressure groups' then the ambitions of its radical spokeswomen far exceeded the demand for equality in every sphere – they wanted regeneration throughout the public and private worlds as well as justice for women. But Victorian feminism did not simply overcome male phantasy by representing the actual or real economic conditions of women; like all political movements it too was founded on imaginary identifications.

Feminist thought in its moments of emergence in nineteenth-century democratic movements, always returns to the individual subject to discover the identity of woman and her difference from man. Part of this process is the phantasy of a powerful masculine subject – the tyrannical men who '*force* women to live in constant masquerade' as 'Sophia' put it in the mid-eighteenth century; the mythical fathers and brothers whom Harriet Martineau strove to emulate in the 1850s; the 'powerful bodies of men' evoked by the Women's Trade Union League. It's not that male power does not have real effects (most of the political institutions of Britain before the present century for instance) but that one element in its formation is its imaginary power which in feminist polemic then becomes an exaggerated distinction between the sexes. The other side of the phantasy is the powerlessness and innocence of women. Sylvia Pankhurst in her 1930 history of the Suffragette Movement made suffering and martyrdom one mainspring of women's fight for the suffrage. The assertion of women's difference – without equal in men, to borrow Julia Kristeva's phrasing – is motherhood which many Victorian feminists seized on as grounds for their political aspirations.[15] Every woman has an imaginary relationship to the capacity for motherhood Josephine Butler believed. For Olive Schreiner motherhood was a beatitude; for Ada Nield Chew, suffragist and woman's trade union organizer, a passion. The identification of womanhood with motherhood was a necessary distinction in the propaganda and rhetoric which asserted women's different needs and status vis-à-vis men. It could be a source of spiritual and political strength to some feminists as long as the different needs and capacities of women as mothers and women as workers or citizens were held separately in the articulation of their demands for political and economic equality. But the emphasis on motherhood, in the absence of an independent feminist voice, risked confirming women's status as one in need of protection, the association of their person with 'sexual slavery' or vice. Before 1918 (when women over thirty won the vote) feminists united women through the demand for the suffrage, not motherhood.

In the forefront of the struggle for political democracy from the 1870s to 1918, the women's suffrage movement pushed the Liberal Party as far as it would go on the issue – as Ursula Bright pointed out, the civil liberties of the Liberal Party stopped short where women came in.[16] But the Liberal Party from Gladstone to Asquith was never a democratic party – its MPs reneged on women's suffrage again and again from 1867. Eventually in 1912 the National Union for Woman's Suffrage Societies (NUWSS), whose President was Millicent Garrett Fawcett, formed a tactical alliance with Labour. In the 1920s, the NUWSS divided on what should unite feminism, equality or difference, and difference – maternity – won. 'We must demand what we want for women not because it is what men have got but because it is what women need' – argued the independent liberal Eleanor Rathbone; her voice broke on the word child when Rathbone delivered this speech, Rathbone's biographer Mary Stocks tells us.[17] After 1928 when women finally achieved the suffrage on the same terms as men, the independent women's movement faded, and egalitarian rhetoric within the Labour Party and beyond collapsed on sexual difference. The emphasis on motherhood enabled the recuperation of the woman question into a narrow domesticity during the 1920s and '30s in the political rhetorics of both labour and conservatism as indeed the Liberal, Millicent Garrett Fawcett, who had been defeated in that crucial debate in 1924 had foreseen that it would. Sexual difference proved no stable basis for a politics of equality.

The essays in Part Two and 'Bringing Women into Line with Men' together outline this analysis. The break with historical materialism was unavoidable once this historical narrative of feminism had been outlined if only because it insisted on the active historical presence of subjectivities other than class. The breaking point was sex and reproduction – the bedrock of sexual difference – how was it to be organized and how to be thought. Who will bear and bring up the children; and where and how publicly to articulate and curb the violence and anguish that perverse sexual desire provokes. Feminisms and the women's movement addressed those questions, as well as the terms and conditions of political power, and when they did they provoked antagonism. This break I could not gloss, since I continued to be interested both in the political economy of relations between women and men in everyday life and feminism, which quarrels with everyday life. I remained interested too in writing history which linked the political economy of women with unconscious mental life. 'Women, Class and Sexual Difference' marks the turn away from historical materialism as the basis for writing history. It was the outcome of fifteen years' feminist research in study groups and adult education – my personal history is there too in the full-stops and the commas.

It took me a long time to write up my critique of marxism. The delay was in part a response to the changed political conditions at the end of the '70s. By 1976 divisions within the Women's Liberation Movement – over political lesbianism, separatism, and ethnic differences – coincided with radical reversals in the political culture at the end of the 1970s. Margaret Thatcher's pledge to eliminate socialism – and to reconstitute the nation through home-ownership, easy credit and the memory of empire and war (Churchill was her ego-ideal) not to mention her enmity towards the political institutions of the 1940s and the 'legacy' of the '60s – made the repudiation of historical materialism seem like a betrayal. Historical materialism was the super-ego of radical history in the '60s and '70s – I had forgotten how much my habits of thought owed to the marxist historians with whom I argued.[18] At the same time the mantle of dissent passed from women and the working class to race and ethnicity as the amnesia of imperialism was decisively challenged by a young generation of black Britons in the 1970s. (One response of historians to these changes has been the shift of emphasis from cultures of resistance to the formation of consensus: from Edward Thompson's 'radical artisans' to Linda Colley's 'Britons' at war.)[19]

The vulnerability of the women's movement to changes in the political and economic culture in the 1980s had parallels with the fading of the women's movement after 1928. During the 1930s high levels of male unemployment, the health, housing and poverty of children in working-class families, and the spread of fascism all assumed much more political significance than women's inequality. The Republican cause in Spain – the Spanish Civil War – was one of the democratic touchstones of anti-fascism throughout the western world and signalled the rejection of pacifism as an anti-fascist strategy for many women. 'Women's Voices from the Spanish Civil War' and the interview with Yvonne Kapp talk about why, and the meaning of Spain among educated and relatively privileged as well as working women.

In both the 1930s and 1980s women had a high economic profile; then as now women could find work in the new industries and men could not, a development with as yet indigested political implications for social or liberal democratic nations.[20] In the early 1980s as in the 1920s the political spotlight passed from woman to child.[21] The relationship between feminist political demands, industrial restructuring, women's work and changing family size are under-researched and difficult to measure. Juliet Mitchell suggests that women are used by capitalist industry to prepare the way for what might become a new class formation or mode of production. She suggests that the demands of women's liberation in the 1970s might have eased this transition.[22] The position of women in society – the early nineteenth-century utopians believed – was the litmus test of social evolution. Perhaps they are too, she ventures, the precursors of social change: where women are at moments of economic dislocation and social disintegration, there men will be. Women are used in moments of social transition, she seems to be arguing, to imagine the future. The 1920s and '30s were such a moment of industrial and political transition yet it is clear that there is more at work in historical causality than market forces and the political demands of feminism. Universal suffrage (1918; 1928 finally) made women a political constituency for all parties to address; the cinema transformed young women's (and men's) pleasure and sense of themselves; while migration – both internal and international – introduced layers of cultural diversity into the affective life of the nation. It is at least arguable that women's refusal of large families was the feature of modernity with most far-reaching effects between the 1920s and the 1960s. It changed women's relationships to their body, to men and to the economy and political parties have had to address those changes. (In a sense the Women's Liberation Movement can be understood as *one* political effect of that change.) In 'Becoming a Woman' and 'Two Women's Lives' I want to rethink the periodicity of early twentieth-century Britain through women's memories and lives. Like Carolyn Steedman, I'm speaking of the mental and historical landscapes, and of the everyday lives of individuals and generations.

After 1976 the essays belong to an ongoing feminist project rather than to the political curiosity of the women's movement.[24] One move they make – from the power of the father to the instability of the subject (which is roughly located in the transition from Part Two to Three) reflects this intellectual change.[25] Patriarchy was the transitional term which was to link women's oppression with economic exploitation via the family. Used by Fabian and other feminisms in the nineteenth and early twentieth centuries to refer to paternal authority, patriarchy was rethought in the early '70s through Jacques Lacan's 'name of the Father'. Ironically, Lacan's phallus – though his prose proved difficult for the empirically trained English speaking historian to read – was less shocking to the feminist sensibility than Freud's penis-envy.[26] Lacan's stress on language and speech in the acquisition of sexed subjectivity at the oedipal moment may have overlooked the body in favour of the signifier, but by recalling the unconscious – its presence and absence in speech and its silences – it offered access to the psychic roots of subjectivity through listening and reading. It seemed possible to rethink not only who 'we' were but also – in my favourite phrase of Juliet Mitchell's – how we 'live as ideas'.[27] Other historians at the same moment of transition in political culture – the exploration of power through image and language – pursued deconstruction and the play of the signifier.[28] This is not a path I chose because the tension between the trials of subjectivity and historical agency and processes on which I am trying to focus increasingly in these essays cannot be adequately grasped by the concept of an endless destabilization of language. Sexual difference is mediated by the body as well as phantasy, and subjectivity is grounded – provisionally – in specific historical forms.

For me however, sexual difference has been unavoidable and I read Lacan (though much more of Freud) in the spirit in which he intended, as a poet and speculative analyst. On reflection my thinking had been prompted as much by random conversations – the history of everyday life – as study groups, or so I remember. For instance, Rosalind Delmar and I visited the Upper Clyde Shipbuilders work-in in Glasgow in 1970, on behalf of *Red Rag*, a marxist-feminist journal of the 1970s. We talked with shop stewards about equal pay and sex discrimination at work, and we asked about sharing the washing up. They were agreeable to every demand of the women's movement except allowing their wives to go to meetings in the evening. How would they know, they asked us, where she was? Conversations like these were repeated in the summer schools I taught with Jim Fyrth for the Extra-Mural Department of London University, the socialist and labour movement talks all over Britain that Sheila Rowbotham and I took on in the 1970s. In 1974, several of us visited the Women's Trade Union Congress in Eastbourne and I was struck by hearing the delegates using the pronoun 'we'. In the Women's Liberation Workshop in London, a woman could only ever speak for herself.[29] I remember Alison Fell's discovery of Althusser's argument about the materiality of ideas; reading Freud's 1933 essay on 'Femininity' and almost fainting with the shock of recognition? ... I remember the three-year-old boy in our house rushing round the kitchen telling his mother and me that he would give us each a baby and his father too. These and other moments imprinted sexual difference – and its imaginary power – on my mind. Feminism and psychoanalysis, I began to think, (and I was reading Freud avidly inside and outside study groups) as bodies of thought had some of the same epistemological roots: listening to women's speech.

I use the term sexual difference because I want to draw attention to the unconscious dimension of subjectivity. Subjectivity and sexual difference have life breathed into them by the unconscious. Gender may be an adequate shorthand for the social forms that sexual difference sometimes takes through its uneven articulations in kinship, property relations, labour and law but gender obscures the difficulties – of the 'sex-relation' to repeat the term of Fabian feminism – that sexual difference foregrounds.[30] Lived unconsciously and consciously sexual difference was unfamiliar territory twenty years ago to the historian.[31] But clues to its meanings are there in colloquial speech: the Leeds clothing worker on the 1960s picket line in the essay 'Women's Factory Work'; I 'fell' pregnant ('Two Women's Lives'), 'I want to grow up to be a man' (Becoming a Woman').

The resistence to femininity – I want to grow up to be a man – spoken by a young woman in the 1920s, anticipates Freud's observation at the end of his life, that both men and women repudiate femininity.[32] Why? In the first decades of the twentieth century – the period of modernism – passivity, hysteria and masquerade are spoken and acted out through both feminism and femininity in the literature of psycho-analysis – though life and history suggest they are part of the human condition. Femininity for Freud was one route to the study of psychic instability – another was himself. Perhaps women, positioned equivo-cally in political cultures both inside and out of the constitutional forms of government and power, were vulnerable to psychic instability in particular ways. I have argued that the politics of feminism in the past two hundred or more years have focussed on sexual difference, and been accused of unsexing women, or behaving hysterically (whether sexual difference is in the mind or the body to fall the wrong side of it in demotic speech is to become hysterical). Neither feminist nor Freudian rhetoric have yet escaped the conventional divide between masculine strength and feminine passivity. To trace some of the same ground – the conditions of women's lives giving precedence to memory and speech – seems a useful way for a historian to follow both feminism's quest for a more generous liberal or social democracy and Freud's (and the poets) for the enigma of femininity. Colloquial speech is less discreet than other discourses, it draws on many idioms. The historian's task is to rework them.

The difficulties of writing a history of twentieth century feminine subjectivity with an awareness of the timelessness of the unconscious; the contingency of memory and desire; the incommensurability of the inner with the outer world are raised in 'Psychoanalysis and Feminist History', and 'Repetition and History'. By invoking the unconscious dimension of all processes of thought, including the constitution of the self and political belief – we encounter ambivalence, and the endpoint of comprehension. Two reminders that knowledge is provisional and that without a faith or political belief we have to think for ourselves what are the determinations in the dynamic between phantasy and the real. The unconscious lengthens modern memory enabling the historian to recover the mythological and spiritual dimensions of thought as well as the literal and empirical. It reminds us too that all the components of political belief are composed with the help of the register of phantasy and the unconscious. I would like to write a history which makes the gap between phantasy and reality more comprehensible.[33] The essays 'Two Women's Lives' and 'Why Feminism' are just a beginning.

1994

Part One

WOMEN AND WORK

Women's Work in Nineteenth-Century London

A Study of the Years 1820–60s

— *Introduction* —

Most historians define the working class *de facto* as working men. Occupations, skills, wages, relations of production, the labour process itself, are discussed as if social production were an exclusively male prerogative. Consciously or unconsciously, the world has been conceived in the image of the bourgeois family – the husband is the breadwinner and the wife remains at home attending to housework and child-care. Both the household itself, and women's domestic labour within it are presented as the unchanging backcloth to the world of real historical activity. The labour historian has ignored women as workers – on the labour market and within the household. Consequently women's contribution to production and as well to the reproduction and maintenance of the labour force has been dismissed. This is partly because the labour and economic historians who first wrote about the working class, wrote about the organized and articulate labour movement – accessible through its trade union records, its newspapers and the occasional autobiography. Only recently have the inaccessible areas of working-class life been approached, but even here the focus has remained on the working man. In every respect women's participation in history has been marginalized.[1]

Feminist history releases women from their obscurity as the wives, mothers and daughters of working men. This does not just mean that family life, housework, the reproduction of the labour force, the transmission of ideology can be added to an already constituted history, but the history of production itself will be rewritten. For the history of production under capitalism, from a feminist perspective, is not simply the class struggle between the producer and the owner of the means of production. It is also the development of a particular form of the sexual division of labour in relation to that struggle.

The focus of this essay is women's waged work in Victorian London. London in the period of the industrial revolution has been chosen for two reasons. Firstly because London's diverse economy offers both a wide spectrum of women's employment within a reasonably coherent geographic unit and the multiple effects of industrial change on women's work, reminding us that the industrial revolution brought with it more than just machinery and the factory system. Secondly, this study will reveal how even a preliminary survey of this kind requires the building of a new feminist conceptual framework to make women's economic activity comprehensible. It is one of the contentions of this essay that women's work is one sensitive indicator of change in the production process.

The working woman emerged as a 'social problem' in the thirties and forties. Indeed, it is as though the Victorians discovered her, so swiftly and urgently did she become the object of public concern. The dislocations of modern industry, the rapid increase in population, the herding of the population into the towns, dramatized class antagonisms and forced the condition of the working classes onto the attention of the propertied classes as a mass of documentary evidence reveals. The effect of these dislocations upon working-class wives and children became one major focal point of this anxiety. The short-time movement (the struggle of the factory operatives in the Lancashire and Yorkshire textile mills to limit the working day), in particular Sadler's Commission of 1832, first highlighted the problem of the female factory operative. Ten years later, the Children's Employment Commission (1842–3) exposed a string of female occupations in the mines and the traditional outwork trades, where wages and conditions were no less degrading than those in the textile mill. These revelations shattered middle-class complacency and aroused the reformatory zeal of evangelical and utilitarian philanthropists. And it is from the philanthropists as well as factory inspectors and Parliamentary Commissioners and journalists, that we receive most of our information on women's work. For most of these people the poor were utterly unknown except as domestic servants or tradesmen.

This sense of shock at 'the condition of England', as contemporaries termed it, in particular the apparent destruction of the working-class family, cannot be understood simply from the dread conditions in the factories alone.[2] The British industrial revolution did not take place in a neutral political context. Its formative years, 1790 to 1815, were years in which England was engaged in counter-revolutionary war against France. Jacobinism (the democratic republicanism of the French revolutionaries) and industrial discontent were fused by England's rulers into an indiscriminate image of 'sedition'. Industrial political unrest was severely repressed with military as well as legal force if necessary. Out of this repression emerged the distinctive features of Victorian middle-class mentality – a blend of political economy and evangelicalism. The one an ideology appropriate to the 'take off' of the forces of production – the industrial revolution; the other a doctrine demonstrating the fixity of the relations of production. While political economy asserted that the laws of capitalist production were the laws of nature herself, evangelicalism sanctified the family, along with industriousness, obedience and piety, as the main bulwark against revolution. The Victorian ideal of womanhood originated in this counter-revolutionary ethos. The woman, as wife and mother, was the pivot of the family, and consequently the guardian of all Christian (and domestic) virtues. Women's waged work, therefore, was discussed insofar as it harmonized with the home, the family and domestic virtue.[3]

Because of women's intimate responsibility for society's well-being, it was the woman working outside the home who received alarmed attention from the parliamentary commissioners, and to push through legislative reform, emphasis was placed, not on the hours of work, rates of pay, and dangers from unsafe machinery – although all these were mentioned – but on the moral and spiritual degradation said to accompany female employment; especially the mingling of the sexes and the neglect of domestic comforts. 'In the male the moral effects of the system are very sad, but in the female they are infinitely worse', Lord Shaftesbury, the evangelical Tory, solemnly declared to a silent House of Lords, at the end of his two-hour speech advocating the abolition of women's and children's work in the mines ... 'not alone upon themselves, but upon their families, upon society, and, I may add, upon the country itself. It is bad enough if you corrupt the man, but if you corrupt the woman, you poison the waters of life at the very fountain.'[4]

Respectable opinion echoed Lord Shaftesbury's sentiments. On the whole both evangelicalism and political economy attributed the sufferings of the poor to their own moral pollution. Their viciousness was variously ascribed to drink, licentiousness, idleness and all manner of vice and depravity, for which religion, temperance, thrift, cleanliness, industriousness and self help were advocated as the most potent remedies. But, if there was any reason for these evils – beyond the innate moral depravity of the individuals concerned – the one that commended itself most readily was the negligence and ignorance of the working-class wife and mother. It is true that enlightened public opinion – enlightened, that is, by an acquaintance with the poor acquired through visiting them for religious or reformatory purposes – recognized that the crowded courts, tenements and rookeries of the cities, so deplored by Octavia Hill, the housing reformer, and her associates, hardly stimulated the domestic virtues nurtured in the suburban villa.[5] Nevertheless, the very squalor of working-class housing could be blamed upon the slender acquaintance with domestic economy possessed by working women whose 'want of management' drove their husbands to the alehouses and their children onto the streets. The Children's Employment Commission of 1843 reported that the deficiency in female education was the 'one great and universally prevailing cause of poverty and crisis among the working classes.' The remedy was succinctly expressed by Mrs Austin, an ardent advocate of 'industrial' housewifery – education for the working girl – 'our object', she wrote in the 1850s, 'is to improve the servants of the rich, and the wives of the poor'.[6]

Every Victorian inquiry into the working classes is steeped in the improving moralism we have been discussing. The poor were seldom allowed to speak for themselves. 'What the poor are to the poor is little known,' Dickens wrote in the 1840s, 'excepting to themselves and God.'[7] And if this was true of the poor as a whole, it was doubly true of working-class women who almost disappear under this relentless scrutiny. It was not that the Victorians did not expect women of the lower classes to work. On the contrary, work was the sole corrective and just retribution for poverty; it was rather that only those sorts of work that coincided with a woman's natural sphere were to be encouraged. Such discrimination had little to do with the danger or unpleasantness of the work concerned. There was not much to choose for example – if our criteria is risk to life or health – between work in the mines, and work in the London dressmaking trades. But no one suggested that sweated needlework should be prohibited to women. To uncover the real situation of the working woman herself in the Victorian period, then, we have to pick our way through the labyrinthine mystifications of the middle-class mind, and resolve questions, not only that contemporaries did not answer, but in many cases did not even ask.

This applies in particular to women's employment in London. Some trades it is true, received a great deal of local attention. The declining Spitalfields silk industry was investigated as part of the national inquiries into the hand-loom weavers; dressmakers and needlewomen received the notice of a House of Lords Select Committee; while starving needlewomen and prostitutes were the subject of anxious concern in a host of pamphlets. But the factory girls of Manchester and the West Riding who so traumatized observers in the 1840s could have no place in London where few trades were transformed by the factory system until the twentieth century. High rents, combined with the high cost of fuel and its transportation, inhibited the earlier development of the factory system in inner London. What changes did occur in the sexual division of labour as a result of a change in the production or labour process, took place beneath the surface, in the workshop, or the home. Most women workers in London were domestic servants, washer-women, needlewomen or occupied in some other sort of home work; they were charwomen or lodging housekeepers, street-sellers, hawkers or women of the town. Many married women worked with their husbands in his trade. Except for prostitution, these traditional forms of women's work were compatible with the Victorian's deification of the home, and so passed almost unnoticed.

Proof that women's waged work was not just less noticeable in London but often completely overlooked is found in the Census of 1851 which was the first to record the occupations of women in other than 'domestic duties'. The number of women over twenty who are listed as being without occupation is 432,000, i.e. 57 per cent of all women over twenty living in London. In round numbers, this figure of 432,000 is broken down as follows: 317,000 wives 'not otherwise described', 27,000 widows 'not otherwise described', 43,000 children and relatives at home 'not otherwise described', 26,000 persons of rank or property, 7,000 paupers, prisoners and vagrants, 13,000 'of no specified occupa-tions or conditions'.[8] If we exclude the 26,000 propertied at one end, the 7,000 or so paupers at the other, and a proportion of propertied widows and dependent relatives in between, that still leaves over 50 per cent of women 'with no occupation'. And yet among the vast majority of the working classes all members of the family were expected to contribute to the family income, for even when the wages of the male workers were relatively high they were rarely regular besides which central London had 130,000 'surplus' or 'unprotected' women.[9] We know therefore that 50 per cent of adult women would not have been able to live without any independent source of income. Obviously the statistics require explanation.

There were several reasons why the occupations of working-class women might not have been declared in the Census, some more speculative than others. The work of married women for instance, was often hidden behind that of their husbands. Previous historians of women's work, Alice Clark, Dorothy George and Ivy Pinchbeck, have each shown that although the separation of workplace and home (introduced by merchant capitalism) was one of the factors reducing the opportunities for women to learn a skill or to manage a small workshop business, nevertheless, the process was gradual and never complete, especially in the numerous and diverse London trades which, well into the nineteenth century, were characteristically conducted in small workshops, often on a family basis. Clara Collett, describing the trades of east London connected with poverty in the Booth Study of the 1880s, noted the prevalence of family workshops there then. Some women were listed in the Census as innkeepers', shopkeepers', butchers', bakers' and shoemakers' wives; but often a wife's work within her husband's trade would not have been mentioned. Many trade societies forbade the entry of women. Also, because the head of the household filled in the Census, he – especially if he was a skilled artisan or aspiring tradesman – probably thought of his wife as a housewife and mother and not as a worker.[10]

Wives of skilled workmen may be glimpsed, however, through conversations recorded by Henry Mayhew, the *Morning Chronicle* journalist and 'friend' of the London poor. Sawyers' wives and children, for instance, did not 'as a general rule . . . go *out* to work' (my italics),[11] and coachmen's wives were not in regular employ for the slop-tailors, because, as one confided in Mayhew, 'we keep our wives too respectable for that'.[12] Nevertheless, according to Mayhew, 'some few of the wives of the better class of workmen take in washing or keep small "general shops"'.[13] Taking in washing, needlework, or other sorts of outwork was the least disruptive way of supplementing the family income when extra expenses were incurred, or during the seasonal or enforced unemployment which existed in most London trades. Home-work did not unnecessarily interrupt a man's domestic routine, since the wife could fit it in among her household chores; it simply meant she worked a very long day.

But only a minority of women would have been married to skilled artisans or small tradesmen. Mayhew estimated that about 10 per cent of every trade were society men, and Edward Thompson has outlined the 30 shilling (£1.50) line of privilege in London, while suggesting that Mayhew's 10 per cent was probably an exaggeration, 5 or 6 per cent being a more realistic figure.[14] Society men were becoming more and more confined to the 'honourable' sectors of every trade in the 1840s (the honourable trades were those which produced expensive well-made goods for the luxury and West End market and the workmen dealt directly with the master without the intervention of a middleman), whereas workers in the unorganized, 'dishonourable' sectors were rapidly expanding in the period 1815–40, and they made a much more precarious living.[15] Women (and children) of this class always had to contribute to the family income, indeed, in the 1830s and 1840s, a time of severe economic hardship, the London poor drew more closely together, and it was often the household and not the individual worker, or even separate family, that was the economic unit. A mixture of washing, cleaning, charring as well as various sorts of home- or slop-work, in addition to domestic labour, occupied most women throughout their working lives. The diversity and indeterminancy of this spasmodic, casual and irregular employment was not easily condensed and classified into a Census occupation.

Other women who were scarcely recorded in the Census, though we know of their existence through Mayhew, were the street traders, market workers, entertainers, scavengers, mudlarks;[16] also those who earned a few pence here and there, looking after a neighbour's children, running errands, minding a crossing, sweeping the streets, in fact, most of the women discussed in the final section of this paper. Lastly, perhaps the most desperate source of income for women, and one which provoked a great deal of prurient debate and pious attention was prostitution. This too was often intermittent and supplementary and found no place in the Census.

Despite the fact that working women emerge only fitfully through the filter of Victorian moralism; in spite of the tendency to view women as the wives and dependents of working men rather than workers in their own right; in spite of the particular problems of uncovering women's occupations in London; nevertheless, some distinguishing characteristics are beginning to appear.

Firstly, London offered no single stable employment for women comparable to that in the northern textile towns so the study of women's work in this period in London yields a different industrial history from the one with which we are familiar; secondly, in a city of skilled trades and small workshops, women, although long since excluded from formal apprenticeship, often worked with their husband in his trade; thirdly, much women's work inside and outside small workshop production was intermittent and casual, which meant that most women's working lives were spent in a variety of partial occupations most of which escaped the classifications of the Census.

These features of women's work must be looked at against the wider background of the London labour market, and the sexual division of labour within it, but first, to help fix the locality, a brief topographical sketch of London follows.

— *London Topography* —

In the 1830s Fenimore Cooper described his journey through the outskirts of London as one through a 'long maze of villages'. Even then the description was a little whimsical. London's first period of expansion had been the late sixteenth and early seventeenth centuries, since when it had continued to extend its influence as the political, commercial and manufacturing centre of England. London was also the largest single consumer market in the country. Between 1801 and 1851 London underwent another burst of expansion; her population increased 150 per cent from 900,000 to 2,360,000, many of them migrants from the countryside, with a vast influx of Irish, fleeing the famine in the 1840s. Industrial and commercial innovations were affecting every aspect of its economic life. Railways as well as migration were transforming not only the topography, but manners, morals, customs, the very tempo of life. London was becoming much more accessible to the rest of Britain. Finally, if industrial productivity and expansion in trade and shipping had made Britain the workshop of the world by 1851, developments in banking, shareholding and company investment were making the City its most important financial centre.

London — world centre of commerce, shipping and trade — does not correspond to the image conjured up by Fenimore Cooper — the force of these developments could wipe out the smaller rhythms of local economies and rituals — and yet there was a sense in which London remained a rambling collection of hamlets. Certainly, its local government before the 1890s lent reality to that myth, if myth it was. G. L. Gomme, looking at a map of London in the 1830s, suggested it resembled an octopus, the boundary of whose body passed from Vauxhall Bridge, to Park Lane, then followed up the Edgware Road, along Marylebone Road, City Road southwards past Mile End, reaching the Thames at Shadwell Basin. Apart from the almost independent enclaves of Greenwich and Deptford, the south of the river began with Bermondsey — separated from Deptford by Rotherhithe. By the middle of the century, according to John Hollingshead, it 'wriggled' its way 'through the existing miles of dirt, vice and crime as far as the Lambeth marshes'. Between 1830 and 1850, London was greedily swallowing up the surrounding villages, and transforming them into the 'stuccovia, the suburbs, the terminus districts', which from the 1840s onwards, appeared with increasing frequency in the novels of Dickens.[17]

The process of incorporation was rapid, but their transformation gradual, the peculiarities of London districts remained very marked. Their geographic, social and economic distinctions more than the preservation of quaint custom. In 1830 Hampstead, Islington, Hackney and east of Bethnal Green and Stepney were rural or semi-rural. So was south of the river beyond Southwark and Bermondsey. In the early morning the park side of Piccadilly was crowded with women carrying baskets of fruit and vegetables on their heads on their way to Covent Garden from the market gardens of Hammersmith, Fulham and Chelsea, where the river ran through fields.[18] Every street was filled with costers on their way to market. Sophie Wackles in *Great Expectations* for example, married Mr Clegg, a market gardener from Chelsea.

Between the semi-rural outposts in the north and the north-east, and central London, were waste districts, great tracts of suburban Sahara, such as Dickens described in a walk from the City to the outskirts of Holloway, 'where tiles and bricks were burnt, bones were boiled, carpets were beat, rubbish was shot, dogs were fought, and dust was heaped by contractors'.[19] Hector Gavin in his 'sanitary ramblings' through Bethnal Green in the 1840s similarly found yards for the collection of dust, refuse and ash, overflowing sewers and open drains and other 'nuisances'. These had gradually been encroaching on the plots laid out as gardens where he saw 'the choicest flowers', dahlias and tulips.[20] The railway, that harbinger of progress, left chaos in its wake in outlying parts of the East End – contributing to its general atmosphere of desolation and disease by the destruction of streets and alleys and the accumulation of rubbish yards and dung heaps flung in their place. The summer houses belonging to the gardens of Bethnal Green were being used for 'human habitation', and every bit of spare ground was being built on: houses that were neither paved or boarded, lacking in sanitation and built below ground level.

Jerry builders were busy throughout suburban London. The hasty conversion of sheds and shacks into homes in Spitalfields; the cheap building in these waste districts of the East End and on the outskirts of the City – Shoreditch, St Pancras, Agar Town for example, once described as 'a squalid population that had first squatted'; the rows of small houses that were built with 'mere lathe and plaster' purely for quick profit, all these had their central London counterparts in the decaying tenements of the City and the West End, and south of the river in Southwark and Bermondsey.

The intervening waste lands between London and its outlying villages were being plundered and abused on the north and north-east sides of the City – between London and Finchley for instance, or the hills and fields of north Holloway and Hackney, or the semi-rural outpost of Bethnal Green. The west end and north-west of the city had long ago been colonized by the propertied and professional classes. As one moved

from west to east, in a sort of arc from Charing Cross, fashionable
society gave way to the aspiring and respectable, but definitely lower
middle classes. Here, in Somers Town and Camden Town, were the
clerks who toiled all day at their desks in the City or the port; whose
wives kept up appearances, and whose daughters struggled in select
'seminaries' to acquire such diverse but necessary preparations for
marriage as 'English composition, geography, and the use of dumb-bells
. . . writing, arithmetic, dancing, music and general fascination . . . the
art of needlework, marking and samplery . . .'[21] Further east, drawing
inwards towards the City, lived lacemakers, drapers, embroiderers, the
straw-hat and bonnet makers and the milliners of Marylebone and St
Pancras, the artificial flower makers, bonnet and cap makers of Clerkenwell and St Luke's.

The nucleus of London is the focus of this study: the City and its
perimeter, the East End and south of the river from Rotherhithe to
Lambeth. Although, in these predominantly manufacturing regions of
London, the polarization of classes was still far from complete – 'in the
Bethnal Green and Whitechapel unions, in which are found some of the
worst conditioned masses of population in the metropolis, we also find
good mansions, well drained and protected, inhabited by persons in the
most favourable circumstances', wrote Edwin Chadwick in 1842 for
instance, in his *Sanitary Report*[22] – the migration of the middle classes
to the suburbs was under way.

Omnibus and rail were beginning to make possible this migration,
but the principal metropolitan trades and manufactures remained in the
centre – and the working classes with them. The industrial districts of
London had established themselves east of the City and south of the
river in the sixteenth century. During the eighteenth and early nineteenth
centuries, the ground between the City and the East End had been built
over; workshops and warehouses were built in and to the north and
east of the City, while docks and shipyards were beginning to stretch
eastwards from the Tower. These developments had pushed many
workers out of the City itself, and, between 1700 and 1831, its
population dropped from 210,000 to 122,000.[23] By 1800 then, artisans
and labourers were well established in the industrial belt encircling the
City, and over the river in Southwark and Bermondsey. There they
dwelt in their 'haunts of poverty' and 'pockets of vice' in the first half
of the nineteenth century where Railways, docks and other 'improvements' failed to dislodge them. In Whitechapel, for instance, between
1821 and 1851 the population increased from 68,905 to 79,759,
although several thousand houses and 14,000 persons had been displaced by the building of the London (1800–1805) and St Katherine's

(1828) docks, together with railways and other enterprises. The result was that the 'labouring class' crowded 'themselves into those houses which were formerly occupied by respectable tradesmen and mechanics, and which are now let into tenements'.[24] Further west, the effect of pushing New Oxford Street through one of the most populous districts of St Giles was that whereas in 1840 the houses in Church Lane had twenty-four occupants each, by 1847 they had forty.[25] Indeed, with the exception of parts of Bethnal Green, Mile End Old Town, St Olave's Southwark and southern Lambeth, all the inner industrial perimeter of London was overcrowded, with between fifteen and forty houses per acre – and the population of every district in this area increased between 1831 and 1851.[26]

The overspill of the working classes in central and east London and their relative isolation from the middle classes, even within a particular district, were a source of perpetual anxiety to Victorian philanthropists, city missionaries and social reformers. Separation of the classes was dangerous since it bred class hatred; proximity of the poor among themselves led to contamination; overcrowding encouraged promiscuity and all manner of depravity. Nevertheless, the poor continued to crowd in on one another because they had to live near their place of work, which in the 1830s and 1840s was still largely localized in the inner industrial perimeter and rents were high in tenements and lodging houses which housed most of the poor, families of several children and more living in one room. There were no cheap transport facilities until the last third of the nineteenth century, and much employment was casual – that is, the worker was employed on a day-to-day or weekly basis. Every trade had its casual fringe and in many partial and improvised occupations (of which London, as a capital city, had an abundant supply), employment sometimes only amounted to a few hours a week, and even then was contingent on being immediately accessible. Even workers in the 'honourable trades' had to be 'on call' daily, which meant it was impractical to live further away from the place of work than a couple of miles.[27] But for the most part it was women who worked closest to their home, who, on the whole, lacked the mobility of their men. Women's trades established themselves accordingly.

There were working-class communities beyond the industrial perimeter of course – the potteries of Kensington, for instance, colonized by pig-keepers, and later brickmakers, in the early part of the nineteenth century. And communities founded on cultures more deeply rooted than work. St Botolph's in the City of London for instance, where congregated 'people of the Jewish persuasion', described by the local vestry-clerk as a 'busy, active and thriving community . . . whose habits and character are much misunderstood'. The Jews were sustained by a range of occupations – mechanics, brick-layers, carpenters, plasterers, porters, braziers, jobbing tailors and shoemakers, hawkers, their wives street-sellers, manglers, with charities of their own.[28] Jewish immigration to London's poor districts between the City and the East End had increased from the second half of the eighteenth century. Excluded from apprenticeships, they filled the casual trades, as did the Irish who appear to have lived more promiscuously among the different working classes. Mayhew mentions Italians, Ethiopians, negroes and Lascars too among the street-sellers and others living in the industrial and riverside regions. In every wealthy district, 'from Belgravia to Bloomsbury – from St Pancras to Bayswater' – there was

> hardly a settlement of leading residences that has not its particular colony of ill-housed poor hanging onto its skirts. Behind the mansion there is generally a stable, and near the stable there is generally a maze of close streets, containing a small greengrocer's, a small dairy's, a quiet coachman's public house, and a number of houses let out in tenements. These houses shelter a large number of painters, brick-layers, carpenters, and similar labourers, with their families, and many laundresses and charwomen.[29]

But while these groups are important insofar as they serve as a reminder that London was the centre of wealth, luxury, fashion and conspicuous consumption – they were part of a different city and a different economy from those of the East End, the City and its boundaries north and south of the river.

Within the industrial perimeter and the East End, work specializations on a local basis reinforced the separation into distinctive communities. In the 1850s, Mayhew listed, apart from the Spitalfields silk weavers, 'the tanners of Bermondsey – the watch-makers of Clerkenwell – the coachmakers of Long Acre – the marine store dealers of Saffron Hill – the old clothes men of Holywell Street and Rosemary Lane – the potters of Lambeth – the hatters of the Borough'.[30] More could be listed, all of which, with the exception perhaps of the laundresses of Kensal Green, or the milliners of the West End, would be designations by masculine trades and occupations. But the correlation between district and trade was never absolute, except perhaps in a place like Bermondsey, south of the river, virtually surrounded by water and uninviting to outsiders because of the 'pungent odours' that exuded from the tanneries, glue, soap and other manufactories of the noxious trades. In general, it was poverty and common want that drew people together in the tenements of St Giles's, or parts of the East End, haunts of the poor as Dickens describes in *The Old Curiosity Shop*:

> ... a straggling neighbourhood, where the mean houses parcelled off in rooms, and windows patched with rags and paper, told of the populous poverty that sheltered there ... mangling women, washer-women, cobblers, tailors, chandlers driving their trades in parlours and kitchens and back-rooms and garrets, and sometimes all of them under the same roof.[31]

The women of these districts are the subject of this essay.

— *London Trades and the Sexual Division of Labour* —

Women's waged work was not immediately conspicuous in London in the early Victorian period. Women were not found in the skilled and heavy work in shipbuilding and engineering, two of London's staple industries in the first half of the nineteenth century. Neither were they employed in the docks and warehouses, nor their subsidiary trades. There were no women in the public utilities, (gas, building, etc.) or transport, nor in most semi-processing and extractive industries – sugar refining, soap manufacture, blacking, copper and lead working and the 'noxious' trades – which were London's principal factory trades in this period. Finally, women were excluded from the professions, the civil service, clerical work, the scientific trades, and had been excluded from the old guild crafts (e.g. jewellers, precious instrument makers, carriage builders, etc.) since the fourteenth and fifteenth centuries. If women were not in the heavy or skilled industries, in public service or factory, in the professions or clerical work, then where were they to be found?

The 1851 Census tells us (in round numbers) that of the 330,000 or so women aged twenty or over listed as occupied in other than domestic duties, 140,000 (or 18 per cent of women of that age group) were employed in domestic service; 125,000 (16.3 per cent) were in clothing and shoemaking; 11,000 (1.9 per cent) were teachers and 9,000 (1.2 per cent) worked in the silk industry. The bulk of the remainder were employed either in other branches of manufacture (artificial-flower making, straw-hat and bonnet making, etc.) or as licensed victuallers, shopkeepers, inn-keepers and lodging-house keepers, or else they were listed as the wives of tradesmen and manufacturing workers. Bearing in mind the limits and idiosyncracies of the 1851 Census as a source, we can see that women's work fell into four principal categories: firstly, all aspects of domestic and household labour – washing, cooking, charring, sewing, mending, laundry work, mangling, ironing etc; secondly, child-care and training; thirdly, the distribution and retail of food and other articles of regular consumption; and finally, specific skills in manufacture based upon the sexual division of labour established when production (both for sale and domestic use) had been organized within the household. That is to say: the sexual division of labour on the labour market originated with, and paralleled that within the family; or, women's waged work mimicked that which they did in the household.

This sketch of women's waged work in London is not an over-simplification. A closer examination of the Census and other sources reveals an apparently wider variety of women's work. Arthur J. Munby, for instance, a careful observer of working-class women, described in June 1861 a miscellania of occupations:

> London Bridge, more than any place I know here, seems to be the great thoroughfare for young working women and girls. One meets them at every step: young women carrying large bundles of umbrella frames home to be covered; young women carrying cages full of hats, which yet want the silk and the binding, coster-girls often dirty and sordid, going to fill their empty baskets, and above all female sack-makers.[32]

And in the same year Munby met or noticed female mudlarks, brick-makers, milk-girls, shirt-collar makers, a porter, a consumptive embroiderer, a draper's shop assistant as well as servants and some agricultural labourers from the country. Mayhew also talked with women in heavy manual work: dustwomen, milk-girls, porters, market girls. Nevertheless, most women's work fitted into the categories described above or if they didn't, then observers said that they did. Poverty had always forced some women to seek employment in heavy, unpleasant, irregular work, especially those women outside the family, or with no male wage coming in regularly. Dorothy George wrote of women among the eighteenth-century London poor, for instance, that there is no work 'too heavy or disagreeable to be done by women provided it is also low paid'.[33] And an investigation by the Statistical Society into the poorer classes in St George's in the East, uncovered the same characteristics of women's employment in 1848. Whereas men's wages

> varied as usual, with the degree of skill required in the several trades, the lowest being those of the sailors, 11s. 10d (55p) per week beside rations, and of the mere labourers, 15s. 7d (80p) per week, on the average; the highest those of the gunsmiths, 41s. 9d. (£2.5p) per week; the general average being 20s. 2d. (£1) per week . . .

The average wage of single women and widows wa
(about 35p). The average earnings of 'widows with enc
9s. 11d. (50p). The report blamed those 'limited means' (
range of employments available for female hands, especial
panied by a vigorous frame and habits of bodily exertion   ⌐ugh
the sexual division of labour was seldom static on the London labour
market, or rather the several labour markets within each trade and
district as we shall see, the designation 'women's work' always meant
work that was unskilled, overcrowded and low paid. Consequently
men, whether in the relatively highly paid skilled trades, especially in
the honourable sectors or in the lower reaches of unskilled work,
jealously resisted the entry of women into their trades and excluded
them from their trade societies. Indeed, such was the force of custom
and tradition in the structures of the London labour markets that the
appearance of women in a previously male-dominated trade or skill
indicated a down-grading of the work involved, and this was generally
achieved through a change in the production process itself.

— The Capitalist Mode of Production and the Sexual Division of Labour —

The sexual division of labour – both within and between the London
trades – in the 1830s and 1840s had been established in the period of
manufacture (roughly from the sixteenth to the eighteenth century). It
was predetermined by the division of labour that had existed within the
family when the household had been the unit of production. The epoch
of modern industry, far from challenging this division further demarcated and rigidified it. Historically many steps in this process must be
left to the imagination. Its progress anyway varied from trade to trade
and was modified by local custom. But a schematic outline can be given
of the way in which capitalist production, as it emerged and matured,
structured the sexual division of labour.

Capitalist production developed within the interstices of the feudal
mode of production; it emerged alongside of, but also in opposition to,
small peasant agriculture and independent handicrafts.[35] Capitalist
production first manifests itself in the simultaneous employment and
cooperative labour of a large number of labourers by one capitalist.
Cooperation based on division of labour assumes its characteristic form
in manufacture, which, as a mode of production arose from the
breakdown of the handicrafts system.[36] Each step in the development of
capitalist production is marked by a further refinement in the division
of labour, so that what distinguishes the labour process in manufacture

...m that in handicrafts is that whereas the worker in the latter produces a commodity, the detail labourer in manufacture produces only part of a commodity.[37] Nevertheless, the technical basis of manufacture remains the handicraft skills. However, these skills become differentiated:

> Since the collective labourer has functions, both simple and complex, both high and low, his members, the individual labour-powers, require different degrees of training, and must therefore have different values. Manufacture, therefore, develops a hierarchy of labour-powers, to which there corresponds a scale of wages. If, on the one hand, the individual labourers are appropriated and annexed for life by a limited function; on the other hand, the various operations of the hierarchy are parcelled out among the labourers according to both their natural and their acquired capabilities. Every process of production, however, requires certain simple manipulations, which every man is capable of doing. They too are now severed from their connection with the more pregnant moments of activity and ossified into exclusive functions of specially appointed labourers. Hence, Manufacture begets, in every handicraft that it seizes upon, a class of so-called unskilled labourers, a class which handicraft industry strictly excluded. If it develops a one-sided speciality into a perfection, at the expense of the absence of the whole of a man's working capacity, it also begins to make a speciality of the absence of all development. Alongside of the hierarchic gradation there steps the simple separation of the labourers into skilled and unskilled.[38]

The accumulation of capital was held back by the handicraft base of manufacture, which enabled skilled workmen to exert some control over the labour process through combination in a trade society. Entry into the trade was restricted and knowledge of the skills involved in the work process was confined to those who entered formal apprenticeship. But these limited privileges were gained at the expense of the 'unskilled'. Excluded from trade societies most workers were denied a specialized training, and hence lacked bargaining power against capital. The transition from handicrafts to manufacture relegated most women to this position.

By the fifteenth century many craft guilds were excluding women, except for the wives and widows of master craftsmen. Even when women were admitted there is little to indicate that they had ever been formally trained in the technical skills of the labour process itself.[39] But the guilds had been organizations of master craftsmen. With the accumulation of capital, and demarcation of economic classes within a

An OUTLINE of SOCIETY — in . OUR OWN TIMES —

SPECIMENS FROM MR PUNCH'S INDUSTRIAL EXHIBITION OF 1850
(To be improved in 1851)

handicraft, the practice of a craft or trade required more capital. The proportion of masters to journeymen altered on the one hand, while, on the other, the impoverished craftsmen (masters or journeymen) practised their trade outside the jurisdiction of the guilds. As more journeymen became wage-earners at their masters' workshops, they organized themselves into societies to protect their interests, which, insofar as they preserved work customs, coincided with the master craftsmen against the domination of merchant capital and the encroachment of the unskilled. These journeyman societies also excluded women. Women, who were now denied access to socially recognized skills, formed a source of cheap labour power for the unskilled unorganized branches of production developing outside the corporated guilds. This pool of female labour formed one basis of the industrial reserve army, which was at once both a precondition and necessary product of the accumulation of capital.[40]

Women's vulnerability as wage-workers stemmed from their child-bearing capacity upon which 'natural' foundation the sexual division of labour within the family was based. Because, in its early organization (the putting-out, or domestic system), capitalism seized the household or the family as the economic and often the productive unit, the sexual division of labour was utilized and sustained as production was transferred from the family to the market-place.

The pre-industrial family had a patriarchal structure. This was true of the working-class family in the period of manufacture (sixteenth to eighteenth centuries), whether the family was employed directly on the land, in an urban craft or trade, or in a rural domestic trade. The father was head of the household, his craft or trade most often determined the family's principal source of income, and his authority was sanctioned by both divine and natural law. Nevertheless (except among the very wealthy minority), every member of the family participated in production and contributed to the family income. A woman's work in the home was different from her husband's, but no less vital. (Most women were married or widowed in the pre-industrial period except for those in service.) Her time was allocated between domestic labour and work in production for sale, according to the family's economic needs. And sometimes a woman's economic contribution to family income was considerable (especially in rural industries). But a wife's responsibility for the well-being of her husband and children always came before her work in social production, and in a patriarchal culture, this was seen to follow naturally from her role in biological reproduction.[41]

The intervention of capitalism into the sexual division of labour of the patriarchal family confirmed the economic subordination of the wife. By distinguishing between production for use and production for exchange and by progressively subordinating the former to the latter, by confining production for use to the private world of the home and female labour, and production for exchange increasingly to the work-shop outside the home and male labour, capitalism ensured the economic dependence of women upon their husbands or fathers for a substantial part of their lives. In these conditions, each further step in the development of capitalist production – breakdown of the handi-crafts system, division of labour, exclusion from the skilled craft guilds, separation of workshop and home, formation of trade societies – further undermined women's position on the labour market. Manufacture provided the economic conditions for the hierarchy of labour powers, but it was the transference of the sexual division of labour from the family into social production which ensured that it was women who moved into the subordinate and auxiliary positions within it. (The other main area of women's employment, domestic and personal service, cannot be analysed in these terms, since it remained outside capitalist production proper arguably into the twentieth century. This did not prevent it however, from sharing the general characteristics of women's work, low pay and low status.)

The reservoir of female labour was an immediate source of cheap labour power ready for utilization by capitalist production when a revolution in the mode of production altered the technical base of the labour process, as for example the introduction of the sewing machine in the clothing, or the type-writer in the clerical trades. For as long as production depended upon the workman's skilled manipulation of the instruments of labour, the capitalist could not dislodge his skilled workmen. Only the decomposition of that skill into its constituent parts, which was brought about by a revolution in the instruments of labour, could break up workmen's control over the labour process. It was this revolutionary progress in the division of labour which marked the advent of the epoch of modern industry. Machinery and the factory system abolished the material base for the traditional hierarchy of labour powers and so for the first time the possibility of the introduction of cheap unskilled labour on a large scale:

> Along with the tool, the skill of the workman in handling it passes over to the machine. The capabilities of the tool are emancipated from the restraints that are inseparable from human labour-power. Thereby the technical foundation on which is based the division of labour in Manufacture, is swept away. Hence, in the place of the hierarchy of specialised workmen that characterises manufacture, there steps, in the automatic factory,

a tendency to equalise and reduce to one and the same level every kind of work that has to be done by the minders of the machines; in the place of the artificially produced differentiations of the detail workmen, step the natural differences of age and sex.[42]

In this sense, modern industry was a direct challenge to the traditional sexual division of labour in social production. In the Lancashire textile industry, for instance, women and children were the earliest recruits into the factories. But in London the ways in which the labour power of women was utilized in the transition from manufacture to modern industry was more complicated, because that transition itself, when it was made at all, was made differently in each trade.

Some traditional areas of the London economy, the small, specialized and luxury trades for instance, which depended on proximity to their markets and skilled handicraftsmen, were scarcely at all affected by modern industry. Indeed in a few cases, they had been only minimally affected by the transition from handicrafts to manufacture. There were still handfuls of women working in these skilled crafts – engraving, precious metals, instrument makers, watchmakers, and others – who served as a reminder of the position that women had once occupied in production during the handicrafts era. Yet even in the trades most directly affected by the industrial revolution there was no single process of adaptation. Of those which had transferred to the factory, there were one or two in which the introduction of machinery at certain stages in the labour process was forcing a realignment in the sexual division of labour. In the Spitalfields silk industry, for example, William Wallis, a weaver, stated that 'the winding is almost wholly done by machinery now consequently it is performed by girls only', and that '. . . winding under these circumstances obtains the best wage of any other branch of trade in Spitalfields'.[43] Further examples in book-binding, hatting and rope and sailcloth making are discussed in the following section. But, on the whole, those trades with a potential or actual mass market found the high costs of rent and fuel and its transportation in central London, made the introduction of machinery and factories quite impracticable. Other techniques with which to counter provincial factory and foreign competition were found. The large supply of cheap labour favoured the development of sweated outwork and other slop-work, not modern industry proper.

— *Industrial Change in London 1830–50: Slop-work* —

The slop trades produced cheap ready-made goods for retail or whole-sale shops, showrooms and warehouses, in the East and West Ends of

London, and the City. (These show-shops and emporiums were the commercial equivalents of the spectacular gin-palaces which so awed contemporaries and which, some complained, likewise displaced the small man and his wife who served in the public house.)[44] They were based upon the same principle as that which permitted the introduction of machinery in cotton textiles, the breakdown of the skilled labour process into its semi- or un-skilled component parts. They depended upon the unlimited exploitation of an inexhaustible supply of cheap unskilled labour. Women and children formed the local basis of this labour force, as well as the pool of casual labour that had always belonged in London. But from the end of the Napoleonic Wars, this labour pool was swelled by growing numbers of immigrants from Ireland and the agricultural districts.[45] As the men sought work in the docks and the building industries, their wives and children flooded into the slop trades. Long hours, irregular employment and wages often below subsistence were the marks of these industries, as the wholesalers or 'warehousemen' adjusted the labour supply to fit the demands of the market.[46] A host of new techniques – 'scamping methods' – were introduced which shortened the length of time it took to produce an article. The division of labour, and lowering standards of workmanship enabled the influx of unskilled labour. A shoemaker in Bethnal Green in the 1840s describes some of the effects of slop-work in his trade:

> It is probable, that independent of apprentices, 200 additional hands are added to our already over-burdened trade yearly. Sewing boys soon learn the use of the knife. Plenty of poor men will offer to finish them for a pound and a month's work; and men, for a few shillings and a few weeks' work will teach other boys to sew. There are many of the wives of chamber-masters teach girls entirely to make children's work for a pound and a few months' work, and there are many in Bethnal Green who have learnt the business in this way. These teach some other members of their families, and then actually set up in business in opposition to those who taught them, and in cutting, offer their work for sale at a much lower rate of profit; and shopkeepers in town and country, having circulars sent to solicit custom will have their goods from a warehouse that will serve them cheapest; then the warehouseman will have them cheap from the manufacturer; and he in his turn cuts down the wages of the work people, who fear to refuse offers at the warehouse price, knowing the low rate at which chamber-masters will serve the warehouse.[47]

In every slop trade, there were middlemen between the warehouse or showroom, and the producer. The work was sub-contracted out to the lowest bidder, who was usually a small master or mistress; the sweater in tailoring and the other clothing trades, the chamber-master in men's, women's and children's shoemaking, the garret-master in dressing-case, work-box, writing-desk making and other branches of the fancy cabinet trade (which Mayhew described as among the worst trades even in Spitalfields and Bethnal Green). Outwork was an effective counter to factory competition because it saved on overheads, required small capital and isolated workers, thus preventing their effective organization. Small masters employed their wives and children, and apprentices or other workers more destitute than themselves, to assist them. By constant undercutting and all the methods of slop-work, wages sank beneath subsistence and the small master undermined his own livelihood.

This sort of 'domestic industry' had always existed beyond the skilled 'honourable' sectors of the London trades, but in the lurching economy of the thirties and forties, even workers in the 'honourable' sectors felt threatened by the expansion of slop-work, and especially by its erosion of customary skill differentials. A journeyman tailor, for instance, describes the blurring of distinction between men's and women's work:

> When I first began working at this branch there were but very few females employed in it; a few white waistcoats were given out to them, under the idea that women could make them cleaner than men – and so indeed they can. But since the last five years the sweaters have employed females upon cloth, silk and satin waistcoats as well, and before that time the idea of a woman making a cloth waistcoat would have been scouted. But since the increase of the puffing and the sweating system, masters and sweaters have sought everywhere for such hands as would do the work below the regular ones. Hence the wife has been made to compete with the husband, and the daughter with the wife; they all learn the waistcoat business and must all get a living. If the man will not reduce the price of his labour to that of the female, why he must remain unemployed; and if the full-grown woman will not take the work at the same price as the young girl, why she must remain without any. The female hands I can confidently state, have been sought out and introduced to the business by the sweaters from a desire on their part continually to ferret out hands who will do the work cheaper than others.[48]

It is easy to see why the journeyman tailor, the shoemakers and indeed most of the workmen who spoke to Mayhew at the end of the 1840s, might attribute their lowered standard of life over the previous fifteen years to the influx of cheap labour. Many trades had bitterly fought (tailors' and woodworkers' strikes in 1834 for instance) and failed to resist the erosion of skills, work customs and wage rates in those years.[49] But their diagnosis was over-simple. The flow of unskilled labour into a trade was the *result* of the dissolution of a skill. This, and the opening up of mass markets was made possible by the strengthening and concentration of capital within a trade, generally in London in the form of the wholesale or retail warehouseman. In this way the skilled workman lost his bargaining power against capital.

But the income differential between men's and women's work did not simply measure the distance between skilled and unskilled. The idea of the family wage had been transferred onto the labour market with the male worker. Although few men's wages actually did provide for all the family, one of the marks of a 'society' man was supposed to be his ability to take home a family wage, and the *assumption* that a man had to support a family, whereas a woman did not, was echoed throughout all but the most casual reaches of the labour market. That this assumption was unjustified, is testified for example, by the Statistical Society's inquiry in east London in 1848. There were 229 'unprotected' women compared with only 125 'single' men:

> A glance at the table which shows their scanty earnings, and the numerous families which are dependent upon two thirds of them, will convey a sufficient idea of the position of moral as well as pecuniary difficulty in which they are placed. Some of the women included in this class are, indeed, widowed only by the abandonment of the husbands. All, however are living unprotected with families dependent on them.[50]

Women's casual status as an industrial reserve army for most of London's manufacturing trades was buttressed therefore by their work in the family and the assumption that a man earned a wage to support the family. The implications of this were far-reaching. Whereas the unskilled countrymen who flooded the slop trades were eventually organized, women workers remained almost entirely outside the trade union movement throughout the nineteenth century, and into the twentieth. Their position as home workers, slop-workers, sweated workers and cheap labour both made them difficult to organize, and reinforced the ideology which prohibited their organization. By excluding women from trade societies, men preserved their patriarchal authority at the expense of their industrial strength.

The sub-contracting and undercutting of slop-work which reduced so many London workers to near destitution in the thirties and forties, were as much part of the 'industrial revolution' as the machinery and factories of Lancashire. And the employment of women and children at less than subsistence wages in the slop trades was as symptomatic of the concentration of capital and the maximization of profit within an industry as the mill girls in cotton textiles.

— Hierarchy of the London Labour Market: Women's Skilled Work —

In such a state of flux within the labour market it would be difficult to construct any hierarchy of employment. But since most women's work was lumped together at the bottom of the social and economic scale, stratifying it is almost impossible. There are none of the familiar landmarks which help us to assess the relative status of a working man on the labour market. Few women's skills had any scarcity value or socially recognized status. Most of them – food and clothing, and the service trades, for instance – had only been transferred to the market in the previous 150–200 years. They had no experience of combination, no sacrosanct customs, no tradition of formal apprenticeship – all of which established a skill.[51]

What skilled work there was for women, however, fell into three categories: the exclusively female trades; women's work in the 'honourable' sectors of men's trades, and factory work. These are the occupations which, as far as we know, required some formal training, where the wages were relatively high for women's work, and where there was the possibility of secure employment.

Dressmaking and millinery
Dressmaking and millinery, were trades traditionally in the hands of women and they remained so throughout the nineteenth century. Mayhew distinguishes between the two branches of the trade:

> The dressmaker's work is confined to the making of ladies' dresses, including every kind of outwardly-worn gown or robe. The milliner's work is confined to making caps, bonnets, scarfs, and all outward attire worn by ladies other than the gown; the bonnets, however, which tax the skill of the milliners, are what are best known as 'made bonnets' – such as are constructed of velvet, satin, silk, muslin, or any other textile fabric. Straw bonnet making is carried on by a distinct class, and in separate establishments. The milliner, however, often trims a straw

bonnet, affixing the ribbons, flowers, or other adornments. When the business is sufficiently large, one or more millinery hands are commonly kept solely to bonnet-making, those best skilled in that art being of course selected; but every efficient milliner so employed is expected to be expert also at cap-making, and at all the other branches of the trade. The milliner is accounted a more skilled labourer than the dressmaker.[52]

Dressmaking and millinery offered girls both skill and respectability – a quality indispensible to the Victorian lower middle class. But when looked at more closely, we discover that the opportunities they offered were limited, and these available only to a select few.

No working-class household could afford the £30–50 premium which was the price of a two- to five-year apprenticeship in a respectable house. Most girls served their apprenticeship in the country and came to London to be 'improved' – a process which took another nine months to two years, and cost a further £10 to £15 fee, in a fashionable West End house. There were at least 15,000 dressmakers' and milliners' assistants employed in about 1,500 establishments in London in 1841, aged between fourteen and twenty-five according to one improvised estimate. A small number of these were indoor apprentices and 'improvers' in the first-rate houses. Mrs Eliza Hakewell, who, with her sister, had kept such an establishment at Lower Brook Street, Grosvenor Square, for the previous twenty years, employed six or seven 'improvers' (but no apprentices). She told the House of Lords Committee in 1854, that they were 'very respectable young people (who) would not like to mix with common young people. They were the daughters of clergymen and half-pay officers and of first-rate professions.' Mrs Hakewell added, 'I have had many officers' daughters, many young people of limited incomes and many who come up to learn to make their own clothes.'[53]

Some of these girls fall outside the scope of our survey. So do the first hands, showroom girls and fitters, all the women Mrs Hakewell describes as 'the first-rate talent'. But most dressmakers and milliners came from less elevated social backgrounds; they were either 'out-door apprentices' – that is, they paid no premium and received no wages; or else they were day workers employed for the season (February to July; October to Christmas) and paid perhaps £12–20 for the year. These workers, according to Mrs Hakewell were 'quite common people: little tradesmen's daughters', or even the daughters of the poor. As a young day worker who supported herself and her mother on the 7s. (35p.) she earned for seven or eight months of the year (and 1s. 6d. (7½p.) a week average for the remainder) told Mayhew: 'There are several respectable tradesmen who get day work for their daughters, and who like that way of employing them better than in situations as assistants because their girls then sleep at home and earn nice pocket money or dress money by day work.' 'That,' she added, 'is a disadvantage to a young person like me who depends on her needle for her living.'[54]

Dressmakers' and milliners' assistants were excessively overworked. Ill-health often forced retirement from the trade. During the season which lasted about four months in the spring and early summer an eighteen-hour day was the norm, and it was 'the common practice', Commissioner Grainger reported, 'on particular occasions such as drawing-rooms, wedding or mourning orders for work to be continued all night'. Another reports that as well as long hours, treatment was harsh, food coarse and meals hurried which was felt very acutely by young girls 'kindly and tenderly brought up.'[55] The result was that girls working at this pitch from the ages of fourteen to sixteen, suffered from 'indigestion in its most severe forms, disturbance of the uterine actions, palpitation of the heart, pulmonary affections threatening consumption and various affections of the eyes', together with fainting and distortion of the spine. Consequently those young women who had families to retreat to, did so. Those who survived the rigours of their teens and twenties in the fashionable West End houses (distinguished, according to Mayhew, by the fact that they 'put out the skirts and served the ladies of the nobility rather than the gentry') moved down the social scale to the third- and fourth-rate houses 'where the skirts are made at home (and they) seldom work for gentlefolk, but are supported by the wives of tradesmen and mechanics'.[56]

Long hours, ill-health, and early retirement were the rewards of many of the 6,000 young women employed in the 'better class' house. 6s. to 8s. (30-40p.) a week for a day worker was a respectable wage for a young working girl, but the cost of lodgings was high (not all lived with their parents), and a further expense was the obligation 'to go genteel in their clothes'. In this respect, milliners and dressmakers were on a par with the upper servants, the drapers, or the haberdashers' assistants of whom it was also said that they were 'remarkable for the gentility of their appearance and manners'. Dickens wryly evoked the aspirations of some of these young women in his description of the West End cigar shop in which young men were

> lounging about, on round tubs and pipe boxes, in all the dignity of whiskers and gilt watch-guards; whispering soft nothings to the young lady in amber, with the large ear-rings, who, as she sits behind the counter in a blaze of adoration and gas light, is the admiration of all the female servants in the neighbourhood,

and the envy of every milliner's apprentice within two miles round.[57]

We know little about the organization or work process of women's trades other than dressmaking and millinery, in this period. Sectors of embroidery, tambouring, lacemaking and straw-hat making were among women's skills which required a recognized training. Two other apprenticed trades were pearl-stringing and haberdashery. Some laundry work was also skilled and highly paid, and small businesses were probably run by women. But the numbers of women's trades had declined. Many had passed into the hands of men in the previous hundred years. (Hairdressing, for instance, which had given 'many women in London genteel bread' in the eighteenth century, was taken over by Frenchmen apparently by 1800!) Fewer women were able to set up in independent business because of the separation of workplace and home, and the increase in the scale of starting capital. Some sewing trades remained almost the only manufacture both managed and worked by women on any large-scale basis in the nineteenth century.

Ivy Pinchbeck describes the scope of an embroideress's business, which, she says, hardly changed between 1750 and 1850:

> . . . Women in business as embroiderers were in a very different position from the sweated journeywomen who worked at home on the materials and patterns supplied to them. Sadlers, tailors and milliners were their customers as well as the general public, and for advertisement the more enterprising of them occasionally held exhibitions of all kinds of needlework, including the then popular pictures in silk and materials, for which there was a good demand in a day when needlework was so universal an occupation.[58]

Women's dressmaking and other needlework trades suffered from the competition from slop-work perhaps more drastically than any other manufacturing trades. This was because the demand for cheap readymade clothing increased with the increase in population, the move to the towns and the move towards a money economy (although barter remained a significant element of the household economy of the London poor). The needle was the staple employment for women in London – apart from domestic service – and remained so throughout the nineteenth century. All girls learned needlework from their mothers, schools, charities and philanthropic reforms. Distressed needlewomen were a notorious problem of London life. Economic instability in the 1830s and 1840s accentuated the inherent seasonality of the work making the skilled needlewoman's living precarious. As slop-work increased, so

TREMENDOUS SACRIFICE!

THE BONNET-MAKER'S DREAM

Bubbles of the Year – Cheap Clothing

did the numbers of out or home workers, and the embroideresses, sempstresses, tambourers, artificial-flower makers, makers of fine and expensive shirts were among those who could no longer rely on regular employment, not even in the first-rate (fashionable West End) sectors of the trade. A saw-seller's wife who spoke to Mayhew, for instance, told him that she 'could earn 11s. and 12s. (55–60p.) a week when she 'got work as an embroideress', but 'at present she was at work braiding dresses for a dressmaker at 2½d. each. By hard work, and if she had not her baby to attend to, she could earn no more than 7½d. a day. As it was she did not earn 6d. (2½p.)'[59]

The 'Honourable' Trades

The second opportunity for women's skilled work lay in the 'honourable' sectors of the male trades. Here women were very much in the minority; they were confined to a few specific skills; they were seldom, if ever, included in the trade societies; their wages were very much lower than the men's in the same trade and any encroachment on the traditional sexual division of labour within that trade was zealously resisted by the men. Women worked in the 'strong' men's trade in shoemaking, for instance, where the 'closer's work' which was 'light compared to that of maker' was principally in the hands of females, many of them wives and daughters of the workmen. Mayhew stressed that he was speaking of the workmen who 'in that part of the trade which I now treat of (the West End union trade) work at their own abodes . . .' He added that 'the most "skilled" portion of the labour is, however, almost always done by the man'.[60] In desk making, a branch of the woodworking trades, again our information comes from Mayhew;

> The journeyman executes the ink range, or the portion devoted to holding ink bottles, pens, pencils, wafers, etc., and indeed every portion of the work in a desk, excepting the 'lining' or covering of the 'flaps', or sloping portion prepared for writing. This 'lining' is done by females, and their average payment is 15d. (12½p.) a dozen. Desks now are generally 'lap-dovetailed'; that is, the side edges of the wood are made to lap over the adjoining portion of the desk.[61]

Women in the numerous branches of tailoring were sometimes apprenticed. Women were also employed in some leather manufactories, sewing goat-skins into bags, or as sewers and folders in book-binding, and trimmers and liners in hatting. There might well have been 'honourable' sectors of other trades which employed women, but our knowledge of women's work is still incomplete.

Book-binding

Respectability and gentility were the qualities which set book-binding above domestic service or plain needlework as an occupation for girls in the nineteenth century. Commissioner Grainger approved of women's work in book-binding provided the employers complied with the demands of propriety. He found Messrs Collier & Son of Hatton Gardens, for example, a 'respectably conducted establishment', Mrs Mary Ann Golding, the forewoman, assuring him that her employer only kept on those who had been apprentices or learners as journey-women 'if they conduct themselves properly'. The premises of Mr Horatio Riley of St John's Street on the other hand, were 'rather confined'. Nevertheless, the sexes were kept apart. 'The females work in a separate apartment', and there were 'orders that the boys should not go into this room. There is a discreet person as forewoman in the shop.' Unfortunately, there was only one privy for the whole establishment, but Mr Riley was 'convinced of the importance of having separate privies and (he intended) to make an alteration to effect that object'.[62]

Messrs Westley and Clark, of Shoemakers' Row, also received special credit for the scrupulous care they exercised in 'reference to the character and conduct of the females in their extensive establishment'. 'A single act of levity, or even a look indicative of a light disposition', according to one authority,[63] was 'sure to be followed by the dismissal of the party.' Fortunately for the girls employed in other book-binding houses, this same scrupulous regard was apparently not to be met with everywhere.

Messrs Westley and Clark was the largest book-binding house in London, and was included in George Dodd's examination of London factory trades in 1843, *Days at the Factory*. It employed 200 women in folding and sewing whose weekly earnings ranged from 10s. to 18s. (50–90p.). A small number of girls were taken on as learners each year, paid no premium the first year, and became journeywomen after two years, aged fourteen. Most houses were much smaller, employing only six or so 'learners', and perhaps a few apprentices. The apprentices in the better houses were always boys, who were taught the entire trade for a premium (£25 at Messrs Collier) over a period of seven years. The 'learners' were girls who, according to Mr Collier himself, 'come for about nine months, paying a small premium of two guineas to remunerate the forewoman, who loses a good deal of time in instructing them'. In the lesser establishments it is difficult to distinguish between the apprentices and learners, both of whom served a nine-month or two-year term, and were often girls. Mr Collier went on to describe the lesser parties in the trade who principally or entirely carry on their business by apprentices and learners; in some cases the former are boarded and lodged, and they receive very small wages during the apprenticeship, and in many cases are imperfectly taught the business; the learners, also, are only instructed in the more common part of the work. At the end of the term it often happens that the boys and young women are dismissed, because the master, doing the work at a low price, cannot afford to pay journeymen's wages ... (He) has very frequently had occasion to dismiss women, who have been in such places of business, on account of incompetence. Has in some cases received a premium from parties who have been with small masters, and who have had again to work for some months without pay. Has had frequent complaints of the cruel way in which, in this respect, young women have been treated.[64]

Mr Collier was describing the 'dishonourable' section of the trade. One of the journeywomen at a second-rate house, Mr Cope's in St Martin's Lane, confirmed some of his claims.

Sarah Sweetman, eighteen years old.

Can read and write. Was formerly an apprentice for two years to learn the business; paid no premium; received 1s. 6d. a week; for the last three years has worked as a journeywoman. Mr Cope only executes a part of the business which belongs to the trade. There are some branches which he does not carry on. Apprentices here cannot learn all the branches; so that if they leave at the end of the term, they must go to some other house to learn the business thoroughly. In those houses where they teach all the business a premium is generally paid of [£2.2s.] or [£3.3s.] and sometimes [£5.5s.] for six months; during which time they receive no wages.

Mr Cope's establishment was a second-rate house but not part of the slop trade, since he did not dismiss all his apprentices at the end of their term; most were employed afterwards as journeywomen and received 'wages according to their skill'. 'With regular work from 9 a.m. till 8 p.m. they can generally earn 12s. (60p.) a week', Sarah Sweetman explained. But she had not been taught all the business, and would find it difficult to obtain another situation. She concluded that,

a girl who pays a premium for six months and has no wages, and who is thoroughly taught the business, is better off than one who is not taught the whole of the branches. Those who have been thoroughly instructed, can generally command profitable employment, which the latter cannot. If witness had known when she was bound that she should not have learned all the business, she would not have come here. A considerable part of Mr Cope's business, as far as the females are concerned, is carried on by apprentices; several have left after they have been here a short time, some of the parents thinking the work too hard.

The average day in both large and small establishments was about eleven or twelve hours, allowing one or one and a half hours' break for lunch and tea, some returned home for meals. During the 'busy times' the work is carried on till

10 p.m., 12, 2, 3 and 4 in the morning. Has often worked all night; has done this twice a week, but only on one occasion. The apprentices generally go home at 8 p.m., and sometimes they stay till 9, 10 and 11; on which occasions they receive extra pay.

Several other witnesses confirmed Sarah Sweetman's evidence, and the intervention of parents was often mentioned. Unlike the dressmakers and milliners whose family and friends often either lived out of town, or else were too poor to influence the terms of their children's employment, the parents of book-binders' apprentices probably worked in the trade themselves and knew whether or not their children were receiving an adequate training – hence the relative 'respectability' of the trade perhaps.

Hatting

'It is a fortunate circumstance', wrote George Dodd halfway through his *Day at a Bookbinder's*, 'considering the very limited number of employments for females in this country, that there are several departments of book-binding within the scope of their ability.'[65] Hatting also offered 'reputable employment for females in the middle and humble ranks'. Dodd gave an account of Christy's, allegedly the largest hat factory in the world, which occupied 'two extensive ranges of buildings on opposite sides of Bermondsey Street, Southwark'. Just under two hundred 'females' were employed there in the early 1840s, and they earned between 10s. and 18s. a week, mostly in the manufacture of beaver hats which were fashionable at that time. Christy's was of particular interest since it offered 'some valuable hints' on 'how far female labour may be available in factories where the sub-division of employment is carried out on a complete scale'.

The degree of ingenuity required varies considerably, so as to give scope for different degrees of talent. Among the processes by which a beaver hat is produced, women and girls are

employed in the following: – plucking the beaver skins; cropping off the fur; sorting various kinds of wool; plucking and
cutting rabbit's wool; shearing the nap of the blocked hat (in
some cases); picking out defective fibres of fur; and trimming.
Other departments of the factory, unconnected with the manufacture of beaver hats also give numerous employments to
females.

Mr Dodd did not specify the ages or backgrounds of the women and
girls, although he described the processes in which they were employed
in some detail. He concluded that, 'Where a uniform system of supervision and of kindness on the part of the proprietors is acted on, no
unfavourable effects are to be feared from such an employment of
females in a factory'. Indeed his descriptions of the 'trimmers' underlines
this point for his readers –

> We enter a large square room, full of litter and bustle, and find
> fifty or sixty young females employed in 'trimming' hats, that
> is, putting on the lining, the leather, the binding, etc. Some are
> sitting at long tables – some standing – others seated round a
> fire, with their work on their laps; but all plying the industrious
> needle, and earning an honourable subsistence.

Christy's, in the early 1840s (like Westley & Clark in book-binding)
was exceptional among hatteries. It coexisted alongside the workshops
described by Mayhew in 1849 that were 'almost entirely confined to the
Surrey side of the Thames, and until the last twenty years or there-
abouts, was carried on chiefly in Bermondsey'. The 'tradesmen who
supply the hatters with the materials of manufacture are still more
thickly congregated in Bermondsey than elsewhere', and their numbers
and variety imply that they were still in those years occupied in small
separate workshop production, not combined under one roof as at
Christy's. Women worked as hat binders, liners and trimmers; the
subsidiary trades included hat lining makers, hat-trimming and buckle
makers, as well as wool-staplers, hat-furriers, hat-curriers, hat block-
makers, hat-druggists, hat-dyers, hat-bow-string makers, hat calico
makers, hat box makers, hat-silk shag makers, and hat-brush makers.
But Mayhew gives no account of women's work except in silk and
velvet hats, which he claimed were 'now (1849) the great staple of the
trade'.[66] No man was admitted to the 'fair' sector of hatting until he
had served a seven-year apprenticeship, 'and no master, employing
society men, can have whom he may choose "to put to the trade", and
they must be regularly bound'. The number of apprentices was limited
to two, whether the master had two or one hundred journeymen under
his employ. Daughters of hatters were not formally 'bound' in this

period; they probably received a similar form of training to the girls in book-binding. Hatters were generally married, Mayhew was told, and lived in the neighbourhood of the workshops. 'Some of the wives (of workmen in the "fair" sector) are employed as hat-binders and liners, but none,' Mayhew continues, 'work at slop work.' Again, the connection between kin, knowledge of a trade and access to that trade for women, is evident.

Factory work

The division of labour between the sexes was successfully maintained when book-binding first entered the factory. But it was only much later in the century that the entire 'printing profession' was broken up into a score of different trades, and the subdivision of those trades into each of its detail processes, permitted the replacement of the skilled craftsman by the machine and/or 'cheap' labour. Then women and children moved into work which previously had been monopolized by men, but only into carefully demarcated work, modified by the male trade societies.[67]

Hatting has a similar history. Christy's hat factory, like Westley and Clark's book-bindery, combined under one roof many processes in the manufacture of an article.

> It may excite surprise, [George Dodd warned his readers] to hear of saw-mills, and blacksmiths', turners', and carpenters' shops on the premises of a hat maker; but this is only one among many instances which might be adduced, in the economy of English manufactures, of centralisation, combined with division of labour, within the walls of one factory.[68]

But traditional skill differentials were maintained because the labour process itself had not yet been transformed by the introduction of machinery. Fur-pulling for example, remained women's work whether carried on at Christy's, or in the small workshops described by Mayhew.

Factories like Westley and Clark's or Christy's, for all the modernity which so impressed Dodd, were sophistications of the division of labour characteristic of manufacture rather than of modern industry. Every process in the manufacture of a hat was centralized under one roof. But the replacement of skilled workmen by machinery was rare.

One such change may be detected from Dodd's account of Christy's: women were in charge of the cutting and cropping machines. Mayhew did not mention women in this work in his account of small workshop production, so we may assume that the innovation was the result of a mechanization of the work process. Another isolated and striking example occurs in Dodd's description of a rope and sailcloth factory in Limehouse.

Dodd first of all describes 'all which precedes the actual weaving', which was 'effected in one large apartment; and a remarkable apartment this is, both in reference to its general appearance, and to the nature of the processes carried on therein'. Here, women were employed on the quilling machines, work in which they and children had always been employed even before it was mechanized:

> The quill-machines, . . . each of which is attended by one woman
> have a considerable number of quills arranged in a row, and
> made to rotate rapidly. In the act of rotation the quills draw off
> yarn gradually from reels on which it had previously been
> wound; and the women renew the quills and the reels as fast as
> the one are filled and the other emptied . . . The little quills in
> the quill-machine, rapidly revolving and feeding themselves with
> yarn, require but little care from the attendant, who can manage
> a whole machine full of them at one time.

The much more complicated process of preparing the yarns for the 'warp' of the weaver elicited awe and admiration from Mr Dodd, but he does not specify whether the work was performed by women or not. Most significant, however, was the employment of women on the power-looms. Hand-loom weaving traditionally was men's work (and I'm thinking of tradition here as belonging as much to the mind as to reality), but in every branch of the textile industry, women were replacing men, as machines were introduced and dispensed with the need for strength and skill. In Limehouse, for instance:

> Forty of these, [power-looms] . . . are at work in the weaving
> room of the factory, and may from the noise they create, give a
> foretaste of the giant establishments at Manchester. The
> machine throws its own shuttle, moves its own assemblage of
> warp-threads, drives up the weft-threads as fast as they are
> thrown, and winds the woven canvas on a roller. One woman
> is able to manage two power-looms, to supply warp and weft,
> mend broken threads, and remove the finished material.

But even in sailcloth manufacture, industrialization was not complete. In this factory some men still operated hand-looms, and Dodd's account of that process contrasts strongly with the relative simplicity of the operation of the power-loom. Dodd marvelled at the

> patience with which a man can sit for hours at a time throwing
> a shuttle alternately with his right hand and his left, moving a
> suspended bar alternately to and from him, and treading
> alternately on a lever with one or the other foot; and many have
> perhaps pondered how many movements of hand, arm, and
> foot must be made before a shilling can be earned.

Girls in the quilling factories in Spitalfields were among the highest-paid workers in the silk industry in the 1840s, where depression (and, so the male weavers claimed, the repeal in 1824 of the Acts protecting wages) had reduced the hand-loom weaver's wage to 5s. 6d. (27p.) in 1849. Their relative affluence was displayed in the 'bonnets with showy ribbons, the ear-drops, the red coral necklaces of four or five strings, the bracelets and other finery in which (they) appeared on Easter Monday at Greenwich Fair'.[69]

Lint scraping was also mechanized and operated by young girls who often came from the parish, and were paid 11s. to 14s. (55-70p.) a week after apprenticeship for a twelve-hour day and one and a half hours for meals. The attention of the Children's Commission was drawn to the trade by an 'opinion prevailing' that the children lost the use of their fingers and contracted consumption from the occupation. The witnesses were reluctant to offer such information, however.

An article in *Household Words* tells us that fifteen girls, fifty boys and eleven men were at work in the Lucifer manufactory in Finsbury in 1851. There is no account of the girls' work in the Finsbury factory, but at the lofty and spacious one in Bow, 'Swift-fingered maidens – aged from about twelve to twenty – can earn nine shillings (45p.) a week, or even more; the slowest fingers earning about six', distributing the untipped tapers into frames.[70]

Topping and button-hole making in slop-work was generally done in the factory, but only because the employers feared their low wages would induce women to pawn the clothing if they were permitted to take them home. 'There is a large workshop called the factory, connected with each slop-shop emporium, and in some of them there are over two hundred hands at work' the author of 'Transfer Your Custom'[71] in the 1850s tells us.

Perhaps further examples of women's factory work tucked away in odd corners of the labour market would emerge in the course of research. But it is unlikely if the diligent Children's Commissioners didn't uncover them. The most important invention to affect women's work in London during the nineteenth century was the sewing machine. But this did not necessarily involve the transference of the clothing industries into factories. Usually, on the contrary, it revolutionized the productivity of female waged work within the home. Indeed the effects of modern industry on the London trades in the nineteenth century were neither so uniform nor so *revolutionary* in terms of the sexual division of labour as many contemporaries, including Marx and Engels, had anticipated. Machinery and other changes in the production process were introduced piecemeal and distributed unevenly, and innovation was related as much to the supply, flexibility and available skills of the labour market as to the technical requirements and possibilities within each trade. Industrialization or modern industry in the London trades was likely to mean slop-work and sweating; a proliferation of small workshops, with a handful of workers, not the collective labourer of Marx's imagination.

— Women's Unskilled and Casual Work —

The problems of depicting women's skilled work dwindle into insignificance once we move outside those carefully delineated domains into the vast uncharted world of unskilled and casual employment. Most women were casual workers in the sense that their employment was irregular, or seasonal, or both, and the boundaries between trades were indeterminate as women moved in and out of work according to their changing circumstances. Whether she lived alone, with a man, or with her family, whether she was widowed or abandoned, whether her husband drank, the number of children she bore, her age, all these things directly altered or interrupted a woman's working life to a much larger extent than they did a man's. This meant that there were few occupations a woman could enter and be sure of earning her living at throughout her working life. It also meant that so much women's work tended to be the sort that was easy to pick up or put down – washing or mangling for instance, cleaning, folding, packing, stitching and sewing. It was for similar reasons that married women sought employment near their husband's work. The man's trade usually determined the location of the family home.[72]

A girl's working life might start very young – at five or six – helping her mother, minding a child, cleaning or sewing. An eight-year-old watercress seller had minded her aunt's baby when she was six. 'Before I had the baby,' she told Mayhew, 'I used to help mother, who was in the fur trade; and, if there was any slits in the fur, I'd sew them up. My mother learned me to needlework and knit when I was about five.'[73] Women continued working until illness or exhaustion prevented them.

Few London girls escaped a spell in domestic service. The hierarchy of domestic servants from kitchen to ladies' maid in wealthy houses were often drawn from country estates (like Rosa, Lady Dedlock's favourite in Dickens' *Bleak House*). But servants of the tradesman and artisan classes came from among the London poor. Most working-class homes it seems, employed a young maid of all work, or a nursemaid, when both man and wife went *out* earning. The majority of children at Bethnal Green Market (held every Monday and Tuesday from 7 a.m. to

9 a.m.) were girls of seven and upwards who were hired by the week as nurses and servants mostly to weavers' families. Parish apprentices were similarly launched into 'industrial work'. Mr Fitch, vestry clerk in Southwark, informs us, for instance, that while the boys are apprenticed, 'principally to shoemakers and tailors, some to carvers and gilders, coachmakers, paper-makers, etc.' the girls 'go principally as servants, some as tambourers, straw-bonnet makers, etc.; but in many of these cases they are principally occupied in household work'.[74] Other masters of workhouses or overseers gave similar accounts.

Service offered a girl food and shelter, as well as, if she was fortunate, the possibility of saving some money, which might later be used to set her sweetheart up in a trade. Loss of character, ill-health, inadequate clothing or marriage could all lose a girl her place. But washing, mangling, cleaning or scrubbing (floors, or pots and pans) was often taken up when necessary and available later on. The 1851 Census shows that the majority of general domestic servants were girls between fifteen and twenty-five, whereas the majority of charwomen, washerwomen, manglers and laundry keepers were middle aged and older. A woman who had worked as a mason in Ireland, for instance, 'cleaned and worked for a greengrocer, as they called him – he sold coals more than anything' when she came to England. But her daughter went into service till the fever forced her to pawn everything and left her too 'shabby' to find a place.[75]

The infinite gradations within domestic work were informally measured by skill and respectability as well as income. A woman could earn 1/3d. to 2s. (8–10p.) a day washing and charring. But as with most women's trades work was seldom regular, especially in years of economic depression. A sixteen-year-old coster boy, brought up by his mother, told Mayhew that 'Mother used to be up and out very early washing in families – anything for a living. She was a good mother to us. We was left at home with the key of the room and some bread and butter for dinner,' but he went on – 'Afore she got into work – and it was a goodish long time – we was shocking hard up, and she pawned nigh everything.'[76] Washing and charring were both very hard physical work. Everything had to be done by hand and the working day was very long, from dawn till ten or eleven at night sometimes. The mother of an orphan street-seller 'took a cold at the washing and it went to her chest'; similarly, the widow of a sawyer told Mayhew that she took to washing and charring until 'My health broke six years ago, and I couldn't do hard work in washing, and I took to trotter-selling because one of my neighbours was that way, and told me how to go about it.' Laundresses and washerwomen were continually reprimanded (as were shoemakers), by conscientious city missionaries for Sabbath-breaking. But then a superintendent conceded that it was an occupation 'of so laborious a character, that the Sabbath is, in common with other days generally devoted to that kind of labour'.[77] Quite often a washerwoman's husband helped her with the mangling. The wife of a dock labourer, for instance,

> has a place she goes to work at. She has 3s. a week for washing, for charring, and for mangling: the party my wife works for has a mangle, and I go sometimes to help; for if she has got 6d. worth of washing to do at home then I go to turn the mangle for an hour instead of her – she's not strong enough.[78]

The income was much higher if the mangle belonged to the woman. An old watercress seller's wife earned 3s. a day taking 'in a little washing, and (keeping) a mangle. When I'm at home I turn the mangle for her', he told Mayhew.

A small laundry could be quite lucrative, and often employed several washing women. One street-seller was leaving the streets, she told Mayhew, because

> I have an aunt, a laundress, because she was mother's sister, and I always helped her, and she taught me laundressing. I work for her three and sometimes four days a week now, because she's lost her daughter Ann, and I'm known as a good ironer. Another laundress will employ me next week, so I'm dropping the streets, as I can do far better.[79]

A 'respectable' laundress was paid 'about four shillings (20p.) per dozen shirts, and one shilling (5p.) per dozen small articles'. She pays her washing women 'from two shillings to two shillings and sixpence (10–12½p.) per day and her cronies from two shillings and sixpence to three shillings per day (12½–15p.)'.[80] Ironing, which was very skilled work, requiring careful handling of delicate materials and intricate fashions, was usually the highest paid in laundry work, receiving perhaps 15s. (75p.) per week in those years.

The shopkeeping classes were as miscellaneous as those employed in domestic labour. Shopkeeping had always been women's work. The wives of small craftsmen or tradesmen traditionally handled the retail and financial side of the workshop. The Census lists women greengrocers, bakers, confectioners, dealers in vegetable foods, licensed victuallers, as well as a few grocers, tobacconists, drapers and stationers. There were also women dealers in timber, carriage building, and other allied trades, probably widows and relatively well off. A small general shop, like laundry work, was perfectly acceptable employment for the wife of a skilled workman. The most typical was the general, or chandler's store similar to the one patronized by a street sweeping gang in the Strand, which dealt in 'what we wants – tea and butter, or sugar, or broom – anythink we wants'.[81]

Street-selling was distinguished from shopkeeping by the fact that the goods were taken to the people, rather than the people seeking out the goods. It was an occupation that many women avoided unless they were born to it, because it was a hard life, with the taint of poverty. . . . 'When they keeps away from here' a buxom dealer in Farringden market confided to Mayhew, 'it's either the workhouse or the churchyard as stops them.' Street-sellers eked out a precarious living, dependent on the spending power of the working classes. Work started with the early morning markets, and the street-seller sat at her pitch or walked the streets all day in all weathers.[82]

Mayhew, an inexhaustible classifier, divides street-sellers into Irish women and English women. The Irish sold mainly flowers, fruit and vegetables – especially oranges – which trade they usurped from the Jews, so some told Mayhew. The latter he subdivided into four groups: firstly, the wives of street-sellers; secondly, mechanics' or labourers' wives who go out (while their husbands are at work) as a means of helping the family income; thirdly, widows of former street-sellers; and fourthly, single women. There was a sexual division of labour in street-selling too – women were principally engaged in selling fish (especially shrimps, sprats and oysters), fruit, vegetables (mainly sold by widows), and firescreens, ornaments, laces, millinery, artificial flowers, butflowers, boots and stay-laces, or small wares: wash-leathers, towels, burnt linen, combs, bonnets, pin cushions, tea, coffee, rice-milk, curds and whey; also dolls, nuts, mats, twigs, anything cheap and small.[83] Stock was either bought from markets, swag-shops or other street-sellers, or the women made it at home. There were women street-sellers of crockery and glassware, too. They were called 'barterers' and usually worked in partnership with their husbands. The serviceableness of a woman helpmate in 'swopping', or bartering was great, according to one of the men of that trade.

The costermongers formed a distinct and 'irreligious' community within London life, entertaining as they did 'the most imperfect idea of the sanctity of marriage', and allowing their children to grow up with 'their only notions of wrong . . . formed by what the policeman will permit them to do'. Mayhew tells us that at about seven years of age the girls first go into the streets to sell.

A shallow basket is given to them, with about two shillings for stock money, and they hawk, according to the time of year, either oranges, apples, or violets; some begin their street education with the sale of water-cresses. The money earned by this means is strictly given to the parents . . .

Between four and five in the morning they have to leave home for the markets, and sell in the street until about nine . . . they generally remain in the streets until about ten o'clock at night; many having nothing during all that time but one meal of bread and butter and coffee, to enable them to support the fatigue of walking from street to street with the heavy basket on their heads. In the course of a day, some girls eat as much as a pound of bread, and very seldom get any meat, unless it be on a Sunday.

A coster-girl's courtship was usually short because 'the life is such a hard one', a girl explained to Mayhew, 'a girl is ready to get rid of a *little* of the labour at any price'.

They court for a time, going to raffles and 'gaffs' together, and then the affair is arranged. The girl tells her parents 'she's going to keep company with so-and-so', packs up what things she has, and goes at once without a word of remonstrance from either father or mother. A furnished room at about 4s. (20p.) a week is taken, and the young couple begin life. The lad goes out as usual with his barrow, and the girl goes out with her basket often working harder for her lover than she had done for her parents.[84]

Costermongering proper was mainly (as it often still is) a hereditary trade, but the wives of labourers went out selling, so did the children of the poor. The children sold oranges and water-cress – anything needing only a few pennies' outlay. Old women resorted to street-selling to avoid the workhouse. Parishes often provided them with money or a small stock (for example bootlaces from the haberdashery swag-shops) to enable them to scrape a livelihood, relatives and friends donated the same. An old lady in the East End who had broken her hip when washing and walking in her pattens (clogs) had a basket of 'tapes, cottons, combs, braces, nutmeg-graters, and shaving glasses, with which she strove to keep her old dying husband from the workhouse'. Her husband was very sick now, but he 'used to go on errands' she told Mayhew, 'and buy my little things for me, on account of my being lame. We assisted one another you see'.[85]

Apart from domestic service, household work and the retail trades, women worked in manufacture. Mayhew's inquiries into 'poverty, low wages, and casual labour, its causes and consequences' in the 1840s uncovered the hitherto unrecognized extent of this work. He showed that the expansion of slop-work probably increased women's participation in the actual work-process of some trades – notably shoemaking, cabinet-making and tailoring – especially with the increasing phenomenon of the small master.[86] The home of a woodworker, tailor, or shoemaker was transformed into a workshop and the entire family was employed in the production of the article. Wood-workers sold on 'spec' to slaughter-houses, upholsterers, linen-drapers, or warehouses; tailors, other clothing workers, and shoemakers worked on order from the shops and showrooms in the City and East End. As we have seen family work in these circumstances often became the last ditch stand of the worker pitched from the 'honourable' sector of his trade onto the casual labour market. The elderly Spitalfields garret master who made the tea caddies which he hawked to the 'slaughter-houses' told Mayhew, 'My wife and family help me or I couldn't live. I have only one daughter now at home, and she and my wife line the work-boxes as you see.'[87] Tailors' wives fetched and carried the goods to and from the slop-seller; the wives of woodworkers went hawking. Sometimes the small master employed other workers besides his family:

In a small back room, about eight feet square, we found no fewer than seven workmen, with their coats and shoes off, seated cross-legged on the floor, busy stitching the different parts of different garments. The floor was strewn with sleeve-boards, irons, and snips of various coloured cloths. In one corner of the room was a turn-up bedstead, with the washed out chintz curtains drawn partly in front of it. Across a line which ran from one side of the apartment to the other were thrown coats, jackets, and cravats of the workmen. Inside the rusty grate was a hat, and on one of the hobs rested a pair of cloth boots; while leaning against the bars in front there stood a sack full of cuttings. Besides the workmen on the floor sat two good-looking girls – one cross-legged like the men – engaged in tailoring.[88]

The multiplication of small masters was a response to the opening up of cheap mass markets, and to economic hardship caused by the perilous fluctuations of the trade cycle. Both phenomena were integral to the industrial revolution. But family work, or small workshop production was not always the grinding struggle that it became in the worst years of economic recession. Piece-rates and work conditions varied to some extent with the skill and quality of the workmanship, and these were not entirely exclusive to the 'honourable' trades, in spite of the better bargaining position of workers in those sectors. Sometimes, the distinction between 'honourable' and 'dishonourable' simply described the division between the fashionable west end trade, and the city or east end warehouses. In toy-making for instance, the principal division was between those who made for the rich and those who made for the poor. And although the Spitalfields silk industry was suffering severely, as it always had done, from economic fluctuations in these years, pockets of family workers remained relatively securely employed:

> When we speak of families [William Bresson told Commissioner Hickson in 1840], we must remember that in a family, when the trade is in a good state, there is invariably more than one loom employed. One man at a loom earns, perhaps, but 10s. in a week, but when able to employ the labour of his wife, children, or apprentices, perhaps three looms, and often four, are kept going, so that I cannot say. I know many families who, when in full work, earn, or might earn, 20s. per week. My son-in-law, for instance, lives with me in the house, and earns about 18s. This would be a poor sum for his family to live upon; but then his wife, my daughter, is very quick at the loom, and earns as much, or rather more, than he does himself.[89]

In spite of its decline in this period there were few trades, as William Bresson explained, 'in which a woman is able to earn as much as my daughter gets by working at the loom; although I must say', he added, 'it is a sort of slavery for a woman'.

The clothing trades offered most employment to women. Women worked in every branch of tailoring (outside the honourable sector) – on their own account as home-workers, as female sweaters, with or without their husbands. Coats, waistcoats, vests, trousers and juvenile suits were in turn divided into different branches according to the section of the garment as well as to material, style, fit and quality, and payment was by the piece. The poorest slop-worker always had to find her own trimmings, thread, candles and coal. An old lady when employed 'at all kinds of work excepting the shirts' told Mayhew

> I cannot earn more than 4s. 6d. to 5s. (22–25p.) per week – let me sit from eight in the morning till ten every night; and out of that I shall have to pay 1s. 6d. (7½p.) for trimmings, and 6d. (2½p.) candles every week; so that altogether I earn about 3s. (15p.) in the six days. But I don't earn that for there's the firing that you must have to press the work, and that will be 9d. a week, for you'll have to use half a hundred weight of coals. So that my clear earnings are a little bit more than 2s., say 2s. 3d. to 2s. 6d. every week.[90]

Trousers were her best paid work, they brought in 4s. 5d. a week clear, and shirt making was the worst, leaving only 2s. 3d. (22p, 11p.) a week clear.

There were a multitude of skills concealed in the bald categories – needlewomen, seamstresses, or dressmaker. As a pamphleteer acknowledged in the 1850s: 'There is no style of cutting and fitting with which the intelligent seamstress is not perfectly well acquainted and must use her scissors in trimming and fitting.'[91] The Census (1851) lists 44,000 dressmakers and milliners of whom the majority were outworkers. Those who received their work direct from the West End fashionable houses ('defined as those that put out the skirts') were mostly between twenty and thirty and lived in St Martins in the Fields, the Strand or St Giles, near by the houses. 'I know of no old woman who is a day worker in the superior trade.' A young day worker told Mayhew, 'You must be quick and have good sight.'[92] Others, working for the less exalted dressmaking establishments, or for the slop-trade, lived all over London (especially in the East End); they were all ages but were not necessarily paid lower wages.

All women's needle-work was very low paid. The West End outworker was as exploited by the fashionable houses as the East End labourer's wife was by the showroom or warehouse – sometimes more so. Both were dealing with middlemen desperately undercutting to sustain a livelihood. Shirt making for the wholesale warehouses of the Minories was perhaps the least remunerative of the sewing trades, partly because the prices were undercut by the prisons, workhouses, and schools which produced shirts at starvation prices.[93] But government contract workers, who made the clothes for the army, navy, police, railway, customs and post office servants were even worse off. We learn from a maker of soldiers' trousers ('the Foot Guards principally'), that

> The general class of people who work at it are old persons who have seen better days, and have nothing left but their needle to keep them and who *won't* apply for relief – their pride won't let them – their feelings object to it – they have a dread of becoming troublesome. The other parties are wives of labourers and those who leave off shirt-making to come to this. There are many widows with young children, and they give them the seams to do, and so manage to prolong life, because they're afeared to die, and too honest to steal. The pressing part, which is half the work, is not fit for any female to do. I don't know but very few young girls – they're most of them women with families as I've seen – poor, struggling widows a many of 'em.[94]

More research might lift the clouds of almost unmitigated destitution which appears to have been the fate of practically all needlewomen in the 1830s and 1840s, indeed throughout the nineteenth century. Is it over-optimistic to imagine that some sewing performed at home, or in

1849
NEEDLE MONEY

George Cruikshank

the small workshops scattered throughout the East and West Ends of London (as well as most of the suburbs), was less exhausting and demoralizing than the general image of the 'distressed needlewomen' evokes? Mrs Rowlandson's evidence for instance, to the Children's Employment Commission in 1841, while it exposes child labour, low pay, and long hours, reveals the different strata within the shirt-making industry, and presents a slightly more dignified if severe aspect to some of the work:

No. 758. 19 July, 1841. Mrs Rowlandson
Executes orders for Messrs Silver and Co. Employs 50 women who make shirts, blouses, caps, collars, etc. These women work at their own houses, and many of them employ 2 or 3 hands each, some of whom are children. All the plain parts can be done by girls of 8 or 9, this is the usual age at which they begin. The regular hours are considered to be from 8 to 8; one hour and a half being allowed for dinner and tea. If an order requires it they work longer, but the children are never kept more than an hour, which is paid as overtime. Girls begin with 1s. (5p.), in a week or so they have 1s. 6d., and increase to 2s. or 2s. 6d. as they improve. A good adult hand, if she has good work, can earn from 10s. (50p) to 12s. Employs at this time three sisters, who can earn as much if they have regular work, which is not always the case. For making the best shirts she pays 1s. 8d. to 1s. 10d. each, having herself 2d. to 4d. for cutting out, taking in to the warehouse, etc. Some mistresses charge as much as 6d. and 8d. for giving out the work; some of the workwomen have complained of this; it has lowered the wages very much.[95]

But Messrs Silver was one of the oldest warehouses in the City, with a relatively established clientele and was conducted along marginally more reputable lines than many of the flash showrooms.

The clothing trades were the most overcrowded, but many others employed women home-workers who made boxes, brushes, brooms, envelopes, matches, mats, paper bags, silk stockings, umbrellas and sacks, who were engaged in fur pulling or card folding. Wages were paid by the piece, and work was irregular so that even the quickest hands were often close to destitution if there was no adult male wage-earner in the family.

Women with a little capital set up as small mistresses in other than the needle trades, in book-folding and binding for instance, and matchbox making. A small capital was necessary either to offer as security to the warehouse which gave out the work, or to get started on one's own. The most notorious method of raising capital was by taking on parish apprentices who paid a £5 premium each.

I have distinguished between two principal areas of women's unskilled work – in the retail/service, and the manufacturing sectors of the London economy. But these were not strictly demarcated. Women moved from one to the other as their circumstances changed. There was the mother of the coster girl whose father 'used to do odd jobs with the gas pipes in the streets', who . . . 'when father's work got slack, if she had no employment charring, she'd say, "Now I'll go and buy a bushel of apples," and then she'd turn out and get a penny that way'.[96] There were the street milliners who 'have been ladies' maids, working milliners, and dressmakers, the wives of mechanics who have been driven to the streets, and who add to the means of the family by conducting a street-trade themselves, with a sprinkling from other classes'.[97] There was the ex-servant girl, married to a smith, who had once owned a house in the Commercial Road where they had let out lodgings. Misfortune reduced her to making 'a few women's plain morning-caps for servants', which she sold to a shopkeeper until that outlet dried up and she sold them herself at the New Cut.[98] There were the women who turned child minding for neighbours into a small Dame School. These received short shrift from the tidy minds of Benthamite educators. Fourteen in Bethnal Green were insultingly described by a British Schools Inspector thus:

> They are in general good for nothing. A broken down mechanic's wife, fit for nothing but the wash-tub, or perhaps as a last resource to keep her from the Poor-house, sets up a dame school and gets a few children about her, who learn scarcely anything.[99]

The inherent seasonality of the London trades accentuated the casual nature of most women's employments. But irregularity was not always oppressive; many London women workers took off in the summer months, for instance, to the market gardens and hop fields of Kent and Surrey. This unfettered anarchy of the female labour market gave women's work a sort of pre-industrial character strangely at odds with a self-consciously industrial age. Even Mayhew seemed to chastise casual workers for simply being casual:

> During the summer and the fine months of the spring and autumn, there are I am assured, one third of the London street-sellers – male and female – 'tramping' the country . . .
>
> A large proportion go off to work in market-gardens, in the gathering of peas, beans, and the several fruits; in weeding, in hay-making, in the corn-harvest (when they will endeavour to

obtain leave to glean if they are unemployed more profitably), and afterwards in the hopping. The women, however, thus seeking change of employment, are the ruder street-sellers, those who merely buy oranges at 4d. to sell at 6d., and who do not meddle with any calling mixed up with the necessity of skill in selection, or address in recommending. Of this half-vagrant class, many are not street-sellers usually, but are half prostitutes and half thieves, not unfrequently drinking all their earnings, while of the habitual female street-sellers, I do not think that drunkenness is now a very prevalent vice.[100]

Many women's employments merged almost imperceptibly into the many partial and residual forms of work which were the mark of poverty or even destitution. The dividing line as far as it existed, was determined not so much by the demands of the economy as by sickness, accidents, old age or the death of a husband or lover. The most frequent visitors to the night refuge in Playhouse-yard, Cripplegate, for instance, were 'needlewomen, servants, charwomen, gardenwomen, sellers of laces in the street and occasionally a beggar woman'.[101] Into this amorphous residuum were tossed all those occupations which respectable Victorians identified with 'vagrancy' and 'vice' – slop-workers, hawkers, trampers, street-sweepers, mudlarks, the inmates of lodging houses, the pickpockets who slept in the baskets and offal around Covent Garden. 'We can take nearly a hundred of them', a Covent Garden policeman told a parliamentary committee in 1828, 'particularly at the time the oranges are about. They come there picking up the bits of oranges, both boys and girls, and there are prostitutes at eleven, twelve and thirteen years of age.'[102]

Prostitution or the workhouse were imminent and real threats to the woman without a trade or other employment in periods of economic distress, and prostitution was often the chosen, desperate alternative to the workhouse. There is no space here to sketch the multifarious wealth of ingenious and pathetic forms of clinging to a livelihood, nor to trace the twists of fortune that regularly deposited the women in these twilight regions of the labour market. Let one 'needlewoman' rescued for posterity by Henry Mayhew speak for all of them.

I am a tailoress, and I was brought to ruin by the foreman of the work, by whom I had a child. Whilst I could make an appearance I had to work, but as soon as I was unable to do so I lost it. I had an afflicted mother to support . . . I went on so for some months and we were half starved . . . I could only earn from 5s. to 6s. (25–30p.) a week to support three of us, and out of that I had 1s. 6d. to pay for rent, and the trimmings to buy which cost me 1s. a week full. I went on till I could go on no longer, and we were turned out into the street because we could not pay the rent — me and my child; but a friend took my mother . . . At last of all I met a young man, a tailor, and he offered to get me work for his own base purposes. I worked for him . . . till I was in the family way again. I worked till I was within two months of my confinement. I had 1s. a day and I took a wretched kitchen at 1s. a week, and 2s. I had to pay to have child minded when I went to work. My mother went into the house, but I took her out again, she was so wretched and she thought she could mind the child. In this condition we were all starving together . . . (my mother) died through a horror of going into the workhouse. I was without a home. I worked till I was within two months of my confinement, and then I walked the streets for six weeks, with my child in my arms.

At last I went into Wapping Union . . . [where both children died in the workhouse].

I came out again and went into a situation. I remained in that situation fourteen months, when I was offered some work by a friend, and I have been at that work ever since. I have a hard living, and I earn from 4s. 6d. to 5s. a week. My children and mother are both dead. The tailor never did anything for me. I worked for him and had 1s. a day . . . From seven in the morning till one or two o'clock I work at making waistcoats, and coats. I have 5d. a piece for double breasted waistcoats and coats, and 10d. and 11d. a piece for slop coats. I can assure you I can't get clothes or things to keep me in health. I never resorted to the streets since I had the second child.

— *Postscript* —

It seems premature to 'conclude' on the basis of research that remains preliminary. Nevertheless, this outline of women's work in London does highlight some neglected aspects of the 'industrial revolution' — in particular, the effect of that process on the sexual division of labour, and vice versa.

The industrial history of London in the nineteenth century demonstrates the strength of Marx's dictum that the capitalist mode of production revolutionizes the character of every manufacturing industry, whether or not modern industry is introduced. Machinery and the factory system were neither as universal nor as immediate in their application, as many had predicted in the 1830s and 1840s. Industrial transformation in London was characteristically expressed in the expansion of the slop and sweated trades which resisted the factory throughout the nineteenth century, founded as they were on a minute division of labour and having at hand a plentiful supply of cheap manual labour. Women (and children) formed the basis of this labour supply. But women's waged work extended beyond the manufacturing industries. Demand for female labour in the service and retail trades ebbed and flowed with the fluctuations of the trade cycle, and so – outside social production – did the prevalence prostitutes, thieves and other 'fallen women'. Needlewomen and homeworkers, small mistresses and their apprentices, charwomen and maids of all work, fit uneasily into the conventional image of 'the working class', but these were the expanding areas of the female labour market in nineteenth-century London; and in none of these trades and occupations were women's wages ever high enough to secure for them and their children economic independence from men.

Throughout the nineteenth and twentieth centuries, amid all the technical changes within trades as well as the industrial transformation of London as a whole, a survey of women's work reveals the tenacity of the sexual division of labour – a division sustained by ideology not biology, an ideology whose material manifestation is embodied and reproduced within the family and then transferred from the family into social production. As technical innovation toppled or abolished old skills, new ones replaced them, creating yet another male-dominated hierarchy of labour powers in trade after trade. It is the consistency of this articulation of the capitalist mode of production through a patriarchal family structure – even at the most volatile moments of industrial upheaval – which must form a central object of feminist historical research.

1974

'BRINGING WOMEN INTO LINE WITH MEN'

THE WOMEN'S TRADE UNION LEAGUE: 1874–1921

— *'Powerful Bodies of Men'* —

The history of trade unionism, wrote Sidney and Beatrice Webb in 1894 'is the history of a State within our State, and one so jealously democratic that to know it well is to know the English working man as no reader of middle-class histories can know him.' The Webbs' two-volume study of the British trade union movement told the story, gave it its heroic cast, largely created its conceptual architecture and their history is indeed peopled with men: engineers, masons, carpenters, weavers, spinners, hatters, miners, tailors, transport workers, agricultural labourers – and from the 1890s, general labourers. The Webbs' trade union officers were all men: the paid professionals who from the turn of the twentieth century formed the union movement's 'governing class' were the direct descendants of the 'diligent unlettered secretaries' of the eighteenth and early nineteenth centuries' trade societies, the true historians of a great movement'.[1]

The Women's Protective and Provident League (WPPL) founded in 1874 by the suffragist Emma Paterson, which inaugurated the only sustained phase of women's independent trade unions in Britain between 1874 and 1920, was relegated to a footnote in the Webbs' *History*.[2] In their second volume the Webbs explained why women 'were the most dangerous enemies of the artisan's Standard of Life'.[3] Women were notoriously difficult to organize into trades unions in the nineteenth century. Of the approximately four million women waged workers over the age of ten in the 1870s, only about 19,000 were in unions, and of these nearly all were in the cotton textile unions; by 1896 the numbers had risen to approximately 142,000, of which 86,000 or 60 per cent of those were in cotton textiles. This compares with the 2,025,000 men out of a total manual industrial workforce of eight million in unions in 1901.[4] The numbers of women in unions did not substantially rise until the First World War – so the Webbs' claim for the democracy of the 'State within our State' needs some modification. Nineteenth-century trade unions were established to protect their members from unlimited entry into the trade – 'illegal men', 'knob-sticks', 'black sheep' or 'scab labour' as well as to raise the level of wages. Female labour was often indistinguishable in the mind of the trade unionist from scab labour.

The Webbs' portrait of the male trade unionist is deliberately seductive. They wrote to convince the British governing class that representatives of Labour with their long tradition of self-government should be allowed to join them. To this end the early trade unionists were depicted as exceptional men in their trade or community, men of 'marked character and ability' who met to educate themselves, to protect the customs of their workshops and to restrict entry into their trades; they were men whose delegates and representatives turned naturally to national government – Parliament – for the redress of wrongs if local arbitration or magistrates failed to secure settlement in local trade disputes. These men invented collective bargaining, according to the Webbs, whose essence by the 1860s was the standard hourly rate, and the 'normal' working week. Drawing on the accumulated wisdom and rituals of their trades, gradually, patiently through the nineteenth century, unions established the principle of the 'Standard of Life' (forerunner of their own national minimum) and imprinted it on the public mind. They founded libraries for their membership, sickness, funeral and other benefits, provision for unemployment, tramping houses of call, recognizing that the accumulation of both funds and knowledge were vital in the struggle to raise the Standard of Life. If the public behaviour and language of these men sounded sometimes stilted and formal, then local descriptions reveal their human hearts and minds: 'The Paisley operatives are of a free, communicative disposition' one of them wrote in 1809,

> They are fond to inform one another in anything respecting trade, and in order to receive information in a collective capacity they have for a long course of years, associated in a friendly manner in societies' denominated clubs ... When met the first hour is devoted to reading the daily newspapers out aloud ... At nine o'clock the chairman calls silence; then the report of trade is heard. The chairman reports first what he knows or what he has heard of such a manufacturing house or houses ... Then each reports as he is seated; so in the period of an hour

not only the state of the trade is known, but any difference that has taken place between manufacturers and operatives.[5]

Little is known about the eighteenth-century societies of men of 'free and communicative disposition' whose oaths of fidelity and shared reading of newspapers and pamphlets informed their sometimes militant defence of wages and customs, until the Acts prohibiting Combinations of Workmen as conspiracies 'in restraint of trade' were passed in 1799 and 1800. These acts were accompanied by debates in and outside Parliament, petitions to the House of Commons and local disputes and riots, information about which – tainted with government paranoia – is lodged in the Home Office records.[6] The acts formed part of William Pitt's notorious 'Gagging Acts' which were an attempt to keep republicanism, Painite and other egalitarian or imagined 'seditious' doctrines at bay among the operatives.[7] Combinations continued illegally throughout the Napoleonic Wars until repeal in the mid-1820s.

The Webbs' hero of the repeal legislation was Francis Place, the radical master tailor of Charing Cross, who had been converted to trade unionism through conditions in his own trade, and whose 'chief merit' according to the Webbs 'lay in his thorough understanding of the art of getting things done'. Place trained and drilled witnesses – the leaders of the Radical working men all over the country – to the Select Committee on Artisans and Machinery (1824), while Joseph Hume, leader of the Philosophic Radicals in Parliament directed proceedings and acted as chief interlocutor of the workmen in Committee.[8] Two acts were passed before the limited legalization of trades unions satisfied hostile employers and their Parliamentary representatives that combinations of workmen would neither interfere with Britain's manufacturing superiority nor reduce the employers to penury.[9] Thereafter the union movement – no longer criminal – enjoyed a limited existence.[10]

The next period of 'prolonged crisis' came in the 1860s provoked by the traumatic revelations (and admission) of violent crimes by some Sheffield trade unionists and a legal decision which withdrew protections from union funds. A new generation of union leaders had emerged, who eschewed the millennial and utopian dreams of the Owenite Grand National Consolidated Trades Union of 1834, and who advocated caution, the moral force of funds, education and political influence. Collaboration between the new informal union leaderships and their 'middle-class' friends, the Positivists, secured legislation to protect union funds, the right to picket, and the replacement of the Master and Servant Act by the Employers and Workman Act – 'a change of nomenclature which expressed a fundamental revolution in the law'.[11] Frederic Harrison, the Positivist, skilfully put the case for trade unions to the Royal Commission of 1867–9 spelling out the principles of trade union legal existence, which informed the legislation of the following six or seven years. Trades councils, Trade Union Congress and International Working Men's Committees were evidence of the newly confident and political trade union movement which put its weight behind Reform between 1865–67, and in the 1870s the first working men stood for Parliament.[12]

I emphasize the Webbs' history, because its heroic masculine portrait of the trades union movement gave authoritative shape to the historical imagination of the Labour Movement until the 1970s; it linked working men's political lives to their industrial history in ways which are only now beginning to be unravelled; and their economism and reverence for skilled men's institutions fixed working women in the Labour Movement's mind irrevocably as industrial dependants. The Webbs' intention – to rescue these 'powerful bodies of men' from their image of origin as violent insurrectionists of riotous disposition succeeded magnificently. In the Webbs' capable hands trade unions were scions of law and order – both harbingers of class struggle and progressive forces in industry. Modern trades unions for the Webbs, were the working man's response to the clash between Capital and Labour which technical innovation – factories and machinery – introduced and made inevitable. Trade unions ameliorated class-war by raising the working man's Standard of Life, and by enforcing Common Rules they assisted in the elimination of inefficient sectors of production.[13] The union movement's 'world of its own' – sectional and intensely local, moved inexorably – in the hands of the Webbs – through its institutions and procedures towards an engagement with and transformation of the national political culture. The fundamental principles of trades unionism were laid down between 1867 and 1876. Seventeen years later when the Independent Labour Party was formed in 1893 its demands were the right to work, provision for unemployment and a minimum wage; when the Labour Representation Committee was established in 1900 it was to elect working men to Parliament.

However the union movement described itself during the nineteenth century – by George Howell, building worker, historian, Liberal MP for Bethnal Green in the 1870s as 'voluntary associations of workmen for mutual assistance in securing generally the most favourable conditions of labour', or more ambitiously by Ben Tillett, the socialist organizer of the 'unskilled' in the 1890s as 'a self-supporting, self-directing, conscious, practical and intelligent administration to govern in all things' – unions were predominantly the organizations of skilled working men until the end of the nineteenth century, and women were excluded.[14] 'Exclusion', as the Webbs made clear, was one of the 'functions' of the trade union movement, founded as they were on a Standard of Life which discriminated against women (women had a lower standard of life, less skill, and fewer dependants).[15] The enforcement of 'Membership' – which necessarily involved 'exclusion' – was as significant the Webbs believed, as the enforcement of citizenship to the emancipation of workmen.[16] Women were doubly excluded: from men's work and unions and from political representation until 1918. What's more, women's conditions of work militated against their industrial organization.

Feminists of the League, some of whom, like the Webbs, were Fabians were faced with a dilemma. How could women workers become part of a political and industrial movement whose ideals were masculine and whose institutions were formed to exclude them? This vision of 'powerful bodies of men', independent, resourceful, heads of families, masters of their trades who were heirs not only to a trade (literally true in some cases, where apprenticeship was confined to the male relatives of the workman) but to a memory, history, tradition of organization may have been a phantasy but it had powerful political and economic effects.[17] Women could share neither men's customs nor their mentality; they could address neither employers nor government as equals, indeed they had no procedures through which to address either – except the strike, demonstration or petition. Women lacking skill and trade societies, crowded into those inefficient sectors of production – casual, sweated, domestic trades – which the trade union movement was historically disposed to eliminate.[18] Consequently the 'average working man regarded the idea of women entering his trade', the Webbs pointed out, with 'an intensity of resentment and abhorrence' based on three things; men's belief that women's rightful place was in the home; the 'instinctive distaste' of the respectable artisan for 'the promiscuous mixing of men and women in daily intercourse whether this be in the workshop or in a social club' (a point to which the Webbs added a stringent footnote on the immorality that followed if this instinct was ignored), and women's lower wages.[19] The Women's Trade Union League had its work cut out. Women workers signified low pay and sexuality: a potent combination, a potential menace to organized labour.

In her *Labour News* article of 1874, which initiated the League, and signalled the beginning of independent unions for women, Emma Paterson pointed out that women had to become accustomed to the idea of union. The Trades Union Congress had for three years' running ruled out discussion of organizing women because somebody always stood up and argued that women could not form unions.[20] Perhaps women had not formed unions because they did not know how to, Emma Paterson suggested. Women workers had been organized before; they had been drawn into the waves of unionization of the unskilled in the early 1830s, and early 1850s. The expansion of trade in the early 1870s was a similar propitious moment for the formation of unions, but the impulse was feminist. Working men in the towns had been enfranchised in 1867; women's suffrage movement was angered by both the Conservative and Liberal Governments' rejection of women's suffrage.[21] The strategy of the League held within it a tension, or contradiction endemic to feminism: women workers were to be separately organized in unions of their own, an aim which carried with it the implication that both the 'needs' and interests of women workers were different from those of men; on the other hand, the feminist leadership of the League maintained throughout the whole period of women's independent organization (1874–1920) that women's separate unions were only a temporary expedient. Women's unions would disappear, or affiliate with men's, the League believed, once women workers had been educated into the 'habits' or 'rules' of trade unionism and men had rid themselves of their prejudice against and fear of female labour. As Mrs Mason, a Leicester hosiery worker and secretary of the Seamers', Stitchers' and Menders' Union, reasoned at the third annual meeting of the League in 1877, men's 'jealousy' of women will disappear 'wherever women show the desire to protect themselves through unions'.[22] Or as Lady Dilke, leader of the League in the 1890s willed in her speeches, 'Labour knows no distinction of sex'.[23] But the principles of trade unionism were masculine, industry divided into men's and women's work, and men's unions excluded women. How the issue of sexual difference in industry was articulated by the League, its irresolution in the first thirty or so years of its history is the subject of this essay.

— *'Degraded and Injurious'* —

The WPPL was set up at a conference (held at the Quebec Hall in Marble Arch) in July 1874 called by the twenty-five-year-old suffragist Emma Paterson. Its purpose was to encourage the growth of women's trades unions in the belief that combination was the first step towards the alleviation of women's 'disgracefully low' rate of wages. Emma Paterson, inspired equally by the discovery of independent unions of working women in the United States (which she visited on her working honeymoon in 1875), and by the example of the Agricultural Labourers' Union (which since its formation in 1870 had grown to 150,000 and increased its wages by one third) published her article in the *Labour*

News inviting 'all persons interested in improving the social condition of women to communicate with her with a view to action in this matter'.[24] In spite of her plea to women 'engaged in trades' for their views and suggestions, the Conference was attended by feminists like herself (Jessie Boucherett, Harriet Martineau (aged 72), and Anna Swanwick); Christian Socialists (Canon Charles Kingsley, the Rev. Stewart Headlam) as well as two influential trade unionists who were to prove steadfast allies of the League, George Shipton, a former building worker, one of the leaders of the London Trades Council, and Mr King, from the Bookbinders' Union (Paterson had been an apprentice bookbinder).[25] A meeting of Christians, feminists and philanthropists which explains the League's rhetorical embrace of both Christian empathy for the outcast (which could verge on the maudlin) with a direct appeal to women to help themselves.

Christian socialism and Comtism were strong influences in the League's work and motivation through its feminist leadership as well as its supporters from the clergy, philanthropists and among the 'ladies' who donated funds. Christian identification with the poor and suffering blended with Auguste Comte's Religion of Humanity, or Positivism, which inspired feminists in part because it proclaimed that regenerative social change would come from the domestic and industrial spheres and so from women.[26] The Christian focus on suffering and sacrifice together with Comtism's moral elevation of public opinion offered feminists an irresistible ethic of femininity which enabled pity and justice to combine with practical reform.[27] There were many different voices on the Committee and Council of the League and among its women workers, but the tension between the pragmatic demands of the unions affiliated to the League, and its philanthropic anxiety (should women work as barmaids; the rescue of prostitutes, for example) reached a momentary climax in the rhetoric of Lady Emilia Dilke, President of the League from 1889–1904. Ironically Emma Paterson, advocate of an *entente cordiale* between responsible employers and women workers, of swimming pools and provident funds, rejected Christianity with impatience; while Emilia Dilke, a socialist who joined the Labour Party in 1904, spoke with religious zeal of her Crusade and its working women.

Emma Paterson's personal history repeats and anticipates that of many nineteenth-century feminists. An impoverished educated woman, she wanted respectable employment and an equality of status with men in every sphere. Emma Paterson was born Emma Smith in 1848, the daughter of a headmaster of a Pimlico church school for children of the poor. Her father made sure that she had a thorough education but he died when Emma was sixteen leaving her and her mother without income. She and her mother made two attempts at running a school. Both failed. Emma then worked as a governess (she could speak and write in three languages) which she disliked so she trained in clerical work. In 1872 she was secretary to the Women's Suffrage Association in Langham Place when she moved to become assistant secretary to the Working Men's Club and Institute Union in Clerkenwell. There she met her husband, a cabinet maker and wood carver.[28] A determined critic of the conventions of political economy, Thomas Paterson, who repudiated his Calvinist faith but remained a Christian, was a self-taught public speaker. He attended lectures on science and philosophy at the Birkbeck Institute, was a member of the Workmen's Peace Association, a campaigner for the suffrage, land reform and education for the working classes; he worked for fifteen years on his book on the new mental sciences which his wife published after his death. He was also on the Council of the Working Men's Institute Union.[29] Together the lives and work of the Patersons exemplify the critical reforming mind of radical liberalism in the 1870s and '80s and its feminist spirit. Individualists, they embraced the belief in a new collectivism as a response to the 'helplessness' of the individual worker in his or her bargain with capital. Both were deeply convinced of the need for the working classes and women to combine to overcome the degradation of poverty; the poor themselves were the regenerative forces in society.

Paterson's description of women's status as workers in relation to men trade unionists in her *Labour News* article became League orthodoxy: women were paid one-half to one-third the wages of men for doing work 'as well and as quickly as men' and work that was often skilled. Whereas men's wages had risen in the previous twenty to thirty years, women's had fallen or remained stable. Even the most skilled workwomen earned less than an unskilled male worker (11s.–15s. (75p.) and 18s. (90p.) respectively).[30] Working men will always look on women with suspicion, and pass rules excluding men from working with women she continued, 'so long as women are unprotected by any kind of combination, and are wholly at the mercy of employers for the rate of their wages and the length of their working hours'.[31] At that very moment men together with 'benevolent persons' were supporting a bill to reduce women's hours of labour in factories and workshops classing women with children, thus perpetuating the idea that women are entirely unable to protect themselves, a position 'degraded and injurious'. It was low pay that above all distinguished women's work from men's. Low pay that reduced women to degradation and vice – (many London workwomen, Paterson told a Sheffield meeting in her characteristic plain speech, 'were half-starved, half-clothed, looking like outcasts, who had committed some crime rather than honest hard working people . . . women who lived by vice were better off materially . . . women's wants were no fewer than men's').[32] Low pay left women defenceless in the face of unscrupulous employers who could impose fines, long hours of work and arbitrary injustices without fear of reprisals from women themselves. The essay opened with an example of a factory worker and mother who literally drove herself to death for the sake of earning a few shillings for herself and her children.[33]

The causes of women's 'degrading remuneration' in their most comprehensive statement were put by Emma Paterson ten years later to the Industrial Remuneration Conference in 1885. This conference (a public enquiry into the best means of 'bringing about a more equal division of the daily products of industry between Labour and Capital') enabled the League to address political economists, civil servants, male trade unionists and MPs interested in the relation between Capital and Labour and the vast gulf between wealth and want.[34] In summary, Paterson stressed equally the conditions of the labour market listed above, arbitrary injustices from the employers and men's 'prejudice'. Added to these were arguments against 'unfair legislation' (which were supported by other contributors to the conference)[35] and women's 'deep sense of injury and wrong'.

The economic thinking was not revolutionary but it opened up the categories of political economy to feminist enquiry. It leaned heavily on the notions of unequal exchange, unfair legislation and unscrupulous employers, imitating in essentials the industrial analysis of the craft unions with its emphasis on the ineffective operation of the market at the level of the demand for labour. Like skilled men, League spokeswomen distinguished between different grades of labour: throughout their literature and public propaganda at the factory gate, Temperance or Church Hall, the League claimed that women's work demanded skill, forethought, training and industry. Only the emphasis on skill, the demand for equality before the law and women's right to economic independence, identified women as a distinct category of labour disadvantaged in particular ways in relation to capital, and discriminated against by men. Emma Paterson and her colleagues did not *dwell* on the deficiencies in the supply of female labour or none that combination and the elimination of both unfair competition from married women homeworkers and men's policies of exclusion would not remove. What distinguished the League's analysis from skilled men's was their focus on working women's relation to the family and domesticity.

Skilled men assumed that a man's wage had to support dependents. The unmarried working woman often appeared in League propaganda as a deliberate challenge to the notion of the man's 'family wage'. She was often the first to join a union, and she represented a source of knowledge and potential strength to the League.[36] But in most speeches and articles on the empirical conditions of women's work it was pointed out that wages and skills were affected by age, marital status, and family need; and that women often worked for or were partially supported by 'fathers, husbands or lovers', and that local trades divided into women's and men's work. The effect was often to concede women's lower value as workers than men.[37]

— League Strategy —

The League, like the wider Victorian women's movement, wanted work in the public world and a new self-hood for women whose expectations otherwise were of 'dependence', domestic 'servitude', the ignominy of charity, the workhouse, or vice.[38] Relations between the League and the *Englishwoman's Journal*, the Society for the Promotion of Women's Employment (both run from Langham Place, the London centre of the women's movement) were cordial. Frances Power Cobbe, Edith Simcox, Martineau (and Lydia Becker) appear in the 1870s at League meetings. But there were differences of emphasis. Whereas the Society for the Promotion of Employment for Women argued that men must step aside to let women into trades hitherto closed to them, the WPPL between 1874 and 1914 perceived not just selfishness on the part of working men, but different material interests of men and women that could only be overcome if women refused to undercut men and combined to obtain advances in wages.[39]

The League formed unions wherever there was a demand from working women, always insisting that women run them themselves once they were established. A model constitution of low dues, benefits and registration was established, and in the first years unions were formed in some skilled London trades, among bookbinders, upholsterers, dress-makers, shirt and collar makers, women's under-linen, tailors, milliners and others; in rope making, shirt-making, confectionery, laundry work in east London; as well as workers in textiles, hosiery, china clay, compositing and other trades outside London.[40]

Few of these unions had a long life, and membership seldom rose above a few hundred. Stories of their formation are often melodramatic. Several hundred women might turn up to meetings held in public halls, or at factory gates, which became much more frequent after the formation of the National Federation of Women Workers in 1906. Sometimes women struck work and formed a union on the spot.[41]

Those unions that survived were formed among first of all women's skilled occupations: the upholsterers, bookbinders, weavers; secondly, among women workers in the 'white blouse' occupations which grew steadily from the early 1900s, women clerks and shop-assistants for example; thirdly those trades in which the women received the co-operation of the men; and finally, sometimes a whole factory or firm would organize.[42] Women workers were militant, but few women's wages could sustain the weekly dues.[43]

The League took every opportunity to influence – indeed form – public opinion. They organized conferences, lobbies and deputations to Ministers, gave evidence to public bodies, and conducted their own investigations into women's trades. From the 1890s the League employed two paid organizers who travelled the country for a few weeks at a time, reporting on conditions in the regions (women who worked in the offices were often unpaid. Gertrude Tuckwell mentions several Newnham graduates and one debutante!).[44] They worked closely with the local trades councils, Women's Co-operative Guilds and suffrage societies. The League and its general union the National Federation of Women Workers (NFWW, 1906) never abandoned hope of agreement with men's unions, in spite of regular attempts at the annual TUC by different groups of male workers to exclude women altogether from their trades. The League's aim was always that women should join men's unions where possible and only if barred from membership should women form their own.[45] From the mid-1880s, some skilled men's unions opened separate women's sections in the attempt to stave off competition from female labour. They were not very successful with women who paid lower dues than men, took less part in union business and were confined to low-skilled work. General and black-coated unions were open to women from the beginning but indifferent to the needs and representation of women workers.[46]

Almost every characteristic of women's labour signified a barrier to union membership. Of the approximately four million women workers in the second half of the nineteenth century and before the First World War, one and a half million were domestic servants and the League did not try to organize them.[47] Of the numbers who worked in manufacturing many were listed as wives. Wives worked for husbands, daughters for fathers and the division of labour, family occupation, income and need varied according to locality even within one trade. Women crowded into a few manufacturing industries (clothing, textiles, food and drink, metals, and other small crafts) many of which were 'sweated'. The majority of homeworkers were women, and competition from married women homeworkers the League argued, was one of the prime causes of women's low pay.[48] Most regularly employed women were young, under twenty-five years, more inclined to spend their money on finery than union membership (although good clothing was also a sign of respectability). And finally, there was an antipathy towards unions among many working women. Letters and reports of meetings in the League literature speak of women's resistance and men's contempt.[49] Some of the white blouse trades (clerks and shop assistants) regarded themselves as too respectable for union membership, while others, the Arsenal girls in the 1900s apparently worked for 'pocket-money' and had a 'false gentility' which prevented them from seeing the value of organization.[50]

The League's attitude towards protective legislation has often been misrepresented. Mrs Paterson did not oppose shortening the hours of women's work. What she objected to was the passing of ineffective legislation about which women were not consulted and which reduced them to the status of children.[51] The League held regular conferences to inform men trade unionists and civil servants of the reasons for their opposition to 'restrictive' legislation. Paterson never failed to point out that men's hours were shorter than women's in 'restricted' trades. Symptomatic of women's lack of political power was the fact that Home Secretaries of both (Liberal and Tory) governments refused to receive deputations of women workers on this and other issues during the 1870s and 1880s, while they did receive deputations from men.

The League began to rethink its attitude toward legislation in the 1880s and this was due to several changing circumstances. Both the revived hopes for women's political representation from the late 1880s, and the socialist revival tipped the scales towards collectivism and hope for a 'renewed state' among the League's industrial leadership. Something radical had to be done to curb the failure of so many small women's unions and to bring the minds of women workers around to the need for trade unions. Spirits were low among the feminists of the League after Emma Paterson's death. Clementina Black, secretary of the League for a year in 1886–7, had left to set up the Women's Trade Union Association in East London.[52] Emilia Dilke, the art historian and member of the League Council since the 1870s, became the new Secretary of the League in the late '80s and, influenced by her husband Sir Charles Dilke, Barbara Drake suggests, pushed the League in favour of legislation.[53] Finally, the experience of two trades in the 1890s were crucial to their change of mind. Laundresses canvassed in 1891 proved eager for legislation to curb excessively long hours, damp, foetid atmosphere and insanitary conditions.[54] Emilia Dilke led an investigation into the dramatically dangerous conditions in the white lead industry which were 'especially poisonous' to women. Workers in these and similar unskilled industries 'stand in dire need of the protection and consideration of the state'.[55] The League was conceding that women workers did not only occupy a different place in industry from men, but that for them, legislation was necessary to help women help themselves.[56] 'Think not of the Empire on which the sun never sets,' pleaded Lady Dilke, 'think of the wage that never rises.' Britain's industrial greatness she argued, was built on the labour of women and children.[57] By the 1890s legislation was being thought of by the leaders of the League as the preliminary to industrial organization.[58]

— Sex-War? —

The economic analysis of the causes of low pay, and co-operation with skilled men's unions – a policy confirmed by Emilia Dilke's presidency in the 1890s – were intended to reassure working men of women's wish to end the 'sex-war' in industry, nevertheless the very claim that women's work was as good as men's (or could be), and that women's right to work meant that more employments should be opened to them seemed to be a provocation and a threat to men's unions, skilled and unskilled. Throughout the nineteenth century the spread of modern industry rendered men's trades vulnerable to the influx of cheap labour. The demand from some feminists that women wanted men's wages was bound to alarm.

From 1877 the League always held a 'Women's Conference' at the TUC to which they invited representatives of men's unions. These occasions, which evoked chivalrous tributes to the gracious and educated ladies of the League in later memoirs, often followed undignified arguments on the floor of Conference. They sometimes drew fire between the sexes. At the TUC itself ritual battles over women's work, wages and organization recurred every year from 1876. In the localities, whenever employers used women workers in a process previously done by men, antagonism flared into open conflict.[59] The quarterly reports of the League, which from the 1890s included the reports of the League's paid travelling organizers sometimes read like despatches from the battlefront.[60]

The problem was always cheap labour – undercutting. Ben Tillet, the socialist organizer of the unskilled, and a sombre presence in the columns of the League Journal, spoke ominously at the TUC in 1894, of the effects of machinery and the increased employment of women and children, and declared that the day was 'coming when husband and wife will fight at the same factory door for work'.[61] Scuffles did break out at factory gates and in public meetings. Male trade unionists either urged organization upon women, or belligerently insisted on exclusion.

In either case they would send for the League – in the first place, to negotiate the terms and conditions of women's entry into their unions; in the second to get the League to help the women to form unions of their own. Annie Marland's report for instance, in April 1895, described the situation in the Lancashire textile districts where women could find employment and not men:

> You see the men hanging about the street idle (I have even seen them scrubbing floors) whilst the women and children are at the mill.[62]

A despairing tale from the Coventry cycle making industry in the same year described the 'struggle between women and men in its intensest form' as the men in trades unions whose rate was 11/2d (5p) were offered five pence (2p) an hour, while the women were employed for half that amount and they themselves 'dread(ed) replacement by the crowd of unskilled women at the factory gate'. This report concluded,

> Day by day the same story, men who are husbands and fathers of large families have been discharged, and wife, or daughter, or sister, have supplanted them at a wage of 9s (45p) a week.[63]

Adult women were sometimes ousted by young boys at a penny an hour, but boys grow up and revolt 'while the women are content to let themselves be exploited because they are women and weak'. The men in the cycle trade opposed women's entry into the men's union because 'if we organize we recognize' – a dilemma indeed.[64]

In 1895 there were bitter struggles in the pottery districts over women replacing men as wages fell. The hosiery workers in Leicester, the clothing and leather workers in Walsall, the chain makers of Cradley Heath were among those workers similarly facing wage cuts, replacement of men ('1,000s of husbands and fathers idle') by women and the threat of lay-off if the women joined a union.[65] Throughout the 1890s employers of Lancashire, Yorkshire, the Midlands, Essex and London were wage-cutting, introducing machinery and cheap labour, taking advantage of disorganization among the labour force and the competition between women and men.[66]

A resolution (introduced by Clementina Black) in favour of equal pay was passed every year at the TUC from 1888, and the League returned in kind exhorting working women through the journals and reports, at public meetings, outside the factory gates, not to undercut the men.[67] This was the principal plea of the League under the leadership of Emilia Dilke and the two women paid organizers through the 1890s. Lady Dilke's speeches beseeched her working women audiences to relinquish the perils of apathy, of low wages, and warned of the ill-effects on family life of women forced out to work for wages of only a few shillings a week, while their men sat idle at home. She addressed some women for instance 'who looked wretchedly ill and half-starved' from Shoreditch and Bethnal Green after tea in a coffee tavern in Bethnal Green in 1892. These women made cigars in a factory for a few shillings a week, whereas several years before men had been employed for 30 shillings (£1.50p). Some workers took work home where their children helped them: 'it comes hard on the children and of course we cheats the School Board' one cigar maker told the audience in a quote which was recycled in Dilke's speeches and articles, 'Folk must live, and them that has five or six children is best off, because their little fingers are so quick'.[68] The problem with this approach was that the focus on women's different needs and conditions of work from men's, while it evoked pity, distracted from demands for higher wages for their women's work.

The exasperation and desperation of the men is palpable through League reports as they complain that women workers stubbornly resisted the habits of steady trades unionism: . . .'As the breadwinner of his family,' George Shipton of the London Trades Council admonished in 1892, 'a man is bound to defend himself by organization, and we ask you to put yourselves on a level with the best workmen of the country.'[69] Men, as the Webbs pointed out, feared that the distinction between men's and women's work would disappear, they wanted women at home. Kidderminster Carpet Weavers in the (unsuccessful) strike over women in their trade in the mid-1880s, underlined the point. They

> paraded the streets, wheeling infants in perambulators, display-
> ing placards of men cooking and turning mangles, and trying
> by means of ridicule to persuade the women from employment
> . . .[70]

— Why were women so difficult to organize? —

The League organizers had always appealed to women to look to their own interests as women, to rely on their own efforts to help themselves – ways of thinking that were unfamiliar to women. 'Much has been written and said,' declared the editorial in the second issue of the *Women's Union Journal*,

> respecting the duties and responsibilities of women as wives,
> mothers, daughters and sisters. How little has been taught them
> of the still higher duty they owe to each other and themselves,
> as women! All classes and grades of men cleave to, and assist
> each other in difficulties and privations. Individually there are
> countless instances of self-sacrifice, self-immolation on the part
> of women for husband, lover, family or friend, but they have

been lamentably deficient in achieving or attempting aught which would improve their own condition as working women.[71] Paterson's advocacy of a re-education of femininity was endorsed by her successors who linked, as she had done women's low self-respect and poverty to their lack of political status. Isabella Ford, a radical suffragist wrote from Leeds to the League to say that when women did 'grasp the aim of trade unionism, (they) grasp it, I think, more firmly than men, because more religiously', but, she went on,

> Trade unionism means rebellion, and the orthodox teaching for women is submission. The political world preaches teaching woman submission, so long as it refuses them the Parliamentary franchise, and therefore ignores them as human beings.[72]

Ford's remarks were a response to a League enquiry into the difficulties of organizing women workers, to which women responded more positively than the men. (The men thought that women knew nothing about administration, could not build a union up, and anyway one said, men didn't like 'go-to-meetings-women'!)[73]

From the 1890s working women organizers for the League, all of them suffragists, saw it as evident that women workers needed political education. Ada Nield Chew, a former tailoress, and a League organizer in the early 1900s, wrote about the need to awaken women to the degradation of their status as dependants as a preliminary to collective organization:

> My distinct impression is that wherever the educating, awakening influence of Suffrage workers has been at work, there one finds it much easier to induce women to see the necessity for industrial organization . . . The practical impossibility of organizing an unskilled, badly paid, intending-to-become-a-parasite-on-marriage worker is a truly formidable obstacle. But it is by no means the only or the hardest one.
>
>   . . . Unless you can get a woman to see the utter degradation of her industrial and political position as a dependant and a belonging of man, there is as little hope of industrial organization for her as for political power.[74]

The 1890s had been a hiatus in the League's thought around sexual difference in industry. Emilia Dilke conceded that women were not always the bread-winners, nor was a woman's labour always as valuable as a man's. Paterson and Dilke had always had regard for the deleterious effects on the home of women's waged work, the disastrous effect on women's and men's wages of the married woman homeworker. But this rhetorical and spectacular focus on homeworkers and sweated workers was accelerated by the Daily News exhibition of Sweated Workers in

1906 which represented women workers as victims, an image at odds with the self-respect needed for the spirit of trade unionism. Simultaneously, within feminist thought there was a resurgence of emphasis on motherhood – for Lady Dilke, women's 'sacred duty' and for Ada Nield Chew, her passion. Altogether it was difficult – a difficulty shared by all women's organizations, the Women's Co-operative Guild (1883) and the Women's Labour League (1906) too – to sustain a rhetoric of equality with men which simultaneously spoke of women's work as sweated, their domestic responsibilities as intrusive and their vocation as mothers paramount.

Mary Macarthur, the new young Scottish worker for the League, founder of the NFWW in 1906, decisively eliminated sexual difference from her analysis of women's capacity for work or organization by separating women's needs as workers from their needs as mothers. 'There is' she said, in a famous formulation,

> no inherent sex incapacity to recognize the necessity for corporate action. The probability of marriage is not the insurmountable obstacle we are often led to believe it is . . . the low standard of living may be stated at once to be the cause and consequence of women's lack of organization . . . women are badly paid because of their unorganized condition, they may be unorganized because they are badly paid.[75]

Macarthur's strategy for equality – a blend of Fabian pragmatism and Independent Labour Party idealism which always prioritized women – was a national minimum wage for women, protective legislation and education.[76] Ada Nield Chew added nurseries and paid domestic workers. Legislation by raising women's wages above subsistence would enable them to regard their situation with intelligence and detachment, as both Emma Paterson and Emilia Dilke had also argued. Motherhood distinguished women from men but motherhood was the responsibility of the regenerated state, not the individual woman.

Before 1914 the WTUL and the NFWW linked economic independence for women with political citizenship – the two principal objectives of the women's movement before the First World War. Issues of sexual difference were momentarily resolved through endowment of motherhood and the minimum wage. (Trade Boards from 1908 were the first step towards the establishment of the minimum wage it was hoped.)[77] How they became severed is partly the story of the fading of the Women's Movement after 1918, and partly the limits of identifying women's needs with those of social welfare, but loss of an independent feminist voice within the Labour movement must bear most responsibility. In a surge of feminist optimism after the war, during which time union membership of women had multiplied, and women's lowest wages had been driven upwards by munitions work, the NFWW amalgamated with the General and Municipal Workers Union, and the Women's Trade Union League with the political Committee of the TUC in 1920, the negotiations led by Mary Macarthur just before her death. The Labour Movement had always found it impossible to imagine women except as wives and mothers. The feminism of the League never shifted this focus. Emma Paterson had tried in the 1870s and '80s. But the resurgence of socialism, the continued alliance with the skilled men's unions and the indifference of the general unions towards women's needs not only undermined women's independent unions, they offered a wider unity of class and a vision of social regeneration in which women's independent needs and voice always risked being forgotten or lost.

Nevertheless, the collapse of a rhetoric of equality cannot be blamed on either men or socialism. Feminists had allowed differential skills and conditions of women's work to undermine claims for equality; elevation of motherhood meant many feminists felt they had to choose between work and maternity. 'I had no vocation for wifehood or motherhood but an urge to serve the Union,' Margaret Bondfield, a League worker in the 1890s, remembered in her autobiography – 'an urge which developed into a sense of oneness with our kind.'[78] Bondfield's identification with women workers implies a sort of malleability of woman's selfhood never available to men.[79] Beatrice Webb's reflection on the woman question is symptomatic of the difficulty of resolving the ambivalence internal to feminist thought whenever it tried to reconcile work and motherhood. Itemizing the qualities she would want in the woman she loved she put motherhood first:

> From the first I would impress upon her the holiness of motherhood, its infinite superiority over any other occupation that a woman may take to.

She went on to wonder what the men and women of a hundred years hence will make of our

> spending all our time and thought on the social organization of adult men and women, and omitting altogether the vastly more important question of the breeding of the generation that is to succeed them.[80]

After the First World War the philanthropic focus did shift from mother to child as object of pity and source of regeneration, and so too did the rhetoric of the feminist movement. But that is another story.

1983

WOMEN'S FACTORY WORK IN WESTERN EUROPE

From Hand to Mouth describes how things are made and the lives of the women who make them. It is an account of women's unskilled factory work in West Germany – and in West Germany 94 per cent of women factory workers are 'unskilled'. In Berlin, Munich and other cities in the Federal Republic women spot-weld tubes for TV and radio, assemble vacuum cleaners, pack olives and spare parts for lorries. The brand-names of the multi-national companies which employ women are as familiar as the household goods which they produce – Siemens, Electrolux, Gillette and others. Equally familiar throughout Western Europe and the USA, indeed every capitalist economy, are the characteristics of the women workers – unskilled, poorly organized. Such is the effectiveness of the division of labour and the separation of classes in Western economies, so completely does the operation of the market (that is, the paraphernalia of distribution and exchange) dominate the visible world and conceal the world of work, that those who do not work in factories know little or nothing about them. *From Hand to Mouth* disturbs this ignorance. Marianne Herzog reaches beyond the language and categories of official statistics to describe the experience of work which those statistics conceal. She itemizes the details of the labour process itself, the composition of the working day and the methods of payment which divide a workforce already divided by sex, language and cultural differences. She describes the isolation of a pieceworker and the strain of reaching a required piece-number minute after minute. A series of almost cinematic images, in a clipped, sparse prose, takes us into different workshops, and through a working day. *From Hand to Mouth* is a convincing indictment of the organization of work under modern industrial capitalism, and in particular of the division of labour which places women and immigrants at the bottom of the job hierarchy.

Because it is a first-hand description of a series of labour processes, *From Hand to Mouth* makes an original contribution to the literature of women's work. It begins to fill a void in our knowledge of capitalist production: the experience of the people who make the goods which we and they consume. The most enduring impression left by *From Hand to Mouth* is its description of modern factory work – not the work performed by an exceptional minority of sweated workers, but the average type of unskilled factory work performed by millions of women workers throughout the advanced capitalist world. This is the importance of Marianne Herzog's book. It lifts the veil from modern industry and reveals the monotony, ill health and debilitation of its working day. It forces us to look at the underside of the glossy commodity spectacle. But Marianne Herzog is not a typical factory worker. She does not speak for the other women with whom she worked. She writes of her own experience and her viewpoint is a distinctive one, that of a socialist and a feminist.

Marianne Herzog was trained as a bookshop worker in the German Democratic Republic. After moving to West Germany she took work in engineering because she had to earn money to live, but also because she wanted to learn about women's factory work – what women earn and what they produce. She deliberately avoided the more conspicuously women's jobs: 'I did not want to be an unskilled childminder, an unskilled salesgirl in a department store or an unskilled orderly in a hospital. I didn't want to be a waitress or a cleaner.' Later, after working in the factories, she wanted to communicate the experiences of work itself, because, as she writes in her Foreword, 'If we are to fight this kind of work – which becomes no more than a few turns of the wrist, if we are to fight this working-to-the-bone, this having to produce five to twelve items a minute for eight hours at a time, we also have to describe it.'

Immanent in her dissection of a working day is a sharp but controlled anger at the way those who actually produce the goods – the vast majority of them women – spend their lives. Too exhausted, drained, enervated to resist the dictates of the factory, these women become mere flexible appendages to the machine. Their labour, in Marianne Herzog's view, is forced labour; the metaphor of the prison is present throughout the text. *From Hand to Mouth*, then, is both a critical description of the capitalist labour process and part of Marianne Herzog's own story of survival. It is a fragment towards the understanding of the collective experience of work – an experience which at present is largely absent from our language, culture and political practice. Through its detailed but unadorned reportage of what factory work on a production line means, each day and each week, *From Hand to Mouth* reveals the ways in which capitalist production utilizes women's subordination in the mechanisms of exploitation.

It is this emphasis upon the process of production and the meaning of the wage relationship for most women factory workers that sets Marianne Herzog's book apart from the large number of official, academic and journalistic inquiries into women's employment that have been piling up in the last decade. This curiosity is in part a response to the increase all over the Western world in the number of women, especially married women, going *out* to work since the end of the Second World War. But it has also been provoked by the resurgence of militant feminism, the Women's Liberation Movement, from the late 1960s. It was in response to this international phenomenon that the United Nations declared 1975 International Women's Year, an event which in turn gave rise to an epidemic of surveys of women's work. Such miscellaneous bodies as the ILO, the OECD and the EEC, as well as the employment departments of respective governments, have all recently issued information, together with a host of more modest reports from trade union research bodies and employers' organizations.

Despite manifest differences in political inspiration and purpose, these surveys characterize women's work and women's place in society in very similar ways. They derive their authority from the official national statistics of population and employment, which, together with the application of conventionally accepted sociological categories, construct both the patterns of female employment and social attitudes. The picture which they present of women's work informs government policy (such as it is), permeates the media, and to a greater or lesser extent informs the way that employers, many trade unionists, and even sectors of feminist opinion think about women and women's work. Because this view of women's waged work is the dominant one, it is worth identifying its central features.

— *Women and work:* *the conventional view* —

Whatever their initial inspiration, most surveys in the past ten years have focused their attention upon women's 'inequality' at work. While this inequality is of course condemned, it is generally placed in a positive long-term context. The opening observation is that more women than ever are entering the labour force and, with some reservations, this is welcomed as a sign of progress. The ILO, for example, in its 1974 report on the position of women workers, notes that there has been

a considerable improvement in the status of women workers in
many countries in different parts of the world, together with a
heightened awareness of the need for women to have equality
of opportunity and treatment with men in the world of work.[1]
Progress is measured not only by women's increased economic activity
but also by the arrival in our streets of policewomen and traffic
wardens, not to mention the oft-cited case of Sweden's women crane-
drivers.

The reports then, however, go on to catalogue the characteristics of
inequality, which identify women as an under-privileged sector of the
labour market: low pay, lack of status and monotonous jobs in a
narrow range of occupations. 'Women's work' is defined most succinctly in Robert Gubber's report to an OECD trade union seminar in
1968:[2] it is 'unskilled'. . . calling for 'great resilience', 'manual dexterity'; it is fragmented and purely operative; it is poorly paid; it involves
no responsibilities. The conclusion is that at present there is still no
proper integration of women in the labour market – they still form a
marginal or reserve labour force.

Some hope in this situation is pinned on technical advance, which is
welcomed as offering new 'opportunities' for women's work participation, although 'mechanization' is greeted more guardedly: 'Certain
branches of activity are becoming more "feminine" in that they require
a lower level of skill owing to the introduction of more highly
mechanized production methods.'[3] But the real motors of progressive
change, as far as women's new economic opportunities are concerned,
are seen as demographic and cultural:

> More women are married: they marry younger; they increas-
> ingly have all their children before they are 30; they have fewer
> children; they have access to more domestic appliances which
> aid housework; they are increasingly better educated and are
> acquiring more skills and qualifications; and they have increas-
> ingly strong incentives to earn and achieve a higher standard of
> living for their families. With changing social attitudes, women
> with higher educational qualifications, and there are increas-
> ingly more of them, tend to have personal aspirations for their
> career advancement, pay and status of employment.[4]

The only clouds on the horizon of increasing opportunities for waged
work are outdated prejudices on the part of society, employers, trade
unions, men, and even women themselves. The suggestion is that the
problem begins not at work but with sex-role stereotyping at school,
and there's a strong emphasis on parental responsibility. According to
the 1975 OECD Report, for example:

The easy logic of each step a girl takes towards her vocational future – each proceeding naturally from all previous steps back to her earliest handling by her parents – is a powerful clarifier in understanding the basis for many of the problems a woman encounters in entering the labour market.[5]

Women themselves are also chastised for their lack of ambition and their too ready acceptance of their own inferiority. Men's hostility to women's entry into new spheres of employment is matched by women's diffidence. Thus the same OECD Report argues with some exasperation that women's persistent educational inferiority cannot wholly be explained by 'discrimination': 'an alternative explanation must be considered . . . [that] women . . . in the nature of things, have been conditioned to expect the role of wife and mother – or perhaps of teacher, nurse or secretary before marriage and children – and . . . have been discouraged from thoughts of a life-long working career.'[6] Women's low expectations, then, their lack of drive and ambition, perpetuate inequality and provoke discrimination; and these expectations are part of women's conditioning which stems from the 'nature of things'.

The remedies proposed are legislative reform of discriminatory practices at work and school, and changes in women's legal status. Some venture the possibility of the socialization of housework, but the real emphasis is laid on vocational guidance and training for girls and women to enable them to seize the new opportunities opening before them in industry and to help them overcome their own sense of inadequacy and inferiority. Since it is the resolute purpose of the surveys to enlighten public opinion, employers, trade unionists and women alike are exhorted to change their ideas and attitudes.

The utility of these surveys lies in the information they provide as well as the occasional random insight. One or two are worth looking at for the knowledge and thought of a particular compiler or author (for example, Evelyne Sullerot in *The Employment of Women*, the Final Report of the 1968 OECD Trade Union Seminar).[7] Nevertheless, while the description of women's work is, in its essentials, accurate, as a full explanation of women's inequality vis à vis men on the labour market, the analysis is inadequate. It never properly probes beneath the surface phenomena of inequality. This is not to suggest that a fiction of women's work has been deliberately or wilfully constructed, but that the picture presented is incomplete. Discrimination and inequality are dealt with as they operate in the market place, but the world of social production is never investigated as a source of divisions and inequalities among the working class. Thus, technical innovation is mentioned as providing

'opportunities' for female employment; mechanization is held responsible for the 'feminization' of many jobs; women's 'dual role' is invoked
as an explanation for the low-paid, part-time character of married
women's work. But the methods of work and payment, the division of
labour and hierarchy of jobs – in other words, the relations of
production and the labour process itself – are never examined. In
economic terms, the weight of explanation for women's lack of status
as waged workers is placed almost unilaterally on the supply side.
Responsibility for the character and quality of women's work is laid at
the door of 'society', particularly its homes, its schools and its legal
codes. It is 'society' which deposits poor-quality female labour at the
factory gates. It is never sufficiently questioned how far the structure of
advanced capitalist production depends upon the large-scale availability
of cheap unskilled labour, and who, therefore, would do 'women's
work' if women ceased to do it.

One reason for this neglect is the vast generality of the project.
Because women workers exhibit similar features across continents –
that is, they have children, sometimes husbands, and always domestic
as well as waged work – the canvas on which they were surveyed can
be literally world-wide. The project of the ILO in the early 1970s, for
instance, aimed to

> bring up to date the report on women workers in a changing
> world, with particular reference to identifying the needs relating
> to equal opportunity and treatment and the problems arising
> from rapidly changing structures and conditions of work.[8]

The report, while inviting admiration for its attempt to comprehend
one half of the human race in a single empirical category, nevertheless
fails to convince. Women throughout the world are divided by differences of race, religion and culture; they inhabit social relations of
production and kinship in different historical contexts. Most international surveys confine themselves more modestly to parts of Western
Europe and the USA, casting only sidelong glances elsewhere. But even
these, while noting uneven economic development from nation to
nation, describe them simply as more 'backward' or 'advanced', depend-
ing on whether the economy in question retains a strong agrarian sector,
and on the relative status of the manufacturing and service (or tertiary)
sectors. The dominant picture is of a series of national economies
moving haltingly but inevitably through successive stages of backward-
ness towards advanced status, opening up new opportunities for female
waged work as they proceed. A progressive relationship is assumed,
then, between women and economic development. The sexual division
of labour, a social relationship between men and women which encom-

passes both productive and domestic work is confused with sexual difference defined by biology. Thus the relations between women and men, both in the family and at work, are obscured by a functionalist notion of social 'roles' which allegedly flow from biology (women's reproductive capacity) on the one hand, and technological innovation (mechanization) on the other. Because the social space vacated by the family and production is filled by biology and technology, any further scrutiny is inhibited. Both biology and technology are treated as natural or at least asocial phenomena, and as such remain unquestioned.

In the combined presence of progressive technology and biological inevitability, the source of 'inequality' can only be attributed to backward attitudes and expectations, residues of 'the past', or of 'tradition'. Thus those obstinate and tenacious problems for feminism – how do ideas about women's place come about and change, and how do we, women and men, internalize those ideas? What are the historical determinants of the sexual division of labour, and in what ways is sexual difference articulated through the sexual division of labour? – these questions, the terrain of feminism, are simply obliterated. If attitudes and expectations are simply old-fashioned ideas then they can be legislated away.

— Equality Legislation and the sexual division of labour —

However desirable in themselves, the recommended reforms (where they have been introduced) leave untouched the place of women in social production. The Equal Pay Act in Britain is a case in point. The Act (introduced by Barbara Castle, Labour Minister of Employment, passed in 1970 and brought into force in 1975) stipulates that, for the law to be operative, women's work must be the same as, broadly similar to, or of equal value to that of men. This definition immediately excludes an estimated three million women workers in the segregated, low-paid, all-female occupations. To be eligible for equal pay, women workers must have men with whom to compare themselves. Even where this is the case, however, the Act offers no simple panacea. Men's jobs are graded more highly than women's in job evaluation or other grading schemes. If women (as individuals or groups) believe their jobs are comparable and of equal value to men's, the responsibility rests with them to take their cases to an Industrial Tribunal. The success-rate at Tribunals is not high. Of the 363 cases heard in 1977, only 25 per cent were successful.[9]

When women workers have achieved an equal basic rate with men, their earnings will be lower. Domestic responsibilities prevent overtime work, much shift-work, bonuses for long service (which some white-collar unions have negotiated), and promotion.

Only through collective bargaining have women workers in some cases established parity with men's rates of pay, and this has usually only been achieved with the support of male workers. For, as the history of successful claims shows, women must remain vigilant lest, on the one hand, their jobs are regraded and they find themselves at the bottom of a new integrated grading system, or, on the other hand, the employers replace them with male workers. In their struggle for equal pay, women must not only combat the resourceful tactics of their employers – when the Equal Pay Act was first introduced the Confederation of British Industry issued a brochure entitled *13 Ways to Avoid the Equal Pay Act*, which has been widely used – but must also confront men's resistance to the notion of parity with 'women's work'. The point is not to argue against legislative reforms, which can be a useful lever of change, but to insist that by themselves legislative reforms will leave untouched deeper inequality. Furthermore, anti-discriminatory legislation, like protective legislation (the justification of which was that women were incapable of self-protection), is no substitute for the collective action of women workers. The Equal Pay Act in Britain deliberately eschews this possibility by forcing a direct relationship between the individual and legal redress.

To summarize the conventional mental picture of the relationship between women, waged work and inequality: legislative reform is only a temporary if necessary expedient, because the real harbingers of change in women's social and economic position are the new opportunities for waged work, the effect of progressive industrialization. The implication is that as more and more women enter paid employment outside the home, the older rigidities in the sexual division of labour (including out-of-date attitudes) will be whittled away. This faith in the essential benevolence of industrialization and the power of rational thought to eliminate prejudice and injustice has a long and respectable lineage. It is reminiscent of neo-classical political economy.[10] Perhaps the most influential and indeed persuasive exponent of this view is Viola Klein, whose many studies of women workers in the years since the end of the Second World War have helped to shape both official and common-sense views of women's place on the labour market:

> At the beginning of industrialization, they [women] were largely
> employed as unskilled factory hands (and, of course, in domestic
> service) ... with the development of light industry and of
> subsidiary services, they entered semi-skilled and white-collar

occupations; during the latest phase of industrial development, they can be found in substantial numbers in executive jobs and are providing the personnel for most ancillary professions, such as medicine, law, accountancy, journalism, etc. Each new stage has, of course, not superseded the previous one, but at each phase another layer was added to the preceding ones and new opportunities were created for female employment.[11]

Viola Klein allows for the influence of feminism, or at least of women's own desires, on their improved social and economic status, but undoubtedly the central stimulus to emancipation is the lure of the factory: 'Work in factories, offices, shops, etc. is alluring to married women (the single ones being already fully employed) who are not sufficiently occupied at home and many of whom feel socially isolated.'

This insistence on the 'allure' of the factory (and office), the 'opportunities' that open up for women in living their 'dual role' denies, inadvertently perhaps, the ways in which unfettered capitalist production perpetually reproduces inequality through division of labour, management and work discipline, the wage-relation itself. Marianne Herzog, by contrast, approaches the production line (via first-hand experience) as a cruel mode of exploitation. Factory work is a particularly pernicious form of work for women, she argues, because it relies on piecework to discipline and undermine through the less than subsistence basic wage, while women's family responsibilities ensure that women have no choice in the jobs they take. But before examining these issues I want to pursue the historical relationship between female labour and capitalist industry in the specific instance of Britain, in order to challenge the belief that waged work itself emancipates women.

— *The increase in women's employment* —

Increasing numbers of married women are going out to work in most West European economies and the USA. In Britain, for instance, almost 40 per cent of the labour force is female and nearly two thirds of these are married. Or, to put it another way, there are almost six million married women workers in the 1970s, compared with just under one million forty years ago. An increasing number of these women have children under five and research shows that more mothers of young children would go out to work if there were adequate provision for childcare. According to the *Economist* (18 May 1978) married women are the growth sector of the labour force at the present time. But is this a sign of progress or of women's changing role? Since the origins of wage labour, wives and mothers have contributed to the family income whenever work is available, domestic responsibilities permit and economic need dictates. The recorded increase in married women's work in Britain in the past twenty years is evidence that more and more families are dependent on two incomes. The increasing proportion of married women in the labour market in the past five years or so must be set in the context of increasing male unemployment. The evidence suggests that women workers have been introduced into some sectors of the economy, particularly many branches of manufacturing industry, to pull the general level of wages downward. The picture is a complex and difficult one to interpret, but there is no evidence that the increase in married women's waged work is in itself an indication either of improved status or of changing role.

What is changing, however, is work organization and work methods. Much of the work that women once performed in their own or somebody else's home has been transformed, or rather reorganized, by the intervention of the market. Until the Second World War, for instance, many married women took in washing or took it to the local baths to wash; women still wash other people's clothes, but nowadays they do it in launderettes or laundries. Similarly, today there are more office cleaners working for contract cleaning companies, and waitresses, maids and cleaners in hotels and restaurants, than there are domestic servants in private houses. Women are doing the work they have always done, only now they are employed by a firm or company, their hours of work and methods of payment are to some extent regularized, their relationship to the state through taxation and national insurance formalized. In these ways married women's waged work has become more visible. The rapid expansion of the service sector in most capitalist economies has been mainly responsible for the filling out of the statistics of women's economic activity rates in the Censuses since 1945. But what this marks is the extension of commodity production, not a change in women's role.

— Women's place in industry: women as 'cheap labour' —

Historically, female labour has always provided a strategic source of cheap labour for industrial capital in its restless search to maximize profit and reduce costs. The breakdown of handicraft skill into separate tasks and the introduction of machinery and cheap labour are the fundamental principles of modern industry. But this tendency of capital to reorganize skill is hindered by the resistance of the workforce whenever possible. Control over workshop custom and practice (i.e. knowledge) by the workmen themselves was the phenomenon identified and abhorred by Frederick William Taylor, high priest of scientific management, in the Pennsylvania Midvale Steel Company in the late nineteenth century. Distressed to discover that workshop practices were determined by custom and rule of thumb, that men learned their jobs and acquired knowledge by watching others, he wanted to eliminate industrial inefficiency, that is, 'the old system of management', whereby 'each workman shall be left with the final responsibility for doing his job practically as he thinks best, with comparatively little help and advice from management'.[12] In place of this anarchy in production he urged that management's task must be to appropriate the collective knowledge of the entire workforce, collate and tabulate it, and then reissue it to the workers in the form of written instructions. Management should also select and train the workforce carefully, encourage competition between workers and bargain with each one separately.

These two principles represent the 'science' in scientific management. They attempt to systematize and legitimize the logic of capital, ease the advance of modern industry by the seizure of real control over the labour process, and provide the ideology of 'rationalization' elaborated since. Ideally, skills are concentrated into special departments under the supervision and instruction of layers of management. (Henry Ford: 'I have put skill into management planning and building and the results are enjoyed by the unskilled.') The workforce is carefully selected and graded with the majority of manual workers – indeed almost all of them – ignorant of the work outside their shop or department. The entry of female labour into an industry has also been part of the employers' strategy to reduce costs, an accompaniment to the fragmentation of skills and the 'degradation of work', to use Harry Braverman's phrase.[13]

The classic instance of this process, the use of women in textile factories in the Industrial Revolution, is well known. Another example is the conversion of the engineering industry during the First World War to the mass production of armaments. Women had to be trained rapidly for the munitions industry from the end of 1914. They were drawn in from the more orthodox 'female trades': dressmakers and milliners' assistants, laundry workers, textile workers, confectionery workers, light metal workers, together with recruits from domestic service and the sweated trades. Skilled work was subdivided, women performing one or two tasks under male supervision to start with, moving on to more complicated processes as they progressed in skill and training. But the majority of women were employed on simple repetitive operations: 'We put the brains into the machines before the women begin' was how one manager of a shell factory described it.[14]

The principles of 'dilution', as the progressive replacement of skilled men by women and machinery was known, were enshrined in the Treasury Agreement of March 1915, an agreement made between the employers, the government and representatives from the skilled men's unions. Women workers, the principal object of the negotiations, were not present at the meeting, nor were their interests represented. It was not until July 1915 that the National Federation of Women Workers (NFWW), under the leadership of Mary Macarthur, reached a working alliance with the largest skilled engineers' union, the Amalgamated Society of Engineers. Its terms echoed the main points of the Treasury Agreement, and it was subsequently followed by agreements with craft unions in other trades. The Engineers agreed to cooperate with the introduction of women workers into their shops, provided that women received 'the rate for the job', and that they undertook to leave men's jobs at the end of the war. In practice, female labour, where it replaced that of skilled or semi-skilled men, was introduced through negotiations with rank-and-file or union representatives on the shop-floor.

Between 1918 and 1922, women were thrown out of most of the jobs which they had not occupied before the war. They were expected to return to domestic service or the home. The next mass introduction of female labour into manufacturing industry occurred with the development of the 'new light industries' in the inter-war years.[15] Because the 1920s and '30s were years of economic depression and unemployment, entrepreneurs could dictate their terms. British industry was restructured (experienced its second 'industrial revolution') while the Labour Movement was on the defensive. Industrialists borrowed the techniques of mass production learned in wartime and drew on fresh supplies of cheap labour. Referring to the new industries in a government inquiry, the Board of Trade spokesman stated:

> Industries using automatic or semi-automatic machinery and requiring for the most part only semi-skilled labour have tended to become established in districts with adequate supplies of labour with the necessary experience or with the reputation for adaptability. Often female or juvenile labour has been thought to be suitable for such industries.[16]

A report to the ILO in 1936 went so far as to argue that the employment of women in these jobs was a 'technical necessity' . . . 'their delicacy of touch is indispensable for a large number of tasks in which most men would be completely incapable or deplorably inferior.[17] Women's manual dexterity and quickness of eye, their delicacy and lightness of touch, made them cleaner, neater and quicker at noticing defects, sewing up bags, assembling and packaging goods and minding machines. Femininity is apparently a special qualification for repetitive, sedentary, monotonous and low paid occupations.

Women workers have served as a cheap and flexible labour supply for capitalist industry, both in the 'old' manufacturing trades – textiles, clothing, printing and others – where they displaced skilled men and in the 'new' industries – light engineering, food processing and, today, electronics. The expansion of the service sector, characteristic of capitalist economies since the Second World War, has similarly been built on the subdivision of labour, the fragmentation of skills, the separation of mental and manual labour, and the employment of women and girls. (The expansion in part-time work underlines the flexibility of these grades of labour.) The two principal ways in which the sexual division of labour is structured in modern industry from the production point of view are therefore the following: first, the concentration of women into a few industries – in Britain in 1974, 60 per cent of all female employees were in occupations where more than three quarters of all employees were female;[18] and second, the restriction of women to low-paid unskilled work.[19]

— Skilled men and exclusion —

Some feminists in search of an explanation for this ghetto-ization of women workers, and for the seemingly unbreakable connection between women's work, low pay and lack of skill, have claimed that this relationship is the result of women's exclusion from skilled work by men's unions. (Millicent Garrett Fawcett, President of the National Union of Women's Suffrage Societies until 1918, argued this view.) And the history of the British trade union movement to some extent supports this belief. 'Between skilled and unskilled workers a gulf is fixed,' wrote Thomas Wright, a journeyman engineer, in the 1860s, and the gulf was unbridgeable between skilled men and female labour. Skilled men, defending the customs of their craft from the depredations of 'rationalization', regarded with fear and contempt the demands of women workers or their union leaders for entry into skilled work during the First World War. 'Industrial feminism is full of menace to the labour movement,' wrote G. D. H. Cole, Guild Socialist, leading member of the Labour Party and spokesman for the Amalgamated Society of Engineers, in 1917.

Despite the fact that the concept and application of skill have been revolutionized continually since the time when handicraft was the technical basis of the mode of production and the 'mysteries' of the trade which constituted the craftsman's knowledge were the collective

property of the craft workers, union organization and collective bargaining in Britain still lean heavily on this notion that an identity of
interest among a group of workers is established through common
practice of, if not exclusive possession of, a skill. 'Exclusion', or at least
segregation, remains a principle of organization in many trade unions.
The survival of craft consciousness is part of the legacy of Britain's
position as the first industrial nation, the 'workshop of the world'. Even
the unionization of the weakest workers can be thought through in craft
terms. When, for instance, London's night cleaners were attempting to
organize in 1971–3, they were advised by the secretary of the window-
cleaners' branch of the Transport and General Workers' Union that the
first step towards self-help was to establish a skill.[20]

While industrial self-protection inevitably involves recognition of
occupational distinctions between one group of workers and another,
men's resistance to women workers is in part a response to the ways in
which women workers have been used as blacklegs or scabs to undercut
men's skills and rates of pay.[21] (Men also prefer their women at home
where their presence materially affects the family's standard of life.)
Therefore skilled men have sought to protect their interests through
excluding women always from formal apprenticeship and often from
union membership. This, however, is an effect, not the cause, of
women's structurally vulnerable position on the labour market.

It is easier to describe women's work than to speculate how change
might come about. Understanding the sexual division of labour as a
historical relationship which structures both economic relations and
unconscious mental processes will give some measure of the task.
Marianne Herzog does not address herself directly to these questions.
But implicit in her text is a two-fold explanation of women's especial
vulnerability as waged workers. The first is the emphasis that she places
upon piecework.

— *Piecework* —

For Marianne Herzog, piecework, characteristic of women's work in
manufacturing industry, underlines and perpetuates women's vulnerability as waged workers. Seventy per cent of all women factory workers
in the Federal Republic are on piecework, and for them it means an
eight-hour day (or longer) with unpaid breaks for lunch and tea, visits
to the lavatory or to collect raw materials or equipment – unpaid
because a pieceworker is only paid for the time spent producing at the
machine. Piecework means that wages have to be beaten out of the
machines, often with the aid of painkillers; that women work so close

to the machines; they almost seem to 'crawl into them'. It means a work cycle of a few seconds, sometimes more, but always under a minute. These are the conditions described by Marianne Herzog and they are echoed throughout British industry.[22]

Worn out or fed up, pieceworkers can always leave. They will be replaced by young school-leavers or immigrants willing to work for much lower wages. Most large towns have a pool of unemployed or under-employed women workers, many of whom are immigrants (West Indian, Asian and Irish in North London, for instance). During a recession the numbers will multiply.

To the naïve or uninitiated, piecework appears the most rational and indeed equitable method of payment because wages are seemingly directly related to output. For this reason Marx described piecework as the method of payment most in harmony with capital. In fact the distinction between piece and time wages is more apparent than real, since piece-rates (or any form of payment by results) are calculated on a time basis – so much has to be produced in a given time, with some form of reward if the output is faster.

For employers, piece-rates have a pleasing simplicity in that they offer an incentive to the worker to work harder; the faster the output, the higher the earnings, or so it seems. In the language of late-nineteenth-century neo-classical economics, the efficient labourer will raise his or her wages by 'a superior intensity of exertion'. Piecework therefore controls the quantity and intensity of work, and it achieves this through the self-supervision of the worker. Persuading workers to contribute voluntarily a 'superior intensity of exertion' is at the heart of all productivity deals, even if businessmen in pursuit of good public relations often like to imply that it is about something quite different. For instance, according to Jack Greenborough, Deputy Chairman of Shell UK and President of the CBI, 'There is a mistaken notion that "productivity" is all about making people work harder. It is not. It is about equipping, organizing and motivating them to work more effectively.'[23]

For women workers in the engineering industry in the FDR, the incentive to work hard is produced by the basic rate being set beneath subsistence. The effort necessary to push earnings comfortably above subsistence is neither constant nor predictable. The women who work fastest to push up their earnings not only have their piece-rates re-assessed and subsequently reduced but wear themselves out in the process. Furthermore, piece-rates are calculated in such a way that payment per piece decreases proportionally as output rises. In this way extra effort replenishes capital, while the costs of that extra effort (the strain on physical and mental health that it involves) are borne by the pieceworker. For instance, the method of payment by results that operates on an assembly line in a North London light engineering firm was described to me as follows:

> [During the dispute] . . . we discovered that to reach the basic rate we only have to produce one third of what is actually produced during the day. But the workers have no control over the number of instruments they do; when the light flashes, the operator at the front of the line puts out a tray with two instruments in it onto the line. The frequency of the light flashing is set by the chargehand and there is a laid-down interval between flashes for each set. For example, on the Princess, the light flashed every two minutes, and we did 60 an hour, whereas on the Maxi there were 36 trays an hour, which means 72 instruments an hour and 576 a day. This system enables the firm to have two thirds of its speedos assembled for about £6 per week per operator.[24]

In theory, the piece-rate is agreed between workers and management. In practice, there can be no bargain between management and unorganized workers (especially if those workers have an incomplete grasp of their legal rights, and English is not their first language). A rate-fixer, trained in work-study techniques, is brought in by the management to time the workers' actions and measure their 'effort'. New piece-rates are then imposed. The rates are set individually and at strategic moments in the year (busy periods before holidays and Christmas, for example), thus further undermining workers' resistance to them.

Because it presupposes the separation, organization and measurement of tasks to the point where all initiative on the part of the worker is eliminated, piecework of this kind is especially applicable on the production lines of consumer goods industries where mass production of a standardized product turns the worker into part of the machinery. These are the manufacturing industries we have already identified as those in which women predominate: clothing, textiles, electrical goods, light engineering, food processing, the tobacco trades, etc. Despite significant differences in the methods of work in each industry, the sexual division on the shop-floor has a remarkable uniformity. Many examples could be given; typical is this situation in a London toy factory, described by an English feminist:

> Of the 2,000 women, about half work on assembly lines and half on individual machines. Both are run on a 'basic rate plus piecework' basis. The men are all mechanics, chargehands, etc., except for the skilled men in the toolroom and the semi-skilled

men in the foundry and tumblers. The men and women are completely divided by job categories and rates of pay.[25]

Piecework – undercutting, and basic rates below subsistence are however, again like skilled men's exclusion, a symptom rather than a cause of industrial weakness, for what distinguishes women's work from men's is not piecework *per se*, but the low level of earnings which that system of payment in the case of women reinforces and perpetuates. Of the size of this differential there can be no doubt. In England before the First World War, the average wage of a woman manual worker was one third to one half of a man's. Today the average hourly earnings of women manual workers are just over 60 per cent of men's. Many women workers in offices, shops and launderettes, as well as factories, earn less than 50p per hour, and those who do not have a man's wage to help support themselves and their children take two jobs or work overtime to make ends meet.

The principal justification for women's low wages has always been that women's earnings are only supplementary to family income. It is indeed the supplementary character of much women's work which explains the general rate at which their wages are set. But this justification wholly ignores the large number of households which are supported primarily or entirely by women. The 1971 Census of England and Wales showed that nearly two million women under retirement age were the chief economic supporters of their households. To recognize the claims of these women would be to contradict the dominant familial ideology. The idea of women as dependants has not only justified private industry's gross underpayment of women workers, but has also informed the trade unions' demand for a family wage and is fundamental to the social security system and, indeed, the whole apparatus of the welfare state. More fundamentally, it has often prevented women themselves from organizing to demand higher wages or equal pay with men.

Women workers and the family

If methods of payment cannot in themselves be considered a cause of women's industrial situation, the second source of women's vulnerability as wage workers emphasized by Marianne Herzog – their position in the family – certainly can. Commodity production dictates the forms of wage work available to women, but the 'ties' they experience – their children, other dependants and domestic work – 'force' women's economic dependence on the factory. The focus of *From Hand to Mouth* is wage work – the world of the factory – but underlying the factory is the other world of the family. The account of the family in the book exhibits the familiar ambivalence of feminism towards the home, domestic work and relationships within the family. On the one hand, the family is the source of love and warmth and human relationships, on the other hand, it extends women's working day, puts their time and energy always at the disposal of other people, limits the possibilities for training or industrial organization and dictates that women's participation in waged work is necessarily discontinuous and intermittent. Indeed the family largely structures women's particular position in the labour market, for, by inhibiting their ability to organize industrially, women's double workload leaves their wages to be set simply by competition. But the competition between women in the labour market is not that of workers in equivalent material circumstances. Some women gain a large part of their subsistence through the earnings of the male breadwinner, some are single women with only themselves to support, some must support dependent families solely through their earnings. Inevitably, in the absence of collective bargaining, unskilled women's wages will be set at the lowest level the market will bear – in practice, that sufficient to induce into employment married women requiring a supplementary income. (The value of female labour power, whatever the individual domestic situation, never includes the costs of the reproduction of the labour force.)

Many attempts to organize women at work have foundered amid the seemingly inflexible demands of women's domestic life. For the consequence of women's domestic work is not simply a restriction of time and activity; it also shapes women's conception of themselves. The home and its responsibilities persistently invade women's thoughts, fragmenting and diluting their sense of themselves as wage workers. A woman involved in the Leeds clothing workers' strike in 1970 explained the effects of women's divided loyalties:

You see, a man's job is to be a breadwinner, isn't it? To earn a wage to keep his family. And he wants what is due to him by hook or by crook . . . Now a woman has a lot more other things to think about. Families and pressures at home, and owt like this. And they cannot be militant enough. If they're militant they're losing . . . Now a woman comes out to work that day; now if she's going to come out to work and strike, well, her home . . . is going to suffer . . . A woman *has* to go out to work, and she works. And a man can stick up for his rights and all stick together, but a woman has a lot more things on her mind. Feeding her family, you know . . . and you think to yourself . . . [on strike] the first hour you thought to yourself, you're militant, you know, and then by the second hour, you're thinking – 'Oh,

I could be doing my washing . . . I could be at home, doing my shopping.' And that's the whole difference.[26]

Women's divided subjectivity demonstrates that Lenin's belief in the spontaneity of trade-union consciousness cannot be unproblematically extended to women workers. Women wage workers have been persistently militant throughout the nineteenth and twentieth centuries, but it is much more difficult for women to sustain long-term industrial organization. In earlier phases of capitalist development – in the domestic system, for example – production and family often coincided and women were often then the most prominent in everyday economic struggles. But when work and family are separated, a strategy of resistance which depends upon the industrial organization of women is unlikely to succeed. For this is to treat women as though they were men, to ignore domestic work, childcare – women's double workload – and the complexities of social-sexual relations. Feminism is often accused by the labour and socialist movements of creating divisions among the working class, but men's and women's material circumstances are different, and so their consciousness of themselves will be different from men's. To ignore this is to overlook the political implications of the sexual division of labour. The industrial organization of women in modern industry is a consequence and not a precondition of political consciousness – precisely the obverse of the Leninist formula.

The structural weakness of women's position in industry will only be changed by an alleviation of their double workload. This can only be accomplished by political and ideological means, through changes in the sexual division of labour in the home and a stronger political presence of women in national politics. Marianne Herzog paints a grimly pessimistic picture of women factory workers as the helpless victims of capitalist exploitation. There is no conscious collective resistance, only occasional solidarity or momentary escape through dreams, though even these are shaped for them by capital, through the words of its pop songs and its consumer goods. Women's deepest longings remain within the bounds of wage labour: a better-paid job, a small shop. The factory totally dominates the lives of the women and the implication is that there is no separate space for the creation of a disruptive politics or culture. This desolate view perhaps underestimates tensions and contradictions in the women's situation as well as in capitalist production itself. There is no inevitable logical chain connecting factory and mentality. Forms of resistance are much more unpredictable. The past ten years have seen a resurgence of militant feminism. In Britain, equal pay and anti-discrimination legislation and more liberal laws on abortion and contraception are not just paternalistic impositions, they are the results of the political organiz-ation of women and the feminist presence in the Labour Movement. These are precarious achievements, but nevertheless indications that women are voicing their demands, that women are speaking and being listened to. What the outcome will be who knows.

September 1978.

Part Two

FEMINISM AND SOCIAL MOVEMENTS

WOMEN, CLASS AND SEXUAL DIFFERENCE IN THE 1830S AND '40S

SOME REFLECTIONS ON THE

WRITING OF A FEMINIST

HISTORY

... it is impossible ever to govern subjects rightly, without knowing as well what they really are as what they only seem; which the *Men* can never be supposed to do, while they labour to force *Women* to live in constant masquerade.
'Sophia', Woman not Inferior to Man, 1739

This desire of being always woman is the very consciousness that degrades the sex. Excepting with a lover, I must repeat with emphasis, a former observation, – it would be well if they were only agreeable or rational companions.
Mary Wollstonecraft, A Vindication of the Rights of Woman,
1792

Throughout history, people have knocked their heads against the riddle of the nature of femininity –
... Nor will you have escaped worrying over this problem – those of you who are men; to those of you who are women this will not apply – you are yourselves the problem.
Sigmund Freud, Lecture on Femininity, 1933, Standard
Edition, vol. xxii

For a long time I have hesitated to write a book on woman. The subject is irritating, especially to women; and it is not new ... The voluminous nonsense uttered during the last century seems to have done little to illuminate the problem. After all, is there a problem? And if so, what is it? Are there women, really? ... One wonders if women still exist, if they will always exist, whether or not it is desirable that they should, what place they occupy in this world, what their place should be.

Simone de Beauvoir, *The Second Sex*, 1949

— I. The Problem: Woman, a Historical and Political Category —

The problem: woman, the riddle: femininity have a capricious but nevertheless political history. Capricious because they surface at different moments among different social milieux, within diverse political movements; and a history in the sense that the social conditions and political status of women have undergone changes which may be traced, and with them some of the shifts in the meanings of femininity. As we become acquainted with the historical range and diversity of women's political status and social roles, the enigma itself occupies a different place. It is removed outside history to some other realm beyond the reach of social analysis or political theory. Since there can be no aspect of the human condition which is not social where could that other place be?

If the meaning of femininity, the political implications of Womanhood have at moments in the past 300 years been contested, then it must be that what they represent is not some eternal and universal essence of woman, but the difficulty of the sexual relation itself between women and men which is always a social ordering, and one where the unconscious and its conflicting drives and desires presses most urgently on conscious behaviour, where political thought, though capable of producing principles of equality and justice in its delineations of the proper relations between the sexes, nevertheless cannot always anticipate or circumscribe the urgency of those conflicts as they are lived.

Feminism, the conscious political movement of women, has been since the seventeenth century the principal contender in the struggles for the reorganization of sexual difference and division, and hence the social meaning of womanhood. If feminism's underlying demand is for women's full inclusion in humanity (whether that inclusion is strategically posed in terms of equal rights, socialism or millenarianism) then the dilemma for a feminist political strategy may be summed up in the tension between the plea for equality and the assertion of sexual difference. If the sexes are different, then how may that difference (and all that it implies for the relative needs and desires of women and men) be represented throughout culture, without the sex that is different becoming subordinated.

History offers many symptoms of this difficulty; from the sixteenth-century Royal Edicts which prohibited women's public gossip, to the nineteenth-century House of Commons references to women as 'the sex' or feminism as the 'shrieking sisterhood'. Whether dismissed as a 'monstrous regiment', 'set of devils' or a 'menace to the Labour movement', feminism both arouses sexual antagonisms and invokes a threat which cannot be explained with reference to the demands of the women's movements – nothing if not reasonable in themselves.[1] By suggesting that what both feminism and femininity stand for is not Woman – who like Man is no more nor less than human – but the social organization of sexual difference and division, I am refusing to abandon femininity to an enigma/mystery beyond history. But then the problem becomes how to write a history of women and feminism which engages with those issues . . .

— II. 'A History of Our Own' —

It is difficult to remember now how there could have been such a gust of masculine laughter at the 1969 Ruskin History Workshop when a number of us women asked for a meeting of those present who might be interested in working on 'Women's History'. I do remember the bewilderment and indignation we felt as we walked away from the plenary to plan another of our own. It seemed to be the word – Woman – which produced the laughter. Why? Those plans became the first National Women's Liberation conference held at Ruskin College, Oxford in early 1970 (an event which wiped the smile off the male students' faces. The television room had been taken over by the creche (run by men), and the college was swarming with women, women and women. Student Union meetings for weeks afterwards rang with incoherent but passionate antagonism to the Women's Conference, focusing on the violation of students' freedoms that it had imposed. The different implications it seems of women's liberation were lived vividly, though differently, for some men and hundreds of women that week-end.) So my interest in women's history coincided with the beginning of my own education as an intellectual at a trade union college (I was a student at Ruskin from 1968–70) and the emergence of the Women's Liberation Movement from the late 1960s. The dichotomies – Women and Labour, Sex and Class, Feminism and Socialism have been the intimate inhabitants of both my psyche and my intellectual work (if the two can be separated) as they have been for many women of my political generation.[2]

Intellectual Feminism

In the early 1970s socialist-feminists struggled to transform those dichotomies into political and theoretical relationships through campaigns and study groups. We diligently appraised and attempted to secure for our own purposes some of the traditions of marxist thought, appropriating the concepts of political economy, historical and dialectical materialism and assessing the revolutionary practices they had inspired through a feminist lens. If I ask what was/is the relationship between class struggle and the sexual division of labour, then historical materialism's focus on the mode of production is illuminating and suggestive. It imaginatively speculates on labour both as a form of activity which involves a relationship between Man and Nature, and as a system of social relations between women and men. But if the categories of political economy can sometimes reveal the operations of the labour market convincingly, the political traditions of marxism have had little to say about feminism or the needs and aspirations of women; while historical materialism, by identifying class struggle as the motor of history, pushes the questions of sexual divisions and difference to the periphery of the historical process. Whether posited as objects of analysis, or included as part of the narrative, sexual divisions can be present in marxist – and most labour – history, only as digressions from the real subject of history – class struggle; and their theoretical status is subservient to the study of modes of production.

If feminism has been only one of the detonators of 'crisis' in marxist thought and practice it has been the most insistently subversive because it will not give up its wish to speak in the name of women; of women's experience, subjectivity and sexuality. 'A history of our own', 'a language of our own', 'the right to determine our own sexuality', these were the distinctive themes of rebellion for the Women's Liberation Movement in the early 1970s. We were asking the impossible perhaps. As a feminist I was (and still am) under the spell of those wishes, while as a historian I write and think in the shadow of a labour history which silences them. How can women speak and think creatively within marxism when they can neither enter the narrative flow as fully as they wish, nor imagine that there might be other subjectivities present in history than those of class – for to imagine that is to transgress the laws of historical materialism? This is a difficulty to which I shall return.

Other intellectual traditions and ways of thinking about women, sexual divisions and feminism pushed the categories Woman and Labour, Sex and Class, Feminism and Socialism apart in my mind, refusing any analogy between them, or any mutual set of determinations and effects. The discovery of histories of women written by earlier generations of feminists showed how women's experience is remembered anew with each resurgence of feminist consciousness; between times it leaves scarcely a trace. Why this recurring amnesia, and why the attenuated feminist voice?

Radical feminism (from the United States: British radical feminist history surfaced later in the decade), offered a breath-takingly audacious understanding of relations between the sexes in history. Sexual divisions prefigure those of class was the message that Shulamith Firestone and Kate Millett flung at a male dominated intellectual world; patriarchy the concept which they restored to the centre of debates around social formations and social relations between the sexes.[3]

Since the seventeenth century feminists have railed against the tyranny of men, male power, male domination and in the idiom of the 1970s, sexism and patriarchy, but those categories, while retaining a polemical conviction, I believe, have to be transcended too in any full history of women or feminism. Ironically radical feminism writes women's subjectivity and active agency out of history as effectively as any marxism. Little girls become women because of what male dominated institutions tell and compel them to do. History is simply one long death knell of women's independent activity and consciousness. There were witches, but men killed them; women were sensual, erotic and adventurous but men used and abused them; women loved each other, but men forbade that love to be spoken; women were wives and mothers, but only because men wanted them to be; women were workers, but men seized their skills, and so on. Men have much to answer for, but the envy and fears and desires of one sex can't carry all the determinations of history. If they do, then we enter again a world where women's identity, action, speech and desires are all explained in terms of something else, in this case, the male psyche. Women are subordinated and silenced because they live in a world shaped in the interests of and dominated by men. Only a political revolution of women could ever destroy male power if it is conceived as so absolute in its effects.

But the writings and campaigns of previous feminisms exhibit contradictions and difficulties internal to the thoughts of both individual feminists, and the movements for which they claimed to speak and these internal contradictions cannot be explained by the tyranny of men. As the vindicator of women's rights, Mary Wollstonecraft, for instance, did not absolve women from culpability in their own history: she castigated the coquetry of women of the leisured classes, condemned their feeble development of reason and virtue, their excess of sensibility, their false modesty. All this she attributed to an education which fitted women exclusively for marriage and the pleasures of men. But reading her letters and novels brings the irresistible recognition that she could diatribe so thoroughly against the thrall of men's authority and desires because she herself fell so violently and seemingly arbitrarily a prey to them herself. Do we reject the authenticity of those conflicting desires because men have placed them there for us? And if we do, how do we explain disagreements among women within the women's movement itself?

Just two historical examples: in the 1870s the suffrage campaign refused to endorse publicly the Ladies' National Association's Campaign against the Contagious Diseases Acts. Josephine Butler and the 'grave and educated ladies' who reached out to their 'fallen sisters' acquiesced in this suffragist silence, a denial as profound as any repudiation of a common sisterhood of women that came from outside the women's movement.[4] The suffragists' decision was made for reasons of political expediency. The second example indicates deeper tensions and divisions within the women's movement on the same questions: the identity or nature of woman, and the political representation of sexual difference.

The coalescence of feminist organizations broke up with the partial achievement of 'Votes for Women' in 1918. From 1917 the largest suffragist organization, The National Union of Societies for Equal Citizenship (formerly named the National Union of Suffrage Societies) had been debating political priorities, culminating in Eleanor Rathbone's attempt to place the endowment of motherhood and birth-control as the new unifying aims in 1924. Eleanor Rathbone argued that what distinguished women from men was motherhood; from maternity the natural feminine dispositions flowed and should be acknowledged in the economic policies and social provisions demanded by the women's movement. 'We must,' she argued in a Presidential speech to NUSEC early in the 1920s,

> demand what we want for women, not because it is what men
> have got, but because it is what women need to fulfil the
> potentialities of their own natures and to adjust themselves to
> the circumstances of their own lives.[5]

But any projection of motherhood into the political arena had always been strongly opposed by those who, led by Millicent Garrett Fawcett, had always maintained that to emphasize sexual difference, or women's 'maternal function', would jeopardize women's claims for equality. The theme of this disagreement was insistent: equality or difference, and if difference, then how could that difference be represented within politics without it being used to submerge women in domesticity, to deny them the full fruits of equality – to justify their economic dependence and political subjection? The extent of sisterhood, the political implications of womanhood have proved as elusive and divisive within the women's movement as between feminists and the government, political parties or the male dominated labour movement in the past 150 years.

Every moment of dissonance and disagreement within feminism, as well as between women and men, demands recovering and disentangling – demands a historical reading. Neither marxism nor radical feminism yet offer a history which can grasp the issues that feminism both stands for and raises. If marxism persistently avoids sexual anatagonism by relegating sexual difference to a natural world, then radical feminism conceives of women as shaped literally by men's desires. Histories of femininity and feminism have temporalities of their own – apart from those of class or men. The political narratives of feminism are as diverse and fractured as the vocabulary of individual rights and egalitarian aspiration itself is, when it surfaces now among the ascendant bourgeoisie in eighteenth-century Britain, now among the English Jacobins in the 1790s, among the Owenites and Unitarians in the 1820s and '40s, and in Victorian Britain, accumulating an intensity of grievance and yearning among women from very different social and political milieux.

The emergence of a mass feminist politics is most often attributed to the effects of the industrial revolution and the ideological hegemony of the bourgeoisie.[6] The former, by separating work from family, the latter by instilling ideas of domesticity among the working classes, allocated women and men to the private and public domains respectively. But we come closer to the terrain of feminist grievance and capture a decisive moment in its political temporality if we examine the forms of working-class politics or radical social movements in the 1830s and '40s, their language of demand and aspiration.[7] If the working class emerged as a political category in those years (remembering its long history of gestation) then Woman emerged as a social problem. The emergence was simultaneous, the roots of grievance and their political representation different.

Feminist Consciousness and Class Struggle

Feminism, as a self-conscious political movement appears when women, or some women in the name of their sex, distinguish themselves and their needs, from those of their male kin within families, communities and class. Feminism's protest is always posed in terms of women's perceptions of themselves and their status in relation to men. From a litany of their discontents feminism gathers an identity of women, and formulates the demands and aspirations that will transform the social relations/conditions in which women and men will live. Whatever the starting point of its dissatisfactions – lack of education, men's property over women in marriage, 'domestic drudgery', the prohibitions on female labour, the double standard of sexual morality, exclusion from the franchise – feminists from the seventeenth century have refused to concede that relationships between the sexes belong outside history in any conception of the natural world, which is where philosophers, poets or marxist historians, until provoked, have been content to abandon or place them. Feminism looks outward at the social forms of sexual division and the uneven destinies that claim the two sexes, but the critical look becomes an enquiry into the self and sexual difference and asks 'what am I a woman, and how am I different from a man?' No social relationship is left unturned, if only by implication, in this endeavour.

Feminism's return to the individual subject in its attempt to distinguish woman as a social category from man is one clue to some of its moments of emergence. There must be available a language of the individual political subject – a language which articulates the dissemination of a political order through the individual's identification with (and subjection to) its law. Some seventeenth-century protestant sects which proposed the unmediated communion between the Soul and God and dissolved the family in the community of all believers enabled women to claim an equal right with men to 'preach and prophesy', for the 'soul knows no distinction of sex';[8] and in the eighteenth and nineteenth centuries feminism seized on the language of democratic rights within both liberal and utopian political discourse. But for the individual voice of a 'Sophia' or Mary Wollstonecraft to become a movement there had to be not only feminine discontent but also a widespread yearning for another way of life. Before a language of rebellion can pass into general speech it must appeal to the imagination of a wide social group. Thus feminism appears at moments of industrial and political dislocation when disparate social groups are struggling to 'find a voice' in the emerging order, when seemingly stable forms of social organization are tumbling down, as in the English and French revolutions stimulating practical attempts to imagine anew proper relations between the sexes. Some of these conditions were present in the 1830s and '40s.[9]

In speaking of the self and sexual difference feminism is at its most disturbing. Sexuality, intimacy, divergent conceptions of need are evoked and haunt the marxist historian with the spectres of bourgeois individualism, gossip, and the crumbling of working-class unity. Ten years of women's history has calmed immediate fears. Few labour historians now hesitate to write of women's work, to mention the family or note the absence of women from some forms of political life. Working class 'experience' has been stretched – though the political significance of those worlds beyond the workplace, ale-house, club-room, union branch meeting are still argued about.[10] But if we are to pursue the history of women's experience and of feminism there can be no retreat from a closer enquiry into subjectivity and sexual identity. For if feminism insists on the political significance of the female subject and on the urgent need to reorganize sexual difference and division, it is to convey a more generous conception of human consciousness and its effects at the levels of popular resistance, collective identifications, and forms of political address and organization.

Social Being: Consciousness or Subjectivity?

The focus on the self and sexual difference throws into disarray the smooth elision assumed within marxist thought between social being, consciousness and politics. Two distinctions are drawn: between material and mental life and true and false consciousness. Mental life flows from material conditions. Social being is determined above all by class position – location within the relations of production. Consciousness and politics, all mental conceptions spring from the material forces and relations of production and so reflect those class origins.[11] Collective class consciousness is the recognition of the shared experience of exploitation, and working-class politics its expression, which in its most advanced form is revolutionary socialism. Thus there are graduated levels of consciousness (from spontaneous to political) before the historic destiny of the working class can be realized.[12] When historical materialism is compressed in this way into a series of laws, they are abandoned only at the risk of jettisoning the dynamics of history.

Let a more skilled philosopher unravel the polarities: material/mental; true/false; cause/effect. Here I only want to point to the absence of the individual sexually differentiated subject in marxism. The question marks hover over social being, and how it is experienced – by women and by men.

'Experience' of class, even if shared and fully recognized, does not, as Edward Thompson and others have suggested, produce a shared and even consciousness.[13] Class is not only a diverse (geographically, from industry to industry, for example) and divisive (skilled/unskilled; male/female labour, generation difference) 'experience', but that experience itself is given different meanings. For marxists, meaning is produced through ideologies. The bourgeoisie as the dominant class has control over the relations and the forces of production and therefore the production of ideologies, which mask the reality of social being to the working class. Thus ideologies serve the interests of antagonistic classes.[14]

Debates within marxism which attempt to release ideology from its economic/material base are inexhaustible. Engels and Lenin have been perhaps the sternest advocates of the grip of the base on the superstructure; Gramsci and Mao Tse-Tung elaborating on the continuum and flux of ideas among the people, the tenacity of traditions, and the irrepressible capacity of human consciousness to produce forms of communal order and ways of thinking independent of the sway of hegemonic ideologies.[15] But if we step aside from these debates to ask not how ideologies are produced, but how, in Juliet Mitchell's phrase, do 'we live as ideas', then we enter the realm of social being and experience along another path – the path of subjectivity and sexual identity.[16] Against marxism's claims that the determining social relationship is between wage labour and capital, exploiter and exploited, proletarian and capitalist, feminism insists on the recognition that subjective identity is also constructed as masculine or feminine, placing the individual as husband or wife, mother or father, son or daughter, and so on. And these subjectivities speak through political language and forms of political action, where they may be severed from class or class interests, indeed may be at odds with them.

In order to place subjectivity and sexual difference firmly at the centre of my research and historical writing I draw on the psychoanalytic account of subjectivity and sexual identity. Psychoanalysis offers a reading of sexual difference rooted not in the sexual division of labour (which nevertheless organizes that difference), nor within nature, but through the unconscious and language. This poses the issue of psychic reality – a reality which like Marx's concepts of commodity fetishism and exploitation, will not be encountered through empirical observation. Psychoanalysis allows for a rich elaboration of subjectivity, identification and desire – essentially psychic processes which give a political movement its emotional power.

The French psychoanalyst Jacques Lacan's re-emphasis on the part played by language – the symbolic order – in the production of meaning, and unconscious phantasy in the construction of subjectivity has been taken up by some feminists because it retrieves sexual difference from the seemingly obvious 'anatomy is destiny'. Perhaps this needs further elaboration. Those who prefer to move straight to the political language of working-class movements in the 1830s and '40s should skip this following (selective) exegesis.

Subjectivity, Sexual Difference and Language

For Lacan the acquisition of subjectivity and sexual identity are a simultaneous and always precarious process which occurs as the human infant enters language; that is, as s/he is spoken to and about and as s/he learns to speak. The human animal is born into language and comes into being through its terms.[17] Or, to put it another way, language, which pre-exists the infant, identifies us first as boy/girl, daughter/son. Language orders masculinity and femininity, they are positions which shift between and within discourses. The infant takes up these positions and moves between them as s/he journeys through the oedipal trauma, which marks the entry into human culture for every infant. The infant is compelled to acknowledge the significance of sexual difference through the presence or absence of the phallus – the primary and privileged sign of sexual difference. Neither little boys nor little girls possess the phallus; they are placed in a different relationship to it through the threat of castration and prohibition, which have different implications for femininity (lack) and masculinity (loss). The relationship to the phallus is mediated through phantasy; recognition of loss/lack, absence/presence is prefigured from birth as the infant differentiates itself from others – the absence/presence of the desired object (breast/mother); the look and speech of others. Phantasy fills the void left by the absent object. Castration and prohibition represent human law, within which every infant has to take up a place, initially as masculine or feminine, and never without a struggle. A struggle, because it is around these moments – absence/loss, pleasure/unpleasure – that the libidinal organization of need, demand and desire is shaped.[18]

Subjectivity, and with it sexual identity, is constructed through a process of differentiation, division and splitting, and is best understood as a process which is always in the making, is never finished or complete. In this sense, the unified coherent subject presented in language is always a fiction, and so susceptible to disruption by the unconscious (or by a collision with an alternative concept of the self in language). Everyday speech with its discontinuities, hesitations, contradictions, indicates on the one hand the process itself, and on the other, the difficulty the individual subject has in aligning her or himself within the linguistic order, since there are as many different orders as there are discourses to structure them and always the possibility of more. A difficulty which is underlined for the little girl/woman by the impossibility for her of taking up a positive or powerful place in a culture which privileges masculinity and therefore men. Subjectivity and sexual identity are always achieved with difficulty, and the achievement is always precarious. The unpredictable effects of that achievement remain inaccessible to conscious thought in the repressed wishes to be one with the other, to belong to the other sex, as well as envy of and desire for the other sex. Both subjectivity and sexual identity are therefore unstable and involve antagonism and conflict in their very construction. Antagonism and instability are lived out not only within the individual psyche and its history, they mediate all social relations between women and men; they prefigure and cohabit with class and other antagonisms, and, as the history of feminism demonstrates, may well disrupt class solidarities.

Post-Saussurian linguistics' non-referential theory of language and insistence on the arbitrary nature of the sign, marks these instabilities. Meaning is produced through the chain of signifiers – the way words are strung together and organized into conversation, narratives, analysis, systems of thought – and may be gleaned from the study of those, rather than from reference to the objects and phenomena which they only designate, leaving them always open to dispute and redefinition.[19] (A salutary, if familiar, reminder to the historian that historical reconstruction of the past is always through interpretation of the sources, which serve like memory-traces for the psychoanalyst, as the raw material through which we impose or offer, our own interpretations and causalities.) There is no relation of sex, Lacan cautions us (meaning no natural relation: no relation that can be read off from anatomy, biology, or the demands of procreation) except, I would emphasize, as it is articulated in language and through phantasy.

It is partly because feminism enquires into the self in its concern to distinguish woman from man as a social category, and because one of the points of that return for my generation of feminist historians has been a dissatisfaction with historical materialism's raising of class (narrowly defined) as the determining social experience, economic relation and agency of political change, that the limits of historical materialism's notions of social being, consciousness and politics, and the articulations between them are so clearly revealed. Feminist history has to emancipate itself from class as the organizing principle of history, the privileged signifier of social relations and their political representations.

Marxism and other sociological theories of social being are resistant to any psychology which could be read as proposing a universal human nature. If they allow for a human nature at all it is one that is produced by the environment (shadows of the Enlightenment). The subjectivity of psychoanalysis does not either imply a universal human nature, it suggests that some forms and capacities of mental functioning – the unconscious, phantasy, memory, for instance – seem to be so. Subjectivity in this account is neither universal nor ahistorical. First structured through relations of absence and loss, pleasure and unpleasure, difference and division, these are simultaneous with the social naming and placing among kin, community, school, class which are always historically specific.

Why open up history to the unconscious? But historians are as familiar as the analyst, poet, philosopher, everyone in their daily lives, with the power of the imaginary: dreams, phantasy, desire, fear, envy. Historians of pre-industrial society have fewer inhibitions about speaking of myth, ritual, magic and their significance in human organization. Perhaps the fear that by introducing the unconscious and phantasy into social history is to open a pandora's box, to deny the rationale of political and social life, is stalled by the distance of pre-industrial societies from our own. Against these reservations, I only suggest that the persistent problem of femininity and the presence of feminism indicate that the box is already wide open – its contents working like alchemy among us.

It is not my intention to reconstruct the individual unconscious, or individual subjectivity (which may be glimpsed nevertheless by the historian through autobiography, memory or speech). Merely to emphasize that the symbolic sets the terms through which any social group must position itself and conceive of a new social order and that just as the symbolic has a life of its own so too does the individual (and perhaps the collective?) unconscious, and both the unconscious and the symbolic are changed in the course of their encounter. Human subjectivity shapes, as it is itself shaped by, political practice and language – it leaves its imprint there.

This reading of subjectivity as an essentially volatile and precarious process suggests that a political movement which organizes itself around a fixed notion of a collective subject as its agency of political transformation – whether that subject is class, sex or ethnic group – is vulnerable to the volatility of identification among its people and so to conflict within the movement (as Clement Attlee, pragmatic leader of the Labour Party in 1945, pointed out, 'the same man in the capacity of a Trade Union official may take a slightly different attitude from that which he does as a member of the Party Executive, or Member of Parliament').[20] The more so in a movement which gives the individual – through representative or direct democracy – the right to participate in the delineation of the new social order, the articulation of strategy and tactics. Radical movements are bound together too by ethical aims – justice, freedom, law, for example – these are juxtaposed to common lived grievances and these, though sometimes divisive in their achievements, are less emotionally corrosive.

There are just one or two further thoughts to leave in the mind of the reader before turning to the social movements of the 1830s and '40s. The first about law and desire; the second about the mobility of sexual difference: its historical and psychic repetitions.

Histories of all mass movements in the epoch of industrial capitalism reveal the power of language – oratory, polemic, propaganda – both to capture the allegiance of the constituency addressed, and to formulate social visions, to translate need and desire into demand. Insofar as the political vision is in combat with the present rule of law, then the question of strategy, how that law is to be encountered and negotiated, will depend on – among other things – the relative balance of visionary aspiration and concrete political demand within a political movement. The strength of desire in utopian visions of transcendence means that there is little incentive for negotiation with government, law, or any other existing domains of authority. We may glean an insight into the mentality of transcendence from Lacan's exploration of desire, which is predicated on loss/absence, is always in excess of demand, but is only knowable through language. The desire for harmony, a world free from conflict, is – like the unified subject – a wish whose realization is elusive, though a wish that compels. Since even utopian visions, when translated into living communities, must impose their own moralities and laws, they too become open to challenge from those who wish to disobey, or to imagine another order. What happens when the visionaries become the lawmakers?

Both feminism and psychoanalysis suggest (in different ways), and history appears to confirm their findings, that antagonism between the sexes is an unavoidable aspect of the acquisition of sexual identity, and one that can be explained neither by anatomy nor environment alone. If antagonism is always latent, it is possible that history offers no final resolution, only the constant reshaping, reorganizing of the symbolization of difference, and the sexual division of labour. The questions for the historian of feminism are why at some moments does sexual difference and division take on a political significance – which elements in the organization are politicized, what are the terms of negotiation, and between whom?

— *III. Radicalism and Women* —

Humble Petition of the Poor Spinners ... Sheweth, that the Business of Spinning, in all its branches, hath ever been, time out of mind, the peculiar employment of women; insomuch that every single woman is called in law a Spinster ... that this employment above all others is suited to the condition and circumstances of the Female Poor; inasmuch as not only single women, but married ones also, can be employed in it consistently with the necessary cares of their families; for, the business being carried on in their own houses, they can at any time leave when the care of their families requires their attendance, and can re-assume the work when family duty permits it; nay they can, in many instances, carry on their work and perform their domestic duty at the same time; particularly in the case of attending a sick husband or child, or an aged parent.

Humble Petition of the Poor Spinners, Leicester, 1788

Now the doctrine of the Free-trader is, that no law is given – no responsibility is incurred! That wealth cannot ... be misapplied ... The Free-trader, therefore, laughs at the idea of Christian laws interfering with him. He rejects the interposition of the Almighty; he is an independent agent. He cannot be a Christian. Every Christian believes that man has fallen from perfection, that he is selfish, covetous, and that he needs the unerring teaching of the Almighty. The Christian must require that all human law shall be founded on the laws revealed in the Word of Truth.

The Christian will never forget, the Free-trader will never remember, that the head and eye must never be permitted to invade the rights of the hands and the feet. The Christian knows that Society is one compact body, each individual member being dependent on the rest, each requiring the protection of all. The Free-trader on the contrary, persuades himself that each member is a separate piece of independence, an isolated self.

Richard Oastler, 1847

We do not hesitate to say, that the tone of mind and thought which has overthrown authority and violated every code human and divine abroad, and fostered chartism and rebellion at home is the same which has also written *Jane Eyre*.

Quarterly Review, 1849

If we turn to the 1830s and '40s with these reflections in mind and ask why some women were able to speak of their right to sexual and economic independence and to deliberate on the formation of the new morality and sexual order within Owenism and not within contemporary movements of similar class composition undergoing similar experiences of industrial dislocation, then the focus on subjectivity and language is suggestive.

The decades after 1815 (the end of the wars with France) were immensely unsettled. The revival of political reform (crescendoing in 1819 and 1829–32), legalization of trade unions (1824–5), Catholic emancipation (1829), the abolition of slavery in British colonies (1833), the passing of the new rational but punitive Poor Law (1834), were enacted against a background of desperate struggles over enclosure in the countryside, machinery in the textiles industries, famine in Ireland and poverty everywhere, but most dramatically visible in the burgeoning industrial towns of Britain. A number of movements of the self-declared poor, the working classes took their histories into their own hands, negotiating with government and its local representatives, educating themselves in the process and speaking a vocabulary drawn from a reservoir of political philosophies of promiscuous origins. The Short-time Committees from the 1820s, Anti-Poor Law struggles, Owenism and Chartism in the 1830s and '40s involved women; speaking for the poor, the working classes, the unenfranchised, the dispossesed, they included both sexes and all generations. But if we listen more closely to the common elements in their analysis of discontent and language of aspiration we discover firstly that women could only speak as political subjects at selective moments, and within the community. Men spoke in the first person for the community as a whole when appealing to a wider public opinion; while political demand, communal rights, distribution and dispensation of the law was a dialogue of negotiation between the men of the communities and the 'capitalists and lawgivers'. And secondly, the place in the vision of the new social order that these movements afforded women was founded on conceptions of the sexual division of labour, property, laws of inheritance and the relative 'capacities' and status of women and men within marriage prevalent among rural and urban industrial communities from the eighteenth century which had never scrupulously observed the principle of equality between the sexes. Sexual difference was intimately bound up in notions of labour, property and kin in popular radical thought, and through their respective organization women's access to knowledge, skill and independent political subjectivity depended.

When whole communities rebelled against punitive legislation, or the depredation of customary rights, against unemployment or starvation – as they did in different parts of the country through the Factory Movement, Anti-Poor Law campaigns and Chartism – then women rioted, attended public assemblies and processions, formed committees, though women and men were often segregated. In active resistance against proletarianization the political subject was the community and radical rhetoric addressed wives as well as husbands, mothers as well as fathers, female and child labour as well as male. Nevertheless, whenever community resistance was formally organized into democratically elected committees with powers to negotiate with employers, justices of the peace, government representatives, then men were in the forefront and the spokesmen of those committees. Women were excluded from these forms of public speech not through the separation of workshop and home (though their increasing distance did underlie the 'separate spheres' emphasis of some nineteenth-century feminist thought, and the different forms of political and industrial organization of women and men in the second half of the nineteenth century) they had been excluded from formal political organization and conceptions of the individual legal, political and economic subject since the end of the seventeenth century.[21]

The legal, political and economic subject in radical popular speech reaching back to the seventeenth century Levellers, was the propertied individual, and the propertied individual was always masculine – whether head of household, skilled tradesman or artisan whose property was his labour, or the evocation of the Freeborn Briton. Early nineteenth-century radicalism did not so much refer to the 'experience' of the dispossessed communities as draw on the rules of association, the idiom and rhetoric of the leaders of their struggles: the small master craftsmen, the displaced domestic worker, the artisan and mechanic, the skilled factory operatives. Men with a long history of trade association, for whom custom and status as well as skill determined the level of wages, length of the working day, and entry to a trade; for whom the collective wisdom and knowledge of their skill was lodged in the custom and practice of the workshop, and whose authority and control extended through apprenticeship rules to their children and other kin. Skilled men outlining the grievances that fuelled the factory reform movements in the textile districts from the 1820s to the 1840s, the several attempts at general unions, spoke of being 'robbed' or 'disinherited' of the right to practise their trade; of the 'slavery' of the mills; of their resistance to becoming the 'hired servants' of the 'new breed of employers'. The vocabulary of grievance is similar among the tailors, shoe-makers and cabinet makers in London resisting the 'sweating and puffing' system; and it stretches back to the small master clothiers in the North and West of England who gave evidence to the 1806 Royal Commission on the Woollen Industry, Britain's first and major capitalized industry, and one which employed a majority of women and children through the seventeenth and eighteenth centuries. In the minds of these different groups of male workers their status as fathers and heads of families was indelibly associated with their independence through 'honourable' labour and property in skill, which identification with a trade gave them.[22]

It was as fathers and heads of household that the radical artisan spoke of the loss of parental control and authority over kin, the predatory sexual freedom of the mills, the destruction of 'habits and morals'. Despair and anger still reverberates through the speeches, petitions and addresses to the public, the employers, the people, or Parliament, at the destruction of a whole way of life wrought by the 'despots of capital', the factory, the workhouse or 'class legislation'. But it was the anger of men threatened in their whole being with loss of skill, sexual and economic authority. John Doherty, mule-spinner, radical, factory reformer, trade unionist, commenting on the manufacturer who advertised in a Glasgow newspaper for women to work in his mills:

> ... if he could not find in his heart to employ, and pay men for doing his work, he should look out for women whose morals are already corrupted, instead of those whose lives are yet pure and spotless. For everyone will admit, that to place persons of both sexes, of fifteen or sixteen years, indiscriminately together, and put them in receipt of 12s and 16s a week, which is entirely at their own disposal, without education and before their habits are fixed, and their reason sufficiently mature to controul (sic) their passions and restrain their appetites ... such persons will (not) grow up as chaste, moral and obedient to their parents, as if they had still not remained under the salutary restraint of parental controul (sic). If the practice were to become general, of employing girls and boys instead of men, it could place the son and daughter of fifteen, at the head of the family, to whose whims and caprices the father must bend and succumb, or in many cases starve.[23]

Popular Political Economy

John Doherty and his contemporaries resisted 'capitalists and lawmakers' as deeply because they usurped 'parental controul' as for any change in the work process. Underlying this resistance were the two themes which spanned all visions of a new social order, whether for a General Union of the trades, social regeneration, co-operative communities, or the Charter: first that labour, as the producer of wealth and knowledge, should receive its just reward; and second, that kinship was the natural and proper relation of morality, authority and law.

The labour theory of value expounded in radical political economy assigned neither labour nor responsible parenthood exclusively to men. Thomas Hodgskin, for example, philosophical anarchist and influential pamphleteer read by chartists, factory reformers and others, stated only that labour's share of wealth should provide the

> necessaries and conveniences required for the support of the labourer and his family; or that quantity which is necessary to enable the labourers one with another, to subsist and to perpetuate their race without either increase or diminution.

Skilled labour is the labourer's knowledge, and 'the time necessary to acquire a knowledge of any species of skilled labour . . . is, in many cases, several years'. Hodgskin describes the 'most important operation' in the accumulation and transmission of knowledge and skill – the parents' work in rearing and educating the children:

> The labor (sic) of the parents produces and purchases, with what they receive as wages, all the food and the clothing which the rising generation of labourers use, while they are learning those arts by means of which they will hereafter produce all the wealth of society. For the rearing and educating of all future labourers (of course I do not mean book education, which is the smallest and least useful part of all which they have to learn) their parents have no stock stored up beyond their own practical skill. Under the strong influence of natural affections and parental love, they prepare by their toils, continually day after day, and year after year, through all the long period of the infancy and childhood of their offspring, those future labourers who are to succeed to their toils and their hard fare, but who will inherit their productive power, and be what they now are, the main pillars of the social edifice.[24]

Food, clothing, knowledge, love and labour are equally the possessions and gifts of both parents, and theirs equally to pass on to their children. But this was the world as it should be. Utopian thinkers expunged from their vocabulary any monopoly of men over skill, or inheritance. But if there was in small rural manufacturing communities or urban crafts and trades, a community of skill and knowledge within families, it was not transmitted in public speech – whether the discourse of bargain and polemic with employers and government, or popular propaganda – as it wasn't in the formal rules of the trades or other political, philosophical societies of different communities. Sexual difference and masculine privilege was embedded in popular conceptions of both skilled labour and authority, and inheritance was through male and not female kin.

Women simply could not speak within these terms. From the mid-eighteenth century, though women were sometimes drawn into the informal and intermittent trade associations, they received full authority to practise their craft only through male kin: father, husband, or if a widow, through her eldest son or principal journeyman. Skilled men's unions throughout the nineteenth century excluded women, and the wage 'sufficient to support a wife and children' was the father's and not the mother's. There was reciprocity between the respective 'capacities' of women and men when considered as husbands and wives within a domestic economy or family industry. But somehow there slips into the vocabulary of men as they defend or expound that system, an estimation of women as wives, workers and mothers which belies full equality of status or even, presence. Wives of wool-combers, weavers, cobblers, tailors and all skilled men or small masters 'assisted' their husbands in their trades, besides fulfilling their household duties; with their husbands they 'brought up the children to a trade', until the age of 13 or 14 when the child came under the proper supervision of his father or male relative (which girls seldom did). If women's work was mentioned it was described as an 'inferior' sort of work, always with the implication that it required less skill and strength, or even that such a task as picking or burling was done by 'inferior people, women and children', as one witness explained to the 1806 Royal Commission on the Woollen Industry.[25]

A woman's skill resided in the household and her property in the virtue of her person. Separated from the home, her family and domestic occupations, or outside the bonds of matrimony, a woman was assured of neither skill nor virtue. (Read again John Doherty's admonitions to the Glasgow manufacturer on page 114.)

Engels touched the nerve in his ferocious indictment of industrial capitalism in 1844. Describing in dramatic rhetoric the destruction of the family by the factory system he alights – as did all his contemporaries – on the evil effects of the wife's employment at the mill:

> In many cases the family is not wholly dissolved by the employment of the wife, but turned upside down. The wife supports the family, the husband sits at home, tends the children, sweeps the room and cooks ... in Manchester alone many hundred such men could be cited, *condemned to domestic occupations*. It is easy to imagine the wrath aroused among the working-men by this reversal of all relations within the family, while other social conditions remain unchanged. (my italics)

So much for the equal status of women and their work. Engels' saving grace, from the point of view of the feminist, is the final clause. And he redeems himself forever, as he continues, in some confusion, to argue that if this condition which unsexes the man and takes from the woman all womanliness without being able to bestow upon the man true womanliness, or the woman true manliness – this condition which degrades, in the most shameful way, both sexes, and through them, Humanity . . . then, so total a reversal of the position of the sexes can have come to pass only because the sexes have been placed in a false position from the beginning. If the reign of the wife over the husband, as inevitably brought about by the factory system is inhuman, the pristine rule of the husband over the wife must have been inhuman too.[26]

'The reign of the wife over the husband as inevitably brought about by the factory system' – the 'condition which unsexes the man' – underlined all the polemic and rhetoric deployed by working-class movements against the 'new breed of employers', the 'capitalist lords and despots'. Those who have studied the literature of grievance in the history of the industrial revolution, are familiar with the lament of skilled men threatened with loss of skill and knowledge by the factory or sweatshop, and made anxious about the destruction of the family and the home by the competition of the wives and children.[27] The motivation was not in any simple sense class-war, nor the pursuit of an exclusive economic self-interest, nor even (at least not in every case?) the conscious desire to dominate their women – but to posit a vision of the social organization of labour centred around kin and the household which permitted 'natural affections' and love as well as skill to flow simultaneously from domestic and working life; which allowed for a continuing dialogue between 'masters and men'; and which enabled the 'natural differences and capacities' of the sexes to determine the division of labour between wife and husband, male and female labourer. This was a language of grievance which embraced moral and sexual orders as well as economic discontents – social preoccupations which became severed in political demands within the labour movement (but not the feminist) in the later nineteenth century.[28] In the early nineteenth century this vision was posed again and again by representatives of the working classes as a mode of industrial organization which had once been there, that was natural and that was being wantonly destroyed by capital and the government.

We come closer to grasping the reasons for the emergence of a feminist voice within Owenism and not within other working-class movements (or not in a sustained form) if we consider further their political diagnosis and strategy, their different social visions and the implications of these for the nature and place of women and men.

The People's Charter:1838.

'Fellow Country Women', the Female Political Union of Newcastle upon Tyne declared in 1839 in their Address published in the Chartist newspaper, *The Northern Star*:

> we entreat you to join us to help the cause of freedom, justice, honesty and truth, to drive poverty and ignorance from our land, and establish happy homes, true religion, righteous government, and good laws.[29]

The plea could have been made by Parson Bull, belligerent enemy of the new Poor Law and its implementation in the North of England at the end of the 1830s, Richard Oastler, Tory Radical and 'King' of the factory operative and starving hand-loom weaver whose motto was 'The Altar, the Throne and the Hearth', and whose enemy was the free-trader, or any one of the many radical men active in those campaigns. Chartism was a mass movement of women as well as men which united all those movements against 'bad laws and unjust legislators'. Richard Pilling's – a Lancashire weaver, and leading Chartist – defence speech at his trial in Lancaster in 1843 on a charge of seditious conspiracy, reveals the overlapping of grievance and aspirations in those struggles:

> Suppose, gentlemen of the jury, you were obliged to subsist on the paltry pittance given to us in the shape of wages, and had a wife and six helpless children ... to support, how would you feel? Though you were to confine me to a dungeon I should not submit to it. I have a nervous wife – a good wife – a dear wife – a wife that I love and cherish, and I have done everything that I could in the way of resisting reductions in wages, that I might keep her and my children from the workhouse, for I detest parish relief. It is wages I want. I want to be independent of every man and that is the principle of every man in this court ... it has been a wage question with me. And I do say that if Mr O'Connor has made it a chartist question he has done wonders to make it extend through England, Ireland, and Scotland. But it was always a wage question, and ten hours bill with me.[30]

The 'women of Newcastle' did not demand independence but they did declare their interests to be those of their 'fathers, husbands and brothers', and their place was in the home, from which they had been torn by poverty and the 'scorn of the rich' – 'the brand of slavery is on our kindred' – who, 'not content with despising our feelings, ... demand the control of our thoughts and wants'. The People's Charter at moments between 1838 and the 1840s mobilized the whole of the labouring population behind its demand for universal suffrage, and, at

moments, shopkeepers and tradesmen, as well as humanitarian philanthropists, though it deleted women from that universality,

> lest the false estimate man entertains of this half of the human
> family may cause his ignorance and prejudice to be enlisted to
> retard the progress of his own freedom.

Those women who acquiesced in their exclusion did so because they
shared the social visions of their men. 'Love of God, and hatred of
wrong' compelled the women of Newcastle to 'assist' their men to have
the 'Charter (made) into a law and emancipate the white slaves of
England'.[31] Dorothy Thompson has documented women's participation
in Chartism (as well as its ambivalence on the question of women's
suffrage):

> (women) joined in protests and action against the police, the
> established Church, the exploitation of employers and the
> encroachments of the state. They articulated their grievances
> sometimes in general political terms, basing their case on
> appeals to former laws and to natural rights, sometimes in
> ethical or religious terms, appealing to the Bible for the legiti-
> mation of protest . . .[32]

It was these last – natural rights and Biblical Law – which together with
the evocation of a golden age always prove insecure foundations for
equality between the sexes.

The Golden Age: The Law of Nature and the Law of God

Chartism appealed for a return to a golden age, or at least to an
imagined Eden before the Reform Act of 1832 'invaded' the civil
liberties of the people (in Disraeli's and Oastler's phrase), introducing
'class legislation', and before the factory system reduced the working
classes to 'slavery' and impoverishment. For Chartists the association of
the working classes was one which clung to a hope of industrial
organization rooted in the household and kinship, and based on the
land. The appeal to the land always evokes, when it recurs in English
popular belief a lost and more egalitarian past, one closer to natural
sources of affection, feeling and community. The place of women in
that evocation seldom escapes submission. The tendency is – and I'm
oversimplifying – to place women closer to nature and the animal
world, distancing them from human law and knowledge. Somehow
women are placed under a different law from men because of their
natural function and capacity. Men become the natural protectors and
defenders of women, whose place is in the home, with their children,
providing those comforts which – to quote the Newcastle Chartist
women again – 'our hearts told us should greet our husbands after their

fatiguing labours'. Women's exclusion from independent political subjectivity is then a consequence of their different capacity and place. Valued
for their household skills and domestic virtue as part of the family under
the protection of men, independence is almost inconceivable. This
implication is present even in R.J. Richardson's ardent advocacy of
women's equal right to the suffrage in 1840, where natural differences
between the sexes are given a divine imperative. Surveying women's
labour to substantiate that right, he fumed against 'money-grabbers'
and 'slave drivers' who forced women into employment in fields, mines
and mills, and found only in weaving the ideal occupation for women:

> In hand-loom weaving, it is no uncommon thing to see in a
> weaver's cottage under the window on the ground floor, a loom
> at which the weaver's wife is employed at the same time she is
> surveying her domestic affairs; for instance, she will leave her
> loom, peel potatoes for dinner, put them on the fire, then return
> to her loom; should her child cry in its cradle, she will stop,
> leave her loom, give it the breast, or a plaything, or get it to
> sleep, and return to her loom again, and so on alternately the
> day through.

There are two kinds of women in Richardson's text: the gentle, domestic
persons of his imagination, 'those tender creatures we call ours'; and
those to whom he spoke in their many different workplaces, who
listened patiently as he regaled them on the inappropriate nature of
their employment, its defilement of their femininity:

> This is the work of men . . . and you ought not to perform it:
> your places are in your homes; your labours are your domestic
> duties; your interests in the welfare of your families, and not in
> slaving thus for the accumulation of the wealth of others, whose
> slaves you seem willing to be; for shame on you! go seek
> husbands, those of you who have them not, and make them toil
> for you; and those of you who have husbands and families, go
> home and minister to their domestic comforts . . .

I suspect most replied as the women of the printfields in Leven,
Dumbartonshire that

> they were conscious that they were not in their proper places;
> but that, as they had no voice in making the laws they could
> not help their degraded position.

Richardson's principal and concluding point was that women should be
allowed to intervene in political affairs because 'I believe that God
ordained women "to temper men"', and that

> when we consider that it is to woman we owe our existence,
> that we receive from her our earliest thoughts and bias of our

minds – that we are indebted to her for all that makes life a
blessing – would it not be unwise, ungrateful and inhuman in
man to deny them every advantage they can possess in society?[33]
Such a highlighting of sexual difference cannot help but undermine the
demand for political equality between women and men, especially when
that difference is given a divine authorization.

Christian humanitarianism – of all denominations – distinguished the
emotional fervour of much popular oratory and polemic. The law of
the Bible was employed to defend the rights and liberties of the working
man against the 'Church, the Throne and the Aristocracy', who would
'rob the poor man' not only of his liberty but also 'of his wife and of
his children'.[34] The social vision of the Chartists met the political and
economic critique of Whiggery and Utilitarianism (the landed aristocracy and the free traders) expounded by the Tory democrats. The
meeting point was women: the protection of the rights of the 'weakest
and most defenceless, the widow and the fatherless'; a social order in
which each person had her or his special place, and the appeal to a
benevolent Constitution whose executive exercised political power with
responsibility, always with care for the freedoms and liberties and rights
of the people – a people in whose speech only men could claim status
as independent subjects.

A New Moral World

Owenism differed from radicalism in the possibilities it offered women.
Determinedly secular, Owenism envisaged a new science of human
nature and promised to revolutionize emotions and feelings as well as
labour and law. Since environment not God or nature made character,
environment could be changed. There was nothing natural in the sexual
division of labour, nor in the 'despotic' rule of wives by their husbands.
The confinement of women to 'domestic drudgery' was an unjust
usurpation of human freedom and female capacity (the difference
between the radicals and the Owenites echoes the quarrel between
Rousseau and Mary Wollstonecraft). The only natural aspect of the
relation between the sexes was the flow of sensuality, the 'sacred
pleasures of the flesh', about which, as Barbara Taylor drily points out,
female Owenites were more circumspect on the whole (except those
fleeing tyrannical husbands or living the life of the 'liberated libido')
than men. The Owenites imagined a whole New Moral World. Theirs
was a vocabulary of transcendence not negotiation; there was neither a
longing to return to a golden past, nor any submission to the natural
laws of the market. Owenism reached out for new social forms which
would displace industrial competitive society with co-operative modes

of work, egalitarian communities, a reformed marriage and a new religion of reason and universal love. As Barbara Taylor has so eloquently argued, utopian socialism promised the liberation of all humanity at once, of all human relations and social institutions.[35] Egalitarian and democratic in spirit if not always in practice, some women found a voice for their discontents and desires as women there. It was a vision of progress and a renewed humanity; a language of community and co-operation which only sometimes foundered on the democratic rights of the individual.

A new science of human nature, a new moral world, these dreams proved more fertile soil for feminism – the independent voice of women demanding equality with men and their full inclusion in humanity – than natural order and natural difference. And Owenism's vision of transcendence (anticipating the millenarianism of the later nineteenth-century women's suffrage movement) invited some women to imagine a full emancipation. It was when those dreams were put into practice in co-operative communities or new moral unions that the reality principle intervened; women's 'equality' was modified by her economic dependence, her children.

Owenite feminists were wives and daughters of artisans and tradesmen; single working women and widows. They were school-teachers and platform speakers and pamphleteers. They included Harriet Taylor, for instance, Unitarian Radical and friend to John Stuart Mill, and Barbara Bodichon, Unitarian, artist, friend of George Eliot and campaigner for women's education, suffrage and property rights. These latter women were the descendants of John Keats' 'devils ... who having taken a snack of literary scraps, set themselves up for towers of Babel in Languages, Sapphos in Poetry – Euclids in Geometry – and everything in nothing'; they also formed some of the number of 'surplus women' revealed by the 1851 Census.

'Natural' differences between the sexes could easily slip into a relation of inequality between women and men as the possibility of a domestic system of industry, with a family of labourers and household economy, faded, and with that fading the dialogue between masters and men, who sometimes addressed each other as 'men, as husbands, as fathers, as friends and Christians', hardened into the confrontations between capital and labour. Symptomatic of the changing class relations is the changing value and status of 'female labour' as it moved in and out of the home, and in and out of those modes of address. The equivocation of political discourse of working-class movements on the questions of 'female labour' is illustrated by John Doherty's prevarications. Imprisoned for obstructing the use of female 'knobsticks' to break a strike of spinners in Glasgow in 1818, a leader of the mule spinners through the 1820s and early '30s, he opposed the 'cotton lords'' use of female labour to undercut the men. Men's resistance to women spinners – justified on grounds of their lesser strength and skill – was part of the struggle against machinery and an attempt to retain a notion of apprenticeship, which, as Doherty conceded to the Select Committee into the Combinations of Workmen in 1838, did not 'exist formally, but it does frightfully to the workmen'. And Doherty suggests to the same Committee that men's monopoly in mule spinning (except in Glasgow where there had been strikes for equal pay) should be extended to the wheel (prevalent in Manchester). He agreed that women's employment in the mills had a 'bad effect on morals and domestic habits', and that the greater strength required on wheels in Manchester would 'shortly put women out'. On the other hand, Doherty, a humanitarian and Owenite, as well as a trades unionist, addressing the London tailors in an article in May 1834, both condemned the 'dastardly stratagem' of hiring female labour to replace the men, and urged on the tailors that this undercutting would not be possible if they themselves acknowledge 'the natural equality of women; include them in all your schemes of improvement, and raise them as high in the sense of scale and independence as yourselves'.[36] But natural difference fitted ill with 'natural equality'.

Male Fears and Female Labour

The spectacle of female labour aroused the deepest fears among many different sectors of public opinion not just the radicals, in the mid-nineteenth century – alerted as they were by a prolific and diverse literature to the 'condition of England' question. The disintegration and demoralization of the working-class family in the midst of economic growth and imperial power haunted social consciences among both Whigs and Tories as they pondered the possibility of social revolution. This fusion of anxiety is less surprising when we remember that what women stood for was not simply domestic virtue and household skills, but sexual ordering itself. If men represented – to such different groups as radical artisans, Tory democrats, utilitarian legislators – labour, then what woman represented first of all was sexuality – which, if not harnessed to reproduction threatened sexual anarchy and chaos (epithets applied to both the prostitute and the militant feminist in Victorian England). Men's desire to confine women to their proper place must be understood – at least in part – as a desire to control (legally) and order (morally) sexuality. Women's capacity to bear children made her one with God in creating life. It was the power of this thought that eventually persuaded even such die-hard opponents of the Ten-Hour Day as Sir Robert Peel to, if not relent, at least adhere to the principle of the protection of women. *The Northern Star* put their case on female labour in the mines rather more bluntly:

> Keep them at home to look after their families; decrease the pressure on the labour market and there is then some chance of a higher rate of wages being enforced.[37]

Through the history of wage labour female labour has meant 'cheap labour' to working-class men, and the threat of cheap labour sets sexual antagonism, always latent between women and men, into livid activity at the workplace and in the unions. Reorganization of the labour process produced continual shifts in the sexual division of labour, provoking anxiety about the destruction of the home and family which had been imprinted in the language of popular resistance since the late eighteenth century. There is a sense in which the vocabulary and rhetoric of the radical artisan in the first half of the nineteenth century evoked a memory of a past that never had been there – except in aspiration. It nevertheless retains a powerful hold still over the political imagination of the labour movement, bequeathing a vocabulary of loss and nostalgia to working-class struggle. The appeal to the family, home and hearth and women's place beside it is its conservative edge – though the yearning for harmony and for sources of emotional satisfaction for which they stand are more tenacious and ambivalent. The labour theory of value remains alive in the labour movement, too, lending weight to men's demands for a family wage. But except when held within egalitarian principles of community and equal rights of women and men in marriage, the notion of the family wrapped up in that theory was (and is) inimical to the 'full and complete' emancipation of women. Because whereas for men the threat of cheap labour means *loss* of employment, status and skill, to women workers their cheapness represents *lack* of independence, status and skill. Feminism's demand for work, training, and economic independence has always unnerved the male-dominated labour movement, while 'lack' of those things permeates the idiom of nineteenth-century feminism. Ironically what women lacked became one of the defining features of femininity, and on the shop-floor, in the unions and working-class political parties this lack could become politically divisive. In fact, women's special needs received short shrift in the labour movement in the first decades of the twentieth century whether femininity was defined positively as motherhood, or negatively as lack. The former produced demands for birth control, family endowment, easier divorce – which never received more than a luke-warm reception in the labour movement as a whole until the late 1930s; and the latter produced the demands for equal pay, equal right to skill and training, to which men's response was always the reassertion of their status as breadwinners for the family.

I am not suggesting that the public speech of skilled men as they addressed their employers, the public or the government, was the only form of popular discourse. That communities imposed their own moral laws, as well as conceptions of the value of women's and men's different social skills and responsibilities is certain. And women themselves often spoke a different reality. But we capture only fragments of those customs. Many of them were conveyed through oral traditions destroyed (if not altogether lost or forgotten) by the swell in population, movements into the towns, destruction of crafts and dismantlement of apprenticeship rules, wage controls, etc. What we are witnessing from a distance is the uneven erosion of local cultures and the submergence of political communities into a national political order which through representative government gradually (and unwillingly) drew the individual into a contract with government. The process was uneven and did not immediately replace other forms of communal relations of power and law, but increasingly came to dominate all public political discourse as the Parliamentary legislature became more intrusive and claimed to be the seat of representative democracy.

Whatever their intentions, the Chartists by deleting women, the factory reformers by submitting to the principle of the protection of women and every working-class custom, insofar as it refused an equal status to women, placed women in a different relationship to the law from men.[38] Women fell under the protection of their fathers, husbands or Parliament and were denied an independent political subjectivity. When feminism emerged as a self-conscious and sometimes mass political movement of women in the nineteenth century it was to demand economic independence and the full rights and duties of citizenship – to combat the exclusion of women from a 'common humanity' and women's lack of masculine privilege. Women's protest gathered force until nothing less than the 'whole world of labour' and nothing short of Womanhood suffrage would satisfy the most radical feminists. Both women and the working class emerged in the 1840s, two universal social and political categories which demanded universal rights and liberties in, as Ethel Snowden, feminist and socialist, carefully phrased it echoing Mary Wollstonecraft – 'all those matters of their common humanity where sex does not enter and impose an impassable barrier'.[39] But if there is nothing 'impassable' about the social ordering of sexual difference, representing difference as a relation of equality in language through political culture was – and remains – elusive.

1983

EQUAL OR DIFFERENT

THE EMERGENCE OF THE

VICTORIAN WOMEN'S

MOVEMENT

The following essay introduced a collection written by students attending an adult education course, The History of the Women's Movement, run jointly by the Extra-Mural Department of the University of London and the Fawcett Library in 1981–2. They were published as a pamphlet in 1984 by the Extra–Mural Department. I have cut the opening pages because they described a feminist pedagogy; the essay is published here in its original, fuller version.

We asked of the material three – rather crudely formulated – questions. Why at certain moments do women emerge as a distinct social group with political demands? What is the meaning of sexual difference at those historical moments and what are the sources of sexual antagonism? Finally, and perhaps most enigmatically, what do women want – or rather, what do feminists think women want?

The questions arose partly out of a frustration with histories which attempt to align the many different voices and campaigns included under the rubric of the Women's Movement with either the feminists' class position or with the principal, mid-Victorian political parties. Feminism – Victorian feminism in particular – is most often designated middle class and liberal. But these designations are only part of the story. Feminism as a body of thought and practice is eclectic – but it always introduces the social ordering of sexual difference and the formation of Woman as a political identity into the political domain. The demand of feminists for equality with men is often at odds with an equally powerful assertion of the difference between the sexes. This tension between equality and difference in feminist politics provoked (and still provokes) unexpected alliances in the nineteenth and early twentieth centuries, as well as fundamental re-readings of the meaning, for instance, of liberal democracy, civil liberties, the rights of labour, and even the cherished categories of political economy. Let me illustrate these points briefly.

— *Equality and Difference* —

Men are the people with whom women compare themselves. If feminists have asked since the seventeenth century 'what does it mean to be a woman' then it is because they have felt that women have lacked the privileges that men have enjoyed: they have been excluded from fulfilling their human potential. And so feminism is most easily understood as the demand for equality with men voiced in a vocabulary of exclusion and lack. But there is always an excess — in the rhetoric of feminism beyond the seemingly reasonable content of the demands themselves. How quickly the wish for equality spills over into a passionate and antagonistic polemic on difference and power: 'I shall also occasionally examin (sic)' exclaimed Sophia, an eighteenth-century rebel, in the middle of a peroration on Reason,[1]

> whether there be an *essential difference between* the *sexes* which can authorise the *superiority* the *men* claim over the *Women* . . . other . . . than what their tyranny [sic] has created (Sophia's emphasis).

'Then' she went on,

> it would appear, how unjust they are in excluding us from that power and dignity we have a right to share with them; how ungenerous in denying us the equality of esteem, which is our due; and how little reason they have to triumph in the base possession of an authority, which unnatural violence, and lawless usurpation, put into their Hands. Then, let them justify, if they can, the little meannesses, not to mention the grosser barbarities, which they daily practise towards that part of the creation whose happiness is so inseparably link'd with their own.

There is no just cause, Sophia argued, why men should have power over women if men have not the monopoly on reason — reason is a human attribute, not a masculine one. Neither should men have exclusive right to knowledge, law, or government (elsewhere in the essay she dwells on men's bestial natures, their susceptibility to the baser passions . . .). Women are the weak creatures they are, she opines, because men have made them so. Women, Sophia is bold enough to suggest, should have the right to enter science, don a military uniform, even to govern for —

it is impossible ever to govern subjects rightly, without knowing as well what they really are as what they only seem; which the *Men* can never be supposed to do, while they labour to force women to live in constant masquerade.[2]

Women, for Sophia, were the governed, subjected, the *seeming* sex, men the 'tyrannical' 'unlawful' governors who sometimes resort to 'unnatural violence'. Fifty years later, in Mary Wollstonecraft's *A Vindication of the Rights of Woman*[3] the grievances regather with intensity as she declares that women are 'outlaws' and 'was not the world a vast prison, and women born slaves?' For three hundred years, before and after Sophia and Mary Wollstonecraft, feminists have fulminated against male tyranny and lust, appealed to reason and individual liberty in their Cause. Polemic whose unavoidable sexual antagonism will not fit comfortably into the vernaculars of liberalism, conservatism or socialism.

At first glance, the Victorian Women's Movement when it emerged in the 1850s and '60s in Britain, though fired with deep feeling, was altogether more circumspect in its initial manifestations than its eighteenth-century predecessors. Coming together at 'drawing room meetings', forming committees under the patronage of the National Association for the Promotion of Social Science, setting up an employment register, reading room and a Middle Class Emigration Society in Langham Place, London, were the wives and daughters of clerics, landowners, small and not so small merchants and businessmen.[4] Impoverished (some of them) gentlewomen indeed, careful in their outward observations of propriety. The image they wished to present to the public – and their purpose was the persuasion of public opinion, the creation of new public opinions – was refined, rational, decorous. 'Educated women', 'women of the middle and lower classes' and 'working women' were their own self-identifications, they wanted improvements in the condition and status of *all* women. Convinced of the justice, morality and reason of their Cause, their reforms were radical: reform of the property laws, work and training for women, and women's suffrage.

Look more closely, read more carefully and rage, resentment, envy, above all, transcendental aspiration infuse the rhetoric. In the 1850s and '60s for instance, the demand for labour – one of the detonators of the mass movement – was modestly listed. Printing, hairdressing, watchmaking (tentatively proposed) the education of children, superintendence of workhouses and hospitals were seemingly the extent of feminist employment ambitions.[5] In 1859, the Association for Promoting the Employment of Women was formed from Langham Place. The energy behind the Association was Jessie Boucherett, who in her mid-thirties came to London from a landowning and unitarian family to work for the cause. The aim of the Association was work and training for women, the tone and the language were something more:[6]

> ... what is it we working women ask? What is it we are made to think and feel through every fibre of the frame with which it has pleased God to endow us as well as men, and for the maintenance of which in health, ease, and comfort, we, with men have equal rights?
>
> It is work we ask, room to work, encouragement to work, an open field with a fair day's wages for a fair day's work; it is injustice we feel, the injustice of men, who arrogate to themselves all profitable employments and professions, however unsuited to the vigorous manhood they boast, and thus usurping women's work, drive women to the lowest depths of penury and suffering.

The authors in this and other writings were careful to blame society not individuals for women's misfortunes and 'disabilities'. Custom and prejudice were the principal sources of women's 'impecunious' condition. But anger at men insisted on being spoken, fuelled by the revelations of the Census, confirmed by Government Blue Books. Forty-three per cent of women over twenty years old were unmarried, declared the Census, that 'melancholy anomolie' was cited at every opportunity in order to dispel the notion that every woman had a husband to protect her and to whose person she submitted her own and those of her children.

The 'excess' in feminism's demands played on a dilemma central to all radical thought since 1789, the contradiction between individual liberty (Mary Wollstonecraft's insistence that there could be no virtue without freedom) and equality. Feminists wanted the education, political representation, participation in public life that their brothers, fathers and husbands had and they argued for these on the grounds of their common humanity. But in justifying women's political (or any other) equality they spoke as women. Ursula Bright, suffragist, put it succinctly in a letter to Henry Fawcett (husband of Millicent):[7]

> ... I never myself hesitate to tell men when asked about my 'ulterior ends' that I mean to have everything in the shape of a right or a privilege which they think worth having for themselves – no more and no less. No one is really frightened of a woman with a babe in her arms.

She was wrong of course. It was the spectre of the 'woman with the babe in her arms' that marked the limits of liberal democracy. It also rendered alliances between feminism and either Liberals or Labour unstable in the nineteenth and twentieth centuries. Whatever its political or philosophical vocabulary, feminism pushes the troubling question of sexual difference into the political domain where it defies conventional political categories, touches fears and desires rooted deep in the unconscious minds of women as well as men, and arouses antagonisms between and among the sexes. Feminist demands for individual liberty, economic independence, full citizenship and an equal moral standard provoked argument and instability of political allegiance across the body politic.

— *Liberalism and the Women's Movement* —

Liberalism drew many women into its shadow through its emphasis on the political rights and civil and economic liberties of the individual. Liberalism as a creed attempted to hold together (among other things) a free market economy with equal opportunities, the liberty of the individual with a pluralism of interest groups.[8] John Stuart Mill's espousal of their 'cause' gave masculine weight to the movement.[9] And yet many Victorian feminists bore testimony to the limits of the Liberal Party's liberalism when it came to the 'woman question'. The Liberal Party under Gladstone (and later Rosebery and Asquith) was never persuaded of the need to or wisdom of extending the franchise beyond a selection of propertied male householders. Similarly during the 1870s, Josephine Butler and the Ladies' National Association (LNA) in their campaign to repeal the Contagious Diseases Acts, were only some in a continuum of feminists from Wollstonecraft to the libertarians of the 1970s who attempted to extend the scope of civil liberties to include women's rights over their own person. The CD Acts, the LNA argued, instituted the slavery of women: they were unjust laws which degraded and violated the civil liberties of all women, which punished the victims of injustice and not the beneficiaries of vice. The LNA's opposition to the imposition of law upon a helpless and defenceless social group was spoken in the rhetoric of liberalism. Nevertheless their natural allies, Josephine Butler recalled, were the radical working men in their communities.[10]

On particular issues between the 1870s and 1914 it was the labour movement, not the Liberal Party, which formed effective alliances with feminists. The Women's Trade Union League (1874–1920), like the LNA, negotiated with individual leaders and some skilled men's unions on issues such as the formation of a female union, or the defence of women's jobs; while the suffragists – the largest non-militant

suffrage organization, the National Union of Women's Suffrage Societies, under the presidency of Millicent Garrett Fawcett (a liberal by
both temperament and conviction) – formed an electoral alliance in
1912 with the nascent Labour Party. Before 1918 the Labour Party
was the only Party prepared to support women's franchise on the same
terms as men.[11]

Yet relations with the labour movement as a whole were fraught and
often contradictory. While feminists claimed women's right to work,
training and 'adequate remuneration', they were opposed by some trades
unionists as well as some political economists and the government, all
of whom regarded female labour (when they regarded it at all) as a
'problem of modern industry'. On the other hand, labour men were
notoriously unwilling to consider women – in the abstract that is – as
anything other than wives and mothers; and feared women's 'unsexing'
as much as did members of parliament when women's right to waged
work undermined or threatened men's own.

Women who wrote and campaigned on behalf of their sex were as
self-conscious about class as were most thinking men in the nineteenth
and early twentieth centuries. But what united women, feminists
thought, was not class (which more often divided them one from
another) but their shared experience of femininity: inadequate education; lack of status under the law; their position as cheap labour in
industry; exclusion from politics and public life; their capacity for
motherhood. Domestic duty was the 'connection' between women,
according to some voices in the English Women's Journal; Emily
Faithful and the Victoria Press were in pursuit of a woman's aesthetic
and culture; women were outside the law, excluded from skills and
earning power; women were united in their wish for peace; and one of
the emphases of the Women's Co-operative Guild from the 1880s to
the Second World War was the influence that married women would
bring to the democratic rights and duties of citizenship through their
role as consumers.

Feminism cannot be aligned either with the orthodoxies of Victorian
political thought, nor can it be reduced to an expression of class feeling.
Feminists practised mesmerism, phrenology, deism and theosophy; they
included free thinkers, co-operators, republicans and Tories. We may
trace the influence of political economy, evolutionary social theory,
elements of liberal as well as utopian socialist and conservative thought
in the polemic and rhetoric of feminists and Comte's religion of
humanity runs through them all. But the Women's Movement as it rethought and re-worked the meaning of and social organization of sexual
difference and its divisions is contained by none of these traditions.

— *Why the 1850s?* —

For the individual voice of 'Sophia' or Mary Wollstonecraft to become a movement there had to be discontent and a widespread longing for another way of life. Victorian feminism arose from a sense among many women of social injustice and grievance. We can date some of the immediate provocations of that sense of grievance. In 1832 the Reform Act inserted the word 'male' in front of 'persons' admitted to the franchise for the first time, and this was extended to all local political franchises in the next few years. Women's suffrage was one of the forces transforming the conception of government from that of a privilege or duty of property to the right of every adult citizen. Secondly, in the 1840s, factory legislation, known as protective to its advocates and restrictive to its feminist critics, excluded women from working underground in the mines, and limited the hours of female labour in the cotton mills.[12] Women, the economic dependants of men, were in need of 'protection' it was argued, because of their special needs, and their interests, like those of children, were bound up with those of others. Thirdly, the 1851 Census, as we have already seen, revealed not only the millions of poorly paid women domestic servants, factory and workshop hands, and sweated workers, but also the half million 'surplus' women. These women – the 'melancholie anomolie' of the *English Woman's Journal,* violated the assumption that all women were in fact supported by either their fathers or husbands. Meanwhile, as the conditions of the poor in the new factory districts horrified those Victorians with a social conscience and the destitution of the poor in the 1830s and '40s provoked an epidemic of reform, 'Woman' emerged as a social problem in the 1840s.[13] But it was groups of enterprising women organizing to remedy women's lack of political status, their humiliating status as the dependants of and under the protection of men, who transformed that social problem into a political category.

There is no space here to outline the contours of the Women's Movement in the following eighty years. We can simply note that the themes of feminism – marriage, work, women's culture, legal status and morality – met and mingled in ways which extended the imaginative scope of political thought and practice through the nineteenth and early twentieth centuries. The women who organized around these issues and spoke for their sex were delineating the meaning of sexual difference as they imagined a new social order. The writings of feminists as they advocated first one and then another aspect of their Cause was not confined to grievance. It was suffused with a spiritual yearning which reached a crescendo in the years immediately before the First World

War. Ideals of equality, democracy and womanhood surpassed party political labels and became symbols of hope and transformation in the relations between the sexes and indeed of all social relations and forms of government.[14]

What feminists wanted was education, knowledge, economic independence and the full political rights of citizenship. They also wanted an end to the double standard of sexual morality, women's control over their fertility and the guardianship of their children. What all these demands amounted to was a radical reorganization of marriage and property law, of production and of sexual morality – disturbing unconscious phantasies of sexual difference in spite of themselves. The issues of sexual difference and sexual antagonism were never far from the surface, however powerful the wish – on the part of many feminists themselves – to push them out of the political arena into the realm of natural law and however careful many of them were to pursue only the *facts* of women's conditions and legal and political status. These 'wants' forced autonomy on the Women's Movement. No political party ever has placed them in the forefront of the political agenda, most political theory slides over them, and most men and some women claim they do not want them. Feminism, then, and the women's movement, are still engaged in articulating and creating a politics that will convince.

1984

WHY FEMINISM?

THE WOMEN OF

LANGHAM PLACE

Re-reading Leonore Davidoff and Catherine Hall's *Family Fortunes* (Hutchinson, 1987) I rediscovered Miss Sparkes – the Wollstonecraftian in Hannah More's *Coelebs in Search of a Wife* (1803):

> . . . a single lady of 45, who has pretensions to be a scholar, a huntress, politician, and a farrier, essentially unfeminine charac- teristics. She is witty, bold, fond of the marvellous and the incredible; she is sure of herself and the only woman in the book to 'speak'. She arrives at The Grove on her horse carrying a whip and wearing a cap, claiming to know all about horses, an essentially male terrain. She likes men better than women, but of course they do not like her. Above all she is contemptuous of domestic economy and her estimation of these 'plodding employments' which 'cramp the genius, degrade the intellect, depress the spirits, debase the taste, and clip the wings of imagination' provokes all the gentlemen at The Grove to the defence of the central importance of domestic skills. But Miss Sparkes is not silenced. She rises to the bait and expresses her envy of the advantages which men have in the world, their access to power and glory.

Feminists, then, we learn from Ms More, evangelical, spinster, educator of the poor and enemy of Ms Wollstonecraft, are those women who – bold, adventurous, speakers and actors, despise domestic drudgery, are envious of and want to be like men and are ridiculed for so wanting. The point of the novel, of all Ms More's teaching (and it had the weight of evangelical as well as many other opinions behind it) was that femininity should confine women to the home, not send them out on adventures. Hannah More's mockery is the more mysterious since she herself was neither married nor domestic but like Mary Wollstonecraft an independent woman: ambitious, a writer, an educator, and a moralist. The two women had much in common. Both had a sense of mission. Both criticized the outward forms of femininity as they were lived among rich and poor. But whereas Mary Wollstonecraft wanted women to be educated into independence of mind and body, Hannah More believed that women's inferiority of status sprang from their femininity. Since to be unstable and capricious is but 'too characteristic of our own sex' she wrote, 'there is no animal so indebted to insubordination as woman'.

This is what I wanted my paper to be about: What makes a feminist? Why did and do some women – born into similar historical circumstance – become feminists and others not? In particular, why, in the 1850s and 1860s, when a clamour of feminist grievance ignited a wide public consciousness of women's wrongs, were Harriet Martineau, Bessie Raynor Parkes, Barbara Leigh Smith Bodichon, Emily Davies, Edith Simcox for instance, all feminists (I'm using the word retrospectively), and George Eliot, a friend of them all, not? George Eliot, born in 1819 (Marian Evans), translator of Strauss's *Life of Jesus* (1846), editor and novelist, counted Owenites and co-operators among her friends; she lived with a man already married, signed the Married Woman's Property Petition in 1856, gave monies to selected women's causes in the 1870s, and yet she remained distant from the movement all through her life and doubtful about the wisdom of women's suffrage. Why? Some would say that political conviction explains all – (compare Hannah More's high Toryism with Mary Wollstonecraft's sexual as well as political radicialism). But how is political conviction formed?

Oddly, this is a question that has excited little curiosity. Historians of the women's movement, content to position feminists among the political orthodoxies of the early Victorian intelligentsia and propertied classes, forgetting those orthodoxies were anyway in flux, have often overlooked the distinctive characteristics of feminism both as a movement and as a body of thought. If feminist rhetoric borrowed from the vocabularies and imagery of every radical individualist philosophy of the early and mid-Victorian age, then feminism's distinguishing feature was its focus on sexual difference and its uneven representations in law, language, the economy, domesticity and politics. This focus draws attention away from the ethical aims of politics to its subject; it divides the liberal citizen; cuts across political alliances by raising the spectre of sexual antagonism. Feminist anger and polemic is directed against men.

Both feminists and their historians are drawn perilously close to the formation of psychic life by this endeavour. If what interests me is the mental world of the feminists, their subjectivity even, this is because there is a proximity between the political narratives in which we situate ourselves which articulate in different ways the relation between need and demand and the psychic foundations of the self. Both are grounded in identification and desire. The self, the ego is formed through identifications: phantasised and with real and unreal objects. The processes of subjectivity and political belief must be sometimes similar. I do not want to pathologize feminism but to uncover its distinctive sources of psychic energy. George Eliot evidently demurred from raising those spectres of sexual difference, desire and antagonism in her political allegiances, if not in her books or her personal life. Always conscious of her public image, Marian Evans in this respect shared the reservations of other conservative women in public life who questioned the wisdom of associating themselves with the cause which spoke openly and sometimes stridently about the sex-relation, and which provoked unruly and possibly irresolvable antagonism between women and men. As *The Times* newspaper retorted on the passage of the 1870 Married Woman's Property Act in 1870 – the world is now divided again into men and women.

If there were common psychic foundations of feminism or of feminist discontents, as some of its accusers have suggested (envy for instance or hatred of men) then this could be because from the seventeenth century the political subject's claims to virtue and independence of person were spoken through the masculine subject. One of the starting points of the women's movement was women's participation in the movements for anti-slavery, the Charter, for the reform of the Corn Laws, peace and temperance where young women learned to articulate a fierce sense of injustice and a democratic vocabulary of grievance and aspiration. Women's activity in these and other movements had been – as Alex Tyrrell has pointed out – both separate and unequal but they took their new found knowledge into the campaigns for married women's property, education, work, the suffrage, the campaign against the Contagious Diseases Acts, where feminists calibrated their tactics (petitions, tea-parties and bazaars; prayer meetings; public meetings) with the masculine forms of parliamentary politics – (debate, polemic, caballing), giving Josephine Butler – a democrat through and through as one friend described her – some grounds for her assertion that women's forms of political organization were more democratic than men's. As Emily Davies remarked wryly to Barbara Leigh Smith in 1862 in regards to the trials and tribulations of the *English Woman's Journal* (EWJ), there was nothing new about women working together; all over England women were working together, in schools, hospitals, philanthropic committees and elsewhere: 'the new and difficult thing is for men and women to work together on equal terms'.

The women's movement's unsettling focus on sexual difference offers insights into the emotional processes of political conviction and action that other movements obscure. We are used as historians to distinguish between the historical and the psychic. In discussion of the 'Woman Question' in the mid-nineteenth century that distinction is blurred. Women's exclusion from the parliamentary and other political franchises for example, was founded on the fiction of their need of protection: women's status as a 'problem of modern industry' on the myopia of political economy which erased women's need for work. In the first case, the justification was women's sexual vulnerability, their maternal capacity and lesser physical strength than men; in the second, the erasure of women's own economic dependants and needs. In both instances, these economic conditions and differential needs of women were glossed over in the name of a natural sexual difference. Feminists' response was to assert need and to attempt to articulate those needs in the political idioms of the time. Inevitably feminism changed those idioms.

I have confined my enquiry – to think the question of the formation of feminist political consciousness – to the diagnosis and grievance of the Langham Place women from the 1850s, in particular through their demand for work. How did those women identify themselves and their cause? What did they want? And what do we discover about the impulse and purpose of feminism (both the thought and the movement) from the answers?

My interest in George Eliot's lack of enthusiasm for The Cause was stimulated in part by a disagreement among friends as we chose the readings for the Wollstonecraft Centenary evening (held at the Conway Hall in June 1992). I wanted to include a quote from Wollstonecraft on the difficult relation between women and creative work. Sometimes spoken of as a wish for an end to idleness and a need for work (the EWJ and the Langham Place women); sometimes as longing for time to write and think (Virginia Woolf's A Room of One's Own); sometimes simply as the wish to escape from domestic life (Florence Nightingale's plea in Cassandra, published as an appendix to The Cause, Ray Strachey (1928) Virago), feminist desire sprang from the lived restrictions of femininity and domesticity. But my friends and collaborators for Dangerous Reputations – Ursula Owen and Jean McCrindle – disagreed. The problem of creativity is not an especially feminist problem they argued, nor does it concern all women. No, I replied, but feminists are not all women. Feminists are frustrated with the conventional forms of femininity and the historical conditions which seem to confine their very selves; a frustration which is then extended – in polemic – to all women.

The Langham Place women for instance, longing for worlds beyond their families, wanted *work* for women: and in that demand they recast themselves in both the image of man and God:

> When we venture to pronounce that as the daughters of Deity, as part of that humanity common to both sexes, women, besides being created for wives and mothers, are also created for themselves and for that Deity, we are sensible that only by great and long continued efforts, can they hope to gain the position of workers in the world's affairs, instead of the idlers they have been hitherto. (*EWJ*, vol. 1 No. 6, Aug 1, 1860 p. 362)

There was nothing that women could not do, the leader averred in an access of aspirational hubris – '*of whatever women are capable, for that they were intended*'. In this sense the demand for release from the subjection to and tyranny of men, from the drudgery of domesticity sprang not only from the economic need for work. It was also an appeal for the release of female creativity.

The ladies of Langham Place in the late 1850s set up a reading room, an employment register, an emigration society, and housed the Society for the Promotion of Women's Employment, and a school for industrial training (as clerks, cashiers and book-keepers) as well as the *EWJ*. Limited, financially pressed, sustained through determination and private donation and always fraught with internal political and personal conflict, Langham Place women strove for knowledge, for enlightenment, for the transformation of women's lives through work. The deity as well as political economy were invoked to teach that the earth is only possessed by those who work for its possession. To this end, women must be prepared for martyrdom, the editorial of 1858 exhorted, if 'we are to take the citadel'.

The wish for work if we are to take seriously the appeal to God and the resort to martyrdom, was perhaps the most deeply felt demand of the 1850s. Reform of married women's property laws was the first campaign, several moves for education and training followed. Feminists wanted release from subjection, male tyranny, domestic drudgery and an end to the elision of women's legal, civil and political identity with that of their fathers and husbands. Female independence was the aim, and this, in the atmosphere of political disenchantment after 1848 (the defeat of Chartism shadowed the failed revolutions in Europe), was to be achieved through social reform rather than political representation. The new ethics, it was believed, would emerge not from the political but from the industrial and domestic sphere and women were the harbingers of this change.

Since the 1790s, as Gareth Stedman Jones has argued, among the questions that radicals (whether dissenters, millenarianists, and now

Comtists, utopian socialists and others) asked was what comprises human happiness; what were the sources of human virtue? Also since the 1790s the force for improvement in social justice would come from an emphasis on human (Comte's religion of humanity) and natural (the radical dissenters from unitarians to deists) rights rather than the ruthless pursuit of equality. Independence was the key. Independence in Mary Wollstonecraft's thought and that of the Langham Place women, was the basis of human virtue, and the opposite of slavery. Slavery or slavish dependence was the most ubiquitous metaphor of women's subjection in early and mid-nineteenth-century feminist rhetoric. Used to describe their domestic thraldom, their submission to male lust and the abnegation of identity on marriage, slavery evoked female degradation. Labour, the human attribute which distinguished mankind from the beasts, provided the means through which women could enter the public world, and realize the full potential of their shared humanity with men.

Mary Wollstonecraft, for instance, striving for self-improvement through occupation, reading and study, had emulated those she admired (first her girlhood friend Fanny Blood, later the dissenting circles in Stoke Newington) before declaiming against idleness as an ideal for women. Her wish that women should subvert through labour the 'necessity of being always woman' was echoed later in Barbara Leigh Smith's essay on women's work (1857) that 'love should not be women's sole profession'.

The struggle against idleness and the strenuous pursuit of self improvement is writ large in the journals and memoirs of nineteenth-century feminists. They are full of references to early morning study, struggles with mathematics, political economy, theology for several hours before the daily grind of 'poor peopling' and other domestic occupations. Several modern and one or two ancient languages were a commonplace among educated women. These young women wanted the education their brothers had received, they wanted knowledge and the right to political representation. They weren't afraid to risk ridicule. Mary Wollstonecraft had feared she might excite laughter with her wish for representation. Bessie Raynor Parkes in an essay on work in 1859 knew too that the need and wish for work would provoke sneering accusations. 'Strong-minded women', 'blue-stockings', 'emancipation-ists', and 'Americanists' were some of the epithets applied to the feminists. Undaunted by ridicule she rejects the poets' abjuration that women should be content to *be* – women wanted and needed to *do*. Passivity not activity was the fear.

The self-discipline, imitation and envy of men, anger at the fathers who refused to educate their daughters, and the world which allowed women workers to endure poverty rather than to train and pay them appropriately combined to form a structure of feeling in which the philanthropic impulse jostled with dawning industrial consciousness; in which learning and labour were closely associated. These proximities and emphases have given the Women's Movement its designation as middle class; and they do belong to the heroic age of the middle class, when the romantic vision of industry transforming the world shaped liberal and conservative philosophies and Harriet Martineau was not the only political economist to argue that ethical regeneration would spring from natural economic laws.

Langham Place's circumspection of demand should not mislead the historian. Their ambitions out-reached those of Mary Wollstonecraft because they had a movement as well as a vision to compel them, only the vision was translated into political demand and social reform. As daughters of the deity, the *EWJ* appealed to an authority above that of fathers, priests, governments, which became invested in the female soul through identification with the Holy Spirit, or Christ himself, whose sexual identity in the Bible and its commentaries, was ambivalent.

The identification with God, the use of the metaphors of martyrdom to sanction their cause, and slavery to ubiquitize it, have several roots. Firstly, the search for truth, the source of virtue, the proper basis for government, even the reforms of health and education were conducted with reference to spiritual and religious values and beliefs. Theology was part of philosophical dispute in the early and mid-nineteenth century.

So many feminists experienced a religious crisis – which was also a crisis of self – during their adolescence. Educated women cut their teeth on theology. Many of the first Victorian feminists also came from unitarian reforming families. (Unitarians put works before faith.) They imbibed political reform from childhood. The new religions of the age – the moral regeneracy of Comtist humanism for example; the new moral world of Owenism; the female messianism of Saint-Simonianism or Fourierism – all spoke a language of moral absolutes, and challenged orthodox Christianity's claim to truth. Identification with the subject of these different religions enabled women to break out of their prescribed silence and submission. They added to the keen sense of the suffering and oppression of other peoples, the duty of those educated and able to help others. The speeches and essays of Josephine Butler, Barbara Leigh Smith Bodichon, Bessie Raynor Parkes and Jessie Boucherett are alive with references to God and to the capacity to speak the meaning of God through them.

Women who had participated in the reform and millennial movements of the 1830s and '40s had articulated and internalized a moral vocabulary of progress and improvement, and a syntax which placed women closer to spiritual values either on the grounds of their detachment from the public world or because of their capacity for motherhood. This is very well documented. This moralism infused feminist polemic. The identifications through which that moralism was grounded are worth exploring further, however, and may well offer us clues as to the emotional formation of feminism.

Feminists united women through their grievances: inadequate education, lack of political representation, the assumption that fathers or husbands would support them, and poverty, idleness and want. Consciousness of privilege did not inhibit feminists from identifying with their impoverished sisters – all women whatever their wealth lacked occupation and independent status; only the poor suffered more. Governesses, needlewomen, and maids of all work filled the alms houses, the pauper and lunatic wards of workhouses; 'starvation or vice' was exacerbated by masculine jealousy; prostitution (whether legal or not) was an economic question, Barbara Leigh Smith argued in 1857, and the Ladies National Association reiterated through the 1870s. Women suffered under tyrannical laws which placed their property and persons in the hands of husbands and fathers. Only a private income in a woman's own name gave independence.

This rhetorical unity around grievance went with a fine sense of the distinctions in education, income, status, respectability, aspiration among women. Feminists were not unaware of the differences among women. For example, the *EWJ*, Bessie Parkes in a letter to Barbara Leigh Smith Bodichon explained, was to address –

> all women who are actively engaged in any labours of brain or hand, whether they be the wives and daughters of landed proprietors, devoted to the well-being of their tenantry, or are to be classed among the many other labourers in the broad field of philanthropy; – whether they belong to the army of teachers, public or private, or to the realms of professional artists; or are engaged in any of those manual occupations by which multitudes of British women, at home and in the colonies, gain their daily bread.

What united women was their difference in status, income, political representation from men; while sexually women were in thrall to men's lust, and incessant reproduction.

Jacquie Matthews in her excellent study of Barbara Bodichon's life and political thought, asks why she, brought up in a radical household, with an Owenite education, and a father who settled £300 a year on her when she came of age (in 1848, the year of revolutions in Europe) should have thought that women suffered under tyranny. Describing the 'unjust laws . . . which crush women' Leigh Smith continues, 'there never was a tyranny so deeply felt yet borne so silently'. This was written in response to J. S. Mill's *Principles of Political Economy* read on publication in 1848. She was twenty-one. When she wrote her essay on women and work (published in 1857, she was thirty), Leigh Smith spoke of the 'hysteria and illness' that accompanied women's idleness and poverty. The Petition which followed an earlier essay on the Laws that 'crush' women, was addressed to all women, 'employed in manufacturing as sempstresses, laundresses, charwomen, and in other multifarious occupations'.

As a young woman, Barbara Leigh Smith read the *Morning Chronicle* journalist, Henry Mayhew's accounts of *London Life and Labour*, French and American radical literature as well as John Stuart Mill, Robert Owen and Auguste Comte. Travelling stimulated her talents and powers of observation, and an easeful emotional life developed her capacity for compassionate identification with the plight of women less fortunate than herself. Her education in family and school (she attended the Westminster Ragged School; later, Bedford College) had led her to reflect on justice, co-operation and equality as principles of law and government; on liberty as essential for the emergence of human creativity; on poverty as a remediable social evil. All these activities and influences made up her radicalism. And yet its roots lie also in her parental history.

Of illegitimate birth, only her father's affection and honour stood between her and ostracism or worse, destitution. Her mother, Anne had been a 'ravishingly pretty milliner's apprentice of seventeen'. Jacquie Matthews suggests that Barbara's feminism reconciled the 'love and admiration for her generous radical father with the memory of the "poor little mother".'

Other feminists admired and identified with those fathers who advocated their education and instilled a need for social reform in their daughters. Listen to Josephine Butler (born in 1828, into a Northumbrian reforming and landed family) on her father, John Gray's liberalism:

> My father was a man with a deeply rooted, fiery hatred of all injustice. The love of justice was a passion with him. Probably I have inherited from him this passion . . . When my father spoke to us, his children, of the great wrong of slavery, I have felt his powerful voice tremble and his voice would break. You can believe, that at that time sad and tragical recitals came to us

from first sources of the hideous wrong inflicted on negro men and women. I say women, for I think their lot was particularly horrible, for they were almost invariably forced to minister to the worst passions of their masters, or be persecuted and die . . . I remember how these things combined to break my young heart, and how keenly they awakened my feelings concerning injustice to women through this conspiracy of greed of gold and lust of the flesh, a conspiracy which has its counterpart in the white slave owning in Europe.

His opinions she thought –

had their root very deep in his soul and affections . . . God made him a Liberal, and a Liberal in the true sense he continued to be to the end of his life. In conversations with him on any public questions, one could not but observe how much such questions were matters of feeling with him. I believe that his political principles and public actions were alike the direct fruit of that which held rule within his soul – I mean his large benevolence, his tender compassionateness, and his respect for the rights and liberties of the individual man. His life was a sustained effort for the good of others, flowing from these affections. He had no grudge against rank of wealth, no restless desire of change for its own sake, still less any rude love of demolition; but he could not endure to see oppression or wrong of any kind inflicted on a man, woman or child. (*Josephine E. Butler, An Autobiographical Sketch*, eds. George W. and Lucy A. Johnson, with Introduction by James Stuart, Bristol, 1909, pp. 6, 8, 14.)

Everything is there – passion, tragedy, injustice, suffering of women; the source of his political convictions, Butler believed, were deep feeling and the direct rule of the soul; one source of hers – identification with the slave.

Some feminists struggled to imbibe masculine virtues in other ways. The effect could be punitive. Harriet Martineau (also born into a Unitarian family in 1802), on considering an offer to edit her own economical journal in the 1840s:

I must brace myself up to do and suffer like a man. No more waywardness, precipitation, and reliance on allowance from others. Undertaking a man's duty, I must brave a man's fate. I must be prudent, independent, serene, good-humoured; earnest with cheerfulness. The possibility is open before me of showing what a periodical with a perfect temper may be: – also, of setting women forward at once into the rank of men of business. (*Autobiography* 1877, Virago 1983, vol. 2, p. 110.)

No wonder she said no.

These identifications are putative, and no more than suggestive of the elements in the formation of belief and a movement. Freud pointed to the significance of the leader in the formation of Group Psychology (and of the traces of words and thoughts of leaders in the formation of the cultural super-ego), but this brief foray into aspects of feminist grievance and demand suggests the identifications were more promiscuous. The honour and reforming zeal of fathers, fused with the transcending deity and the suffering sisterhood to give the mind of the women's movement its identificatory imagery and polemical power.

Julia Kristeva, whose essay 'Woman's Time' is almost alone in addressing the historical implications of the psychic dimension of feminism – or the women's movements in Europe – has suggested that the political demands of the women's movement follows phases. In the first phase, women ask for equality with men; in the second they assert the distinctiveness of women. What is necessary, Kristeva continues, is a third and final phase (and here she reveals her debt to Hegel) in which the distinction of sex is transcended (forgetting that Mary Wollstone-craft had made that proposal two hundred years ago).

I want to suggest not only that all three phases are present at any one moment in the women's movement; but that this is what defines feminism as utopian and situates the women's movement firmly among the progressive post-enlightenment movements. It emerged in the shadow of the 1848 revolutions, after the failure of Chartism and the demise of utopianisms. This climate in part explains feminism's circum-spection. Feminists through the 1850s and '60s wanted what their brothers and fathers already had in the way of education, occupation, political representation, power; but they argue on the grounds of their femininity. Langham Place women wanted work for women; they wanted to alleviate the 'suffering and poverty' of so many women revealed by the Census to be unsupported by father or husband, or working on their own account. They wanted the education and training that men had, Bessie Parkes and Emily Faithful later urged, and for all occupations to be open to women as well as men, and for wages to be the same for women as for men. In 1865 they organized a petition in support of women's suffrage on the same terms as men.

All this made their men anxious. Jane Rendall has shown how private correspondence reveals that fathers and friends were among the critics who feared that to emphasize the need for occupation might suggest that they ignored women's domestic responsibility. Bessie Raynor Parkes, for instance, then editor of the *English Woman's Journal* hastened to reassure readers that the *Journal*'s concern was with work, education and occupation because that was where women had cause for complaint. Of course the *Journal* knew that the home and family were the foundations of society. (Thirty years later, Emilia Dilke, President of the Women's Trade Union League in the early 1880s, had the same problem: women wanted to be at home with their families, she argued at the Trade Union Congress and in published articles, meanwhile those women at work needed trade unions.)

Victorian feminists argued for equality on the grounds of women's difference from men. In the mid-nineteenth century, motherhood marked the difference between the sexes for feminists (as well as for evangelicals, political economists, utilitarians, Comtists, Darwinists and other Victorian public opinions. Mary Wollstonecraft had made the reform of mothering one of her aims in *Vindication*.) Feminists differed only on the extent to which motherhood, or sexual difference should be emphasized in political campaigns. The dwelling on sexual difference, unavoidable in the campaign against the Contagious Diseases Acts, for instance (and as we have seen, an emotive and formative forcing ground of Josephine Butler's sense of self and politics) was at the root of some suffragists' (Millicent Garrett Fawcett's, for example) anxiety about publicly supporting that campaign.

In other words, the identifications of feminist political speech were always manifold – both masculine: wanting to have what men had already got; and feminine: the demands were made in the name of all women and on the grounds of women's difference from men. The solution was often conceived as an end to the distinction of sex.

One of the distinctive features of the women's movement is its accent on the formation of sexual difference – what makes us women and men? Feminists, discontented with that alignment, want it changed. But in re-aligning the outer forms of femininity and masculinity feminists disturb the inner forms. Those inner forms are grounded in identifications, the processes through which the ego is formed. Feminism thus brings the personal into political life in ways which are disturbing, and some thought inappropriate. George Eliot was one of the latter. Women's suffering was undeniable but she was deeply sceptical (as her novels show) of the reforming power of the ballot box. Laws and institutions should be changed in order to permit women to develop, but there would be no necessary release of virtue or creativity in this way. When she reviewed Margaret Fuller's *Woman in the Nineteenth Century* (1843) and Mary Wollstonecraft's *Vindication of the Rights of Woman* (1792) she admired the first for its 'calm plea', the second for its 'serious, severely moral' tone, and them both for their evidence in each of the 'brave bearing of a strong and truthful nature the beating of a loving woman's heart, which teaches them not to undervalue the smallest offices of domestic care or kindliness' (Thomas Pinney, *Essays of George Eliot*, RKP, 1963). Eliot was convinced by Comte's teaching of resignation and separate spheres, and the necessitarian doctrine that each should obey her own nature. Women should not do any work for which they were unfit. This was quite different from those feminists who placed Comte among a sequence of philosophers who located the foundations of a new ethics in the domestic and industrial sphere, then used them as their springboard for political change. Eliot decried optimism in favour of realism, and realism meant pursuing the common-places, the unpretentious in life as in her writing. Her concerns were with the morals and passions of everyday life and she searched her own heart and the circumstances of the small manufacturers and tradesmen among whom she grew up for their workings. Eliot's father, a midlands estate manager, was a conservative. She described him at the time of his death as her 'one deep love'. She too experienced a deep religious crisis which she resolved with an inward refusal of Anglicanism while her father was alive, submitting to his wish for her dutiful attendance at church. In middle age, a distinguished, revered figure in literature, she named herself mother, and requested that epithet from young women friends. Nevertheless her rebellions were inner, rather than political. It's a moot point whether this was disposition or conviction.

This essay was given as a talk at the Mary Wollstonecraft Centenary Conference held at the University of Sussex, November 1992. It is very much 'Work-in-Progress'.

Note on further reading: Hannah More, *Coelebs in Search of a Wife*, 1803, ran into three editions in nine months, sold 21,000 copies, and entered into the imagination of the educated. *The English Woman's Journal*, the speeches and writings of Josephine Butler, and most of the relevant autobiographies and writings are in the Fawcett Library, London. The Parkes Papers and the Bodichon Collection are in Girton College Library, Cambridge. Candida Ann Lacey's (ed.) *Barbara Leigh Smith Bodichon and the Langham Place Group*, RKP, 1987, is a useful source. Hester Burton, *Barbara Bodichon, 1877–1891*, John Murrey, London, 1949 is still the only biography. Harriet Martineau, *Autobiography*, (1877) 2 vols. Virago, 1983; *Josephine E. Butler, An Autobiographical Memoir*, eds. George W. and Lucy A. Johnson, Arrowsmith, Bristol and London, 1909 are both compulsive reading. Jane Rendall, 'A Moral Engine'? Feminism Liberalism and *The English Woman's Journal*, ed. Jane Rendall, *Equal or Different? Women's Politics 1800–1914*, Basil Black-well, 1987, pp. 112–138; Jacqui Matthews, 'Barbara Bodichon: Integrity in Diversity, 1827–1891', ed. Dale Spender, *Feminist Theorists; Three Centuries of Women's Intellectual Traditions*, The Women's Press, 1983, pp. 90–123; Alex Tyrrell, 'Woman's Mission and Pressure Group Politics in Britain (1825–60)', *Bulletin of the John Rylands University Library*, vol. 63, 1980, pp. 194–230 are three immensely valuable essays with excellent bibliographical references in the notes. Gordon S. Haight, *George Eliot: A Biography*, Oxford University Press 1968, is still a useful if pedestrian introduction to Eliot's life and thought. Julia Kristeva, 'Woman's Time', *Signs, Journal of Women in Culture and Society*, Autumn 1981, vol. 7, number 1, pp. 13–35.

THE FABIAN WOMEN'S
GROUP
1908–52

'How does a working man's wife bring up a family on 20s a week?' *Round About a Pound a Week* made a remarkable impact when it was first published. For four years, from 1909–13, Maud Pember Reeves and other members of the Fabian Women's Group recorded the daily budgets and daily lives of working-class families in Lambeth. The people whose lives formed the subject of the book were by no means the poorest people in the district – the men 'respectable, in full work, at a more or less top wage, young, with families still increasing'. Their wives were described as 'quiet, decent, "keeping themselves to themselves" kind of women'. The book came out at a time when the discussion of infant health, infant mortality and the health of mothers was dominated by the eugenicist rhetoric of race degeneration. Thinking of ways to improve the nation through 'improving' the mother had become almost a national pastime. But Maud Pember Reeves' moving account of working-class mothers in Lambeth showed them to be at once independent, resourceful, hardworking, respectable – and poor, bringing up their families on wholly inadequate incomes.

The national preoccupation with motherhood had its roots in the waning of national economic confidence.[1] Since the last decades of the nineteenth century, under the pressure of German and American industrial competition, Britain had begun to feel its vulnerablility as a world-dominating economic power. Declining births and the high rate of infant mortality had taken on a new significance in the wake of the Boer War. Anxiety provoked by the physical debility of the army recruits had been confirmed by the poverty surveys (Charles Booth in London in the 1890s discovered 30 per cent of the population to be living below the poverty line; Rowntree in York uncovered similar proportions).[2] Because of these revelations of malnutrition and chronic ill-health the governing class acquiesced to the social reforms of the Liberal Government of 1906 (old age pensions, provision of school meals and school medical inspection). And the duty of women to fulfil their natural function of motherhood efficiently and effectively became one predominant theme of liberal individualism and Labour's socialism. Few public figures were unaffected by the idea that mothers were uniquely responsible for the wellbeing of the nation. John Burns, for instance, socialist engineer, then President of the Local Government Board, at the first National Conference of Infant Mortality in 1906:[3]

> At the bottom of infant mortality, high or low, is good or bad motherhood. Give us good motherhood, and good pre-natal conditions, and I have no despair for the future of this or any other country.

Among socialists were many individuals who showed concern for working-class health and many organizations which aimed to overcome the evil effects of poverty on the working-class mother (Margaret Macmillan's Mother and Infant Welfare Clinic in Bradford, for instance).[4] But Maud Pember Reeves and the Fabian Women's Group were unique in investigating the *daily* circumstances of women's domestic labour, how they coped with damp, vermin, inadequate food, how they washed, cooked, scrimped for furniture and clothes, saved for the frequent burials. The book was based on the Fabian Women's Group investigation into the effects on mother and child of insufficient nourishment before and after birth, begun after registering the simple fact that more children grew up undernourished in the working class than in the wealthy districts of London such as Kensington or Hampstead. In telling of these lives – of births, marriages, and deaths, of ill-paid work for men and unending toil for women, Maud Pember Reeves presented to a largely ignorant public the everyday realities of poverty. The conclusions were inescapable – high infant mortality was due not to mothers' ignorance or degeneracy, but that they had not enough money to provide for their own and their families' needs; they lacked decent housing, domestic equipment, adequate food and clothing, and any facilities or opportunities for recreation.[5]

By describing the experience of the poor to a middle-class audience, Maud Pember Reeves was revealing a world glimpsed only – if at all – through the literature and activities of philanthropy. She paid attention, therefore, to the shibboleths of philanthropic thought. She showed why the 'gospel of porridge' was not well received at the breakfast tables of Lambeth; why thrift, cleanliness and order were not the most desirable qualities in an overworked wife and mother; and she makes short shrift of the argument that only the provident should marry and have children.

If the poor were not improvident, she declares, 'they would hardly dare to live their lives at all'.[6]

These detailed observations were to convince the educated public that only the State could remedy such a situation. Beatrice Webb (who was only ever a lukewarm feminist) explains the 'demand for State intervention from a generation reared amidst rapidly rising riches' as she describes her own political awakening in *My Apprenticeship*:[7]

> The origin of the ferment is to be discovered in a new consciousness of sin among men of intellect and men of property . . . The consciousness of sin was a collective or class consciousness; a growing uneasiness, amounting to conviction, that the industrial organisation, which had yielded rent, interest and profits on a stupendous scale, had failed to provide a decent livelihood and tolerable conditions for a majority of the inhabitants of Great Britain.

This 'consciousness of sin' took very strong root in the minds of women of the propertied classes in the 1880s, since whatever restrictions on economic and sexual activity masculine authority might impose, charitable work ('poor peopling' as Florence Nightingale disparagingly named it) was a legitimate activity for even the most sheltered girl in the Victorian period. As Ray Strachey has suggested in her excellent history of the feminist movement, *The Cause*, these middle-class women were moving from dealing with the individual cases of hardship to solving the social problem.[8] Becoming a socialist was often a consequence of that process. Autobiographies of socialists and feminists show the power of *seeing* the slums, the way in which the working class lived, in the conversion to socialism. Doubtless many Fabian women shared the background of one in search of 'social-secretarial or organizational work' who advertised her skills in the *Fabian News*; 'University Education. Experience London Settlement, Charitable Organization Society and Girls' Club.' It was a short step from all these worthy organizations to membership of the Fabian Society.[9]

The society had been founded in 1884 (the name derived from the Roman general Fabius Cunctator whose tactics in his campaign against Hannibal were said to be 'cautious and forthright'). Some of its more famous early members included George Bernard Shaw, Beatrice and Sidney Webb, H.G. Wells, Graham Wallas, Hubert Bland, Edith Nesbit, Annie Besant. From its inception it had always included a large number of women. Fabian socialism – a hybrid of the social conscience, often with strong evangelical roots, of the well-off and well-educated on the one hand and the pragmatism of the new professional strata (civil servants, teachers, journalists) on the other – was essentially a belief in the gradual extension of the State. The Fabians acknowledged class struggle but not its viability as a route to socialism. As social democrats they shared 'a common conviction of the necessity of vesting the organization of industry and the material production in a State identified with the whole people by complete Democracy' (Preface to *Fabian Essays*, 1889). Class antagonisms could be side-stepped by the permeation of the middle and upper classes (and in particular their political and economic institutions) with 'collectivist' ideas. Thus Maud Pember Reeves suggests in *Round About a Pound a Week* that the State 'as co-guardian of the child' must strip off 'the uniform of a police constable with a warrant in his pocket' and 'place all the information, all the security, all the help at its command at the service of its co-guardians, the fathers and mothers'.[10]

Fabian women were content to remain quietly inside the Fabian Society, representing between a quarter and a third of its membership until 1908, when, according to the pamphlet *Three Years' Work*, the period of militant suffragist agitation produced:[11]

> ... unrest among women within the Fabian Society as well as outside. The socialist movement was rapidly growing in volume and force, and encountering increasingly bitter opposition, and many ardent suffragists amongst the Fabian women felt that the society was not keeping pace with a movement to which it recently committed itself by the inclusion of a new Clause in its basis. [A statement of equal rights for women.]

In 1908, Charlotte Wilson, an anarchist married to a stockbroker and living the 'new life' in Hampstead and one of the first members of the Fabian Society, founded the Fabian Women's Group at the London home of Maud Pember Reeves, and in the following year the 'Mother Allowance Scheme in Lambeth' – later to become *Round About a Pound a Week* – began on the initiative of Maud Pember Reeves. According to her daugher, Amber Blanco White, no sooner had the idea occurred to her mother than she set to work on it, enlisting the help of her sister Mrs Lascelles, who had lived with the Pember Reeves family since her husband's death, and Dr Ethel Bentham. They set up a sub-committee for their work, and Charlotte Wilson became the Treasurer of the project, contributing the two final chapters of the book.[12]

The imprint of Fabian socialism on *Round About a Pound a Week* lay in the concern with poverty, the extension of the State; but the emphasis on the houseworker and mother came from feminism.

Numbering only 230 at its peak in 1912 the Fabian Women's Group concentrated on women's social welfare and political rights, and their contribution to the political climate of social reform was important and influential. From a separate office in Tothill Street, Westminster, they published numerous pamphlets and tracts and two highly praised books, of which *Round About a Pound a Week* was one.[13] Less active in the inter-war period, the Fabian Women's Group enjoyed a brief renaissance after 1938 with the re-organization of the Fabian Society until the Group's end in 1952.

The two immediate aims of the Fabian Women's Group were equality in citizenship and women's economic independence. The first was prompted by a suggestion from Beatrice Webb that 'in local government women's citizenship is theoretically recognised but imperfect – ill understood, unappreciated and little used, whilst the evils crying out for women's intervention are enormous.'[14] The Group set out to rectify this with characteristic energy. A sub-committee was formed, and money raised. Ten women were deputed to investigate local bodies in their areas on which women could sit, or with which they might work. They tackled the education of 100,000 women within the London County Council boundaries (formed in 1888), to enable them to acquire the necessary qualifications for becoming electors. As a result Fabian women were elected to Poor Law Boards, and occasionally to local councils; they served as school managers, on care committees and in local government associations. Fabian women were also among the militant suffragists. Several members were imprisoned and underwent forced feeding (experiences which characteristically produced a sub-committee and eventually a pamphlet). And there was no sectarianism within the Group: its members belonged to the range of suffrage societies, to other socialist parties, notably the Women's Labour League (which, after 1918 became the women's section of the Labour Party) (Dr Marion Phillips for instance, and Ethel Bentham) and the Independent Labour Party (Ethel Bentham, Margaret Bondfield, Mary Macarthur).[15]

The distinctive quality of Fabian feminism before the First World War, was its economic individualism. The first aim of the Fabian Women's Group (it was often re-worded) was declared in 1913 to be: 'To study the economic position of women and press their claim to equality with men in the personal economic independence to be secured by socialism.' Socialism would provide complete economic independence for women by three means. Firstly, the full and equal participation of women in paid work; secondly, the training of skilled domestic workers and/or the provision of co-operative households; and thirdly, some form of State support for maternity and the costs of child-rearing, i.e. the 'State Endowment of Motherhood'. Only the Women's Co-operative Guild, an organization of working-class housewives, was more comprehensive in its schemes for maternity and childcare.[16]

The emphasis on economic independence explains why Maud Pember Reeves was so critical of the notion of the 'family wage'. Not that such a wage existed, but in a talk she gave on socialism and women, she stated:[17]

> The family must not be the economic unit. We talk of a wage of 20s., or 30s., or 35s., as a family wage, but it is nothing of the sort. It is an individual wage, paid to one wage earner, quite irrespective of his family.

The elimination of the idea of the family wage and the disintegration of the family as the economic unit of society were ideas based on an historical analysis of the position of women which is still influential today. The industrial revolution, it was argued, had removed industry from the home, driving women into poorly paid factory work, and reducing middle-class women to 'parasitism' – that is, economic dependence on their fathers and husbands, deprived of productive work, diminished in human dignity. This analysis, cogently presented by Mabel Atkinson in *The Economic Foundations of the Women's Movement* is interesting because by distinguishing the effects of the industrial revolution on the two main classes of women, it separated the demands of middle and working-class women, and explained their different consciousness:[18]

> There are two main sections in the modern women's movement – the movement of the middle-class women who are revolting against their exclusion from human activity and insisting, firstly, on their right to education, which is now practically conceded on all sides; secondly, on their right to earn a livelihood for themselves, which is rapidly being won; and thirdly, on their right to share in the control of Government, the point around which the fight is now most fiercely raging. These women are primarily rebelling against the sex-exclusiveness of men, and regard independence and the right to work as the most valuable privilege to be striven for.
>
> On the other hand, there are the women of the working classes, who have been faced with a totally different problem and who naturally react in a different way . . . What the woman of the proletariat feels as her grievance is that her work is too long and too monotonous, the burden laid upon her is too heavy. Moreover, in her case that burden is due to the power of capitalistic exploitation resulting from the injustice of our social system. It is not due . . . to the fact that the men of her class shut her out from gainful occupation. Therefore among the

working class women there is less sex consciousness ... The reforms that she demands are not independence and the right to work, but rather protection against the unending burden of toil which has been laid upon her.

In spite of the different conditions of women in the two classes, the Fabian women argued that their ultimate objective must be the same: the achievement of economic independence. Industrial capitalism was forcing the two groups together, they argued: middle-class women into realizing that emancipation didn't lie in wage labour as it was then organized, working-class women into recognizing firstly the suffering that 'parasitism' brought, and secondly, that their interests were not always represented by those of working men.

The Fabian women believed that State intervention in women's lives through the Factory Acts was made necessary by excessive exploitation of women workers in the new industrial conditions. Thus the precedent was set for the State as 'guardian' of women (and children).

Mary Macarthur, founder of the National Federation of Women Workers 1906–22, and a Fabian, pointed out that historically it had always been easier for women to improve their conditions of work through protective legislation from the State than through self-organization. The State must step in to put an end to women's economic dependence, firstly through the establishment of a legal minimum wage, and secondly through the 'State Endowment of Motherhood'.

These two themes, the harmony of economic interests among women from different class backgrounds, and the emphasis on State provision for women's economic independence go part of the way towards explaining why it was that this unevenly privileged group of women could claim to speak on behalf of all women and not just themselves. But there is also another explanation.

The Fabian Women's Group was the voice of the 'educated' woman. Its members were teachers, lecturers, journalists, writers, dancers, artists and the wives and daughters of educated and professional men. Membership surveys also reveal one or two nurses, sanitary inspectors, gardeners, civil servants, as well as a large number of type-writers and secretaries. Margaret Bondfield (Fabian, member of the Independent Labour Party, shop assistant and the first woman to sit on the General Council of the TUC), gave a talk to the Fabian Women's Group in 1910 on 'Wage-earning Mothers' in which she determined the class position of women by their education: women who had only been to elementary school (compulsory state education up to the age of 14) were working class, all the rest were middle class. This distinction cast most of the Fabian Women's Group into the middle class.[19]

But Margaret Bondfield's division was over-simplified; there were at least two broad groups of women within the Group. The first was the imposing number of intellectual and professional women of independent means. The biographies of all the leading members of the Fabian Women's Group reveal a formidable array of qualifications and achievements. Practically every woman of note in the trade union, labour or socialist movements participated in its conferences, lecture series and research projects, if they did not actually join the Group. The second group of women, and this is more speculative, came from the less elevated branches of the teaching profession, clerks, type-writers and secretaries. There had been a burst of union activity amongst these women workers in the five years before the formation of the Fabian Women's Group. It seems probable, therefore, given the emphasis in the Fabian Women's Group on women's economic independence, that some of these younger women joined the Society.[20]

There was a distance between the older generation of women (Beatrice Webb, Charlotte Wilson and Maud Pember Reeves, for instance), and their younger sisters. The older generation did not take their education and hard-won professional status lightly. Their achievements had been bitterly fought for: some of the younger women, they thought, took these victories and the opportunities they opened up for granted. Victorian propriety hovers about some of the older women. When I asked Amber Blanco White for a description of her mother's friends in the FWG, she replied that there 'was never any time to meet any of them – they were just a lot of women talking about very serious things.' Her mother thought it was important for girls to study their lessons most of the time: having been well educated herself, and her mother before her, she wanted her daughters to grow up in the same way. And so they did – Amber Blanco White abtained first class honours in both parts of the Moral Sciences Tripos at Cambridge, her sister went to the Royal College of Music.[21] Femininity was identified with frivolity – they kept a vigilant watch on this side of their character. In the 1909 annual report of the Group, women were urged to 'cast aside feminine slackness and negligence with regard to their own affairs', and get on with the work of preparing for citizenship.

There was no intellectual dogmatism in the Fabian Women's Group. There were many divergent views, but the unifying theme was the fundamental acceptance of the economic basis of women's subjection. They believed they could speak for the majority of women because their analysis of sex oppression *was* economic.

All women were disadvantaged on the labour market compared with men. While the grossest forms of exploitation were suffered by working-class women, women in middle-class occupations were also struggling under the burden of low wages, lack of skills, and very often had other people to support as well as themselves. And mothers in both classes were unable to support themselves or their children adequately.[22]

It was therefore quite undesirable that men should be paid a 'family wage' – this would simply increase women's subjection to them. It was also a bad idea to send mothers out to paid work. The solution in the eyes of the Fabian women was the 'State Endowment of Motherhood'. The strength in their position lay in their clear conceptual distinction between women as mothers, women as wives, and women as wage earners. This meant that they could thoroughly analyse the problems and organize around them. Its weakness lay in the identification of the State with both the democratic and the national interest. The belief that the individual could have a direct, unmediated relationship with the State, left the door wide open for all sorts of ideas uniting the national interest with motherhood.[23]

The focus on motherhood in the Fabian Women's Group originated in the desire to uncover the essential attributes and implications of sexual difference. In this respect they were quite unlike the more orthodox liberal feminists. Millicent Garrett Fawcett, for, instance, refused to acknowledge the difference of sex. Women as wage earners were neutered units of labour; motherhood did not enter into her economic calculations. She was extremely irritated when Eleanor Rathbone took over the Presidency of the National Society for Equal Citizenship and immediately began to campaign for the inclusion of the endowment of motherhood in its demands. For Millicent Fawcett, the progress of the women's movement was measured by the 'successive removal of intolerable grievances'.[24] Fabian women wanted the reorganization of society, the incorporation of industry into the State, the absorption by the State of all fundamental economic functions and processes. This, they believed, was the road to socialism, and their motive in forming the Fabian Women's Group was to ensure that women too should determine their own fate, should define for themselves the relationship between socialism and economic independence.

In *Round About a Pound a Week*, Maud Pember Reeves was determined to convince the intelligent and liberal middle classes of 'the glorious common sense of socialism', the rightness of State co-operation in parenthood. But the real strength of this most readable book lies in its detailed account of working-class women's domestic work and household management. Maud Pember Reeves did not presume to teach poor women how to run their homes; she wanted to learn about their daily lives from their own lips. *Round About a Pound a Week* is a neglected work by an important group of women; with it, a vital piece is added to our fragmented view of working-class lives in the years before the First World War.

1978

Thanks to Linda Walker and the staff at Nuffield College Library.

FABIAN SOCIALISM AND THE 'SEX-RELATION'

The Fabian Society was formed in London in 1884. One of several socialist sects founded in the 1880s, the Fabians were a breakaway from the Fellowship of the New Life, a small group of women and men who were inspired by the ideas of Thomas Davidson, a wandering scholar, philosopher and advocate of the 'new life'. Davidson taught that the regeneration of mankind would come through regeneration of the self and a repudiation of the waste and excess of capitalism. The cultivation of love, wisdom, and unselfishness would lead to the 'new life' which would be based on mutual though voluntary co-operation.[1] 'Everyman', Davidson believed, 'must be his own philosopher', a tenet which, according to Beatrice Webb (leading Fabian, and autobiographer), was one of the two 'most characteristic assumptions' of the 1870s and 1880s (the other being that 'physical science could solve all problems').[2]

Hampstead, Bloomsbury, and Chelsea in the 1880s were filled with eager idealists searching amid the debris of Christian belief and the fading ethos of liberal individualism for a moral creed powerful enough to vitalize the 'new life'. Those who broke away from the Fellowship were sceptics who modestly feared, in George Bernard Shaw's word, that the ideal society would have 'to wait an unreasonably long time if postponed until they personally attained perfection'.[3] The Fabians wanted the 'new life' too, but they were − as Havelock Ellis, the sexologist and anarchist member of the Fellowship put it − more political.[4]

'Socialist militants' was Bernard Shaw's retrospective epithet. The inner life − though in need of refurbishment − pressed less urgently on Fabian consciousness than the poverty and squalor in which the mass of the population lived and the conditions of which could be seen every day in the streets of London.

In 1884 Fabian Socialism was rudimentary. It meant a belief in collectivism and the priority of the social question: that is, poverty. The huge gap in living standards between rich and poor was *the* social evil in the late nineteenth century. Not only did such gross inequality cast a blight on the prosperity of the imperial and commercial capital of the world, but the predicament of the poor also preyed on the consciences of the well-to-do. Both Shaw in his novels and plays, and Beatrice Webb in her autobiography have evoked the awakening 'consciousness of sin' among the privileged and propertied classes, anxious to hold on to political and economic power and fearful of the newly enfranchised working classes.[5] In the 1880s Britain was in the throes of severe economic depression with the characteristics – familiar again to-day – of lavish wealth of the few, a relatively high level of income among the employed, while the unemployed (a term which entered the English language at the turn of the century) lived in chronic want.

There were bitter divisions among all sectors of public opinion about the solutions for industrial dislocation and its effects. 'Social questions are the vital questions of today', Beatrice wrote in her diary of 1884, several years before she herself became a socialist: 'they take the place of religion'.[6] And indeed, socialism in the 1880s and 1890s had something of the enthusiasm of a religious revival. People of all classes spoke of their 'conversion' and spent much time and energy spreading the word. Hubert Bland, journalist and husband of Fabian novelist Edith Nesbit, referred in his Fabian essay of 1889 to 'the deep discontent, a spiritual unrest' which he experienced at the 'constant presence of a vast mass of human misery'.[7] For the Fabians, it was the spectacle of poverty in the midst of plenty rather than their own or the poor's spiritual imperfections which provoked a vigorous critique of bourgeois economics, industrial inefficiency, and party political inertia. And although a vein of spiritual regeneration ran through the society, the Fabians prided themselves on a 'practical socialism', a determined pragmatism, a refusal – in Shaw's phrase again – of 'sentimental cant'.[8] Their very first tract was simply called 'Why are the many poor?' and Amber Reeves, a member of the Fabian nursery before the First World War, told me that the socialism of her mother and friends had been about 'being fair to the poor'.[9]

Fabian socialism was always intellectual. It took shape in critical dialogue with others. It never had, and only once or twice had any ambition to have, a popular base. The first Fabians were writers, teachers, journalists, civil servants, and one or two stockbrokers and clerks. Mostly young, in their early twenties, several of them poor, they were of heterodox religious and philosophical opinions: unitarians, lapsed Anglicans, secularists, anarchists, Hegelians, Marxists, and feminists. They met in each other's rooms to talk: of Marxist economics or revolutionary anarchism; the causes of poverty or the progress of municipal socialism. And then they went out into the streets or on public platforms to influence hearts and minds through exhaustive propaganda. 'For years past', wrote Shaw in the 1890s, 'every Sunday evening of mine has been spent on some more or less squalid platform, lecturing, lecturing, lecturing, and lecturing'.[10] Since the Fabians included at this time Annie Besant, the secularist and birth-controller, Charlotte Wilson, feminist and anarchist, Ramsay Macdonald, future leader of the Labour Party, and other authors and propagandists including Shaw, their street oratory was as prolific and distinguished as their written propaganda.

All this talk took place against a background of riots of the unemployed in the mid-1880s and the strikes of the matchgirls, dockers, and other unskilled workers in London in 1889 and 1890. Fabian socialism was shaped then and during the equally turbulent years of Irish nationalism, women's suffrage, and syndicalist militancy before the First World War (1906–14) (years when, as Virginia Woolf remarked, the mental life of the nation changed). Some Fabians had participated in these struggles working alongside trade unionists and socialist militants. But this experience of working-class militancy filled them with unease. Fabians had studied Marx and rejected his theory of class struggle as well as the labour theory of value.[11] The collectivist spirit and growth of the state were the motors of history, according to the Fabians, not class struggle. Socialism they conceded might be inevitable, but it would not emanate from the working class. The poor lacked the education and leisure to think and to organize – for this reason, as Ruth Cavendish Bentinck argues in a tract which reveals the élitism latent in some Fabian thought, 'no Socialist has nor ever will come from the slums'.[12]

In this respect Fabian socialism owed more to John Stuart Mill's cautious collectivism than to the revolutionary creeds of Marx or Kropotkin. Their name was taken from the Roman General whose motto was: 'deliberate before striking hard'. And Mill's anxious reservations about the benefits of mass democracy, the fear that the desires of civilized minorities would be swamped by the uncultivated majority was more to the forefront of much Fabian thought than that open-hearted goodwill of, for instance, the Independent Labour Party or even the humanist imperatives of Auguste Comte. Socialism was as necessary as democracy was unavoidable, but it must be a socialism based on the study of facts not the encouragement of feelings (except collectivist ones). As Sidney Webb, husband of Beatrice, admonished the enthusiastic socialist missionary Katherine St John Conway (who like Ramsay

Macdonald and others was a member of both the Fabians and the Independent Labour Party) in 1892, 'study the facts of modern industry' not 'the aspirations of socialists'.[13] Socialist aspirations were unsettling, they were for the unconverted. The characteristics of Fabian socialism identified by Beatrice Webb would certainly have dampened chiliastic ardour:

> They translated economics and collectivism into the language of prosaic vestrymen and town councillors. They dealt largely in statistics; they talked about amending factory acts, and municipalising gas and water supplies. Above all they were prolific of facts, ideas and practical projects of reform. They were, indeed, far more extreme in their opinions and projects than their phrases conveyed to the ordinary citizen. Their summary of Socialism, which was found in the ensuing decade to have a strong appeal, was put in the following terms. It comprised, they said, essentially collective ownership wherever practicable; collective regulation everywhere else; collective provision according to need for all the impotent and sufferers; and collective taxation in proportion to wealth, especially surplus wealth.[14]

There was no mention of the women's movement, the suffrage, or women, which was odd because women formed between one-third to a half of the membership, sat on the Executive, and contributed fully to the political life of the Society. But then, Fabian socialism through Beatrice's lens (and she was one of its architects) was dry and passionless; the product of reason. The Woman Question, on the other hand, aroused passions not always amenable to reason because it opened up (and still does) those vexed questions of marriage, the family, and the 'sex-relation'. The first Fabians refused to think politically about sexual difference, except in very limited ways, which is why some women found it necessary in 1908 to form the Fabian Women's Group. But the Society's commitment to democracy and egalitarianism, their opposition to virile displays of revolutionism, their – on the whole – decorous socialism, created a tolerant atmosphere in which feminists could pursue their aims. So who were the Fabian women, and what were their aims?

The Fabian Women's Group (FWG) first met in the drawing-room of Maud Pember Reeves, wife of a New Zealand diplomat, in early 1908 after a winter of suffrage agitation of increasing violence. Women had not made themselves or their cause felt powerfully enough in the Society, they believed; nor, although Fabian women belonged to about a dozen different suffrage organizations, had they participated effectively in the movement as a group. At the first meeting they resolved first to further the principle of equal citizenship within and without the

Society, and second to 'study women's economic independence in relation to socialism'. To this end they threw themselves into activity: standing for local elections as Poor Law Guardians; joining the Women's Labour League, the women's circles of the Independent Labour Party, and trade unions; working for reform of divorce (they wanted divorce by consent), prisons, and the feeding of London schoolchildren; and running well-attended lecture series and conferences on women's employment and training, motherhood, and domestic workers as well as speaking on socialism and aspects of the Woman Question wherever they were invited. They wanted to forge links between the two most vital movements of their time: socialism and women's emancipation.

Insofar as they conceived of the Woman Question as a problem of 'economic liberty' Fabian women went a long way towards thinking through the connections past and present between this problem and socialism. Their historical writings and empirical research on the economic condition of women still form a vital element in feminist thought. Beatrice Webb's explanations (culled from trade unionists) of women's low pay, her arguments for factory legislation and the 'rate for the job'; Maud Pember Reeves's description of domestic life on a pound a week; Barbara Hutchins's uncovering of the different economic needs of women at different phases in their lives; Barbara Drake's study of women and trade unions; Alice Clark's account of the effects of capitalist production on women's economic position remain unsurpassed.[15]

But it was the 'sex-relation' that was more difficult to reconcile with socialism in thought or practice. In spite of some remarkable women among its membership, the Fabian Society was silent on the Woman Question in its first years. It had something of the character of a men's debating society, and informal reminiscence conveys Fabian men's hesitancy to speak publicly on marriage, divorce, and the 'sex-relation'. However, in the first years of the twentieth century the Women's Movement gathered in momentum and militancy. Women joined trade unions in large numbers, their independent voice as industrial workers being heard through the National Federation of Women Workers (NFWW, 1906–21); while the Women's Co-operative Guild (1883–) spoke with authority for the working-class housewife and mother. Fabian women belonged to these and other organizations and were often among their leadership: Mary Macarthur, the leader of the NFWW, for instance, or Margaret Bondfield, shopworker and first woman cabinet minister; Marion Phillips, educated at Melbourne and the LSE, Hon. Sec. of The Women's Labour League (1912–18), or Susan Lawrence, daughter of wealthy, London professional parents, read maths at Cambridge, elected as a conservative to the London

County Council, converted to socialism by the low pay of school cleaners, became a Labour MP in the 1920s. Like Fabian men, the women were writers, journalists, lecturers, teachers – occupations which had always been open to women of ability and audacity. But they were also drawn from the new – to women – and militant professions: doctors, nurses, local government officers, sanitary inspectors, and trade union officers.[16] Some list no occupation and were perhaps single women of means, or wives and mothers with leisure, property, and servants enough to combine the study of social conditions with plans for their alleviation: Charlotte Shaw, for instance, wife of the playwright and with a private income of her own; Maud Pember Reeves; or Charlotte Wilson, the anarchist wife of a stockbroker in whose Hampstead cottage the first Fabians had met to study Marx's *Capital* in the 1880s. She had then left the Society, rejoining in 1908 to become the first secretary of the FWG.

These women came – in Beatrice Webb's own self-definition – from that class of persons who 'habitually gave orders',[17] which is probably why they could imagine a state, Parliament, and even industrial forces responsive to their collective and egalitarian will. (The other reason, of course, was their optimism. They believed, before the First World War disabused such illusions, both that human nature was perfectable and industrial forces tractable.) More anguished were their attitudes towards domestic servants, most of whom were women and some of whom were absolutely necessary if women like themselves were to live a public life. Some Fabian women refused to employ any but the most essential; others ate with them; most characteristic were the several schemes for their better training and industrial organization. Domestic servants themselves, manual workers, and wives of working men were not visibly or vocally represented in the Group (which numbered 230 out of a total membership of a few thousand at its peak in 1912), though clearly not all the typists, office workers, or the one weaver I discovered, came from the wealthy reaches of the middle class.

Fabian women, then, recognized class difference among women and made it central to their analysis of women's economic condition. The industrial revolution, they argued, had reduced wealthy women to economic 'parasitism' within the family, and confined working-class women to sweated industry and starvation wages. But while they were alert to the fact that class division meant that women's immediate demands might differ, their ultimate interests were the same. First, the parasitic status of women of property obliged them to expose and reform the poverty in which the majority of women lived and died. And second, what united women (apart from their lack of the franchise) was their economic dependence and their 'sex-function'. In the minds of employers, Members of Parliament, male trade unionists, or factory inspectors, economic dependence and sex were linked. Fabian women wanted to separate them. A woman's economic liberty depended upon her either receiving the rate for the job in industry – irrespective of her sex – or a state pension if she were a mother. That the biological function of motherhood had no ill-effects on a woman's capacity and so her economic value was, Fabian women realized, an assertion that had to be proved. Unlike the *Freewoman* (1911–13), an anarchist journal celebrated by Rebecca West because it 'mentioned sex loudly and clearly and repeatedly and in the worst possible taste', Fabian women determined to pin down the differences between the sexes scientifically.[18] But Edith Nesbit, opening the first series of lectures on the subject, cast all caution to the wind by claiming that: 'women . . . are predominantly creatures of sex, whose paramount need is a mate and children, and also they are heavily weighted throughout life by physical and mental disabilities unknown to man'.[19] Not surprisingly this statement aroused 'much opposition' among the women who listened to her and produced an avalanche of argument to prove that women's 'disabilities' of strength and skill were the result not of natural difference, but – in the age-old plea of feminism – of the artificial exaggeration of sex differences. Fabian analysis went on to argue that this exaggeration was historical, patriarchal, and that its effects radiated adversely through domestic and industrial production.

'We women are the slaves of slaves'[20]

Women's economic dependence was twofold: within the family they were subordinate to father, husband, son; while in waged work they were fixed as unskilled and cheap labour. Both positions stemmed from the past and had a single cause: the custom of marriage by capture or purchase (of wives by husbands), and the exclusive focus on a woman's sex which a man's wish for legitimate heirs imposed on his wife. Men had defined women through their sex rather than their common humanity. Motherhood united women, but motherhood was, in Emma Brooke's words, a 'stigma' when it should have been recognized as a 'valuable act of citizenship' and rewarded with state pensions and co-operative households. If a woman's biological function was the explanation of her impoverishment in the home (and Maud Pember Reeves's research into household budgets in Lambeth showed how poor this was) then her sex also lowered her value in the labour market.

Wherever Fabian women looked they found the relentless effects of the sexual division of labour on women. Women were domestic servants, unskilled and sweated workers. Industrial production was not to blame. The factory system 'provides the great market for women's labour', if only women would raise themselves up and organize and refuse to accept wages below subsistence level.[21] Hitherto, women had made 'poor trade unionists', a failing which had perpetuated their cumulation in 'backward' sectors of the economy, the sweaters' dens, and backstreet workshops beyond the reach of factory legislation and trade boards. The unskilled woman worker was her own worst enemy Beatrice Webb had argued in the 1897 tract on *Women and the Factory Acts*, because of her partial subsistence from within the family, her lack of training and skill, her low standard of living, and, as Sidney Webb had noted earlier in an influential survey of women's wages published in the *Economic Journal* in 1891, because she had something to sell other than her labour.[22]

Women then, were caught on a treadmill. Their economic dependence, their poverty, forced them not only into sweaters' dens and a 'narrow range of occupations' in which the unskilled and low-paid woman worker became the 'enemy' of her own sex, but worse, it led them into compulsory sexual relations with men – whether prostitution or marriage, the latter being merely a legalized form of the first. 'To be compelled to marry to escape prostitution' exclaimed Emma Brooke, 'is clearly sexual slavery'.[23] What form free and proper sexual relations should take, Fabian women were not prepared publicly to opine, except to stipulate first, that women should enter them freely and not out of economic need, and second, that women might have both work and sexual fulfilment.

Fabian women's analysis of women's economic dependence was as thorough in its details as it was circumspect in its demands. When they looked into themselves to define women's wants their voice becomes bolder. The modern feminist, declared M.A. (Mabel Atkinson) in her 1914 tract on *The Economic Foundations of the Women's Movement*[24] wants not *either* love or work but both:

> She wants work, she wants the control of her own financial
> position, and she wants education and the right to take part in
> the human activities of the State, but at the same time she is no
> longer willing to be shut out from marriage and motherhood.

These wants (which in the twentieth century have tormented educated and ambitious feminists as much as they have exasperated their socialist male comrades) have ebbed and flowed with the changing conditions of women's lives. Articulated as a dream in the eighteenth and nineteenth centuries, in the early twentieth century industrial development, birth control, and women's suffrage seemed to promise the possibility of a new epoch in the 'sex-relation'. But, at a more mundane level, the demand was also formulated in defiance of the limits, as Fabian women understood them, of the feminisms of earlier generations.

'Serious-minded ladies'

Nineteenth-century feminism, M.A. argues (inaccurately incidentally), was a movement of elderly spinsters, and she quoted Lydia Becker (secretary of the Manchester Suffrage Society in the 1860s) to the effect that 'a good husband is much better worth having than a vote'.[25] Twenty years later Beatrice Webb (Potter as she then was) forcing herself into intellectual work as an antidote to sexual desire, echoed these thoughts: 'I have not despised the simple happiness of a woman's life; it has despised *me* and I have been humbled as far down as woman can be humbled.'[26] Even when Beatrice wasn't languishing in the slough of unrequited love, she firmly believed from her observation of the hardworking philanthropic and socialist women around her, that a woman could be a mother ('the highest calling') or have a career, but she could not have both. The second generation of Fabian women had less respect for custom and public opinion; they were less stoical.

The first generation of Fabian women had the grit of pioneers. They were the 'serious-minded ladies' as Amber Reeves described her mother's friends, whose intellectual path to socialism was strewn with the thorns of theology, political economy, secularism, idealist philosophy, and Marxist economics. They exhorted each other to learn, to educate, spurring each other on with reminders of women's 'undeveloped civic sense', lack of mental discipline, or the habits of trade unionism. Education was the path to collective as well as individual self-improvement as it was for so many working men. The minutes of the FWG reverberate with intentions to pursue and spread rational thought and education in citizenship, and this austerity and single-mindedness is reflected in their personal lives. Beatrice Webb commented, at the end of her life, on the 'bourgeois respectability' of the first Fabians (forgetting perhaps Shaw's philanderings, or Hubert Bland's several sexual liaisons). 'My mother was chaste to the last degree', Amber Reeves told me, 'not a hint of scandal about her', whereas she herself rocked both her family and the Fabian Society in 1909 by having an affair and a baby with H.G. Wells, marrying a loyal suitor (also a Fabian), and then keeping everyone on anxious tenterhooks while she wavered between them.[27] Margaret Cole, a young Edinburgh graduate before the First World War – pipe-smoking and mop-haired – said in her autobiography that feminism to her was about free love as well as economic independence.[28] This was a sentiment that Beatrice's generation of Fabian women was unlikely to have voiced. Beatrice's diary is dotted with interesting asides on the love affairs of younger socialist women, and her accounts of the pre-war Fabian summer schools portray them as evidently glorious opportunities for the young to at least talk about sexual liberation in the 'sex-relation' even if the chaperonage was too vigilant to permit much practice – but among her own generation liberal love had produced heartache and difficulty for women rather than the emancipation she believed. In a letter to Millicent Garrett Fawcett in 1906 she had written – of the present 'gross share' of body and mind and of the increase of 'sexual emotion for its own sake and not for the sake of bearing children. That way madness lies.'[29]

But if sexual desire and its implications could be felt, and sometimes lived, more fully by some younger Fabians before the First World War, sex still remained the most volatile element in the delicate relationship between the movements for women's emancipation and socialism. The time was not yet ripe for their harmonious resolution. Fabian men greeted the 'new' woman more unequivocally than the women; in some sense they invented at least her literary existence. Unwilling or unable to explore the political implications of women's emancipation within the Society, the issue spilled over into men's novel- and play-writing. 'We are discovering women', H.G. Wells wrote with excitement in his autobiographical *New Machiavelli* (1910) which meant that he and other male writers were exploring the literary possibilities of the 'sex-relation' without the marriage tie.[30] Fabian women on the other hand argued, as we have seen, that the Woman Question was essentially an economic question. A woman could achieve economic liberty so long as the laws of the market were tempered in waged work by judicious legislation and responsible trade unionism and in the home by state pensions and co-operative households. What women should not have to do was to rely on men's property or wages for their subsistence. As far as it went, theirs was a powerful and rational analysis.

But the sex-relation could not be compressed into an economic relation. By urging the woman wage-earner to become more like a man, and the state to take responsibility for the maintenance of the child, Fabian women were in fact evading the difficulty of what sort of relation should exist between the sexes. Fabian women sought self-fulfilment. Women were bound to men not just economically, they argued, but by their very identity: 'women [are] bred to please men'. Femininity was merely a veneer. To discover themselves, women had to throw off the chains of economic slavery and mental subservience. Many agreed with Shaw, who wrote in a clever essay on Ibsen that self-sacrifice, the least attractive human quality, was the essential attribute of the 'womanly

woman' in late Victorian Britain.[31] The search for an identity independent of men (and children?) and women's self-fulfilment was hard to
reconcile with the collective socialist will – a dilemma feminists and
socialists have yet to resolve.

After the First World War Fabian feminism faded, individuals moving
into women's or labour organizations, and in the 1930s into the
Communist and Peace movements too. Many wrote books. The Fabian
Society's socialism influenced the Labour Party whose constitution it
had helped to draft. Some Fabian principles of piecemeal reform and a
responsible state, may be discovered in the policies of the Attlee
government of 1945. But the collectivism of the Labour Party has never
been able to contemplate women as other than wives and mothers,
fastened to the home, or else in carefully demarcated sectors of the
labour market. Feminists inside and out of the Labour Movement
during the 1920s and 1930s strove to force a way to make it consider
women as independent persons, but independence does not stick to the
category 'wives and mothers'.

I am left only with a question. Does it reveal the limits of the English
socialist vision that women remain fixed in its thought as wives and
mothers, and as sources of cheap labour? Or is wanting something more
the impossibility of feminist desire?

1988

WOMEN'S VOICES IN
THE SPANISH CIVIL WAR

The Spanish Civil War began in July 1936 when General Franco led an invasion against the government of the Popular Front which had been elected in February of that year. Franco's army and supporters were known as the Nationalists; they were anti-Communist, anti-atheist and anti-liberal. The Popular Front government of the young Republic (1931) were liberals, anti-clerics, anarchists and socialists, who wanted a de-centralized, non-clerical, egalitarian and collectivized Republic (the *Daily Mail* referred to the combatants as the Patriots and the Reds respectively). Britain with France formed the Non-Intervention Alliance in August, one month after the conflict began. Germany, Italy and the Soviet Union were supposed to be parties to this agreement too. The aim of Non-Intervention was to isolate the war; arms were not to be sold to either side. Soon Hitler, and then Mussolini, supported the Generals with arms and men. The Soviet Union supported the Republicans from October. The European context of Spain was Hitler's advance through Europe. Hitler's army entered Vienna in March 1938; Prague in March 1939. The Munich Agreement had been signed in September 1938. In retrospect, the Spanish Civil War has been understood as the beginning of the Second World War.

The response in western democracies to Franco's invasion was immediate. The first Medical Aid Committee in Britain was formed on August 1st, 1936; the first unit left later that month. The International Brigades were formed in October. Over 2,000 Brigaders went from Britain; 500 died. Britain banned volunteering for the Brigades in January 1937. Tens of thousands of people organized fund-raising, petitions against Non-Intervention, for aid and medical equipment in 1,000 committees throughout Britain. Two hundred medical personnel and many more went to Spain to work in canteens, hospitals, with the illiterate and in homes for children. After the fall of the Republic in March 1939, people worked with the refugees who poured across the Pyrennees into the South of France. The historian of the Aid Movement, Jim Fyrth, argues that between 1936–39 Aid Spain bcame the 'most outstanding example of solidarity' in Britain since the mid-nineteenth-century Chartist movement.

I have included this introduction (which is no more than a sketch) because the book it introduces, *Women's Voices from the Spanish Civil War*, recalls an idealism unknown to generations since the Cold War. An idealism about the possibility of a democratic Europe founded on a belief in truth, the simplicity of the people and the moral goodness of those opposed to fascism. A sceptical George Orwell, who had fought in the Militias for six months in 1936–37, then repudiated the confused and sectarian politics of the Brigades in his gripping account of the conflict, *Homage to Catalonia*, nevertheless wrote, in 1953, that there was 'no doubt as to who was in the right'. British opinion was divided in the 1930s. The Diaries of Harold Nicolson will tell the reader why; while, as I write, *The Remains of the Day*, both novel and film (by Kazuo Ishiguro and James Ivory respectively) appraise the English landed classes' predilection for Appeasement which was based on another understanding of truth: one founded on honour, service, Christianity, the paternalism as well as the privileges of landed wealth.

When I was a child in England in the 1940s and '50s my mother dreaded the coming of the third world war. Men were precious to my mother. She had grown up almost exclusively among women in the shadow of the first – the Great – war. 'We never saw a man,' she told us, 'no man ever came to our house.' She lived in the Berkshire countryside, the eldest of four children raised on a peacetime widow's pension and occasional charity – 'We idealized men because we didn't know any.' Her sisters and brother thought her fortunate because she was the only one who could remember her father, and the only one of his children he had known. My mother's father had survived the First World War only to die in military service in Africa in the 1920s before his wife, who had been a nurse before her marriage, could reach him to care for him. My mother's brother had been killed on the last day of the Second World War in Burma. Riding his motor-bike to welcome his commanding officer he was ambushed. So my mother wanted the third world war that she knew was coming – 'world wars come every twenty years' – to happen before my brother grew up. Korea and Suez were met with relief in my family because my brother was too young to go.

As far as I can remember this was my first understanding of war: war was when men killed each other somewhere else, a time of telegrams and death when women were left to live in a world changed by men's absence or mutilation. Gradually I heard other stories: of crouching under the kitchen table with my mother and sister during an air-raid; of banging on the side of the cot when my father came home and got into bed with my mother; of gas masks that were never used; of land girls, evacuees, women in uniform (but not fighting) and foreign lovers. My father's stories were quite different – he and his friends were the first out of Dunkirk; 'if you see the enemy, duck'; 'always be the first to surrender' – and they tempered (as I daresay they were intended to do) my childhood fears. If from my mother I learned about love and loss, then from my father the lessons were as negative if less tragic. He taught me about the disillusionment and impotence of the ordinary soldier, of the humour in self-deprecation (a persistent theme, reaching back through music-hall, of plebeian humour, reinforced in the 1940s, for instance, by the radio broadcasts of Al Read, some of the Ealing comedies in the late 1940s and early 1950s, and in the 1960's television show, *Dad's Army*), but also of the unexpected egalitarianism among fighting men in wartime. My father used the same latrines as old Etonians; all the officers (except him!) were public schoolboys. It is a paradox that while each one of my generation has had her or his psyche marked by their parents' memories of war, their senses and comprehension blunted by incessant images of war, actual and fictional on television, few have had direct experience of war themselves. So I read the testimonies of women volunteers in Spain with the curiosity born of ignorance. What was war like to live, and why did these women choose to go to Spain?

— '. . . a deep hatred of fascism' —

Loathing of fascism, dread of war and belief in democracy drove women to volunteer for Spain on the side of the Republican government, the Communist historian Margot Heinemann remembered fifty years later.[1] Fascism divided Europe, but anti-fascism was an international movement. 45,000 men from all over the world, 2,500 of them from Britain, joined the International Brigades. Like the men, the first women to go on the side of the Republicans or the Popular Front – from New Zealand, Australia, North America as well as Britain – were mostly Communist and socialist sympathizers who had learned from the study of international politics in the previous ten or fifteen years the meaning of fascism.[2] For women fascism meant, continued Margot Heinemann, war, the abolition of civil liberties and the return of women to the status of second-class citizens and to child-bearing as their exclusive socially useful function.[3] Not every woman who went shared Margot Heinemann's retrospective circumspection. A passionate sense of injustice sent Patience Darnton, training to be a midwife in East London: 'I realized at once – I don't know how I had the sense but I did – that this was "us" and "them" and this was a chance to do "them" down.' Lots of young women who had not fully thought through their political response to the civil war reached out to help the Spanish people because they were horrified by the spectacle of a military overthrow of a democratically elected government – the 'invasion' as the Republicans called it, and as Dorothy Parker repeats here. Sheila Grant Duff, a twenty-three-year-old English journalist working in Prague, received a telegram from the Paris foreign editor of the *Chicago Daily News*, asking her to go to Spain,

> I had worked in Edgar (Mowrer's) office in Paris and learned
> from him . . . that the only decent aim for any footfree individ-
> ual at that moment in history was the defeat of fascism.

The first British woman to enter the territory of the insurgents, Sheila Grant Duff's mission was dangerous, but exhilarating: to expose 'appalling slaughter' which succeeded Franco's entry of his troops into every Spanish town.[4]

About half the nurses, secretaries and interpreters among whom Winifred Bates (a teacher and writer living in Spain with her husband) worked, went for compassionate not political reasons: 'They were just nurses, courageous women, willing to work under the most dangerous conditions.' Others went 'only' for humanitarian reasons or to pursue their 'healing mission'. Once in Spain, political awareness was swiftly born. Even the Quakers – officially neutral – wrestled internally against restrictions on their public speech and actions. Ruth Cope, an American Quaker, wrote home, 'There is much we do not agree with and stay silent about.' Pleading for medical supplies and food, she felt bitterly frustrated and shamed – as did so many British women – by her government's policy of Non-Intervention which, by facilitating Hitler's and Mussolini's aid for General Franco and the insurgents, paved the way for the bombing of civilians and for Munich, a much uglier collaboration than the term appeasement implies.

With the exception of the few supporters of Franco (described by one defender of the 'patriots' as a 'shining light', a 'beacon') the dominant political impulse behind support for Spain was anti-fascism, and fascism to democrat, humanitarian, socialist or Communist meant political dictatorship predicated on imperial aggression. Franco's rebellion – although widely anticipated in Spain after the February 1936 election of the Popular Front, fulfilled the worst fears of the anti-fascists everywhere, because it was illegal, brutal and lacked popular support. Since the 1920s British anti-fascists had worked together in organiz-ations like the League of Nations Union, the No More War Movement, the Women's International League for Peace and Freedom, the Peace Pledge Unions, the Women's Committee against War and Fascism and the Left Book Club. For each woman who went to Spain there were thousands of others who formed the Aid Spain Movement between 1936 and 1939.[5]

If Communists speak most insistently in English-language history and memoir it is because their initiatives led the huge popular movement in support of Spain. Communists believed that the struggle against fascism was the class-struggle writ large, and fascism the inevitable if – hopefully – final phase of capitalism. In accordance with the strategy of the united or popular front, their analysis was muted and aid for Spain propaganda was articulated in terms of democracy versus fascism, a formulation persuasive to generations who could remember the First World War, were alarmed by the prospect of a second but still idealistic enough to imagine in 1936 or 1937 that it could be stopped.[6] For if, as Ellen Wilkinson argued to the largely unsympathetic House of Commons in 1938, the civil war in Spain was the 'point of truth' for Spanish people, then many in Britain felt that truth to be their own. 'Our fate as a people is being decided today,' wrote Ralph Bates, novelist and Communist (his collection of short stories on Spain, published before the outbreak of civil war in 1936, marked the beginning of the identification of Spain with 'contempt for luxury and death' and the 'instinct to revolt' which seized the imagination of so many intellectuals among all classes in the 1930s), Storm Jameson, novelist and anti-facist remembered in her *Autobiography*.[7] And in 1986 Winifred Bates, Ralph's wife, reiterated: 'If we could have stopped Hitler from taking Spain, we could have stopped him spreading his evil over the rest of Europe and Britain.'[8] The idealism in some of these voices sounds discordant today. Dorothy Parker for instance remembering:

> I went to Spain (on the side of the loyalists) and I became a human being. I stayed in Valencia and Madrid ... and in the country around and between them. I met the best people anyone ever knew. But I shall see their like again. And so shall all of us ... For what they stood for, what they have given others to take and hold and carry along – that does not vanish from the earth ... truth and courage ... and determination for a decent life.

Similarly, Sheila Grant Duff:

> ... To my generation the Spanish Civil War appeared as one of the great battles of human history and its mythic quality moved us all.[9]

— Civil War in Spain —

The political and moral prescience of those anti-fascists who led the support for Spain in Britain during the 1930s need not deter us from the realization that from the perspective of an Andalusian agricultural labourer, Asturian miner or industrial worker from Barcelona or Bilbao, the divisions of the civil war were more complicated than the opposition of fascist and democrat. When the Popular Front won 4.7 million votes in February 1936, 4 million voters opposed them. Revolutionaries of both sides – Falangists in opposition, and Communists, left-Socialists and Anarchists in the Popular Front – declared that this was merely the first step towards social revolution. The fascist Falangist party, founded in the early 1930s, had formed links then with monarchists and Catholic Carlists as well as with more traditional forces of reaction, the church, landed gentry and the army. In their wish for social revolution, the elimination of large landed estates, the nationalization of the banks and democratic control of factories, the Falangists sometimes had more in common with Communists, Anarchists and Syndicalists than with the élitist monarchists and right-wing Catholics. On the other hand, religious faith could motivate sections of the peasantry, haunted by the spectre of church-burnings, anti-clericalism and the destruction of private property to support the nationalists; or fear of the populism or brutality of Franco's 'Crusade' might persuade sections of the professional or business classes in the towns to support the Popular Front. The populations of the large industrial cities were the most ardent defenders of the Republic, although the brave if tragic defence of towns and villages by the untrained Republican militias, who were gunned down as they fled unarmed and without cover, are testimony to the depth of Republican feeling elsewhere. Political divisions within one family evoke the confusion and tragedy of civil war for the Spanish people.[10]

Ronald Fraser spoke to Juan Narcía the son of a mining engineer in Asturias, sympathetic to the nationalists until he was twelve years old when he saw the corpses of three of their victims brought down to his village in garbage carts:

> When they killed some of them – people who had fled, who were living in the mountains as guerrillas to a certain extent – they celebrated their success with a sort of fiesta, with plenty of food and drink.[11]

Of his four older brothers, the eldest, Jose, was a doctor of liberal beliefs who voted left republican; Francisco, a lawyer and clerk of the town-hall was an 'extreme conservative'; Timoteo a dentist, was a member of the Communist Party; Leopoldo, the fourth, a member of the Falange. Before the war 'we all got on as brothers,' Juan told Fraser, but as his mother was an ardent Catholic and only his father 'a moderate man' there were 'violent political discussions'. When war broke out the brothers joined their respective organizations. Timoteo was executed by the nationalists in Algeciras where he had 'attempted to organize resistance to the military uprising'. When Juan's father heard the news, 'From that time until his own death seven years later, he never raised his head again. He was completely overwhelmed with grief . . .' Both during and after the war there was a silence among the brothers about Timoteo's execution: 'No one wanted to talk about it. After the war it was a question of keeping alive; there was considerable fear.'

— *Women's Work in Wartime* —

The women writing here do not explore the depths of political contradiction and change in Republican Spain, nor do they explore their own motives or selves. This is wartime writing, immediate and often urgent in description. Both letters home and journalism lack metaphor. Nurses, administrators, relief workers, teachers of literacy were each inspired by the strength of the Spanish people's resistance to Franco, their will to eliminate illiteracy and to create a democratic culture, but they were saddened too by the suffering they saw. Letters home cajole or plead for funds and supplies – 'it's no consolation to me to know,' begged Madge Addy, a Manchester nurse in Uclés, 'that aid has been sent to Barcelona, we have a hospital of 800 wounded *here* . . . so please get them to concentrate on us.'

All describe the surface of events. Blood spattering walls, floor, and operating theatres, staining clothing, bodies and pavements red, clogging nails. We hear the unnatural silence before the wounded arrive and feel the exhaustion of the nurse who throws a dead body off her bed before she collapses in sleep. There is horror: packets of chocolate dropped by Mussolini's fascist planes are picked up by hungry children whose hands are then blown off by the hidden explosives. The nationalists commandeer an ambulance which whirls wildly round machine-gunning civilians at random. Retreating ranks of refugees are bombed by Hitler's Luftwaffe. A woman emissary, Marian Merriman, raped by a comrade accompanying her. These non-combatants too experienced battle-fatigue and shell-shock. The symptoms were loss of memory, uncontrollable shaking, indifference to death. Some letters home read as though writing was necessary to expel unthinkable experience. Sometimes there is comfort: 'Walking down twisted cobbled streets with only a narrow strip of star-picked heaven above us, lighted only by the glow of two cigarettes,' wrote Florence Conard, 'tired as I was, the stillness of that Spanish town crept into me and rested there.' There is love too – for the soldiers wounded and dying some of whom were scarcely more than boys; for lovers and husbands briefly and sometimes unexpectedly encountered, and for children, friends and family left at home.

The men's war was very different from the women's. John Richardson, an eighteen-year-old volunteer from Luton, described in a letter the last attack in the battle of the Ebro:

> At dawn we went over the top and the world went mad. Machine-guns sent a hail of bullets at us. Snipers shot at us, shells and trench mortars burst all round. But we reached cover at the bottom of the valley where we lay all day unable to move because of snipers. The heat of the sun became unbearable. The ground scorched and our clothes stuck to our backs. We had no water and my mouth and throat were swollen and hard with thirst.
>
> At 10 p.m. we got the order to attack. We reached the very summit without a mishap. A little while later came the signal for real business. We rose with a yell and rushed forward throwing hand-grenades as we ran. But the machine-guns rained death on us, red-hot lead. Hand-grenades burst all round. Time and time again we attacked only to be driven back. The fortifications were too strong. Solid concrete pill-boxes lined the hill-top and we were only flesh and blood.[12]

The most dramatic accounts in this anthology come from the women who nursed that 'flesh and blood'. 'Bodies torn and limbs smashed' were repaired often with blunt instruments, anaesthetics given by unskilled helpers, injections and bandages applied with shaking hands in hospitals swiftly set up in olive fields, caves, or under a bridge or in a tunnel as the Republicans retreated and the bombers pursued even the wounded. Twenty-four- or forty-hour shifts were followed by tea and cigarettes, as food was scarce and often had to be shared with starving refugees and soldiers. Any passing sturdy person could be hauled into an operating theatre to stroke a man's forehead, to hold an instrument or limb as he underwent an operation. These desperate times were not without their moments of black comedy. What to do with the limbs hastily amputated, flung on the floor, chucked out of windows, dumped in moats of castles where they blocked the sewage and fed the rats, was a macabre preoccupation.

Not everyone who had volunteered for Spain had been allowed to go. The women writing here represented many others left behind. And those who did go had to be content with conventional women's work mostly, because war confirms the sexual division of labour. Some had wanted to fight. Valentine Ackland, poet, Communist and hitherto campaigner for peace, wrote immediately when news of the insurgents' rebellion reached Britain to offer her services. She had a scheme for fifty women like herself, with their own cars, who could spearhead medical as well as military aid.[13] Kay Ekervall, writer and secretary, recalls how she (and her boyfriend) longed to volunteer but were turned down, in spite of training to use a machine-gun until her shoulders were sore.[14] Felicia Browne, artist and Communist, trained in machine-gunning, went to the front and was shot dead. And stories were told, behind the frontlines of battle, of women brave and eager enough to take pot-luck with the militias.

— *Women in Spain* —

In the first months of civil war women had been recruited into the Popular Front militias, ill-equipped and untrained as they were. Women defended their cities and villages by hand, alongside men and children. They built barricades, poured boiling oil on the insurgents and in less pressing moments did as their government directed them to do, and delivered food to their husbands at the front instead of in the fields.

The visible and symbolic presence of women on the Republican side was vital, even after they had been prohibited from fighting. Dolores Ibarruri – Pasionaria – was only the most well-known of women leaders in the Popular Front (admired by British women, as they make clear below, because she was beautiful, of the people, self-educated, principled – *and* a mother). The position of women in Spain was a flashpoint of political conflict. Catholic and conservative opponents of the Republic linked women's emancipation to the destruction of the family, private property and the anti-Christ, while how far women's emancipation should go was as much a bone of contention among Anarchists, Socialists and Communists then as now.

Spanish women had won the right to vote in 1931. In 1934 the Republican government passed Spain's first divorce law. Young women celebrated their new-found freedoms by wearing trousers and make-up, seeking training and work alongside men, and addressing men as comrades and friends as their women leaders did. But some women wanted the changes to go deeper into the structure of relations and feeling between women and men who formed the Republic and were disappointed to find their explorations checked or suppressed. Pilar Vilvancos tells Ronald Fraser about her village in Aragon where the men would permit no women on the village committee, and where her cousin was vilified for living 'like an animal' because he lived with a woman out of wedlock. None of this deterred Pilar from falling in love with a Major, a Republican hero, 25 years her senior, and defying family and friends to live with him:

> I liberated, emancipated myself. We slept together, we became the couple we were to remain all our lives, for we never married. I believe that people respect each other more without marriage. Not being married is a freedom – not a freedom to do as one pleases but the freedom to be oneself in a human relationship.[15]

— Feminism, Pacifism and Anti-fascism —

In Britain Spain was never a feminist issue, but a democratic and humanitarian one. In these respects the Aid Spain movement drew support from both women's organizations and individual feminists. Selina Cooper, for instance, Lancashire radical suffragist, aged 72 in 1936, argued with Sylvia Pankhurst and others that fascism meant 'back to the kitchen sink for women'. After a visit to Nazi Germany in 1935 Selina Cooper discovered that fascism also meant living in constant fear without the protection of civil liberties. Women must oppose fascist brutality she wrote in her report, because they are the 'creators of life and it is their business to preserve it'. She lost no opportunity after her return, to speak to meetings of women and socialists about what she had seen and learned in Germany in spite of the lack of enthusiasm from her Labour Party for what they regarded as a dangerously pro-Communist analysis.[16]

In the predominantly feminist pacifist movement in Britain anti-fascism drove a wedge between those who recognized that fascism could only be reversed by force, or at least the threat of force, and those who believed that no regime, however vile, ever warranted deliberate killing. Storm Jameson's *Autobiography* traces the agony of a liberal socialist driven inexorably by the angry frustration and curt mockery of more knowing European friends, to the realization that fascism was not going to respond to pacifism, or goodwill, anymore than it respected national frontiers. Vera Brittain, on the other hand, whose *Testament of Youth* had shaped so many people's understanding of what war meant to women, never abandoned her pacifism solemnly vowed in a hospital in France in 1916. 'War,' she argued, in line with her mentor the Revd Dick Shepard, 'however "righteous" its alleged cause, was contrary to the will of God and spiritual welfare of man.'[17]

It is doubtful whether this conflict of opinion, echoing that between socialists and feminists before the First World War, and causing estrangement among women of different nationalities in the international women's movement for peace in the 1930s, will ever be resolved. But women's experience in Spain reminds us why women rarely glorify the results of war. Watching so many die (it was often a surprise, how long it took a strong young man or child to die), or starve (the descriptions of refugees wild with hunger are among the most horrible), or people faced with impossible choices (one woman preferred to kill her child, she said, than be separated from her husband) and the gradual defeat of Republican hopes meant that the war these women describe is closer to emotional suffering than the heroism of armed combat.

Women's testimony of their work in Spain is part of a gathering momentum throughout Europe in the past ten or fifteen years, to rediscover the conditions of fascism and opposition to it through the release of memory. Children whose parents lived and worked under fascist regimes in Italy and Germany, Austria and in Vichy France have probed painfully the memories – drab and violent – of collaboration, acquiescence, silence in fascist nations, through film, television, fiction and historiography. The will to forget has been powerful but the anger of younger generations, their determination to know what happened in Europe during their parents' lives has been tenacious too. Every voice in this book has something to tell us of the struggle between fascism and its enemies and it would be wise to listen to them all if the tragic outcome of the 1930s is not to be repeated. For the conditions which gave rise to fascism – political and economic inequalities, militarism, unemployment, racial prejudice, ethnic and sexual divisions – have deep roots in western democracies in the 1990s.

1990

'I HAVE ALWAYS BEEN A WRITER' – YVONNE KAPP

WRITER AND SOCIALIST

I became acquainted with Yvonne Kapp through her two-volume biography of Eleanor Marx, published in the 1970s when the author was in her late sixties and early seventies.* *Eleanor Marx* is a magnificent book, a tour de force, a work of scholarship and literary skill which adds to the histories of Marxism, anarchism and labour in the nineteenth century a feminine dimension. Eleanor Marx, advocate and translator of her father's work, untiring actor in the trade union and international socialist movements, lover of literature and theatre, common law wife of the disreputable secularist and socialist Edward Aveling, belongs with Mary Wollstonecraft and Emily Bronte in the nineteenth century and Virginia Woolf and Sylvia Plath in the twentieth, to the modern feminist imagination. In the 1970s I was absorbed in the Women's Liberation Movement (WLM). In small groups we campaigned, consciousness-raised and studied. In my study group we read volumes one, two and three of *Capital,* Lenin, Mao and Freud – in order, we hoped, to give new meaning to class struggle and the politics of sexual difference. Sex and class were the two insistent preoccupations of socialists in the early British WLM. No wonder then that Eleanor Marx's life and politics should fascinate us. Her socialism – a blend of passionate identification with oppressed peoples, Marxism and a fervent belief in freedom (she yearned and failed to become an actress, declaring once that the artistic life is 'the only free life a woman can lead') – seemed to anticipate the complexities of our own.

1   And the circumstances of Eleanor's personal life – from her father's claim that 'Tussy *is* me', through her despair over housework and the struggle to earn a living, to her ultimately tragic love for Edward Aveling – were bound to intrigue the generation of feminists who voiced the slogan 'the personal is political'.

---

* Yvonne Kapp, *Eleanor Marx*: Volume I, *Family Life 1855–1883*; Volume II, *The Crowded Years 1884–1898*, Lawrence & Wishart 1972, 1976; 2 vols., Virago, 1979.

Reading *Eleanor Marx* then, for a feminist of my generation, was to enter a dialogue with two other political generations: Eleanor's, but also, if more obliquely, the author's. Yvonne's Communism, her knowledge of Marxist theory and practice and determination to raise the events of Eleanor's life above the level of a melodrama shaped the biography. Had one of us written it the emphasis might have been different; less perhaps on the power of the father and more on her emotional ambivalence and self-denials. Those differences were what interested me when I first read the book, and continue to do so. Yvonne, I think, is more exasperated than interested in the differences between us. She wonders at our preoccupation with antagonism between the sexes. Having played down Eleanor's feminism, and emphasized (eloquently and with dignity) what Eleanor gained from her relationship with Aveling, 'Why do all you girls hate men?' she once asked me, 'What dreadful things have men done to you?' . . .

Standing in Yvonne's elegant living room (everything about Yvonne is elegant, from her literary vocabulary to the delicious cake she offers with afternoon tea), gazing out on to her leafy garden in Highgate, I searched for a reply, 'Oh no, no, no, Yvonne. Not all of us do hate men . . . only some of us, and only some of the time . . .', reaching as I hoped for firmer ground: 'Socialist feminists don't hate men. The sexual division of labour is the problem, the undervaluing of femininity, of everything that women do and have done.' I sank into silence.

The different emphasis didn't simply indicate different political formations, but also emotional contours. If, since Mary Wollstonecraft, feminists have struggled to combine work and political being with love and motherhood, then the particular ways in which these seeming incompatibilities have moulded women's and men's lives is the very stuff of history.

Socialism in England, at least since the 1890s, was born partly out of compassion for the poor. Through the early twentieth century the well-educated, the propertied and the wealthy lived worlds away from the working classes. Autobiographies of those many socialist and labour women and men who came from privileged backgrounds are full of the shocked discovery of poverty: the evidence of deprivation and hardship that unemployment and poverty – capitalism's twin evils – bring. Over and over again one reads: I went to the slums, and I saw, and what I saw changed me. I became a socialist. The language is Biblical and so is the experience of conversion. If those with a social conscience submitted themselves to the service of socialism, then faith in the moral and ethical superiority of their service sustained them. Both Yvonne's generation of educated women and men, and my own, are heirs to this tradition of socialist service to which Eleanor Marx's life bore testimony. We rejected Fabian gradualism – ours was a revolutionary socialism. But there are vital differences. My generation, born in the 1940s, accepted education, health and economic subsistence as their right. We grew up with the self-confidence to demand changes in the immediate and most intimate conditions of our *own* lives – not just in the lives of others. How different from Yvonne's generation, who had come to maturity in the shadow of the Great War, when to be alive at all seemed mere chance. In the 1930s unemployment, poverty and fascism over-shadowed the claims of feminism, whereas each political generation since the Sixties has been preoccupied with liberation, personal identity and sexuality. In the 1930s the Soviet Union floodlit the consciousness of Western with the promise of proletarian government, economic planning and the austere paternalism of Joseph Stalin. Indeed, there is no ideal socialist commonwealth, except in the imagination.

When I went to meet Yvonne – writer and Communist – it was with the curiosity of an historian of socialism as well as feminism, keen to discover the ways in which these different social forces might emerge in one woman's long and active life. I was not disappointed.

— I have always been a writer —

Eleanor was not begun until the 1960s, Yvonne having 'discovered' her 'between the lines' of the correspondence of Frederick Engels with the Lafargues (Eleanor's sister and brother-in-law) which Yvonne was translating in the 1950s for Lawrence & Wishart. Nothing was written or known, it seemed, about this interesting person who kept cropping up in the letters. So Yvonne seized the first opportunity she could – which, given the demands and contingencies of the life of a freelance writer, took a while to arrive in the unexpected form of a small inheritance – to devote herself to research and to write the boigraphy of Eleanor.

In a sense all her life had been a preparation for such a task, in particular the central activity – writing. The desire to write seems to have been born out of isolation as a child and galvanized by a combination of rebellion and economic need:

'I have always been a writer. I wrote verse at the age of seven, comic poetry. I did write an awful lot of verse. All through adolescence. I had a short story published when I was about twelve or thirteen somewhere.'

Why had she started writing so young?

'It's very difficult to say. I don't exactly know. I think it may have been influenced by the fact that I was a tubercular child and so I had to spend long months lying on my back and just reading and reading and not going to school.'

Yvonne's pursuit of writing, indeed of education and a career at all, was born out of intense personal struggle with her parents:

'I didn't like my parents very much . . . and as I grew up we didn't get on at all. They wanted me to live a completely conventional life. My father was a merchant. And they just thought I would come out; get married to some nice, presumably well-off young Jewish businessman, or something of this sort. Instead of which, having been to a finishing

school in Switzerland and a ghastly family outside Paris I was determined to go to a university and got myself into King's College, London.
Just after the First World War they took people coming out of the forces
who had not got the qualifications for university entrance. I had an
interview with the head of the English Department and he let me come
in on a special course.' Yvonne believed the course was in journalism,
and London University did offer a Diploma in Journalism in the 1920s
which Vera Brittain claimed was the 'next best thing to a degree as
preparation for a career in journalism' (*Women's Work in Modern
England*, 1928).

'This upset my mother very much. My father was really rather proud
of me. He thought it was a good idea. It did cut me off from the social
swim my parents wanted me to be in.

'I had a lovely time. I edited the college magazine and I enjoyed
myself no end. Eventually there was a real bust-up and I ran away. We
had rows all the time. My father would say, "Daughters don't behave
like that," and I would say, "Well, I'm a daughter and I do behave like
that and if you don't like it I will leave home." And eventually I did. I
literally ran away. I just went out of their flat in St John's Wood and
ran down the road.' This was in 1921 when Yvonne was eighteen.

'I was eleven years old when the First World War started. Anyone
who grew up during the First World War belonged not only to a
different generation but to a different epoch. My parents were literally
Victorians . . . That war made more of an abyss between one generation
and another than anything that's happened since. The world changed in
those years. Ideas were different. I can remember at thirteen saying to
my father that I couldn't possibly believe in God, which shocked him
dreadfully. It could not be possible that there was a God because how
could each side claim that God was on their side? And these appalling
deaths. People who never lived through that would hardly know what
it was like – the casualty lists. I read the newspapers. And all the girls
at school (Queen's College, Harley Street) had brothers in the army.
And people were always being sent for, their brothers being killed.
Their fathers being killed. It was all around you.'

Having left home Yvonne stayed with a girlfriend and launched
herself into a career as a journalist. Her first job was on the *Evening
Standard* which paid £4 a week ' – riches in those days'. Audacity and
good fortune secured her the job:

'I had been a great admirer of Alec Waugh's book called *The Loom
of Youth* which was one of the very earliest books critical of the public
school system. And I'd written a gushing fan letter to Waugh. I expect
he had millions of them, especially from young people. He was my one

hope, so I went to see him. He worked at a publisher's and he knew the editress of the women's page on the *Evening Standard* and she took me on. Then I was seconded from the *Evening Standard* to the *Sunday Herald* to be assistant to the editor – because they needed somebody very quickly. He had clattering false teeth. He was a Manchester man. I had a most extraordinary and interesting job there. I was an errand girl. I was sent out to collect people's articles. I had to correct text. I had to cut articles. I had to do absolutely everything that has to be done on a paper including on a Saturday morning I used to help in the compositors' room. I was a real dogsbody. The tea girl, so to speak.'

This relative affluence was short-lived. Yvonne was sacked after a clash with the editor over a quotation from Shakespeare – 'I was a pretentious little literary snob.' This was August 1922 and she was already in the throes of the final break with her parents that her marriage in that month brought about, her father acting out feminism's paranoia.

'After I had left home, my father made sure that I could not marry under age – and he had given the authorities the names of twelve young men whom I was forbidden to marry. Young men with whom I'd gone out dancing, playing tennis, you know – most of whom I wouldn't have dreamt of marrying. And of course my husband's name was among them. We couldn't do anything about it. I was under age and my father could stop it. In those days fathers didn't have to give a reason at all. The Solicitor-General's spokesman said, "Unless your father is insane" – well, I thought he was, I thought he must be – but that was hardly good enough. There was no way of removing this ban till I was twenty-one.'

The ban was removed in fact when adverse newspaper publicity threatened to escalate. Yvonne was marrying an artist, Edmund Kapp, thirteen years her senior, penniless but with some influential acquaintances in the arts and Fleet Street. A successful exhibition at the Leicester Galleries with an introduction to the catalogue written by Max Beerbohm had begun to make his name known and the story newsworthy. Her parents' retreat was not sufficient to bring them to the wedding. It was many years before a reconciliation was effected.

— *Marriage* —

Yvonne was nineteen years old when she married in 1922. Theirs was an itinerant life in search of artistic integrity and financial solvency. In spite of their poverty and the precariousness of their material existence, fate and friends in uneven combination offered homes and work at vital moments. If Edmund's career set the pace of their married life – at least in the first year or so before the birth of their daughter – then it was Yvonne's work as a journalist that brought in the irregular income.

Edmund had a quest. He returned from the war a staff captain with a distinguished record of service. His talents as a linguist as well as an artist were undiminished in spite of traumatic experiences. But he felt desperately that he lacked an artist's proper training. When Yvonne first met him he had just come through a period of 'curious interior crisis . . . a very self-disciplined and agonizing time'. In pursuit of this training they set off for Rome, rucksacks on their backs, and walked 'the whole of the French and Italian Riviera. It was absolutely marvellous. Stopping with people on the way – Max Beerbohm lived on the coast, and Gordon Craig, my daughter's godfather – we got as far as Pisa eventually.'

They were given a lift to Rome where they lived for six months in a small hotel and then in the summer took a little house up in the mountains:

'We lived a very, very disciplined life. We didn't even, though we were young, ever go sightseeing. It was quite an austere sort of existence. Every Sunday we went to a concert, but otherwise . . . However, we made a lot of friends. And Edmund started to paint.' When short of money in Rome, 'we went begging into cafés playing our recorders, going round with a hat. We made quite a bit.' They stayed in Capri with Edgar Mowrer, the writer, and his wife where Yvonne found herself 'to my very great delight, pregnant', so they wanted to return to England. In Italy they were without 'a home, roots, anything'.

Joanne, Yvonne and Edmund's daughter, was born in a Hampstead maternity home for soldiers' wives. But her presence did not inhibit their footloose and unorthodox life. Chance acquaintances met at a concert offered them a home – a cottage in Sussex where they took their new baby:

'It was a very primitive cottage I may say. My mother-in-law lent me her sweet maid who came and did do a lot of very early things – nappy-washing and so on. And it was all right as long as I was feeding, but you know the difficulties. Anyhow . . . Edmund got a job drawing judges and advocates in the law courts. A marvellous series and very well paid. It was at this stage that I wrote my first book, *Pastiche*: pieces to accompany Edmund's drawings. When the winter came I was left in the cottage with the baby, breaking the ice of the well to fetch water, every drop of which had to be filtered and sterilized before it could be used. And cooking on calor gas. It was pretty terrible, and I really could hardly stand it. Eventually I just didn't stand it: and I got a friend of ours who lived close and who went to London regularly to drive me to London.'

In London they found a flat in 'Orange Street, off the Haymarket. That's where the baby grew up. She was a little Piccadilly baby. She used to be weighed at the Boots that was there. It was a marvellous studio with a flat upstairs that had a parapet where you could just put a baby's cot. It was at the stage door of the Comedy Theatre with Ciro's Club at the other end. And Constable the publishers.'

But Edmund got restless and went off to Spain so that Yvonne found herself alone again with the baby.

'And I must say I was very miserable. It's frightfully difficult being alone with a small baby. I was twenty-one or two, and everyone else of that age was having a wonderful time, going to the Gargoyle and parties and that sort of thing. Everyone danced in those days. The baby-sitting thing hadn't happened. Occasionally a friend would come in and sit in but I felt fettered by the baby if you want to know. It was less a joy than a responsibility and it wasn't very good . . .

'That was in the spring of 1926 and the baby was nearly two. Then we joined up again in Paris and went to live in Antibes, and I did freelance journalism most of the time. In the autumn, though, Edmund was invited by Nigel Playfair to play the recorder in his production of the "Bourgeois Gentilhomme". So he went off again, you see. I was always being left in places [peals of laughter]. And I minded that very much . . . Edmund was a sweet father, a marvellous father. He would wash the nappies and do anything. But he didn't feel bound by the baby. He could drop us. Anyhow, so he left me in Antibes, in a *pension* there, which was all right as long as he was living there but as soon as he left it was dreadful.'

This time Yvonne was joined by a friend, John Collier the writer, and they had also been adopted, as it were, by a young girl who had 'fallen in love with the family' so stayed to help with the baby:

'It was there that I was interviewed for the job for which Rebecca West had recommended me. You know, to work on *Vogue* . . . She was one of the people to whom I'd been sent as an errand girl when I was on the *Sunday Herald*. When I went to her flat and said I had come for her article, she said, "Oh, come in, come in." And she sat me down on the sofa. She was absolutely charming. She wanted to know all about me and she listened to my ambitions as a writer. Then when we were in the south of France we used to go sometimes to the Juan les Pins casino and we were sitting there with some friends, and people from another table came and joined us and a woman across the table said, "Oh, aren't you Yvonne?" She'd remembered my name. And I said, "Who are you?" [peals of laughter]. Isn't that dreadful? Dreadful! She was living in the same *pension* with us, and we had a very nice time with her.*

'Anyhow, I was offered this job – so then in the autumn I left Edmund with the baby and the nanny and went to Paris. And until I'd got enough money I didn't send for them, till Christmas. I had this job as literary editor. It wasn't too bad. It involved all sorts of idiotic things like going to see these fashion house shows. The work was really a matter of putting commas in and taking commas out, because all the people who were really interested in fashion were pretty well illiterate. They couldn't write English and I was quite useful for that. They were absolutely sold on the idea of *haute couture* which didn't interest me at all.'

The job was 'fantastically well paid': £1,000 a year in dollars, tax-free and in Paris. It was 1927 and Yvonne was twenty-four. She lived opposite the Luxembourg Gardens, paid the nanny, took a studio for Edmund and 'we really lived well'.

'The only luxury that I got out of it personally was that I went riding before breakfast [laughs] . . . It was better than doing freelance journalism. I loved being in Paris, and of course we were relieved of money worries for the first time. But here was where the marriage began to crumble.

'He was always in his studio. I don't think he liked being married in those days. I think he would have preferred not to be married although he was a loving person. I don't think he liked having ties. He painted, he was quite happy, and you know – one can't get away from it – people who went through the First World War were damaged personalities. When we were up in the mountains that summer in Italy on every feast day (which in Italy is, as you know, very often) they used to shoot off some little ancient artillery piece. An old gun they'd got. Edmund was always stunned. He would turn absolutely bloodless, and tremble from head to foot. It was as bad as that.

'He spoke about the war very seldom and not for a long time. He'd had a most terrible experience. He was a brilliant linguist and one of his jobs had been to interrogate German prisoners immediately as they were brought in. And he was sent to a forward post which was then completely deserted. It was no more than a dug-out lined with bully beef. He was supposed to be relieved after three days. But the man

* Victoria Glendenning, *Rebecca West, A Life*, Macmillan, 1987, pp. 103–7 gives an account of Rebecca's and Yvonne's sojourn at the Hotel Josse between Antibes and Juan Les Pins in 1926.

who was told to take over was killed on his way up. Then they forgot about him. And he remained there for weeks. And was gassed. When they eventually found him he was deaf, stone deaf, and he had total internal stasis. He'd eaten nothing but tins of bully beef from the sides of this dug-out. He was a complete wreck. This was at the end of 1917. He was in hospital for weeks. And he was never sent back to the front. He'd been in the trenches for over two years. He was in the Sussex regiment. And most of the men who went to France with him were totally, totally wiped out. All that. And then this ghastly experience.'

Yvonne left *Vogue* as suddenly as a few years earlier she had left the *Sunday Herald*, only this time the issue was the appallingly low pay of the clerks and typists:

'I got angry about a number of things that were happening to the lower-paid people. They were very exploited, the typists and clerks. There was a hierarchy and I was at the top of it. Well, I was overpaid really, and these people were dreadfully underpaid. And eventually I said, well, I could be paid twice as much as I'm getting now, but otherwise it's not worth it: double or quit. They said quit, so I did.'

'Back in England Edmund took a cottage just outside Cambridge near some friends of ours, the Bernals. And that's where I began to write the first novel . . . about French people . . . I wrote very slowly. I remember going and reading a first chapter to Rebecca West who thought it was rather good and encouraged me. Some friends of mine had started a publishing firm and said to me, "Why don't you write a novel? We'll give you £50, go away and write." Well now, £50 was a lot of money in those days. You could live on it for six months. So I took my opening chapter and I rented a place in the South of France for a few months very cheaply, and I completed this book. But these young people, these publishers, hadn't got any money of their own. However, one of them had a rich father who was funding the firm. And he insisted on seeing everything on their lists. When I came back and delivered my book, it went into galley proof and was read by the father. It was called *Nobody Asked You* and he sent back the proofs, writing right across them, "I cannot sanction the publication of this book", with his signature. And underneath his name was the title, "Nobody Asked You". So the first thing I did was have this made into a Christmas card and sent it to all my friends wishing them good, clean fun.

'Then I looked through the galleys and do you know he had been so annoyed at certain things, and thought they were so obscene, that he had practically torn the pages with his savage markings. Mind you, it was pretty outspoken, I mean for those days. Anyhow I said to these young people: look, it's all very large and fine but how about giving me some compensation? You've had the type set up, can I have that? And you've got the paper, can I have that? And they agreed. So I had the paper, I had the type. I got a friend of mine, Quentin Bell, to design a cover, I bought a car for five pounds, a lot of stamps and brown paper and so on, and I registered myself as the "Willy Nilly Press". And I published the book myself. I got quite a number of pre-publication orders. And then what do you think happened? On the Sunday after it came out there was a review in the *Observer* by Gerald Gould who devoted two columns to it. He said – unforgettable words – that if he didn't review this book by a remarkable new young writer he might be doing her a grave injustice, on the other hand if he did he might be doing his readers a grave disservice because it was a very shocking book. Well, you couldn't ask for a better review, could you? The next day little men with bag sacks from every bookshop in London were on the doorstep of my house in Brunswick Square. They were taking twelve and fifteen copies at a time and coming back for more. It sold and sold and sold. Within a fortnight it was practically sold out, and I'd made more money than I've ever made in my life on anything I've written since.'

— *Taking Life Seriously: Politics* —

Yvonne's publishing adventure was short-lived. She sold *Nobody Asked You* to a wholesaler for the second edition and settled back into writing. At a dinner-party one evening she met Lindsay Drummond, the head of John Lane, the Bodley Head who, obviously intrigued by the tale of the Willy Nilly Press, paid Yvonne £150 a year for the first refusal of any future novels.

The years of writing novels were a sort of watershed in Yvonne's life. She had taken easy advantage of the opening up of higher education and the professions to women that occurred in the 1920s. Easy, that is, compared with the women who felt they had struggled to intellectual maturity in the years of militant feminism before 1914. Vera Brittain and Virginia Woolf were the public voice of a generation of literary women who felt the disadvantage of being a woman more keenly than Yvonne. But if chance and women's suffrage had lightened Yvonne's path to economic independence and a literary life then the driving forces behind her development as a writer had been personal: rebellion against her parents, marriage and child. Financial necessity drove her on. Her psychoanalysis was mentioned almost as an aside. Otherwise, after the early 1930s, Yvonne's life-story as she told it, although punctuated with references affectionate, enthusiastic, admiring about others (as diverse as the men in the packing department in the basement of the AEU's headquarters in Peckham, as Harry Pollitt, secretary of the Communist Party, or colleagues and immediate employers), did not reveal the same intimate connection between personal relationships and the development of her professional self.

It was the pressures of external events, the need to give political coherence to an increasingly frightening and chaotic world, which changed Yvonne's priorities as well as her perception of her world. A child of her time, her personal transformation marked the shift from the 'careless' Twenties to the sombre Thirties.

'I began to take life more seriously as a result of outside events; which coincided with my being round about thirty and the beginning of the fascist era in Germany. I hadn't really thought about politics before then, though I'd always been on the left side. Having rows with people in 1926 during the General Strike and that sort of thing . . . my brother actually drove a bus and I couldn't stand that. But I was what you might call rebellious rather than politically conscious. It wasn't until fascism in Germany and the burning of the books that as a liberal, and a Jewish liberal at that, I began to feel really involved.'

From 1933 Yvonne used to put up refugees: 'So I became involved in that way and began to work for refugees and anti-fascist organizations. They were peripheral, not directly political. Because I didn't know enough about politics to know if there was a central way in which you could – what's the word I want – I mean, the proper way for people a little more mature than I was to be politically organized and then deploy one's energies. But I went the other way, you see, doing all these things. And then, before you could say Jack Robinson, there was Spain.'

Before the Spanish Civil War began in 1936 Yvonne went to the Soviet Union: 'I was terribly interested in the Soviet Union. It was fascinating and I had this wonderful time . . . I think it's true to say that people see what they want. What they think they're going to see, they see. What I thought I was going to was a country that had got rid of capitalists and landlords and was getting on with social democracy with everything in favour of the working classes.

'On the way home aboard ship, I travelled with Harry Pollitt who was returning from the Seventh World Congress, which was a very, very important congress, as you know, in which great changes were made from the disastrous policy of "class against class" to the popular front. This of course, was after the burning of the Reichstag . . . I spent a lot of time talking to Harry Pollitt on the voyage home saying that I would be more useful not being in the Communist Party. He said that was a great mistake ... He said, "You see, the trouble is you'll be discouraged so easily because things go badly in one country or another and unless you are in an international movement you can very easily feel that nothing is ever going to happen."

'When I got back home I decided that he had been right and I joined the Communist Party and lost a lot of friends ... I had really had, do you see, up to then, a sort of playgirl's attitude.'

Yvonne now led the full life of a political activist. One of her first organizing successes was the 'great meeting at the Albert Hall in 1937 in aid of the Basque children ... which collected thousands of pounds'. Paul Robeson arrived unexpectedly and sang. Picasso sent one of his Guernica sketches for auction and Yvonne also wrote a book on the Basque children in England for their funds.* A little later, Yvonne began to work for a Jewish refugee organization at Woburn House. She was in charge of the department dealing with refugee dentists and doctors.

'When I took over this office was lined with files up to your neck ... And each file represented a human life. Can you imagine anything so dreadful? So with two shifts of four young refugee workers by day and by night, the papers were sorted out and put in order ... And then you found that out of the thousands of pieces of paper that there were, some individuals had already got to England, some to America. Others had died. Some represented urgent cases that had to be taken up immediately. Doctors and dentists were not allowed to practise in Britain and they were refused entry unless they had a guarantor ...

'I spent practically the whole working week with a couple of secretaries preparing six cases. And on Friday afternoon I would go to the Home Office with those six cases and say, can I have these please? And they were so carefully prepared that I always got them. I had quite good relations with all the Home Office young clerks. And I would not spend my time, unlike the voluntary ladies of the past, in chattering with those who had already arrived here, all of whom wanted to say, "Can't I be an exception and practise?" And some of them wept because they couldn't.

'The refugee organization was of course flooded with applications to come to Britain. I mean people who had the faintest chance of

---

* Jim Fyrth, *The Signal was Spain. The Aid Movement in Britain 1936–39*, Lawrence & Wishart, 1986, ch.15. Yvonne Cloud, *The Basque Children in England*, London, 1937

coming out of the Nazi countries. And it's true we did try to get out the people who had the least connections here. Some of them were in concentration camps ... When the war came they were allowed to practise. Three thousand of them were on the department's books altogether.'

Soon after the invasion of Czechoslovakia Yvonne went to work for the Czech Refugee Trust Fund, a government-funded body ('blood money, you might say, to save people who were going to suffer as a result of the sell-out') under the directorship of a retired civil servant, Sir Henry Sunbury. Yvonne became his assistant: 'There were three government-appointed Trustees: a very high-up retired civil servant, a Jewish businessman and a distinguished ex-Trade Union leader.'

Shortly afterwards the war broke out and then, in May 1940, Yvonne was sacked: 'The Home Secretary, Sir John Anderson, sacked me because I was thought to be a Communist ...' Another member of the staff, who had been in charge of preparing material for the refugees' tribunals, was sacked at the same time. They both went away to the country (Yvonne's daughter was away at school) and wrote a book called *British Policy and the Refugees*, 'because we knew it from the inside'. The book was not published at the time because a Penguin paperback on the subject of refugees by François Lafitte appeared before theirs. There was a paper shortage during the war and afterwards.

'Don't forget: this was the moment when it was thought there was going to be an invasion. It was also thought that anybody who was in sympathy with the Soviet Union would become automatically a traitor to Britain and, because of the Non-Aggression Pact, pro-Nazi, if you please. Our sacking was a signal of the Government's attitudes to the Communists in the coming months ...'

— *Working for the Engineers* —

The two women returned to London when the bombing became bad (in 1941) but they were unable to find jobs. Everywhere she applied Yvonne was short-listed, but never appointed. So she did some voluntary work, including some at the Labour Research Department. From there she was recommended for the post of Research Officer for the Amalgamated Engineering Union (AEU) whose president was Jack Tanner. Within a month of the appointment the Soviet Union was invaded 'and the whole atmosphere changed, and I was able to continue being the Research Officer until after the end of the war. And that was a wonderful job.'

At the AEU Yvonne used to prepare the wage claims for the whole of the engineering industry and write Jack Tanner's speeches for him:

'He had a beautiful voice; strongly cockney, very resonant. There were certain words he stumbled over, and certain words he didn't like, and certain words he did like. I studied him like an actor, so that I could write his speeches in the terms in which he would say them. He got so used to this that the bloody man never read the speeches before he had to deliver them, which used to annoy me terribly. He just took it for granted that I would write the speech that he would want to make. He never asked me anything. I used to beg him before the annual congress, "You read it." He never did.'

The AEU had no women members, and so of course no women on its executive. It took time for Yvonne herself to be accepted. Because of the manpower shortage women were conscripted into the engineering industry and in 1943 the AEU reluctantly allowed them into the Union. Women attended the annual conference (the National Committee) for the first time in the spring of that year:

'As we drove down to Blackpool, Tanner said, "Look, would you talk to them. Find out what they want to drink. Give them whatever they want. Introduce them." The AEU never before had a woman in an administrative position on the staff, and they were very thankful for me for once. So I said to the women delegates, "What would you like to drink? Order anything." There I was pouring out these things and one of them got up and said, "Oh, let me do that, I used to be a barmaid!" So she poured the drinks! I told them: whatever you do don't speak of yourselves as skilled workers. You may be skilled but it means something quite special in this Union . . . and don't do this, and don't do that . . . "Skilled" meant you had to be a white card holder, you had to have done your full apprenticeship; served your time, you see. The women were dilutees. They had only come in for the war. They were semi-skilled. They were on the repetitive operations and so on. A toolmaker, for example, was something quite different. And if the women did mention a skill, which they did once or twice, really a kind of rigor went through the men. I mean, they were beside themselves. It was the most macho union.

'The women managed very well. There were a lot of dilutees, also men, young men. They had to accept dilution as men were in the force. But this contempt for people who hadn't served their time. You only get that among the craftsmen, this extreme craft attitude. Terribly old and terribly traditional. I don't know what it's like now but it was a diehard attitude. I was lucky. I managed to overcome most of the prejudice. I don't think anybody really felt hostile to me. And I did actually attend one or two of their excutive meetings.'

Among the most significant achievements of Yvonne's work at the AEU were the wartime Production Enquiries. Many complaints came through from the shopfloor about poor management, and other obstructions to production:

'The very first National Committee for which I wrote Jack Tanner's speech had a lot about incompetent and inefficient management and how war production was not up to what it should be and so on. And the Minister for Production wrote to Tanner and said, "How do you come to this conclusion? We should very much like you to establish your facts." Tanner got in touch with me and said, "Well, what do I do about this?" I said, "That's quite simple. You just get in touch with the members, with your shop stewards. You ask them in every factory." "Oh," he said, "do you?" "Yes," I said, "You do. You send out a questionnaire, that's what you do."

'And in effect, that's what we did ... I drafted a questionnaire of a hundred questions and it went to a thousand factories, direct to the shop stewards. Then I analysed the returns, three thousand of them in all. The upshot was absolutely fascinating.'

Yvonne was allowed to employ a secretary for this work, and her research skills developed so that for the second Production Enquiry six months later, she was using the punch card and knitting needle method!

'I may say that the first enquiry created quite an uproar. It went only to government departments, but Tanner saw that it also went to certain MPs and so on. Questions were asked in the House. Tanner was terribly pleased that the Union should produce this. It was of national importance. So we did it again six months later. By this time I'd also got two more assistants. After that we did a health and welfare enquiry. Because what was turning up more and more were the inadequacies of physical wellbeing in factories – like air-conditioning, canteens, first-aid, rest-rooms and so on. This idea of health and wellbeing in the factory was very far from the minds of the Union officials at the time.'

The introduction of women into the Union and the Production Enquiries were only two of the matters in which Yvonne was involved at the AEU. She also helped to organize the Jubilee of the Union, which was transformed into a cultural event, with an exhibition of pictures, a play and a history of the Union. She wrote the pamphlet on post-war reconstruction for the Union as well as the evidence to the Royal Commission on Equal Pay (which was published later as a separate pamphlet by the Labour Research Department: 'And that is my one contribution to feminism, I may say'), and she also assembled the John Burns Library of trade union and working-class movement literature for the AEU which they later gave to the Trades Union Congress.

At the end of the war, however, Yvonne was again at odds with her employers because of her politics:

'Well, then, of course, as we came to the end of the war, Tanner couldn't make the speeches that I wrote, and I wouldn't write the speeches that he wanted to make. He had hit the headlines by demanding the opening of a Second Front, which pleased him mightily . . . He was a very handsome man and he genuinely liked women and respected them, and was awfully nice about the women who came into the Union. He had a naturally good attitude. He was a Labour supporter who had been a bit of a wild boy in his youth. He met Lenin. At the drop of a hat he would tell you what he had said to Lenin. He never told you what Lenin had said to him [giggles]. I got on with him terribly well. I really liked him very much. But we quarrelled. He became more and more right-wing. And I would not write his speeches. In the end we just fell out.'

Yvonne left the AEU in 1947 and went to the Medical Research Council as part of a group 'doing what they call industrial psychology, which is rubbish. But I didn't really care very much – it took me into factories, which included Silvertown and the dock area of the East End of London.' Each factory – chemical, rubber, engineering, sugar – had its own specific hazards, and intimate acquaintance with Silvertown as well as her work with Jack Tanner at the AEU undoubtedly deepened her later research and writing about Eleanor Marx's political work in the East End of London.

'I got to know the district very well indeed. I went into every factory and found out exactly what the situation was. What they had in the way of doctors, nurses, first-aid, and I even went into the little workshops, where they employed only ten people or so who never came under factory inspection. It was fascinating. But of course that material is not mine. It is theirs. It belongs to the Medical Research Council which never published it. It was a marvellous experience. I enjoyed that. But I got into trouble over the report on the silliness of the job satisfaction enquiry at Vauxhall's, so they sacked me.'

The end of her job at the MRC meant a radical change in Yvonne's working life:

'Once I was freed from salaried jobs after many years, instead of going back to writing as I should have done, I made the mistake of agreeing to do a translation from the French and this led from one translation to another. And I got stuck in this ... like doing cross-word puzzles. Translating is not real at all. It's a ridiculous thing to do.'

But in the course of translating (which she did full-time between 1953 and 1960) Yvonne came across Eleanor Marx. 'I was fascinated. And I thought, what a very interesting person this is, I must find out more about her.'

And so her major project was born. It took ten years, survived a serious accident which left Yvonne flat on her back for five months, and the second volume was subsidized by two small Arts Council grants. 'I've had heaps of careers. But they were all to do with writing finally – in different spheres. I've never stopped writing. I never thought of doing anything else except writing – I've always been learning about writing. You never stop really. [But] I had to be the family support. It wasn't always by choice that I took paid jobs.'

Yet curiously, for a woman who so identifies herself, her attitude towards most of her writing is often casual, if not neglectful. Yvonne's work is scattered in the archives of the Labour Research Department, the AEU, or the MRC, for instance. (It is oddly reassuring to think that some of the massive literary infrastructure of the Labour Movement has been shaped by a woman such as Yvonne.) Some writings have been published without acknowledgement of authorship. Her fiction she dismisses curtly: 'Oh my novels, Sally,' I was told on a second meeting. 'They were *early* writings – pretty trivial and not very important.' Yvonne is severe on her young self. For her, her life and writing fall into two parts – before and after the Communist Party. Young womanhood was characterized by 'lightmindedness'. 'I joined the Party,' she said, 'not for sentimental reasons. It gave me a seriousness which I hadn't had before.' Her writing, like herself, was not to be taken seriously, until it was harnessed to the cause of socialism.*

Listening to Yvonne's story (many of the details of which space and discretion forbid including) I thought how those 'old enemies' evoked by Vera Brittain in *Testament of Youth* (1933) accurately describe Yvonne's early circumstances: 'The Victorian tradition of womanhood,

* Yvonne Cloud is her name as a novelist

a carefully trained conscience, a sheltered youth, an imperfect education, lost time, blasted years . . .' and I revel in the spirited way in which Yvonne subverted them!

1987

Part Three

MEMORY
AND
HISTORY

BECOMING A WOMAN
IN LONDON IN THE
1920S AND '30S

— *Introduction* —

Two visual images of the working class vie for attention in the popular memory of the inter-war years: the cloth cap and spare frame of the unemployed man whose wasted face and staring eyes still wrench pity from the onlooker; and the young working girl — lipsticked, silk-stockinged, and dressed, in the phrase of novelist, playwright, and broadcaster J. B. Priestley, 'like an actress'. The juxtaposition pierced contemporary consciousness. The two figures represented, on the one hand, the means test, hunger marches, and Orwell's 'twenty million inadequately fed'; and, on the other,

> the England of arterial and by-pass roads, of filling stations, factories that look like exhibition buildings, of giant cinema and dance-halls and cafes, bungalows with tiny garages, cocktail bars, Woolworths, motor-coaches, wireless, hiking ... grey-hound racing and dirt tracks, swimming pools and everything given away for cigarette coupons.[1]

This was the north/south divide. It was also a sexual division. Priestley was lamenting the changing industrial structure of Britain, or rather the effects of this change on the people. Nineteenth-century industrial power had been built on the blast furnace, coal-mines, and textile mills of the north and west; labour was manly and strong, its output substantial. Priestley lists twentieth-century industries in contrast: the tea-shops, corsetries, and hairdressers of the south-eastern suburbs and East Anglian small towns; the potato crisps, scent, toothpaste, bathing costumes, and fire extinguishers of West London. Priestley's lament is partly the recoil of the middle-brow man of letters from the influence of the United States — in particular California — on English people's wants and needs: the new forms of mass entertainment, the glare of advertisements, and ephemera of the new consumerism.[2] But there is also the fear that England and the English are in danger of being feminized by their wirelesses, movie-star worship, silk stockings, and hire-purchase: not only is the new working class in these new industries female, but the wants and needs which the new industries supply are feminine.

Priestley's sense that some vital energy in English life was being sapped by the new industries and suburban sprawls in which they were situated or which swiftly surrounded them (like the north of Notting Hill, described by Rebecca West in the 1930s as 'hacked out of the countryside and still bleeding')[3] was echoed by Orwell, the Coles and other contemporaries, and has been reiterated by historians.[4] Feminists too eyed the new young woman warily. 'Clothes, hat, shoes, stockings, furs, bag, scarf – all are standardized,' wrote Mary Agnes Hamilton, novelist and labour organizer in 1936, noting also her make-up and lissom boyish figure. This young woman smoked, she went on; she spoke with confidence, and was no longer interested in feminism. She 'took her freedom for granted'.[5] Most agreed with Ellen Wilkinson, MP for Jarrow, that 'the real difficulty' caused by industrial decline in Britain's staple industries 'is that of the adult male'.[6] Unable to find work, he lost status in his family and community through the indignities of negotiating with the Unemployed Assistance Board. The new jobs of the trading estates trailing the northern towns were, like those in the south-east, principally for young women and youths. Skilled and unskilled men feared the changes in industrial structure and process which made their work redundant and new industries open to women. The stark misery of Max Cohen's *I Was One of the Unemployed*, for example, documents the physical and mental suffering wrought by unemployment. Fear broke into hostility and contempt in some accounts. Those 'silly girls', wrote the socialist novelist John Sommerfield in *May Day*, published in 1936, 'in their synthetic Hollywood dreams, their pathetic silk stockings and lipsticks, their foolish strivings'[7] – dismissing at once both them and their dreams.

The following essay reconsiders some of those dreams and the young women who dreamt them. I want to query the use of the epithet 'feminine' to denigrate both the new consumer industries and the human needs they evoke.[8] Part of the explanation for this denigration lies with the habits of mind of the socialist and labour movements (to which Priestley, Orwell, Wilkinson, and the Coles, cited above, all belong). Both movements – in spite of resolute attempts of feminists – were organized around notions of class whose formation and destinies vary, but in which the individual subject was masculine and founded on the notion of independence through, and property in, labour. Femininity and women themselves, outside of the category 'wife and mother', were a problem associated with either their 'sex' or, worse, the threat of 'cheap labour'. Fear of cheap labour was the rational kernel in the labour movement's antagonism towards the female worker, but the denigration of the feminine should alert us to deeper levels of unease. Since it is through the division into masculinity and femininity that human identity is formed, and sexual desire and reproduction organized, any disturbance of that division will provoke anxiety, and labour is one element in the division of women and men more unstable than popular belief would like. Though the structure of the sexual division of labour in modern industry was set down during the Industrial Revolution – 'women's work' was designated unskilled, low paid, and unorganized – its boundaries constantly shift. The social relations of labour, in other words, are central not simply to the historical understanding of class, but also to the relation of sexual difference.[9]

In the 1920s and 1930s the sexual division of labour and women's sense of themselves – indeed what it meant to be a woman – were changing in significant ways, and the changes were nowhere more apparent than in London. Families were smaller, the working days shorter, wages (for those in work) were higher, and the numbers living below the poverty line fewer than before the First World War.[10] Aspirations too were changing. Women in trade unions, education, local government, and feminists groups, as well as writers of fiction, were articulating women's wants and trying to persuade authorities to consider them, even if they refused to embody them.[11] But most strikingly, advertising and the cinema, playing on fantasy and desire, enabled women to *imagine* an end to domestic drudgery and chronic want. Images of streamlined kitchens, effective cleaning equipment, cheap and pretty clothes and make-up, on hoardings and cinema screens and in the new women's magazines, added a new dimension to romance – a source of narrative pleasure to women since the eighteenth century at least, the scourge alike of puritan and feminist critics of femininity.[12] Few women replaced the copper with the washing-machine or the outside lavatory with the bathroom during the 1930s. But the dream was there and houses were built with these amenities, and by the end of the decade families were moving into them – apprehensive often of the costs of this new life, but moving in nevertheless.[13]

Women were moving into new areas of work too, in offices, shops, and office cleaning (domestic service was notoriously unpopular with London girls). Their numbers in the new and expanding industries – glass, chemicals, light metals, commerce, the manufacture of food and drink, for instance, all of which were growth industries in Greater London – were increasing. But the 'general tendency observed by the *General Report* of the 1931 Census towards the gradual weakening of the influences that restricted an occupation to the members of one sex, especially the male sex', was simply an acceleration in the development of mass production: the division of labour into short repetitive tasks, and the introduction of machinery and cheap labour.[14] This tendency, uneven, local, specific, was shifting the allocation of jobs among women and men, but not undermining the designations of women's and men's work. The content of 'women's work' remained in colloquial speech what it had been since the beginning of waged labour: 'Men done the hard work, the good work,' was how one Woolwich factory worker put it, 'and women done the light work.' And the vital distinction remained what it had always been – pay. 'They'd be out on strike at the drop of a reel of cotton,' Lily, an East London clothing worker, told me, if men had been paid women's rates. 'A man could have done it,' a clerical worker said of her job, 'but they would have had to pay them more.' When women were employed on men's work they were paid less.[15] And employ them they did. The location of the new industries was deliberate: close to their markets and within easy reach of cheap ununionized labour.[16] In the 1920s and 1930s office cleaners, packers, shop assistants, typists became the unlikely and suddenly visible shock troops of industrial restructuring.

Who were these women, and what did they want? Women's political and industrial organization, the vote, and changes in education, publishing, purchasing power, and with them habits of reading, writing, and even remembering have deepened individual subjectivity. And in the past twenty years the voices of some women may be heard through autobiography and oral history. Listening to, or reading, women's own descriptions of their growing up places women's subjectivity, their own sense of themselves, at the centre of historical change. Women's subjectivity is only one element in the relation of sexual difference, but one fraught with difficulties of interpretation because it opens up not only behaviour, thought, opinion, and family stories to historical enquiry, but also unconscious mental processes. That is, we listen to fantasies of desire and loss, the compelling inner directives of the structure of sexual difference. Sceptics wonder whether there can be a *history* of subjectivity which borrows its understanding of that precarious process from psychoanalysis. But fantasy draws on the immediate and historical for aspects of its content, form and context, and the conditions of these are always changing. This essay is part of a longer study. Here I only touch on women's first jobs, and their changing appearance: the one a condition of femininity, the other a sign. Its polemical purpose, of course, is to counter the repudiation of femininity which underlines the visions of England and the English described by Orwell and Priestley in the 1930s.[17]

— *Becoming a woman: the first job* —

For each young girl reaching her fourteenth birthday, the step from school to work was a step towards adulthood. 'There was nothing gradual about growing up,' wrote Rose Gamble in *Chelsea Child*:[18]

> As long as you were at school you looked like a child in short trousers and frocks, and you were treated like one, but when you left school at the end of the term after your fourteenth birthday, childhood ended. It was abrupt and final and your life changed overnight.

But the end of childhood was not so absolute. The end of schooling meant the end of lessons and children's play but not the end of obligations to the family nor yet the achievement of adult status. For a woman, that came with marriage and motherhood; few young women in London in the 1920s and 1930s escaped this destiny. But first there was adolescence — the transition between child and woman when identity itself is in flux and when the wage, new clothes, and the tangle of emotions associated with those years seems to promise the transformation of the self and relations with others. Memories of adolescence are vivid, perhaps because they still carry the weight of possibility — the intense wondering what one might become.

Rose Gamble, one of five children growing up in Chelsea in the 1920s, looked forward to the change from child to woman with excitement and hope. They lived in two rooms in the streets and courts behind Chelsea Town Hall, moving often; their mother earned sixpence an hour charring until she took a job in a mothers' clinic for 25 shillings (£1.25) a week; their father — a feared and intermittent presence — described himself once as 'a wharfinger', though he was mostly unemployed. Dodie, the eldest, 'plunged' from the top to the bottom of the class in 1928 when she saw a job for a greengrocer's cashier advertised in the local tobacconist. Fiercely insistent of her qualifications in spite of her childlike appearance, she was given the job, and the whole family celebrated her achievement. She plaited her hair; her mother showed her how to put it up; and without a backward glance at her abandoned education, she flung herself heart and soul into her new tasks. She was quick and obliging, polite and smiling with both customers and staff. It was not enough to sit behind the cash register. She mastered the books, learned to serve, and began to do small jobs in the florist's department. She made wreaths, and was trusted to collect the rents on her employers' properties. Every penny of her 10 shilling wage (50p) (for a 56-hour week) was handed over to her mother. Dodie's delight and satisfaction were in pleasing her mother – relieving her of some of the financial burden for the family. Her sole personal ambition was to own a bicycle; an ambition not realized until some years later when, still at the greengrocer's, still handing over her full wage-packet – 18s 6d (92p) by this time – to her mother, she heard of another job in a 'posh' shop off Sloane Street. The errand boy at the greengrocer's, whose gran cleaned for them, told her about it one day as they commiserated over their low and seemingly static status. The posh shop was called the Little Gallery and it not only took her on with an advance in wages of 9 shillings (45p) but also employed the second sister, Luli. Both girls learned about fine arts and handicrafts from the ladies who employed them; their young brother and sister also became familiar with the pottery and paintings and quilts on sale in the shop. Rose herself hand-decorated cellophane boxes and cards for sale while still at school. The Little Gallery was owned by two sisters, whose empathy with their young employees prompted them to finance their first ever trip to the seaside and a weekend in France. Dodie and Luli were lucky. Their new jobs opened up physical and intellectual landscapes, extended their knowledge and understanding.

Luli was two years younger than Dodie. Her first venture into employment had been less auspicious. She too had wanted to go straight into a shop and ''ave a black frock an' wavy hair', and had scoured the district around her home in Chelsea to no avail. Hearing from Lily Browning that 'there was a job goin' in 'aberdashery' over in Clapham Junction, she traipsed over there (a distance of several miles) only to be turned down because of the state of her hands; they were ingrained with dirt. Dirt – the mark of poverty and domestic labour – was incompatible with the aura of ladylike respectability which a salesgirl in a large departmental store should exude.[19] These gradations of status were quickly learned. On her disappointed return from Clapham, Luli's mother seized the opportunity. Tactfully, she suggested that, just to begin with, while looking for further employment in a shop, Luli should 'work up' a few cleaning jobs at fourpence an hour, and she could be home to see to her younger brothers and sisters after school. Luli, in despair at the prospect of more cleaning – 'Please, Mum, I don't want to be a char' and 'Oh no, Mum, I done with that' – reluctantly acquiesced, and within a couple of days had fifteen different jobs each week 'worked up' through her mother's contacts at the clinic: a few private homes, a doctor's surgery, scrubbing the stairs in a block of service flats in Fulham, and so on. She walked, like Dodie, from Fulham to Earls Court and Knightsbridge and back each and every day. She was dressed appropriately: 'Dodie made her a sacking apron for scrubbing and Mum cut down a cross-over pinny to wear under her coat.'

Luli was not released from these charring labours until her mother, after an illness, gave up her job at the mother-and-child clinic in Chelsea, and went to work in a factory canteen with 'a nice bit of easy office cleaning in the evening with no scrubbing'. She told Lu about a vacancy at the factory, and after frantic preparations to hair and underclothing Lu went after the job, was taken on, and gave up cleaning. 'With her bosom high up on her chest and her hair done, she was a lady,' remembered Rose, 'and I couldn't understand where the old Lu had gone.'

The story of Luli and Dodie's first steps into employment was the story of many London girls. The labour market was, to begin with, local and specific – 'You all worked in the nearest factory job to your home,' as I was told, or shop, office, workshop, wherever employment could be found.[20] Resistance to domestic service was strong and persistent among London girls. Each factory listed the jobs available on boards outside the factory gates or advertised for 'hands' – 'the only part of my body they was interested in!' – in the local paper.[21] But word of mouth and 'working-in' were the more vital labour exchange, and a mother's occupation and contacts usually more important than the father's, though the father's status if skilled could be decisive.

Jane Smith, for instance, came from a family of artisans on her father's side, while her mother's family were small tradespeople. The youngest of five children (her brothers were all in apprenticed trades; one sister was a tailoress, the other a high-class private domestic servant), she was kept at home in the first year after leaving school to keep house for her father and brothers in Pimlico:[22]

> My father came from people where they were proud of their occupation; where they trained. They were artisans. Daughters were expected to stay at home unless they were able to train, perhaps as a schoolteacher, or train as a ladies' maid where you met a better class of man.

Not until she 'kicked up a fuss' and provoked a 'family conference' could she persuade her father (her mother was dead) to allow her to search for an apprenticeship in her older sister's trade, West End tailoring.

Celia Wilmot, who became a Fleet Street secretary during the 1930s, was the daughter of a printworker killed during the First World War. His widow, Celia's mother, besides a small pension from the printworkers' union, worked as an early-morning cleaner in Fleet Street (and was one of the organizers of the General Strike there). Celia took a job as a clerical assistant to Pitman the printers straight from school. She learned shorthand at evening classes, and taught herself typing in the office, but it was her contact with the print union through their mother by virtue of her father's trade which provided the opening in Fleet Street.[23]

'Skill' was picked up haphazardly – or not at all. Apprenticeships were rare and, because low paid, often impatiently worked.[24] Lily Van Duren's first job when she left the Jewish orphanage in 1929, aged 15, was with a court dressmaker in Conduit Street, W1 – 'The clothing trade was the thing for poor Jewish children to do.' Her pay was 10 shillings (50p) a week. Hurt and angry when she overheard a conversation in which she and the other learners were described by the proprietor as 'cheap little girls',[25] she

> immediately decided to find my own job – which meant I had to root around and I found a job in the East End on the more popular, lower-priced clothing. I discovered that I was no good and I just had to poke around from job to job until I got the experience . . . I trained myself by watching what other girls did, and they would help me as much as possible, and I gradually picked it up until I became an experienced [hand] finisher and I was able to find work during the busy periods.

Soon Lily moved from hand finishing to machining. Machinists (men were called machiners) were paid more than finishers (the difference between 30s (£1.50p) and £2 10s (£2.50) in the early 1930s) because it was a much more skilled job. When Lily switched to the machine:

> I'd go into a factory, and say I was a machinist, get half a day's experience and get the sack because I couldn't do it. Maybe a couple of days later I'd get another job as a machinist and last a day, and so on until I became an experienced machinist and was able to claim I was an able machinist.

Jane Smith, daughter of the Pimlico engineer described above, was equally impatient. She earned 8 shillings (40p) a week as a learner to a waistcoat maker in Soho, a situation which she regarded, in the same way as Lily, as a 'waste of time':[26]

> And I was taught, I had no papers of apprenticeship . . . I was paid a poor wage in order to learn the trade, that's what it amounted to. My father didn't find the job, my sister found the job . . . she worked in a little workshop in Marshall Street, Soho, and they used to let out sittings for tailors. There'd be a

big room and there'd be tables, half a dozen tables, and each tailor had a table with his goose iron (have you ever seen a goose iron? It was a large chunk of iron with a handle which was put into a gas heater, and it was ... used for pressing, shrinking work. It was recognized that women weren't capable of handling this huge iron) and his equipment, and his sewing-machine, and he had what is called his 'hand', that is, a female to help him ... And he was called a journeyman tailor ... And we made clothes for gentlemen, in inverted commas if you like! ... And my sister knew a number of tailors because she'd worked there for some years, and she said to one of them, 'I've got a sister who wants to learn the trade, who we think we ought to teach the trade', and somebody said to her, 'Well I can do with a girl.' And I remember very well I was paid 8 shillings a week by virtue of the fact that I was learning a trade ... Well, now, they estimated that it would take me five or six years. But I learnt it in little over a year, and I branched out on my own ... it wasn't going to take me six years.

Having grasped the essentials of the work, as well as the nicer distinctions between women's and men's skills (women did not become journeymen tailors unless the widow of a tailor, and even then they probably made only the 'smaller garments'), Jane left, and found herself employment as a tailoress to an Irish waistcoat maker for 30 shillings (£1.50) a week. She was determined to set up on her own: 'I was a bit rebellious ... I wasn't the kind of person that was going to be satisfied with anything less than getting what I wanted to get.' When I asked her later what she meant by rebellious, Jane replied that she 'didn't take things for granted. I had my own views.'[27] Presumably it was to protect themselves from the competition of young women like Jane that the West End branch of the Tailors and Garment Workers' Union excluded women from membership.[28] Undeterred by mere custom, Jane began touting for work and joined the union. She paid her subs regularly, had a strong sense of skill learned from her father, and had read widely the labour papers and the books on her father's shelves which included, apart from *The Ragged Trousered Philanthropist*, Jack London, William Morris, and Upton Sinclair.[29] But, as every woman knows, knowledge and skill in themselves are not always enough to overcome male prejudice:

I canvassed the shops, and I went in and said, 'Do you want a good waistcoat maker in this shop?' And, if you'll forgive me for saying this, I was ginger-haired and freckle-faced and quite a lively youngster, probably a bit unusual, not beautiful or anything like that, but I had this pale skin that you do have,

and this ginger hair . . . and I was something of a rebel, a red
from an early age. So it may have been that they were attracted
to me. But I did manage to get work, and I did manage to make
waistcoats.

So a father's trade could impart confidence and raise expectations as
well as provide access to skilled work; wider kin were influential in a
city of small trades and diverse industry and with a huge service sector;
but a mother's word was usually final. She was in charge of the family
budget and, for the first years of earning at least, took most of the
young woman's wage:[30]

You'd walk home, like the men had done in the past, with your
wage packet. She'd open it and give you back your five or ten
shillings. It was a hangover from the Victorian days, and you
were equivalent of the man in the family.

For most young women their first jobs were a compromise between the
rude structure of the local labour market, family need, and their own
hopes. Surprisingly, what emerged in conversation was the extent to
which the women felt they had chosen their occupation. 'I *wanted* to go on
a machine,' said Margaret Payne, the ninth of eleven children in Bermondsey. She was restless until she found her niche in a leather factory, in
which industry she remained, always working in South London, refusing
promotion (she did not want to be in authority over the other women and
girls) even though she designed for the firms and trained the younger
women. When I met her in the late 1970s, she was an outworker,
respected and still designing. 'I wanted factory work,' said another who
became a coil-winder in Woolwich; 'I couldn't stand an office.'[31]

Recognition of social divisions and inequalities slip into speech
unobtrusively, and they mediated choice: girls who went into office jobs
were 'well-to-do' or 'well spoken'; others were the 'commonest of the
common'. The girl who won a coveted scholarship to elementary school
was the 'daughter of a professional man, the local detective': in private
domestic service, or higher-class restaurants and shops, you 'met a
better class of person'. Most women and men from the London poor
still situated themselves within a hierarchy from 'respectable' to 'rough'
which covered the uneven terrain of different religions ('We went to
church three times on Sunday,' May Jones told me; 'we were a cut
above'), degrees of 'slovenliness', book-learning, and levels of skill too.[32]
I say 'still' because this is a hierarchy familiar to all students of late-
nineteenth-century London and one which reproduces itself tenaciously
in popular memory. Divisions within the working class, or among the
poor, are remembered in detail – which is partly the inevitable perspective of the child whose vista is immediate: the family, street, and school.

But the young women born into those families and streets remembered them so intensely partly because they wanted to escape from them. A good job and – best of all – marriage seemed to be the way out.[33]

The exception to this general, albeit attenuated, sense of choice were those girls who had wanted to continue in education. They felt disappointed and sometimes angry that they had been forced to leave school at 14. Even if they had won a rare and coveted scholarship to trade or secondary school the cost of school uniform and the family's need for money prevented them from taking it up. Among the very poor, even a learnership was beyond their grasp; it was too low paid for too many years. 'My mother wanted my dibs from work,' was a mild reproof. 'I wasn't dumb. I passed a preliminary trade scholarship at 14; but she had to have the money come in,' was another.[34] This sense of disappointment never left the women. It had different effects. It left powerful feelings of ambivalence towards both their mothers and the homes they did not want to reproduce (notwithstanding the equally ubiquitous memory of community as a child: 'No one ever locked their door'; 'Everyone was in and out of each other's houses'). In some it contributed to a fine sense of social injustice which led to trade union or political work with the unemployed, against fascism, or for the working class (there was no feminist consciousness *then* among the women I interviewed).[35] But, the sense of disappointment also contributed to the low self-esteem to which many of the women of that generation fell prey. Education was longed for by more than were permitted to have it, and those who 'spoke well' and 'knew a lot' were admired and often envied by others deprived of an education. Those young women who did yearn to improve themselves, attended evening classes, acquiring skills in the ways described above, and cultivated their appearance and social life too for good measure.

Lives were narrowed by the lack of education and by family poverty, but this narrowing was not always immediately clear to the young women themselves. All the women I spoke to felt themselves then, they said, lucky to be in work when brothers and fathers were often unemployed.[36] And there was also the excitement of leaving school and earning a wage, and of long skirts and new hair-styles which seemed to anticipate a new independence, a new self.

— Becoming a woman: dress —

A child's appearance changed when she took her first job. Dodie was scarcely tall enough to reach the cashier's desk when she started work at the greengrocer's; nevertheless her hair was up. Younger brothers and sisters were left behind with the schoolroom, learning by rote, the Saturday job, and street games, as the need to earn a living propelled the child into the adult world of work with new preoccupations and responsibilities. The transition was keenly felt. Rose (Dodie and Luli's younger sister) had won a place at a private school when she was 13. She was able to attend because the earnings of the older children relieved financial pressure on the family; and while she remained in a drill-slip until matriculation at 16, her friends from the old elementary school 'had perms and handbags and ear-rings'. Boys as well as girls underwent this transformation. They appeared immediately after their fourteenth birthday in long trousers:[37]

> If their mothers belonged to a clothing club there was a fair chance of a new pair ready and waiting, but more often their first pair were cut-downs, the slack folded into a belt, and the crotch halfway down their thighs. They slicked their hair with water into a quiff above their foreheads, and half a comb stuck out of the top pocket of every jacket.

Dress not only marked the transition from child into adult, it also carried the visual weight of sexual difference, and held too the promise of daydreams and drama. Images and identifications acquired and rehearsed in play as she was growing up were elaborated and sustained in the imagination of the young woman with every new pair of shoes or special outfit. For, paradoxically, if the changed appearance was the most immediate outward sign of the 'abrupt and final' end of childhood, then as a form of self-imagining it also signified one of the continuities between child and woman. Most little girls (and little boys) loved to dress up. Rose Gamble's description of Lu's love-affair with 'a disastrous black-and-yellow dance dress, the skirt heavily encrusted with jet beads' that she wore to school every day, for instance, recaptures the occasional bliss experienced by a child normally clothed – as so many children of the poor were – by the ingenuity of mothers and sisters putting together bits and pieces brought home from work, or gleaned from jumble sales, or charitable cast-offs.[38] Others remember the white frock worn for coveted ballet lessons, the red tap shoes, 'sexy' black silk knickers under black wool tights for gymnastics in a Holborn trade school, a flowered straw hat, white socks and embroidered frock for Sunday school in Hackney, and so on. Every such memory enclosed an imaginary identification with a graceful or beautiful self which both anticipated the woman she would like to become, and transcended the hard work and poverty around her. And when later on she squeezed into stays and embroidered white cotton knickers, or into brassières and liberty bodices under synthetic silk frocks with perhaps high heels and a piece of fur, she felt herself someone new and different.

English historians often attribute the relative affluence of the young working girl, and her new self-image, to the growth of individualism, the absorption of middle-class values, and the beginnings of the consumerism of the 1950s.[39] These are partial truths but they miss the dynamic of sexual difference. Looks figure in a woman's psyche on the whole more than in a man's. Dress both declares a woman's femininity to the outside world and is one measure of her own self-esteem. Few women neglect to describe their appearance, or forget what they were wearing at vital moments in their lives. Anyway, clothing factories producing cheap frocks and skirts in Tottenham and Edmonton, make-up, cinema, and dance halls were not part of a middle-class culture *before* they were used by working-class girls and boys. Cinema was always a cheap urban entertainment, which had to be cleaned up before the respectable or polite would attend.[40] And although individuality could be accentuated by the new pleasures – if only by lifting each person momentarily out of the uniform drabness of poverty – the process was under way long before the advent of cheap consumer goods in the 1930s.

When I first spoke to women I asked about their first job. I was interested in their work. Only later, when transcribing, did I notice the insistent presence of dress, romance, and leisure. In speech (as in life), work, love, family, and politics have trouble keeping to separate compartments of the mind. Day-dreams and reverie impose continuities across different sorts of activity as well as past and present. Day-dreams – a blend of inner imago or memory-trace with everyday life – gives fantasy its repetitive pull, and gives each of us our sense of self as surely as class position, relation of kin, ethnic identity, or religious or political affiliation. And although the joy of a new frock, the memory of violence, or separation make full sense in their particularity only in the context of an individual life history, they also can outline the contours of a shared emotional economy.[41]

— Memories of authority: deprivation and separation —

Clothing children and keeping the family clean were time-consuming and laborious. One woman's memory of her appearance in school commemorates for many the time and effort put into school 'outfits' by mothers and the way in which the teacher used to single her out from the other girls:[42]

We were very well-dressed in these pieces of material that my mother used to knock up, or have over. Bits from jumble sales and that. 'Cause my mother made everything. I didn't have anything from a shop until I was 16. We were always brought up in front of the class to show how we looked, with a piece of rag machined round for a hankey, and a pin, and all that sort of thing. That was before the secondary school. But we was always that little bit – spotless clean, of course, you know, and always had the shoes for Sunday. We were never allowed to wear the shoes in the week, or the socks, or the rig-out for church, you know, it was death if you ever asked to put it on in the week, because they used to be put away for the weekend . . . You just had them for Sunday, and let me say, it gave you a sense of values that sticks with my sister and I, for ever and a day. Not my brother, he was a spendthrift.

In May's account we glimpse something of the tempo and discipline of the domestic routine of their home in Stepney. May's mother lived with her three children, their grandfather (her father, 'whose word was law . . . everything that was said or done was referred to him. He was the head of the household'), and 'any available cousin' that her mother took into the grandfather's four-roomed house in Stepney. Her husband had been an oyster-sorter on the London docks. He died of pneumonia when May was six weeks old. May's mother worked through the nights making shirt-blouses with leg-o'mutton sleeves by machine and hand-sewing at sixpence a time; she cleaned in the early mornings and evenings and waitressed over the weekends. She dressed their grand-father (who always looked 'very smart, he drove a hearse') and her son in the same way she did her daughters, and took pride in her own appearance. She was, in May's description, 'fantastic! A handsome woman'. May's mother was not exceptional. The working week for mothers was one of ceaseless activity – its rhythm broken only by the Sunday rituals.[43]

The singling out of the respectably dressed child was not an unusual experience either. School was substantially about ordering through example, exhortation, praise, and punishment. Just as children learned by rote, and were lined up by teachers in silent single file in corridor and playground, so too they were regularly inspected for nits and ringworm, their heads shaved if either were discovered. Apart from the damage to the child's self-regard, this could bring painful ostracism from peers. Rules of health, cleanliness, and appearance were imprinted in the child's mind for another reason too. Childhood fears of abandon-ment and separation, of spectral figures threatening severance from loved ones, are probably universal; and in the 1920s and 1930s poverty or illness could make them real. Scarlet fever, for instance, meant having your head shaved, being removed from home and sent to isolation hospital for perhaps six weeks. For May Jones the experience was traumatic. She wore a 'sassafras' cap of carbolic soap on her shorn head, and was sent to the 'depths of Kent':[44]

> You never saw your parents or anything like that ... If you were unfortunate enough to have kidney trouble it was three months before you ever saw your parents. There was no question of them ever coming to see you. You're in tin huts – oh shocking ... there used to be such terrible, terrible loneliness.

May's horror of scarlet fever fused with stories she had heard from mother, grandfather, and sister – 'family stories' – about 'Dr Barnardo's coming with the van' to take three children away after her father had died of pneumonia. Her mother had sent them packing, but no one explained to May why they had come or who had sent them.

The London poor had a long memory reaching back into the nineteenth century of arbitrary intervention into their homes and families. Family stories told of interference from city missionary or charity visitor, and these then reinforced suspicion, alienation, and powerlessness when faced with the relieving officer, teacher, or anyone well dressed and well spoken in authority. (Educated speech was as important a social distinction as occupation or income and gave content to the division between 'them' and 'us'. Rose Gamble's description of the ladies who ran the mother-and-child clinic in Chelsea where her mother worked – for instance, they 'knew exactly what they were going to say before they said it' – is as succinct a description of what class difference could *feel* like as Beatrice Webb's 'I belonged to a class of persons who habitually gave orders.')[45] But from the child's perspective, the public humiliation that the school or official from another world meted out was often less distressing emotionally than the effect of such discoveries on their mother when they returned home. The condition of her children's health, hair, and dress was one measure of a mother's self-respect and status in her neighbourhood. The child's fall from grace was a reproach to the mother's capabilities, a sign to the neighbours or street that she had been momentarily defeated in the battle against bugs, infection, and ill health, which, although the product of bad housing and lack of amenities, was a constant challenge to a mother's skills, and was understood as such by herself as well as others, 'What will your father say? ... What will the neighbours think?' sprang to the lips of so many mothers faced with disaster.

A mother's disappointment or disapproval was often reprimand enough to keep a child in line. Most remember themselves – especially in conversation rather than written autobiography, and probably inaccurately – as obedient. Anger might provoke a smack, or clip round the head, or, in some families, a beating with brush or belt from either parent. Some children feared their fathers. Doris Bailey's father (a french polisher; they lived in Bethnal Green), though kind, generous, and good to the children when sober, became violent and terrifying after drinking:

> Many a night, my young sister and I lay in bed petrified, listening to the almighty din downstairs when someone or something had crossed his path and made him angry. Sometimes Mum came running up the stairs and came in and sat quietly crying on the end of our bed. He would come belting up after her. He would open the bedroom door and point down the stairs. 'Come down and take your medicine,' he would say in a queer and level voice, and she would go sobbing down the stairs, and the thumping began again.

Violence was not part of every child's family life, but it was present in most overcrowded neighbourhoods, as much as poverty and drink. Both were associated with men rather than women. 'Drinking and pubs went with manhood,' Doris Bailey wrote, 'and I knew no different.'[46]

For a whole generation of children raised in an atmosphere of constant anxiety about inadequate clothing – inadequate for warmth or comfort, inadequate to meet the teacher's approved standards of decency and respectability, and inadequate to ward off ridicule from one's peers – the first items of clothing bought with the wage-packet are remembered with undimmed pleasure. Mrs Murphy, a wire-winder from Woolwich, sitting in her daughter's South London council flat fifty years later, gestured with her slender ankle and foot as she recalled the penny-three-farthing pairs of stockings that she and her friends used to buy:[47]

> and, you know, buy myself a 4s 11d [25p] pair of shoes perhaps. The best shoes you could buy was only 6s 11d. Beautiful shoes we used to buy for 6s 11d. They used to be flat heeled, two-inch heels. The best ones were black patent with a lovely silver buckle.

It was as though those shoes eradicated the memory of men's boots, patched and restored, of huge slopping grown-ups' thrown-aways, or stiff heavy uncomfortable new boots that were worn through school-days and form part of every child's memory of the 1920s and 1930s. Every reminiscence describes the misery and discomfort of leaky boots, chilblains, or shoeless feet of the very poor during their schooldays in the inter-war years. No one I spoke to ever went without shoes themselves, but all remember other children barefoot. Shoeless children, like 'nitty Nora', bugs, the pawnshop, guardians, and relieving officer are part of a shared memory of poverty.

— *Rebellion and glamour* —

The new consumerism may be charted in reminiscence. Detonated by mass production, its growth was uneven and rooted in local traditions of distribution and desire. Until the late 1920s, for instance, make-up was primitive, though improvised with inspiration:[48]

> Of course, we were particularly heavily made up in those days. Make-up was, what shall I say, a tin of erasmic, twopence. No such thing as eye-black, we didn't know. We used to stick a matchstick up the chimney and ruin your eyes once and for all. Make a ring around your eyes and cut your eyebrows with a pair of scissors. There were no tweezers or anything like that.

Those who did wear make-up — still quite rare in the mid-1930s — were in the avant-garde of young womanhood. Would-be heroines have pinched their cheeks and bitten their lips to bring colour to their faces since time immemorial. But until the First World War in London, make-up was the mark of the prostitute, the fast woman. Vera Brittain, herself no amateur in the art of self-adornment, dismissed a maid in the summer of 1918 because she was 'clearly an amateur prostitute who painted her face ten years before lipstick began to acquire its present fashionable respectability'. (She also smoked 'pungent cigarettes,' another sign of the modern young woman.)[49]

Dress or self-representation was in this sense a symbol of defiance, a gesture of independence often combined with risqué friendships or love-affairs, each a statement of individuality, of distance from siblings and parents. 'We were living with my father as a family,' the daughter of the Pimlico engineer confided:[50]

> and we were very hard up. We both of us smoked — in defiance as far as I was concerned. I mean . . . I started to smoke when I was something of a bloomer girl, suffragette. Defiance. Had my hair cropped, and I was, you know, childishly to some extent, asserting myself.

Cropped hair and cigarettes, bloomer girl and suffragette: Jane's rebellion, we have seen, took the form of defying her father and learning a trade.

May Jones chose romance for her rebellion. She went dancing at the People's Palace in the Mile End Road with[51] particular girlfriends that hadn't had a disciplined upbringing. You sort of got more saucy and more cheeky in their company, you know ... You went and had a port at the Three Nuns – that was a regular outing, without my mother knowing. This girl and I, we used to get ourselves three penn'orth of port to get ourselves in the mood, so we'd float away in the tango and goodness knows what.

Later, May defied her carefully protective mother by marrying the manager of a public house whom she had met in secret. Theirs was a 'romantic marriage', a deliberate breaking from mother, sister, and the environs of the East End. It did not last long and brought much unhappiness, but in her mind it was associated with romance and everything that her mother's life was not.[52]

Young women growing up in streets and houses overcrowded with dirt and noise, as well as people, watched their mothers and fathers and learned what it meant to be a woman. 'I was never told to do the housework,' May Jones remarked; 'I just saw it done.' 'I want to grow up to be a man,' Rose Gamble had declared. Looking at their mothers, they saw economic hardship, hard work, and neglect from husbands who were often unemployed, who drank, or who abandoned them (a recurring image in reminiscence and autobiography is of mothers waiting for their husbands to return, or watching them leave).[53] They experienced want as girls and young women and heard their mothers talk of it. Overhearing women talking, in the streets or in their kitchens, was a vital source of knowledge. Stories were of childbirth, abortion, death, sex, and money, and listening to them was usually forbidden.

What was allowed to be heard and spoken was surrounded by as much taboo and prohibition as what was, and was not, allowed to be seen. No speaking at mealtimes, no speaking out of turn, no answering back. May Jones remembers standing in the window of their front room in Stepney and seeing a woman with a fat belly walk past. 'What's she got in her tummy?' she asked her mother, and received in reply a hit across her face. The silence surrounding sexuality, particularly female sexuality (there was no word for 'pregnant'; the term for 'menstruation' was 'the curse'; when Angela Rodaway tried to describe what she knew about sexual intercourse she found she had 'no words to say what I meant'), underlined women's lack of self-esteem.[54]

Most young women expected to marry. This 'expectation', reiterated in official sources, denied them training and economic equality, and made them, it was alleged, difficult to organize, preoccupied with romance, and so on. Yet knowledge of sex, reproduction, and their own bodies was random, haphazardly learned, and often wrong. 'We learned the dirty way', was a phrase often heard; or from peers, or sisters, or 'in the playground', but seldom from mothers. Time and again I was told that women went to childbirth 'completely ignorant'.

By the end of the 1930s more and more young women were able to refuse their mother's lives, not because they had new jobs, and cheap clothes, but because they could have fewer children. Everyone I asked said they had had fewer children deliberately. Several had been thus urged by their mothers, like Jean Moremont: 'The only thing my mum ever said to me was, "Don't have a load of kids." '[55]

This wanting to live lives different from their mothers had – if education failed them – enormous impetus from the cinema. By the mid-1930s the department store, Oxford Street, and its local equivalents had begun their reign as the Mecca of fashion for the working girl, site of her much-vaunted new affluence. Court dressmakers continued to turn out stiffened satins and brocades, and shop windows still displayed their clothes draped decorously on plaster busts. But high fashion failed to capture the imagination of the young. Mimetic images of Harlow, Garbo, and Crawford paraded in the high street, as they glowed across the cinema screen. Few, in the 1930s, could afford the new clothes in the shops. Mothers, sisters, and friends hastily put together copies of their clothes with material a few pence a yard from market or cheap department stores.

'I had girlfriends who worked in dressmaking and millinery,' Celia Wilmot explained:[56]

> We'd get them to make us a hat, and it was really something unusual, or they would make our dresses for us, and they could make the dresses for a mere 10 shillings [50p] . . . Oh, I was keen on clothes, very, very keen on dresses . . . As a young girl, basically one considers one ought to be smart. One would buy a black suit with a check colour, and then you would get a white flat hat with a black-and-white ribbon round it, match it all up. And you'd have your white gloves and your black-and-white shoes, or your black shoes, but you would, on occasions, you would be smart. But you only wore them on Sundays to start off with . . . and you only went out shopping just before Whitsun and just before Christmas – twice a year . . . I even changed my bag to make the colours correct.

Shopping was a ritual, a tribute to a special occasion, and one willingly saved up for. Window-shopping, on the other hand, was a more regular enjoyment, like the cinema or dancing. Helena Rubinstein claimed to have democratized glamour, but the sewing-machine, mass-produced in the early twentieth century, often inherited from mother or mother-in-law, bought on hire-purchase, played its part. In this way, via the high street or the sewing-machine, the mantle of glamour passed from the aristocrat and courtesan to the shop, office, or factory girl via the film star.

There is no doubt that the film star transformed popular identities of femininity. Not all women identified with film stars or wanted to be like them. It all depended on what sort of woman you wanted to become. Angela Rodaway, for instance, who discovered ecstasy for the first time when her writing was praised at school, and who like Jean-Paul Sartre took an almost physical pleasure in words and poetic feeling, wore open-necked shirts in imitation of Shelley, and developed a limp in sympathy with Lord Byron.[57] Rose Gamble, we have seen, wanted to become a man when she grew up. Jane Smith, though aware of the appeal of her curly hair and bright blue eyes, had her heart set on a proper trade and socialism. Only some drew a sharpened sense of self from the images on the screen and the stories they acted out (it was extraordinary the number and versions of 'rags-to-riches' which came from both Hollywood and British studios in the 1980s, and how rarely the heroines (Jean Harlow and Ginger Rogers from the US and Gracie Fields and Jessie Matthews from Pinewood) were shown anywhere near domesticity). May Jones spoke for many when she described going to the cinema once a week or more, and then 'You acted out what you saw the rest of the week.' The high heels and tilt of the hat gave the illusion for a moment of wealth, of abundance, of being like Greta Garbo or Ginger Rogers:[58] 'You probably saw the film round two or three times for sixpence, so you got the proper gist of it . . . and you used to walk along the road imbued with it, caught up with it.' The cinema offered to millions *en masse* an alternative to their mothers, schoolteachers ('flat-chested, hair scraped off their faces, tortoiseshell glasses', was one description), and the upper classes. The vamps of the 1920s, Garbo, Dietrich, Carole Lombard and Mae West, were a long way too from the familiar and colloquial sensibilities of Marie Lloyd and her contemporaries, with whom perhaps their mothers had identified.[59]

But these new images of glamour were fitted over old. 'The East End has a long tradition of glamour,' I was told by a friend, born and brought up in Stepney. Most reminiscences include someone like Celia's aunt, a cleaner all her life in Covent Garden, who 'loved it' and was[60]

> very pretty, lovely curly hair, and she dressed well. My impression of her is with a satin hat wrapped like a turban round her head with a rose underneath. That was gay, exciting.
>
> She was a very lovely woman, and very exciting in her dress.

Arthur Harding, East End villain and autobiographer extraordinary, dates the passion for fur coats among the women of Bethnal Green from the beginning of the First World War.[61] Allowing for masculine contempt, his explanation for the phenomenon is probably accurate: it was a time of unexpected affluence, when the men were away, and women 'went mad on furs and pianos'. The point was that furs could be bought cheap. Pieces of fur, like everything else enjoyed by the poor, could be bought in weekly instalments. May told me:[62]

> lots of furs we used to have then. We used to buy them on the weekly ... it was the local coalman used to sell them, you see. He used to sell shoes as well. Coal and shoes always went together, 'cause you used to pay sixpence a week for your coal, and he always used to chip in with the shoes. He was an executive, not the coalman actually who brought round the coal; and you used to pay him, and that used to be your shoe bill and your coal bill ... He used to bring half a dozen pairs for you to try on.

Celia recalls wearing a fur she bought at a jumble sale, cut down and altered to the latest fashion. She wore it on a demonstration against unemployment, with a hat and veil, as they shouted, 'We want bread!' By then she was earning the high wage of £4 a week, and the fur coat had cost her £5.[63] Poverty and unemployment did not preclude small luxuries; nor, in spite of Orwell's famous equation between cheap luxuries and political palliatives, did they necessarily inhibit political consciousness.[64] The unemployed in London in the 1930s did not belong to a separate culture from the young who wore the lipstick and went to the cinema.

The cheap trappings of glamour were seized on by many young women in the 1920s and 1930s, frustrated in their wish for further education, yearning to escape the domestic treadmill of their mothers' lives, haunted by the fantasy, not of the prostitute as in the nineteenth century, but of the glamorous screen heroine who paradoxically could be you, the girl next door. But if adolescence is when everything seems possible and identity is in flux, when the imagination yields to convention and restraint only with difficulty, economic conditions in the inter-war years ensured that the flamboyance and flourish of most working girls symbolized by their dress were brief. The discipline of the production line or typing pool, prefigured as they were by school, public authorities, and parents, curtailed, if it did not entirely repress, high spirits as the young entered the labour force. Speed-up and the piece-work system were blamed for illness and breakdown; supervision was strict, and the hours of work long. Unemployment, of course, was the most severe disciplinarian:[65]

> All I can think of is, you could never be out of work – you could never, ever be out of work ... You left on a Friday to go

somewhere else on the Monday ... you dared not be out of work because there wasn't any work, you see. And now, even after all these years, even now, as you say, I've just practically left at 65, quite candidly, you never lifted your head. It's a remarkable thing, but you don't. You do everything precisely and correctly because you dared not lift your head in those days. There'd have to be a complete revolution for you to leave. You were never out of work. You went sort of from one job to another.

And later, marriage and motherhood produced different aspirations and responsibilities. The self-assertion indicated by the silk stockings or piece of fur were replaced, though not forgotten, by children's needs and the demands of husband and household. Dress for most mothers became a symbol of lack not excess. At least that's how some remember their mothers in the 1920s and 1930s. 'She had no vanities,' Rose Gamble wrote of her mother:[66]

But now and again a pretty pattern would catch her eye, perhaps on a scrap of cloth in Dodie's bucket, or on a roll of lino standing outside the ironmonger's. 'I'd like a frock of that,' she would say, showing just for a moment that she still had an occasional thought for herself.

1988

FEMINIST HISTORY AND
PSYCHOANALYSIS

Feminist history has been slow to draw on psychoanalysis – which is odd given the – to some extent – shared preoccupations of psychoanalysis and the women's movement. Who they were was of absorbing interest to the Women's Liberation Movement in Britain and the USA in the late 1960s and early 1970s. The first British national Women's Liberation Conference held at Ruskin College, Oxford, in 1970 was a history conference.[1] If feminist scholarship in the USA was literary and radical feminist, then English feminist scholarship was historical, its polemic socialist and humanist. Women's history in the early nineteen seventies sprang from that utopian and romantic disposition – 200 years old – which sought to tell women's stories in their own words, to invent new vocabularies for women, and to re-map the divisions between the personal and political.[2] This disposition reaches back to the feminism of Mary Wollstonecraft – at least – which struggled to reconcile a reformed femininity with the revolutionary notion of a democratic political subject.[3] Feminist history's first self-designated task – to recover women's experiences – involved, and was swiftly followed by, the ambition to transform the whole body of historical knowledge.[4]

That first wish of feminist history – to fill the gaps and silences of written history, to uncover new meanings for femininity and women, to propel sexuality to the forefront of the political mind – shares some of the intentions and scope of psychoanalysis. Whether the unconscious is traced through the familiar routes of the early Freud, via slips, jokes, dreams and symptoms; or installed in primal fantasy as Melanie Klein suggested; or inferred, following Jacques Lacan, from the gaps, silences, absences in speech, what is central to both feminism and psychoanalysis is the discovery of a subjective history through image, symbol and language. There is a close proximity between the concept of the

— 225 —

unconscious and the unspoken histories of women's lives at the very foundation of psychoanalysis. In an encyclopaedia entry of 1923, Freud begins with the relationship between doctor (Josef Breuer of Vienna) and patient (Anna O) as the 'best way of understanding psychoanalysis'.[5] By listening to the hysteric and allowing her to speak, Freud uncovered the place of memory and female desire in the aetiology of hysteria, and shifted the constellation of neurosis from women's bodies to the centre of psychic life.[6]

The coincidence of the appearance of psychoanalysis with the gathering of the women's movement in Europe and the USA at the turn of the twentieth century explains the intermittent, if sometimes antagonistic, fascination between the two (like the feminists, Freud referred to his movement as 'the cause' in the early twentieth century). For both Freud and feminism, femininity was a problem to be deciphered and understood. At two important moments – the 1920s and the 1970s – psychoanalysis and feminism have converged in deliberating the question of femininity and sexual difference. Psychoanalysis, concerned with the unconscious and sexuality in the formation of the subject, began to consider the possibility and meaning of female desire – issues which preoccupied feminists since at least the seventeenth century – only after the first world war. During the twenties and thirties, femininity arose as a problem for psychoanalysis; the issue was – how does a woman come into being, was a woman born or made?[7] Feminism in the '20s was also arguing about the nature of woman, this time as a political subject. Should women demand what they want as 'women' on the basis of their different needs, or as 'workers' and 'citizens' like men? Within psychoanalysis, the debate about femininity was eventually suspended, replaced by an increasing focus on mother and child. The women's movement faded too during the thirties, surpassed by the political urgency of unemployment and fascism, but also undermined from within by irresolution and conflict about women's proper place and what women should want.

By the 1970s the protagonists were differently aligned, the debate between psychoanalysis and feminism more direct. In the USA, radical feminism rejected Freud, seeing psychoanalysis as diagnosing a problem – femininity – whose political solution – feminism – it either ignored or repressed.[8] In England, on the other hand, some feminists who had read Freud and Marx drew on Lacan's reading of Freud to explain the constitution of female subjectivity in and through language. The difficulty for historians was how to reconcile this notion of a sexed speaking subject with historical materialism's privileging of class.[9] Cora Kaplan's essay on three centuries of women poets in England and the USA, noting the very high proportion of women's poems which have been about the right to speak and write, suggested that women's poems – romantic and lyric – use metonymy as a 'way of referring to experience suppressed in public discourse.'[10] Luisa Passerini's work on memory and subjectivity in fascism and autobiography, my own on female subjectivity and unconscious fantasy in early-nineteenth-century radical movements, and Alex Owen's exploration of women's mediumship and spiritual possession as forms of resistance and female power in the nineteenth century, all employ a psychodynamic notion of subjectivity;[11] while Carolyn Steedman interrogates dreams, memories and family stories to give an account of the reproduction of mothering in the 1940s and '50s as a process which failed.[12] Poverty, absence and envy shape female desire in Steedman's acid yet poignant counter to the nostalgia of men's autobiographies, which have imprinted a sentimental portrait of mothering on working-class experience in the twentieth century.

And yet, feminist history's interest in Freud and psychoanalysis constantly meets those resistances in the wider profession excavated and so eloquently challenged by Peter Gay. Historians, he discovers, resist any deliberate use of psychology and psychoanalysis, in particular because of its ahistoricism, its inapplicability to anything other than neuroses or the irrational, and its individualism; and they ask anyway how can we analyse the dead? Gay – rare among historians for having undergone a training analysis – asks for a 'welding' of historical method with psychoanalysis's scheme of human nature and development. The historian can, he suggests, interpret dreams, read private journals as though they were free association, understand public documents as condensations of wishes and exercises in denial; he can tease out the unconscious fantasies underlying popular novels and art.[13]

The unconscious fantasies underlying fascism have preoccupied feminist historians since the coming of age of the children of those regimes in 1968. (Psychoanalysis has often been allowed to explore the 'irrational' in history.) Maria-Antonetta Macciocchi argues that an intimacy between women and fascism was carved out by Mussolini in Italy in the 1920s, by the promise of the vote (later withdrawn); the creation of a female death squadron; the production of a 'feminine semiotic'; the injunction to women to give birth; and the use of public ritual and spectacle.[14]

Drawing on Bertholt Brecht's analogy of the pimp/whore relation to describe the relation fascism/women; on Virginia Woolf's assertion that the oppression of women and Nazi repression have the same roots; on Antonio Gramsci for his discussion of the irrationality of fascism; and on Wilhelm Reich's emphasis on the sexual repression which dictator-ship feeds on and which is linked to death, her urgent task is to uncover the extent and causes of women's consent to fascism, in order to place women 'as protagonists, who are responsible, and in any case never innocent'. And in this cause she evokes – though not as a psychoanalyst, only as a 'political militant' – the instincts of women; female masochism and the death drive. The problem of consent, argues Macciocchi, lies within the psychic structures of femininity. There was no rational reason for women's support for fascism under the Duce. Their labour was grossly exploited, their sons killed, their husbands symbolically castrated; they were enjoined in a marriage with Mussolini which was sexless, chaste and deathlike.

Fascism's repudiation of femininity and women's consent are the concerns too of Claudia Koonz's study of women in the Third Reich. No-one was innocent, Koonz argues. While women took no part in the planning of the final solution, nor – except for a few thousand camp guards and matrons – did they administer murder, almost as many women as men voted for the National Socialist Party between 1930 and 1932 and supported the women's bureau under Hitler for as long as it advocated the dream of family and home. In a social order which polarised the sexes down to the last walk – MEN TO THE LEFT, WOMEN TO THE RIGHT – women left the business of genocide to the men, or so they remembered, and so Koonz reconstructs.

Psychoanalysis implicitly informs Koonz's analysis of the Nazi state. National Socialism constituted a special order founded on gender and race, on eugenics and genocide. Whatever its contradictions in practice, the heart of its vision lay in 'a dream of a strong man and a gentle woman, cooperating under the stern guidance of an orderly state'. The SS administrators of the 'death machine' 'managed to remain sane while committing subhuman jobs'. These men were not brutal or hardened sadists, Koonz asserts, but imposed on themselves a split reality. Obeying orders was their public responsibility, while in their private fantasy – sustained by wife, family and home (strong family men were chosen for these jobs) – they deceived themselves into thinking they were not 'bad after all'.[15]

Koonz shares with the Frankfurt school an emphasis on the internal-ization of a punitive and relentless authority in the psychic formation of fascism but, like Macciocchi and Klaus Theweleit, the responsibility for fascism is placed firmly on the mentalities, the psyches of the fascists themselves.

Klaus Theweleit's study of the Freikorps literature (the volunteer armies of 1918–23 which, he claims, prefigured the Nazis) assumes that these men meant what they said. What they spoke about was their hatred of women, their dread of women's bodies and sexuality and their wish to kill them. Anti-semitism discovers its emotional source in this revulsion which itself springs from the infant and its fear of being engulfed, swallowed up, sucked in by the mother's body. Theweleit thinks that these fantasies belong to all men, whereas Barbara Ehrenreich points out first, 'that not all men murder', and secondly, that 'these Freikorpsmen do not emerge on the plain of history fresh from the pre-oedipal nursery of primal emotions, but from the First World War'.[16]

If we follow the logic of fascism's deathly antinomy, the full horror of its unconscious repertoire, then it is easier, perhaps, to understand the recent withdrawal from sexual difference by some feminist historians. Two influential books refuse the 'monotony' of a psychoanalytic understanding of sexual difference.

Joan Scott moves in favour of deconstruction which evacuates the subject from the centre of both history and language. The concept of gender (understood as knowledge of the relations of power between women and men) is divested of any psychic subjectivity and adjudicates the many meanings assigned to sexual difference, class or race (though race, as in most north American and European feminist history is muted).[17]

Denise Riley, poet and philosopher as well as historian, prefers the discursive construction of the category 'women' in the hope, following Foucault, of an eventual dissolution of all identities. Can anyone 'fully inhabit a gender without a degree of horror' she asks, recalling Mary Wollstonecraft's caution that women should forget their sex, 'excepting with a lover.'[18]

The place of the psychoanalytic notion of sexual difference in historical work cannot be insisted upon. A history which takes into account an understanding of memory as contingent, of culture as inimical to the drives, of mental life which is irreducible to consciousness, and of subjectivity which is both forced and irresolute, is in no way an easy one to write. But the problem is that by excluding the unconscious, we lose the concept of psychic instability. We also jettison fantasy, the generative figurative form of psychic life, an integrative moment in all mentalities. Such a loss has implications beyond the reach of feminist history.[19]

Julia Kristeva has written of two notions of time which have haunted philosophy, literature and science since the beginning of the twentieth century: monumental and cursive time on the one hand, and the sequential, linear time of history on the other. Women, she implies, insofar as they are mothers, inhabit the former, which converges with Freud's understanding of unconscious time – timeless and repetitions. Women do seem to slip – in daily life as in philosophy – into this latter temporality. But rather than accept this placing of female subjectivity and the severance of the two temporalities, we could bring to bear an awareness of repetition, fantasy, and the resistances which constitute psychic life, as we write the histories of women, of sexual difference, of mentalities.[20]

1990

MEMORY, GENERATION AND HISTORY

TWO WOMEN'S LIVES IN THE INTER-WAR YEARS

I want to describe two women's memories of growing up in London in the inter-war years. My concern is with the formation and processes of memory, the transference of spoken testimony into written history, and finally, with what an individual's memories might tell us of the history of female subjectivity in Britain in the first half of the twentieth century. Jacqueline Rose, in her study of Sylvia Plath has written of the way in which a personal present may be engendered by a historical past. Sylvia Plath – a poet – used the memory of the Holocaust as a metaphor for her own life. I am interested in the ways in which the individual life-story might engender a deeper historical present, and in the inseparable dialectic of individual and historical memory.[1]

Plath's inventive borrowing suggested two thoughts: the first the unavoidable trauma involved in the constitution of the self; and second, the force of cross-generational memory. Both psychic trauma and generational memory – originary processes of subjectivity – belong to the common mentality through which notions of citizenship in mid-twentieth century Britain were lived.[2] The imagined citizen of the 1940s – a moment to which politicians and the media still persistently return – was a mature and responsible adult, convinced of the need for both democratic domestic provision and individual liberty, decent comfort and educational opportunity; values which were shared across the political spectrum.[3] The formation of that notion of citizenship involved some inevitable forgetting.[4] The aim of this essay is to indicate through two women's life-stories, some of the elements of both that unknowing and forgetting.[5]

The two women belong to the generations of women and men born in the first twenty-five years of this century who left few documents of their own, but whose lives seem familiar partly because their experience is within living memory.[6] The lived experience of this generation both informed and was constituted by a constellation of events which reshaped personal life in mid-twentieth-century Britain, giving new impetus to modernity. Firstly, the epidemic of social investigation from the 1880s into poverty, slums, sweated labour and the health of the imperial people eventually produced William Beveridge's 'five giants' in the 1940s: Want, Disease, Ignorance, Squalor and Idleness. A vast literature on the conditions of the people between the 1880s and 1940s provoked the thinking behind the social policy and legislation of the welfare state.[7] Secondly, these were the women whom Donald Winnicott, the pediatrician and psychoanalyst, watched and to whom he listened as he formed his notion of 'adequate mothering' in the Hackney and Paddington Green hospitals from the 1920s. Their overheard conversations and observed habits and customs prompted his understanding of 'inner reality'.[8] And finally, these were the women whose young womanhood was circumscribed by two world wars whose effects included both the death of men and the shattering of illusion.[9]

Memories of war, welfare and the aspiration of good enough mothering – left their imprint on everyone born in England and growing to maturity during the 1940s and '50s.[10] We know something of their effects: inherited melancholy, four-hourly feeding schedules, strong teeth and bones from the extra milk and vitamin C (malt and minedex), the division of children into grammar schools and secondary moderns, and a new self-confidence that the young had a right to the future.[11] We also know something of the policy inspirations and bias of mid-twentieth century welfare and advocacy of adequate mothering – the poverty surveys from Booth to Cadbury at the turn of the century, for instance, whose revelation that between 30 and 40 per cent of the population live on or below the poverty line has been repeated at regular intervals since; the Webbs' minimum standard for civilised life which they derived from trade union history and collective bargaining; the school dinners, Old Age Pensions and the national insurance of Liberal legislation of 1906–11; unemployment (in particular men's) during the 1920s and '30s, 1940s radicalism and anxiety about 'race suicide'.[12]

In different ways the poverty surveys, welfare legislation, unemployment, 1940s radicalism and population anxiety each foreground domestic life. But as they focused on economic remedies for inequality and poverty (believing that enriched spiritual and emotional lives would develop if the material needs of the mass of the people were met) domestic life was narrowly conceived. The vision of an educated people, housed in homes fit for heroes, with a safety net of social welfare to rescue the unemployed, sick, old and disabled from the contingencies of unemployment was an honourable, necessary but limited response to universal suffrage in the 1920s. The 'citizen' of Labour's new (parliamentary) democracy was made up of – as well as components of labourism itself – Fabian elitism, residues of the deserving and undeserving and flashes of the idealism of the Independent Labour Party; he was usually a man – a soldier, working man or urban householder. From the 1940s he was an undogmatic English patriot too, convinced of the common sense of social welfare, a chastened imperialist. He was formed in the image of those who made him: the professional civil servants, conscientious social legislators, and other left intellectuals who included self-educated men who were driven with a sense of ambition and improvement for their class as well as themselves.[13] The few women who shared in the shaping of Labour's social vision were mostly self-effacing if driven in the interests of clan and national unity.[14] As Margaret Bondfield, former shop assistant, said on becoming the first woman cabinet minister in 1929,

> I am what I am not out of any personal virtue, but because all
> my life has been in the training ground of corporate bodies and
> of different organizations, and I am merely the product of the
> work of hundreds of thousands of unknown names.[15]

Women, though citizens too, were the economic dependants of men and their place was in the home. Social reform and the politics of social conscience since the First World War had been about poverty and education for citizenship. A healthy family life needed homes and 'family planning'. Home in the minds of the English reformers and legislators (who by the 1940s were a more professional class than their predecessors) was the site of domestic comfort and maternal welfare (both family allowance and good enough mothering). In that guise it swiftly (by the 1950s) became surrounded by the dead weight of political inertia.[16] The political imagination failed when it came to the family as, with rare exceptions, it still does.[17] We know already, we think, all there is to know about domestic and family life; this knowingness is one of the deepest psychic political sites of conservatism.[18]

The traces of a generation are remembered and figured through legislation, hospital practice, psychoanalysis, statistics and social policy as well as fiction, film and family story. Thus they work their way into what Raymond Williams has named the 'structure of feeling' of a generation.[19] I find this notion of Williams' evocative though inadequate for my purpose. Perhaps because it's evident from his conversation with the editors of the *New Left Review* that structure of feeling refers to what is left out of a materialist, class analysis of culture. Structure of feeling serves in Williams' thought as a sort of repository for the minutiae of everyday life in a social formation whose determining relation is class. I don't believe that the affective life of a generation can be evoked as the residue of class. I want to retain the affectivity and the reference to generational possession embodied in the structure of feeling while relinquishing that term's dependence on class. Carolyn Steedman recently pointed to the limits of Williams' understanding of history for feminist historians. His history wants to connect everything to everything else; it searches for the totality of a culture, or for the reproduction of culture as a whole way of life.[20] Feminist history on the other hand seeks to identify the gaps, the silences in histories – not only in the hope of restoring a fuller past (though that might be something of the effect) but to write a history which might begin from somewhere else.

Subjectivity could be that somewhere else. I have written elsewhere of my understanding of that concept.[21] Here I would simply underline several of its features: that subjectivity is the location of sexual difference; it links past with present through memory and phantasy; the times of subjectivity are over-determined and composite; subjectivity reveals the relation of phantasy to the real (reveals is not quite the right word, betrays would more aptly describe the inadvertent revelations of the connection between the two); and it always involves an unconscious dimension. Life histories, as they tell us something of what has been forgotten in cultural memory, always describe, or rehearse a history full of affective subjectivity. As with a poem, they may suggest the metonymic signs of femininity particular to a generation.[22]

Both psychoanalysis and feminism in the twentieth century have been intrigued by the words and experience of women. Both have put pressure on women's memories, have drawn them out to yield new forms of knowledge. I situate my own work at the intersection of these two movements. If – as Virginia Woolf once wrote – 'we think back through our mothers if we are women'[23] – then can that thinking, (using 'our mothers' for the moment as a metaphor for those intergenerational lineages of mostly oral and feminine identification and exchange) be used to move beyond the history of femininity to remap the history of twentieth-century structures of feeling? Only whereas in psychoanalytic theory the girl's relationship with the mother remains resolutely in the pre-oedipal domain (Jessica Benjamin, the object relations analyst and writer, recently asked for a developmental theory of femininity which would situate the relation with the mother in history)[24] as a historian I want to write a history which retrieves that maternal dimension.[25]

These issues – of generation and memory; of subjectivity and history

– beg the question of identification between the historian and her subject. Alessandro Portelli has defined the interview as a common project between the historian and his interviewee (reminding us by the way how the partiality and subjectivity of oral material reveals the partiality of all history).[26] Karl Figlio has written of the possibility of transference between the historian and his/her interviewee in oral history.[27] I want both to acknowledge my own investment in Portelli's project with Figlio's transference and to add the dimension of generation. Eighty years ago Virginia Woolf, a 'benevolent spectator' at the 1913 conference of the Women's Co-operative Guild in Newcastle measured the distance between herself and the working women delegates of the Guild: their minds fixed on Divorce Law reform, taxation of land, the minimum wage, education for children over fourteen, labour saving appliances, housing reform, maternity and the vote – preoccupations of women's organisations in the first decades of this century which created that public awareness of the need for reform of domestic and personal life which I have already noted. Woolf noticed the delegates' determination and resolution, their discreet clothing; their bodies 'thick-set and muscular', their hands large with 'the slow emphatic gestures of people who are often stiff and fall tired in a heap on hard-backed chairs'. She felt only an 'aesthetic sympathy' she lamented which touched her through sight and imagination rather than through heart and nerves, and which differed from real sympathy because 'it is not based upon the sharing of emotions unconsciously'.[28] Even if all their demands were granted, Virginia Woolf wrote, they would not touch a hair of her own head. My generation, on the other hand, grew up in the achievement or at least the aspiration of some of those demands. I identify with both Woolf's wish for a room of her own, and those Guild women tired with work, who strove for order and clarity in their lives and communality in their demands. Those women were literally my/our mothers' mothers. If both the political cultures of Bloomsbury Labourism and the Guild's Socialism (which enabled the affinity between Woolf's feminism and that of the Guild) have eroded, then the gulf between rich and poor remains, but it is differently fashioned in political affiliation today. As my generation of historians have 'thought back through their mothers' they have heard more than the wish for decent housing, public health and welfare for the people, but what they have heard has yet to distil – remains turbulent – in the historical mind.

The first of my two women is Lily Van Duren, born in 1914, in Minton Buildings, Brick Lane, the daughter of Jewish parents, who fled to the

East End of London in 1910 from the Russian pogroms. She spent ten years of her childhood from the age of six, in a Jewish orphanage in West Norwood:

> I would have to go back to my parents to explain why I was at an orphanage ... I know this sounds a terribly sad story, but actually it's true – my parents were Jewish refugees from the pogroms. And they – from what I've been told, because naturally I don't remember, I've been told by relatives later in my life – they came here in 1910. And both my mother and father had been married before. And each had a child from the previous marriage. My father had a son, my mother had a daughter. They must have been married in Russia of course, you know, to come over together with these two children. And then there were two subsequent children. There was my brother, who's three years older than I am, and I was the youngest.[29]

Lily's parents came to the East End, where other relatives were living – 'some old grandparents', her mother's sisters, Rebecca and Mary, shadowy figures, and where her father could earn a living as a cabinet maker.[30] Her mother's trade is not mentioned.

The 'sad story' continues with Lily's first memories: of being wheeled round the streets in a 'big basket-work pram' because she had been born with a congenital dislocation of the hip, later cured at Great Ormond Street Children's Hospital. The second memory was of herself crying, and her mother:

> ... my mother coming in with a candle, into the room. And I have the vague impression there was another child or more in this bakery ... That's the first memory I have of my mother. The second memory of her is seeing her at home in bed, obviously very, very ill indeed. And the next thing that I remember is ... I think I was about four years old (my brother) was about seven ... I remember on this particular day, my brother and I came home from school, midday, and we had to go up a flight of stairs, and there was a door at the top, and ... we knocked ... And there was no reply. I assumed ... in my mind, that this was very unexpected. And then my father came home, he had the keys and we got into the flat. And then I could see my mother lying on the floor in a white nightgown. And the next thing I remember was ... a whole lot of adults, all dashing about all over the place, saying, well, 'the gas was on', and 'did she do it on purpose?' and 'why was she lying here? Perhaps she came out to have a cup of water and was overcome by the gas.' But it was obviously a case of suicide.[31]

Lily's relations seemed to want to take one child each, but each 'had their own families', and there were differences between her mother's family, who were Orthodox, and her father's who were not, so Lily and her brother remained with her father. The children's move to the orphanage was precipitated by a scene with Lily's step-sister, sixteen years older than Lily, who finding Lily, dressed for the Jewish Sabbath in her best frock sitting in the middle of the street, punished her by locking her in the lavatory. Lily climbed out of the lavatory window, a sheer drop to the ground below, smashed her face, and spent six months in hospital. Her father then decided that he could not look after his children himself anymore. The first weeks in the orphanage – a 'posh house', an Elizabethan mansion in West Norwood – visiting was once a month – was marked by misery. Separated immediately from her brother, the boys were in one room, the girls in another, she screamed and screamed, 'in such terrible agony, you know, mental anguish' that her brother was allowed to visit her every afternoon.

These stories were told, with digressions to describe details of the working day in Whitechapel (families lived close to work, so they could return home for lunch, hence the discovery of the mother in the middle of the day) in spite of the questions the interviewers threw in. The foundations of Lily's self had a momentum of their own, and the flow of memories only stopped when each sequence – culminating in her arrival in the orphanage – was in place.[32]

Until this point, Lily's narrative coincides with the history of Jewish exile and immigration.[33] Her place of birth was Whitechapel, but her origin is Russia, her position in the family prefigured by half-siblings of her parents' first Russian marriages whose only role in the story (confirmed by tales of subsequent neglect by profligate brothers – compulsive gamblers, they 'left me to starve') is destabilising. Lily's story proceeds: she left the orphanage, becoming a learner at a Court Dressmaker's in the West End, she lived with her brothers who did not pay the rent, she moved from East-End workshops to the factory end of the trade in Tottenham, and learning to machine, she became a finisher by trial and error. Her story becomes one of lonely survival in a brutal world. A world in which the ways she hears herself described – at the orphanage by one of the non-Jewish housekeeping staff as a 'little heathen': at the Court Dressmaker's, as a 'cheap little girl'; and in the factories as a 'hand – the only part of my body they was interested in!' – become dynamic terms of both identification and resistance.[34] Identification because the low estimations from the outside world contributed to Lily's developing sense of herself as a working-class woman, parentless and poor; resistance in that they spurred her to defy the values of those in authority over her. Her search for employment, training, her friendships in the Independent Labour Party and Communist movements were in part driven by a desire for other values; a better life, another set of relations.

The internalisation of such attributions – described elsewhere as 'the hidden injuries of class' – are difficult to evaluate.[35] Lily remarks that the insult to the orphans was 'hid inside every child' where it damaged self-esteem. Memories of insult are often told through humour and mild self-mockery. The anger they prompted could lead to political activity in the labour and socialist movements which were determined to right such wrongs during the 1920s and '30s, and not only in Britain.[36] Lily Van Duren's personal story blends in the telling with the Labour Movement's histories of the working class, and the merging of personal with epic time – the time of class struggle, of progress, of revolution – reveals the psychic potency of such historical identification, whether one believes that it rests on myth or on a philosophy of history which owes something to truth.[37] When Lily moved from the pacifism of the Independent Labour Party to Communism in the early thirties (a move which many others made too) fascism, anti-semitism mirrored the violence of her own origins.[38]

That merging – or rather, the understandable wish to merge – with the subject of historical materialism, with epic time – however, has its limits, particularly if the subject is a woman. Communist and socialist politics were inimical to personal histories other than those that would fit with class struggle, and there are traces of misogyny in their literatures.[39]

As Lily's life-story unfolds (unevenly through four interviews across a period of years) so her sense of self is dispersed across several identifications: as a Jew, her status as the 'apple of my father's eye', an orphan, a neglected sister, a seamstress/machinist, a pacifist and a Communist. The discovery of her femininity as she describes it belongs less to her inner world (no further references to her mother in the interviews which followed) than to an outside world of imposition. Gender division is experienced with the force of inevitability: she was her mother's second daughter, the boys and girls were separated in the orphanage, this distinction reinforced by work. Girls were taught needlework and mending in the orphanage and later domestic science, which 'consisted of washing up'.[40] At fourteen, they were sent to an LCC Housewifery Centre in Streatham for instruction in cooking. From twelve years old the the orphanage girls were informed that they would enter the clothing trades, the boys the cabinet or other woodworking trades.[41] Once in the workshops and factories, men's work and women's were always differentiated; pay was the divide – women's work was cheap labour. Women were not in the unions, or not very many of them. During the early thirties Lily was involved in the attempt organised by the Communist-led breakaway from the Tailor and Garment Workers' Union, to unionise women workers in the Totten-ham factories.[42] They were not interested – 'a dreary lot' she laughed, adding that it was probably the low wages, the expectation of marriage that inhibited them.

Lily's politics were learned from the family into which she was born, the pacificism (of the Independent Labour Party) of the people who ran the orphanage (the early 1920s), the Workers' Circle in the East End in the late twenties, early thirties.[43] In 1936 Franco's invasion of Spain – 'Spain was then a little democracy' – persuaded her, and others of her friends to abandon her pacificism: 'the ballot box was not a good idea'. Lily joined the Communist Party after meeting her future husband in Trafalgar Square at a rally for the unemployed. He was a steward. He asked her what she was doing. She was on her own, looking for her friends. He and his friends would look after her, he said, and they have been looking after each other ever since.[44]

Lily's childhood memories of migration, death, family disintegration, East-End poverty and factory work rehearse in minor key the histories of Jewish settlement in London, labour history and the history of international socialism and anti-fascism in Britain in the inter-war years. Lily draws on each of them to describe her changing sense of self and to give her personal history political definition. Her femininity is only an intermittent often disruptive presence in her life-story. Disruptive in the sense that this feminine self, formed through division (what she can't remember), separation (the 'mental anguish' of death and the orphan-age) and disparagement ('a cheap little girl'), is difficult to combine with the heroine of the narrative of emancipation. Lily began her story with a series of memories organized around loss, death and separation; the loss of her mother was sealed by the loss of language. All the children at the orphanage spoke English:

> ... it got to the stage where – when I would go home for these
> four weeks in summer, I wouldn't be able to talk Yiddish to my
> father anymore, at all – it was, became a lost language to me.[45]

Lily's father died when she was eleven.

The association between sexual difference and loss and death is closer to the surface of Liz's life-history. *Liz* is a fictional first person 'story' of 'growing up in Hoxton', in the East End of London between the two wars. Liz's narrative, like Lily's, tells of poverty, inadequate schooling, casual work in the clothing factories, and like Lily's, Liz's story begins with what has been lost (in this case, youth, employment, life), only Liz's is a story with no heroism – class or socialism – at all.[46] It owes something to romance, more to anecdote and gossip. Liz's Hoxton is the Hoxton of music hall and nostalgia: the weekly bath in the kitchen, street games, 'nitty Nora' and the sanctity of the mother's parlour. There's a glimpse of the modern at the cinema, but Hoxton's 'important places' were the music halls, where pleasure was found; the missions, which fed the poor; the hospitals where care was to be had. Both joy and survival for women in the early narrative depend upon the skilled improvisation of the weekly budget, later on the dangers and excitement of her body and sexuality.[47]

Liz's story is rooted firmly in the geography and landscape of the East End, but its tension unfolds through the changing significance of her body:

> At fourteen Liz had changed in looks and figure. Her hair had developed a natural curl and was a golden brown. Her skin was perfect and her grey eyes, with the help of long eyelashes, were perfect. She knew as she walked through Hoxton market she had more than her share of attention from the stall holders and shopkeepers. 'Hello, beautiful' and 'how about it tonight?' were very common calls the men made to her as she went to work.[48]

Sacked from her first job because her boss paid more attention to Liz than his wife, Liz's story is punctuated with references to her good looks, and those of her friend. Isabelle Bertaux-Wiame, in a study of migration in France, has noticed how women telling their life-stories speak less in the first person singular than men.[49] They use we, or 'one'; their lives are told through the social relations in which they live; in Liz's case friendship, especially with Peggy, and mothers and daughters. Liz and Peggy smooth fully fashioned nylons up their legs, put on a full Max Factor pancake make-up aged fourteen sitting in the backyard with a broken mirror, totter in cheap high-heels, wear french knickers with pretty frocks and suits, and once, a stolen mink coat. All this on a few shillings a week – sometimes. Work is only ever casual. They measure their success in wolf whistles and the envy of older women. If femininity is masquerade, then these girls in Hoxton in the late 1930s are living it to the hilt whenever they can.

The provocative pleasures of young womanhood in Liz's account are haunted by 'menace'. Something 'evil' happened to her when a child of eight. A friend's father took her into a room and 'made her lie down beside him'. She never told anyone anything, and she always felt guilty, just as later, when 'used' by a young man she knew, she never spoke of it, to him or others.[50]

Childhood knowledge of sex came in fragments – fragments of drama and violence: the Old Maid's shop where pills for everything were sold, including miscarriages; the school playground, where Liz heard that when babies were born they 'cut you open' and that as a girl 'blood comes to you every month', something which when it happened made her scared and ashamed. Mothers knew about sex; they decided too whether a girl who fell pregnant had an abortion or kept the child.

Liz's friend Peggy falls pregnant; her mother takes her for an abortion and she dies.[51] Liz is made pregnant by the man who 'uses' her. By then she is a young widow, it is 1945 and the world has changed.[52] The changing context of femininity is signified by Liz's visit to the clinic where a young 'lady doctor' examines her, asks her only if she 'is looking forward' to the child. The doctor is without prurient interest in either her body or her condition. She's a product of the soon to be born NHS. Liz leaves happy, single, pregnant and cared for. She spends the rest of her life working to support herself and her child within London's East End. Her son is the love of her life.[53]

I have tried to show through two women's different telling of their life-stories, firstly, how loss and knowledge of death constitute two psychic motifs of female subjectivity in the twenties and thirties in Britain (and indeed they reappear again and again in the spoken and written life-stories of women of the period); and secondly, how both death and loss were underwritten by the historical conditions in which these women lived. Lily Van Duren's first memories are of loss in which the historical and the autobiographical fuse. The illness and suicide of her mother, the dispersal of kin, the forgetting of Yiddish, the death of her father – were the result of migration and exile; experiences which characterise modern urban life. They haunted Lily's sense of self like a sort of modern possession.[54] London was a city of migrants; wave upon wave came from the countryside in the nineteenth century, migration from Ireland accelerated during the 1840s, and from Russia and Europe from the 1880s. All came in search of work, and were supplemented by small influxes from China, Italy, Spain and elsewhere, especially around the docks and in the new East London suburbs.[55] Dominant political culture remained resolutely English.[56] I mentioned earlier the conservatism in the psychic conception of family life in the mid-decades of the twentieth century. The conservatism stems also from what was repressed from national memory. The body politic was the nation, relations within the nation were those of class, and without were colonial, but the two seldom came together in the political mind. A bizarre illustration of their estrangement comes from Ellen Wilkinson's memoir. As a child in

Manchester at the turn of the twentieth century she learned her skills as a public speaker and performer from the Methodist Sunday Schools, the Band of Hope (temperance) and missionary meetings where she tells us she made speeches 'dressed as a Chinese or Indian girl'.[57] What for Ellen Wilkinson was performance, for many young women and men in Britain was a division lived in private emotion.

Liz's first memories on the other hand evoke a working-class East End cast in a spell of warmth and colour and humour first broken only by sexual knowledge. Liz's sense of self sprang from an awareness of the meanings and functions of her female body whose femininity generated fear and shame as well as fun and anticipation. The female body registered uneasily in public speech: obliquely in the mystical sentences of Marie Stopes in 1919; as a source of female hysteria in the years immediately after the First World War; transmuted through mother-hood – the most important of 'women's occupations' by the end of the 1930s.[58]

If loss and death are two prefiguring motifs of psychic femininity, then they are too those of early twentieth-century modernity. Death of men in the First World War (four million deaths in Europe) marked every psyche and was continued and underlined in the epidemics of shell-shock, VD and influenza which all cast their shadow on the emotional economy of women through the 1920s and '30s. The pogroms of Russia and Eastern Europe continued before and after the First World War. The statistics of infant and maternal mortality in the inter-war districts although declining – among the poor – confirm the psychic association, between female sexuality and death, towards which these life-stories gesture in different ways. The medical profession's tardy support of maternity provision through the national health service in the 1940s were grounded in the details of such women's lives. These conditions of the people whose psychic economies were haunted by emptiness and dislocation, formed the foundations of a new democratic optimism, of welfare politics in the 1940s and '50s – the home was the 'only factor of the democratic tendency in the social system' Winnicott wrote in 1957.[59] The twentieth century needs a new wisdom for a new age, John Maynard Keynes had written in anticipation in the early 1920s.[60] To the extent that that mentality was feminine – its changing conditions concealed both undercurrents of the broken literacies and family lineages of migrant peoples, and the sometimes violence of sexual desire the measure of which – in each case – is only now being taken.

1994

FEMINISM: HISTORY: REPETITION

SOME NOTES AND QUERIES

Repetition in the vocabulary of psychoanalysis refers to the pressure of unconscious mental formations on consciousness which may manifest as 'acting out' in analysis through the transference or in the subject's everyday life.[1] (Freud was careful to distinguish between 'clinical material' and real life only when it suited his purpose. In practice he was less fastidious in the distinction: Freud listened to himself, family, friends and patients to develop and illustrate his ideas.) Acting out is the neurotic's way of remembering. Unless this sort of unconscious material is 'worked through' it will drive us unthinkingly to repeat. If the material is worked through (by remembering, removing resistances, making conscious unconscious thoughts) in an analysis or elsewhere, then it shifts or reshapes itself in a way which leaves the ego less in thrall to myth.[2]

I rehearse the psychoanalytic meaning of repetition from Freud, because I wish to make the point that in psychoanalysis it has a particular meaning: it can refer both to unconscious material, and to forms or patterns of behaviour. Can the historian borrow this term from the mental life of the individual and apply it to social phenomena? Is it appropriate or legitimate to move from individual unconscious processes to forms of national, ethnic and religious conflict in Europe, Ireland, the former Soviet Empire, Africa, the Middle East, or anywhere else in the New World Order today?[3]

If historians do borrow 'repetition' from psychoanalysis' vocabulary, then does that return human mentality to the foreground of determination? Does that invest human nature with more historical force than say – geography, climate, the economy or language? Or does it simply remind the historian, that knowledge of all these phenomena is organized through human mentalities?

If today there is a turn to psychoanalysis for an understanding of the movement of events in time then it is because – momentarily? – philosophies of history have failed us.[4] They no longer provide us with a justification for politics or ethics. Or rather, the justifications they provided for an ethical politics have failed. We can identify aspirations – justice, equality – but for a political generation of historians (those born in the late 1930s, early 1940s) who were perhaps the last to be seduced/convinced by historical materialism, it is no longer clear how those goals may be reached or by now even whether they are desirable. Historical materialism told us which way history would be moving, and who would be its political beneficiaries. Fearing that our parents may have been right, that ideologies are never benign, that no history ever tells the truth, we nevertheless still seek a theory of history which could provide the ethical basis for action. Now we have lost this historicist moralism, or have we? Is the turn to psychoanalysis a repetition of this wish?[5]

There are other reasons for the turn to psychoanalysis. Firstly, the 'new' political movements of the 1960s and '70s raised again the questions of identity and desire, and psychoanalysis offers ways of thinking through these issues from the unconscious formation of desire to the return of the repressed; from the violence of psychic repression to the unconscious power of myth; and identity, desire, myth and psychic violence dramatize every political event.[6] Because feminist politics go to the heart of psychic conflict in their interrogations of sexual difference, feminists appropriated and developed psychoanalysis to explore both identity and desire, and beyond.[7]

Secondly, since democracy – within and between nations – is once more open to re-interpretation, psychoanalysis's focus on the individual subject offers a way to think through political identities whose subjectivities may be divided against themselves, as well as against a common enemy.

And finally Freud's psychoanalysis is relentless in its exposure and explanation of illusion: it refuses icons even as it deals in myths.[8] It tells us that there is no authority over the soul – except the divided self.

When I was asked to reflect upon the ways in which the feminist slogan of the '60s – the 'personal is political' – might be recast in the light of the psychoanalytic concept of time, I thought immediately of the way in which so many of the discontents of feminism are repeated again and again, even in the same vocabulary as far back as the seventeenth century. In the 1870s Lydia Becker, suffragist and Manchester Liberal, echoed the words of the seventeenth-century sectaries, that the Soul knows no distinction of sex. Feminists from 'Sophia' in the 1740s to now, want an end to male lust and speak of masculine tyranny. What women want, feminists have always argued, is independence from men, equality with men, a full and equal citizenship. There is a continuum of fears of male violence, anger at men's tyranny, envy of men's power which runs throughout feminist speech.

Feminists also always identify with other oppressed peoples: slavery was the most common metaphor in the centuries before and after the anti-slavery movement; some feminists from Olive Schreiner and Eleanor Marx in the 1880s to Winifred Holtby and others in the 1930s identified with the colonized peoples of British imperialism; in the 1970s Mary Kelly writing in the Women's Liberation Workshop's journal *Shrew* aligned the women's movement to movements of national liberation, in particular the Palestine Liberation Organization.[9]

What does this recurrence of grievance mean? What is being repeated in feminist discontent? Let us first distinguish between the conditions of femininity of which feminists complain – inequality vis-à-vis men in law, government, the economy, the family for instance – and feminists' perception of those conditions. Are the latter – that is the shared *idea* of women's wrongs – the product of a shared unconscious, the residues or effects of a psychic-symbolic conflict which is simultaneously reproduced within each individual which then some in each generation act out in conditions which are historically contingent? Western politics, literature and conversation are remarkable for the constancy of some women's anger, but that anger does not always take the form of a political movement which then articulates it as a measurable response to legitimate grievance. The solutions to the injustice will differ too: from Friedrich Engels' contention that the entry of women into waged work will liberate women from the patriarchal family, to the wish of Wollstonecraft and Kristeva for the dissolution of the distinction of sex.[10]

If there is repetition in the discontents, there's repetition too in the patterns of the women's movement's demise. The reasons for the demise have always been both internal and external. Disagreements among feminists about the aims and purpose of the movement drives them in different directions, only sometimes taking their feminism with them. In the 1880s the women's movement faltered in the face of the rise of social purity, and disillusionment with the Liberal Government's reneging on women's suffrage. In the 1920s after the achievement of the vote (almost), feminists argued within and between organizations about the priority of equality or difference. Unemployment, malnutrition and the rise of fascism in the 1930s for many feminists seemed more important than sex inequality, leading them into the socialist and Communist movements. In the 1970s and '80s the Women's Liberation Movement (WLM) was internally divided on political lesbianism, separatism and race, while the external pressures undermining unity echoed the 1930s: unemployment; poverty; and the politics of war (the Falklands; the Gulf; and Bosnia).

At every fading of the Women's Movement in the nineteenth and twentieth centuries, the political emphasis has passed from woman to child – a fact which needs more elaboration since it points to feminism's central dilemma – the incessant articulation of woman as mother.

Feminists always emphasize the need for women to demand and organize themselves; but they can't achieve their aims without forming alliances. Alliances with socialists, labourists, communists and liberals always (and I will risk the absolute) break down on the question of the form of the family: who will bear and rear the children; what will be the division of labour; the challenge to the heterosexual imperative?[11] If feminist discontent (and I'm aware this is not a very powerful word to use to evoke a movement which some may feel has life in it yet) is a structure of feeling – present, indeed endemic in the cultural life of a liberal nation, then so too is the desire for sexual difference and family life and child-rearing to remain around the gender divide.

It's worth mentioning perhaps that the political debates and campaigns initiated by feminism which have been most circular and recurring in both the nineteenth and twentieth centuries are those dealing with the most intimate areas of life: housework, male violence, sexuality and domestic living. The repetition here is partly a measure of the difficulties encountered and the limits of feminists' ability to tackle them. Most recently the Women's Liberation Movement's attempts to theorize women's exclusive responsibility for domestic labour failed because housework proved intransigent to the application of value theory. No government has reorganized work or industry in favour of childcare; women, the majority of workers today in Britain simply work part-time with the help of babyminders and schools, or wait for the children to grow up. Meanwhile unemployment, not feminism, has driven men to help with the dishes, when they do.

In the 1850s, some of the women of Langham Place, recognized that one of the reasons why their enterprises were moderate, small in conception, was the collapse of earlier utopian dreams which had been crushed by a combination of economic mismanagement, and the weight and conflict of passionate natures.[12] The communal events of the Women's Liberation Movement of the 1970s have been hardly less dramatic, ending sometimes in violent emotional disarray and despair. This history has yet to be written. Much has already been forgotten.[13]

Why these circularities; repetitions? Why is there no resolution to feminist grievance? Can the issues raised by the Women's Movement never be worked through? The 1990s WLM, like its nineteenth-century predecessors, tried to confound the divisions between the personal and the political and in particular to politicize the sexual. Politicize the sexual and what emerges are incest, rape, war crimes all those abominations about which, as David Owen observed in 1993 of the incidence of rape in the Bosnian war 'What is there to be said?'[14]

In the 1970s, the question of a possible politics of the unconscious was raised and dropped.[15] The question is hovering again on the outskirts of political debate, to remind us (if we needed reminding) of the difficulty that all political affiliations raise. The slogan 'the personal is political' has not exhausted its potential. It has been suggested both that history repeats itself (Marx's suggestion that history repeats itself twice – first as tragedy, secondly as farce) and that history has come to an end.[16] Both propositions ignore the psychic dimension of history. Political histories cannot be reduced to the psychic, nevertheless historians should take note: repetitions in the constitution of human subjectivity – among which sexual difference is the most insistent and irresolute – are structured historically through law, kinship, the economy, for example; they are grounded in the body, figured in space and speech. The human subject is formed through fantasy and identification, processes as historically resonant as Fernand Braudel's *longue durée* and as slow to change. Feminism's recurrence suggests that no resolution to political struggle is ever final; but also that repetition is the time of the unconscious, which is only ever one of the composite times of history.

1993

ADULT LEARNING

RUSKIN, 1968–70

THE UNIVERSITY OF EAST

LONDON, 1992–

I went to Ruskin in 1968. I was a housewife and mother of one daughter, separated from my husband; twenty-five years old. I had worked as an actress since I was seventeen – not very successfully. I was a member of Equity, the actors' union. Uncertain of myself, my future, I had worked with a literary agent named Clive Goodwin, to set up a radical newspaper, *The Black Dwarf* (I had made the tea and collected money); I had done some voluntary work at the Blackfriars Settlement; I had been on demonstrations. I had read a few novels (Sartre, Camus, Murdoch, Margaret Drabble in the early sixties; before that the Brontes and Dickens); I had passed my 11 plus and O levels; I had struggled through English A level by correspondence course. I qualified for Ruskin – just because I had left school at fifteen and was a trade union member with no independent means of support. I wanted knowledge and I didn't know how to acquire it. A friend of a friend told me about Ruskin. I slipped in after an interview with Billy Hughes the Principal, and an essay, a few days before the beginning of term when there were always drop-outs; men who could not leave their families.

I was an unusual student for Ruskin. I was a woman. Most of the women students were on the social studies course training to become social workers. A few studied literature. I began the Oxford Diploma with a term of economics and political theory, certain that this was the way to understand the world outside me. But quickly dissatisfied, I became one of the first students on the History Diploma. (I tried to change to Labour Studies when I realized the Oxford Diploma wasn't for me, but I couldn't attract the attention of any of the tutors.) The 'structure of feeling' at Ruskin then, was very masculine. Men still spoke of skills, of themselves as working men, of apprenticeship unions and of employers as another breed of men. Wives and children were left at home. The politically active combined pride with anger; a sense of exclusion from the establishment with a strong sense of belonging to a labour and often a socialist tradition. My presence was anomalous and I felt silent and inhibited throughout the two years. I lived out of college; my daughter attended nursery. But my diffidence, lack of self-definition, low confidence were typical of Ruskin students – miners, electricians, white-collar workers. So too was my desire to learn, my wish to understand the political and economic world in which I lived.

Studying was an effort; writing a nightmare. I took several hours to read one chapter, or ten or fifteen pages, taking notes, at the end of which I was demoralized and *terrified* by the future essay, tutorial or – worst of all – seminar. I never spoke in a seminar at Ruskin and never presented a paper. The thought made me physically ill. Writing was preceded by paralysis, nausea, despair. Misery. I was talked through the process by men friends: Alun Howkins, Martin; and my tutors helped. Victor Treadwell taught me how to read books, discriminate in argument, follow my own judgements; Raphael Samuel's inexhaustible historical imagination encouraged me to enjoy research, to risk the archives and primary sources, to write history.

Our tutors used Oxbridge methods. We were given an essay title, long booklists and in tutorials our tutors outlined the main themes of the essay. We were sent packing to abundant libraries (we still complained that we couldn't find the books). These teaching methods – jettisoned by the polytechnics during the seventies, eliminated by the expansion in higher and further education in the past ten years have fallen into disrepute. It's true they ran the risk of capsizing students in the sea of their own ignorance, but in conversation, in periods of reflection, students acquired splinters of illumination, an awareness of reservoirs of knowledge elsewhere.

The point of this story is to make a comparison between mature students then, and the students – also mature, similarly qualified (or not) I teach now in east London. My students are the beneficiaries of the expansion in higher education which economic decline has forced on the governments of the past ten years. These students too approach learning with fear and awe, study is strange, writing difficult. Learning and trying to write can arouse feelings of futility and worthlessness. Learning – the pursuit of knowledge – can be as psychically perilous as it is exhilarating. Learning needs time, books, space, sympathetic and intelligent tutors. Ruskin gave students two years of these.

Marxism was the economic and political vocabulary that Ruskin radicals wanted to understand and speak within in the late sixties (as it had been in the 1920s and earlier when the College was founded). Young men then seized on the labour theory of value, the distinction between social labour and labour power and expounded it painstakingly to the rest of us – an admiring and receptive audience. The idea that history had a purpose or a direction appealed to Ruskin students too. There were sceptics: those who believed that the world was governed by self-interest and that the point of Ruskin was self-betterment. The majority of students believed in Labour's (or the Communist Party's) gradualism – democratic ethics. Industrial democracy was close to the heart of most students I knew. Only a minority worked with the revolutionary groups.

I didn't read Marx thoroughly until I left Ruskin. And then I read volumes 1–4 of *Capital* in a Women's Liberation reading group. But my interest in political economy was stimulated at Ruskin. There I read some of Marx's economic pamphlets, his essays on France and extracts from volume one. The mysteries of commodity fetishism; the enigma of the labour theory of value fascinate me still but history captivated me. From Edward Thompson I discovered the literariness and excitement of radical cultures; from Keith Thomas the ways in which belief encompasses magic, religion and science; from Eileen Power a supple and enticing prose. History offered a literature of narrative, causality and agency. It gave me details of other ways of life and thinking. Through reading primary sources I entered other worlds, heard other people speak. I let their words and thoughts enter my consciousness. This changed me.

I emerged a feminist, an apprentice historian with a strong sense of purpose. I read history at University College London, worked one day a week in the Women's Liberation Workshop and spent much more time at meetings – organizing . . . Later in the seventies I taught in adult education, worked in the women's and labour movements, and was a founding editor of the *History Workshop Journal*.

I am now a senior lecturer in history and cultural theory in the Department of Cultural Studies at the new UEL in Dagenham. On the fringes of the Becontree Estate, north of the fast-becoming derelict perimeters of Ford (which looks like a cross between the straggling main streets of a small mid-western town and the outskirts of an airport) among housing estates built in the late '20s and '30s (Attlee House; Mandela Street; shades of labour and empire) the university, when it was a poly, pioneered the recruitment of mature students (only 25 per cent of students are aged between eighteen and twenty-one) and discriminates positively in favour of women, ethnic groups and the local population. So I am appropriately placed. I teach nineteenth and twentieth century mostly British history, psychoanalysis, feminist history and theory to students, the majority of whom work between eight and twenty hours a week (or more) for wages as they study.

I came to the poly from the extra-mural department of London University, where I had taught (part-time) courses which were worked out with the students themselves, broadly in the realm of feminist history and theory; socialist history and social movements. The students I teach now are poor, ethnically diverse, and have less say in what they learn or how they learn it. What is different about them in expectation from both Ruskin students in the sixties and the extra-mural students of the eighties is their sense of being rushed through a degree with very little preparation or resources. Not all of them, but many, come without A levels, without books in their houses. They may have taken an access course which has helped them to rifle textbooks for information, to write the standard essay, but has not given them time to think nor a sense of the abundance of the historical imagination. My students are now working towards a degree, and their minds are focused on assessment (continuous). They hope a degree will bring employment.

My students differ too from the Ruskin students I met twenty-five years ago. Few belong to trade unions, and except for those with a labour or socialist background, few see their relevance. Music shapes modes of thought, articulating grievances and passions. Most still live within diverse and unorthodox family histories and hierarchies since few can afford (as my generation could in the late fifties/early sixties) to leave home completely, many returning in the holidays, even those over twenty-five. Issues of feminism, sexuality and race speak more directly to the concerns of their daily lives it seems than class; and ecology and environmentalism surface as political issues sometimes. Ireland and Britain's ugly imperial history often politicize as the students read and write about them. Student politics, even at the level of the department, seldom engages them. Some protest and demonstrate over grants, accommodation (there are rats in students' flats in Stratford, for instance); fewer still complain about the miserable numbers of books in the libraries, or the lack of quiet study space, or even the most rudimentary student common rooms. But, several – mature – students, were arrested and imprisoned after the poll-tax demonstration two years ago.

In the intellectual culture which my students encounter and which they help to produce, questions of identity and ethnicity predominate. Edward Said's analysis of Orientalism, Michel Foucault's discourse analysis and feminism's emphasis on gender and sexuality form a matrix of concerns, in which the notion of the 'other' helps their understanding of relations of power. Language and texts are the object of study, not reality or history; and labour, as unemployment has risen through the eighties and the authority of the labour movement has diminished, has become the repressed of culture.

I have no conclusions, only these comparisons. I am grateful to Ruskin. It was the crucible in which my sense of myself as a woman, as a historical subject, and my wish for knowledge, distilled. In specific ways both the *History Workshop Journal* and feminist history in England owe much to the political and emotional economies of Ruskin.

1992

APPENDIX

THE NIGHT CLEANERS

AN ASSESSMENT OF

THE CAMPAIGN

The night cleaners' campaign occupies a special position in the history of the women's movement. It was the first time, in London at least, that women's liberation became actively involved in a struggle among working women to organise themselves, the WLM worked together with other leftwing groups and cleaners, under the leadership of May Hobbs, to unionise nightcleaners. For Marxist feminists therefore, the cleaners' campaign raises fundamental questions of theoretical and practical significance. In the first place, the cleaners' situation reveals important insights into the position of women within the labour market: i.e. the relationship between sex oppression and class exploitation. Because the Women's Liberation Movement was and is primarily a middle class movement this question sometimes posed itself in the form of the relationship between WLM and working class women. Secondly the campaign raised the strategic question of our attitude towards the trade union and socialist movements.

This article cannot resolve these questions, it will simply describe the context in which they arose and offer some observations which might be useful for the future political practice of the women's movement. First of all, it is necessary to give as concise an account as possible of the campaign. (For fuller details, see *Nightcleaners Shrew*, Dec 1971; ed. Michelene Wandor, *The Body Politic: Writings from the Women's Liberation Movement*, Stage 1, 1972.)

— *How did the WLM get involved?* —

In Oct 1970 May Hobbs, a night office cleaner who had been trying to organise cleaners for the previous eight years, approached the International Socialist (IS) group. Through them she was asked to go along to a meeting of the Dalston Women's Liberation Workshop. Almost

immediately women from IS and the workshop started leafleting cleaners outside their buildings as they went to work. The leaflets explained
the purpose of collective action, and urged the women to join the union.
An incident on a Board of Trade building in which two women were
sacked gave impetus to the campaign, and an atmosphere of urgency
was generated by the wider struggle of the labour movement against the
Industrial Relations Bill. In spite of the unfavourable outcome of the
Board of Trade picket there was lots of enthusiasm and optimism in the
early months.

— *The formation of the* CAG —

It soon became clear that helping the cleaners meant more than catching
them as they went into work at 9 or 10 o'clock and persuading them to
sign a union form. In order to unionise cleaners we had to organise
ourselves. We formed a collective Cleaners' Action Group which at
different times fell under the domination of the IS and the International
Marxist Group (IMG). Probably because they were more articulate and
self-confident and had a definite 'line' towards the TU movement, but
May was always the most vocal spokeswoman. A film collective of 3
men and one woman also formed to document the campaign. After
some months both IS and IMG dropped out of consistent active
participation in the campaign although they provided valuable support
on the strike last year.

The collective met at regular intervals for several months; lists were
kept of which group was leafleting which building; other women stepped
in if a leafleter went on holiday or dropped out. Leafleting a building
meant visiting it every week on the same night, and getting to know the
cleaners, who were often too nervous to speak to us for fear of
victimisation or intimidation. When or if the women joined the union,
we continued to visit the buildings to collect their dues, and to establish
a link between them and the union. This was much more difficult than it
sounds. In the first place the women work in small groups on separate
buildings scattered throughout central London, which makes any contact
among themselves almost impossible. Secondly, and even more important, the union, the Transport and General Workers Union, the TGWU,
was extremely reluctant to take the cleaners seriously as an area of
recruitment. We found that we had to put on the pressure at two levels:
the women to join the union, and the union to take the women seriously.
Partly because of these difficulties there was a rapid turnover of leafleters
in the first 1½ years. As one person dropped out, however, another
woman from the Workshop stepped in to take her place.

— *Strategy* —

The CAG developed and discarded several different campaign plans. In the beginning we did not seriously question the feasibility of union organisation for the night cleaners. We simply decided to organise the cleaners into one union – the Transport and General Workers' Union (T and G) – and to aim at setting up a cleaners' branch within it, with May Hobbs as branch secretary. Meanwhile the night cleaners entered the window cleaners' branch. Next we turned to the problem of recruitment. The first plan was to systematically leaflet every building being nightcleaned in London. Lack of resources made this plan completely impracticable. There were not enough leafleters and too many buildings. The second plan, was to concentrate on the buildings of one individual employer. This also proved unsuccessful for several reasons. It was not always possible to discover the contractor on a building, also leafleters worked better if the building was near their own home. More important was that the contractor would either move or sack a cleaner he suspected of joining the union. To be moved onto another building can be an effective form of victimisation. Many cleaners, particularly the ones who have stuck in jobs for several years, have chosen their place of work with some care. Either it is near their home, or on an easy transport route, or the pay and conditions (which vary considerably) are better than most, or they are working with their friends. It is difficult to prove unfair dismissal since the cleaner is always sacked on some pretext, e.g. inefficiency, late attendance, or changing over from night to morning and evening cleaning. May did take a case through court last year, but the contractor won it.

Our third and final plan was to unionise one large building, employing lots of cleaners. This group of women could then form the nucleus of the cleaners' branch. The two Shell Centre buildings in Waterloo were selected because May knew that the T and G had always been interested in them. By this time it was beginning to appear as if the union's apathy towards the night cleaners was insurmountable. May's demands and protestations merely aggravated the union officers, while at the same time they were wary of the publicity she might provoke. The cleaners, and ourselves, were treated with almost total indifference. There had been some discussion within the CAG of forming our own union. The problems facing Pat Sturdy and her co-workers demonstrated the futility of attempting to build up a strong workers' organisation outside the official trade union movement, however. We also considered the possibility of forming a cleaners' co-operative, but this would have meant starting a business, which neither women's liberation nor the cleaners themselves wanted to do! We had begun by this time (summer '71) to recognise the limitations of trade union activity, and the particular resistance male trade unionists put up towards women workers, but we decided to have one last attempt at arousing their interest and assistance. Shell Centre was the carrot we hoped to dangle in front of the union official's eyes. It almost worked.

Shell Centre and the T and G

About half a dozen women from the Pimlico and Chiswick workshop groups started leafleting Shell. From the very first weeks we made friends with three of the cleaners, and soon we were visiting every week to collect the dues, bring new forms, and liaise between the women and the union officials since most of the women were not on the phone. Several meetings with the union officials were arranged, and each time the women put forward their demands firmly and articulately. To start with the women had lots of 'small' complaints about their conditions of work. For instance, in the summer the air conditioning was turned off, the heat was stifling but they were not allowed to open a window. In the winter it was the central heating that was turned off so there was the opposite problem. The women were not given proper facilities for making tea, so unless they brought a thermos they went without. There was one dinner break at 1 a.m. for one hour, but no other tea or coffee break. The women were locked in at night, and were not allowed to leave their own floor to visit a friend. There were also the usual demands for three weeks' holiday with pay, adequate staffing, proper equipment, notice of dismissal. After two meetings between us and some of the cleaners in a cafe near work, we drew up a very long list of demands and asked for a meeting with Mr Ferriman, and Mr Churchouse of the T and G. In spite of the union's insistence that cleaners never turn up for meetings, about 7 or 8 came, as well as May, the leafleters, and the film group. We had the names and addresses of the other twenty-five or so women on Shell who had joined the union. They were up to date with their union dues but were unable to attend because of babysitting problems. The officers did seem impressed by our efficient paperwork, and thorough record keeping. They must have been grateful that we were doing their work for them. In fact, we wanted to be certain that we would not be dismissed with the usual complaint about women not joining unions. On the contrary, having visited Mr Fred Sage, the window-cleaners' branch secretary ourselves, we discovered that in the previous couple of years almost a hundred women night cleaners had joined the T and G.

The two union officers assured the cleaners they would write to the employers asking for union recognition. They explained that when the union puts in a wage claim, the other conditions necessarily follow, so this list of demands was superfluous. The first step anyway was to win union recognition, the union would then put in a wage claim when one from the women themselves had been turned down. The situation was slightly complicated on Shell because the two buildings – the upstream and the downstream – were contracted to different cleaning firms. To overcome this sort of problem, Mr Ferriman explained, the union was working to establish a national negotiating structure with the employers' association, the CCMA (Cleaning Contractors Maintenance Association) but this of course might take years. Perhaps the most urgent demand of the cleaners was for union meetings at their place of work. Babysitting is a constant problem and the weekend is spent shopping and catching up with domestic chores. More importantly, the cleaners who were too nervous to openly join the union would be more reassured by the presence of a union officer at work than by women from the Women's Liberation Movement.

There were several other meetings with Mr Churchouse, Mr Ferriman, and other T and G officers. Sometimes we visited their offices, once we sent a petition to Jack Jones (President of the T and G) signed by all the Shell cleaners asking for their own branch. We, the leafleters, talked to the women regularly as they went to work or before work in the cafe. We took as many who could manage it to other meetings and demonstrations relevant to the trade union or women's struggle. We also leafleted the TUC and the T and G Women's Conference and attempted to make links with other groups of women workers. We spoke to every officer in the T and G who would listen to us. May travelled to different parts of the country where cleaners were organising. The CAG began to build up national contacts, its magazine, *The Cleaners' Voice* helped to spread news and keep everyone in touch.

In spite of all this activity, however, Mr Churchouse, the officer responsible in the T and G for the night cleaners was very elusive. He seldom replied to letters or telephone calls, twice he did not turn up for meetings and specific requests for help on issues such as victimisation, unhealthy conditions etc. were ignored. We made two formal complaints. Eventually Mr Ferriman, a Group Secretary, agreed to replace him. Both these officers eventually met the employers, however, and on one occasion took the two shop stewards from one building to negotiate with them. One or two small gains were made. The cleaners were given two rises of 50p within a few months (their first for two and a half years), making their wages up to £13, and the cleaners on the up-stream received a bonus in Christmas '71 and '72. Since then, there has been another small wage increase. Each time the rise has been given independently of union negotiation. The contractor's representative did not turn up to the second meeting arranged between them and the women shop stewards, and the union officers never took the matter up. Some of the union's attitudes were ludicrous. For instance, the shop stewards were told by Mr Ferriman, in all seriousness, that when they asked for open windows the contractors refused on the grounds that, as it was well known that women are hysterical, they might throw themselves out.

The Fulham Cleaners' Strike

Meanwhile the leafleting on other buildings gradually stopped. Finally in the summer of '72 when the number of leafleters was sadly depleted, and May and the CAG were growing despondent, the cleaners on the Ministry of Defence building came out on strike for more pay, adequate staffing etc. Two other government buildings followed suit. These three buildings were in the Civil Service Union (CSU) which had been mounting a campaign to unionise night cleaners. The CSU made the strikes official and paid ten pounds a week strike pay. Other cleaners, trade unionists, and groups of workers came along to support the picket line which had to be maintained throughout the day and night. The left groups and women's liberation were also there in strength. The atmosphere was one of great excitement, and enthusiasm. The cleaners brought their children and husbands down to the picket line, they spoke at workers' meetings, and visited other cleaners as they went into work. The strike received sympathetic media coverage, especially in the liberal press. Nightcleaning has always been a potent liberal issue. (In the 1930s for instance, the women's co-operative guild raised the question of nightcleaning in the media whenever they could.) The *Morning Star* also gave the strike much sympathetic and encouraging support.

Victory was won after two weeks but the cleaners had to stand firm to maintain it. On one building the contractor changed over to morning and evening cleaning and none of the women strikers who applied were given their jobs back. The conditions of the Fulham cleaners have been maintained and improved by the action and solidarity of the girls themselves. Their wages have just been raised to £21 a week. Not very high but 6 or 7 pounds higher than average.

Since last summer the CAG has concentrated on two issues. First of all, the cleaners' branch in the T and G with May as branch secretary is still being pursued. It was promised in Christmas 1972 and we are still waiting. May is becoming more involved in other issues especially housing and women's prisons and has less time to devote exclusively to the cleaners, so that unless other women put themselves forward to actively engage in union work, the branch might never materialise. The second issue is to raise the question of contract cleaning on government buildings in the House of Commons. Joe Ashton heads a lobby of sympathetic MPs, and he has arranged meetings with the relevant minister. In 1968, Harold Wilson successfully cut down the size of the civil service by sacking all direct cleaners, and contracting the work out to office cleaning firms. This means that the lowest bidder receives the job, and since labour is the biggest single cost factor, wages are reduced to the absolute minimum. It is hoped that by abolishing contract cleaning on public buildings, something can then be done in the private sector. The abolition of contract cleaning will not unionise night cleaners, but will raise their wages by removing the middle man between the cleaner and their employer.

The CAG is now much smaller than it was a year ago and more diverse. There are men and women from the labour movement and the Communist Party in as well as WLM. There are no longer regular meetings, and leafleting has stopped. But it is still hoped that when the film of the campaign is finished it will be used to publicise the cleaners' situation, and to recruit more leafleters. Meanwhile, however, there is no doubt that the campaign has encouraged cleaners in different parts of the country to organise themselves. May and the CAG often receive news of cleaners waiting to participate in the campaign, or asking for information and support.

— *Women's liberation and the night cleaners* —

Women's liberation first began to work with the night cleaners because May Hobbs asked for help. Our participation was not a strategic intervention in the working class struggle. In the true spontaneous tradition of the women's movement organisation, politics and strategy developed as we went along (as hopefully the previous account has shown)! The contrast between the cleaners' lives and our own was one of the initial influences on us.

There are between 2 and 3 thousand night cleaners in England, of which about 1,800 are working in London. This is probably an underestimate as many women work without cards, moving from job to job. Cleaning workers have always been one of the most exploited groups on the labour market, but the exploitation has dramatically increased with the introduction of contract cleaning in place of direct employment. (For information about the contract cleaning industry see PIB Report 1971.)

Labour is the biggest single cost factor in the industry, so contractors ruthlessly compete with each to win contracts by lowering wages. Today, on average, night cleaners receive between £12 and £14 for a 40 hour week. Three years ago, the average wage was £9 a week.

The cleaners are mostly between the ages of 20 and 60, but there are a substantial number over 60. They are almost all married, divorced or widowed, with several children, the youngest under school age. Lack of nursery facilities forces women out to work at nights. The women are either the sole providers in the family, or their husbands are low-paid. Some do two cleaning jobs, one in the day or early evening as well. Others take different part-time work during the day. A large percentage of the women are immigrants; West Indian, Asian, Greek, Spanish, Irish. Immigrant women are uncertain of their rights, cannot always speak English very well, and are the most easily intimidated. Cleaners work in small groups on different buildings throughout London. This isolation is accentuated by the different nationalities, or rather the attempts of the supervisor or firm's manager to victimise one or two 'troublemakers', and to provoke racial tension. In fact, the women work together very well, but you never meet a black supervisor, although over half the cleaners are black.

Very few supervisors are sympathetic to the union. They often have their employers' interests at heart. But also a great deal of fiddling goes on in contract cleaning and sometimes it suits the supervisor to be able to manipulate the women by threatening their jobs. When economic pressures are so great, fear of losing one's job or even a week's pay keeps the cleaners quiet. It is important to be on good terms with the supervisor because taking a night off to care for a sick child will depend on her goodwill, so will 'cover' work, which brings in an extra few shillings a week.

The contractors themselves vary in their attitude towards the unions. Generally the larger the firm the more indifferent they are to it. Because the small firms are gradually being swallowed up by the larger ones they desperately undercut to stay in the market. Their survival depends on paying subsistence wages. Obviously therefore they will actively oppose the union.

These facts, and many more, we learnt as we worked and talked with the women. The dreary round of housework interspersed with a menial job during the day, then more housework all night for a pittance, with little sleep all week, aroused our sympathy and concern and made us do all we could to support the cleaners. Loyalty to the women with whom we had made friends prevented us from dropping out when we felt most inadequate.

We leafleters were mostly young women in our twenties or early thirties: students, teachers, young mothers. There is a strong tradition of co-operation, between middle-class feminists and the working class in the history of the labour movement: Annie Besant and the match girls, Eleanor Marx and the gas workers, Sylvia Pankhurst and the East London Federation. Because of the cleaners' isolation, they need help in maintaining contact with each other. Lack of time prevents them from attending every meeting, and keeping up with the bookwork. However, our role can only be very limited, and we were never sure quite what those limits were.

The CAG indulged in self-criticism on several counts. Perhaps our most serious failing was that we never managed to develop leadership and direction among the women themselves. We should have raised the money to support one or two cleaners while they worked on the campaign for a few months. We could have used the film (or part of it as it is not yet finished) to help raise this money, at the same time as publicising the night cleaners' campaign among other groups of workers, men and women. It is possible to leave groups of cleaners on specific buildings to their own devices until they ask for support, but there is no way of spreading this self-activity. Part of the problem has been that as feminists, we tend to reject the concept of leadership. We recognise the need for self-activity, and for direction within a campaign, but we associate leadership with domination and lack of democracy. We ignored the fact that May at least was already providing leadership, and that the strain of that responsibility was too much for one person. The women's liberation movement was also, de facto providing leadership. In practice we tried to avoid this. We shifted nervously from one foot to the other, explaining the unions to the cleaners, and the cleaners to the unions, feeling unable to identify strongly with either, albeit for different reasons. We could neither urge the women to strike, since the effect of militancy on their lives was so uncertain. Nor could we open the attack on the unions, since there was no other way of helping the cleaners.

It was difficult to raise the subject of women's liberation with the cleaners. Most of the women could only spare a couple of minutes outside the door before they rushed into work. Those who arrived earlier were obviously more interested in hearing about the union. We were known among the women as the union girls. Whenever women's liberation was raised there was an initial self-consciousness on our part, and probably a joke about bras or man-hating on theirs. The cleaners often talked about their feelings as women, and especially the burden of two jobs, in the home and at work. It is easy to talk to any woman about children, schools and shopping but some of the problems that occupy the feminist consciousness raising groups feel awkward in discussion when lived experience is so different. Abortion is an obvious example. The difference between a middle-class private abortion (unpleasant though that can be) and the abortions of women who have neither the money to pay nor the self-confidence and discrimination to obtain one from the national health, need hardly be emphasised. The class differences were complicated by our own reticence as a movement about ourselves. This was much truer two or three years ago than it is today. There is a strong belief that the movement should speak for itself, that we will not proselytise or harangue, women will discover us when they need to. The media will always distort everything we say so say nothing. This is an overstatement, of course, but when that belief – inarticulate though it might be – is accompanied by middle-class self-awareness of privilege it can be quite an inhibiting force. The women's movement like the rest of the left, still has to learn how to popularise its ideas and politics successfully.

— The night cleaners, trade unions and women's work —

Several unions have night cleaners in their membership, but cleaners are only effectively organised in factories or firms where there is a strong closed shop already operating, e.g. some engineering works, or government buildings. Otherwise night cleaners have remained outside the trade union movement both because their work is classified as unskilled and casual, the sort of work which historically has always been more difficult to organise, and because they are women. Low pay inevitably accompanies women's work and casual status. But high wages are determined by the firm's profitability and the collective militancy of the workers, not the degree of skill. So, why aren't the cleaners organised?

When women's liberation first began to help the cleaners we were very conscious of our naivity and ignorance and sought the advice of experienced trade unionists. Some women in left groups tended to be combative in their attitude towards the unions, we felt perhaps we might make more progress if we adopted a conciliatory approach. We listened as male trade unionists inside and outside the T and G patiently explained the problems of organisation, emphasising the limitations of trade union resources. Few were as succinct as the 1971 PIB report on the contract cleaning trade which stated that trade unions have not promoted the campaign because 'workers are widely dispersed, in isolated small groups and working at inconvenient times for union organisation'. Some were more helpful than others. Fred Sage, for instance, the window cleaners' branch secretary emphasised the need to establish a skill. All that most emphasised, however, was that women are notoriously hard to organise because they are home-orientated, they are not interested in union work, and they are easily intimidated.

Some of these arguments carried more conviction than others, particular the problems concerning the organisation of casual workers, and the cleaners' vulnerability to intimidation. Like most women workers cleaners have interiorised their inferior economic status. They see themselves primarily as wives and mothers, and regard their job outside the home as a necessary but temporary expedient. They feel fatalistic about changing this situation. However, those who do have the courage and energy to start helping themselves and their workmates, quickly generate enthusiasm and optimism. The cleaners are not disinterested in union work. They are sceptical of a trade union's effectiveness. Their scepticism has been nurtured by the union's neglect. When the officers fail to reply to letters or phone calls, do not arrive for meetings, ignore their most deeply felt demands paying out a shilling or more a week becomes an unnecessary strain on a tight budget.

Male trade unionists have always had an ambivalent attitude towards women workers. On the one hand, their wives go out to work, and they recognise the need for working class solidarity. On the other hand they believe that a woman's place is in the home and that she should stay there. This support of working class men for the sexual division of labour within the family is not just backward ideas in a few men's heads about women and sexuality. Its origins are complex, but one of its deepest notes is the very real fear that the entry of women into a trade or industry will reduce wages, lower job status and throw men out of work. Historically, women have been used to break strikes and undercut men's pay. From the beginning of capitalism women, restricted by child bearing and rearing, and discriminated against on the labour market, have accepted the most unpleasant jobs, for the lowest wages. This situation was accentuated by the separation of home and workplace (e.g. women's work in the mines; the early unskilled factory work; sweated trades, etc.). Women on their own have always been the worst off: Denied proper education, apprenticeship, or training, and without a male wage to prop up the family income, they have had to accept any work available even if it has meant blacking a strike.

But women's exclusion from the trade union movement has confirmed and perpetuated their weak and secondary status on the labour market. As Audrey Wise has shown in her pamphlet 'Women and the Struggle for Workers' Control' (*Spokesman*, no. 33) women are at present 38% of the labour force, but concentrated in the lowest paid jobs, and this situation is getting worse. Many women work part-time and intermittently throughout their lifetime, and this is termed 'casual' and given a lower status by employers and trade unionists alike. It is no more regarded as real work by male trade unionists than housework and childcare. Nightcleaning occupies such a position. It is termed 'casual', although the women work a 40 hour week. It is outside commodity production, and it is done by women and immigrants. In fact this work is not peripheral to capitalism, the service sector is an expanding sector of the economy.

Like many women's jobs nightcleaning is labour intensive, i.e. it could not survive without a large supply of cheap labour. Two demands of the women's movement – nurseries and equal pay and job opportunity – would remove the worst conditions of nightcleaning and other night work, since women would then have an effective choice of employment. However, these aims recede into the distance in the present economic climate. Women workers must therefore organise themselves at work, both to win better pay and conditions, as well as to effect wider changes in society.

Male workers will have to radically change their attitude towards women. Trade unions more or less are the working class movement in this country, and they are bastions of male privilege. At every level in the hierarchy of the labour market women occupy a weaker position than men. The unions are doing nothing to alleviate this situation. Out of 600 full-time officers in the T and GWU for instance only one is a woman.

— *Conclusion* —

By arguing for women to organise at work outside their homes I am not advocating that all women should go out to work and thus ease the road to socialism. Neither am I advocating trade unionism as the panacea for women's oppression, nor as an alternative to organising around the family or in the community. The struggle against capitalism and sexism must be fought at every level – trade union organisation is only the first tentative step towards workers' self-consciousness and strength. The women's liberation movement must actively support it.

But the night cleaners' campaign has also revealed two other urgent priorities for the women's movement. In the first place, we vacillated between co-operation with an ineffectual criticism of the unions because we never resolved the dilemma of being neither the cleaners nor the union. Strategy is learnt through political practice as well as from theory. As we had no immediate experience of our own to draw on, and as political practice is hard to learn out of books, it is not surprising we were hesitant. But marxist feminists are not redundant in the labour movement. We must develop a guideline for action within the trade unions. At the same time, of course, the most effective support for women working on that front is a strong articulate feminist movement whose ideas and actions penetrate and influence the class struggle.

The second strategic priority the campaign revealed is for an historical materialist analysis of the position of women's work within the labour market, the relationship between women's work and capitalism. This need is being realised in fact, as there are many women and women's groups studying this question. At present women are designated a secondary status within the class struggle because they are casual workers, because they are low-paid, un- or semi-skilled, work part-time because they are wives, and mothers. We are not asking to participate in the class struggle: the women's liberation movement must redefine it.

First published in *Red Rag* no.6, 1973(?).

IN DEFENCE OF
'PATRIARCHY'

— Written with Barbara Taylor —

The major problem with the theory of patriarchy, Sheila Rowbotham claims, is that it ascribes women's subordination and men's domination to their respective biological roles – a politically dangerous position which can only lead to a call for the abolition of all 'biological male persons'. Feminists must realise, she says, that 'it is not sexual difference which is the problem, but the social inequalities of gender': it is not men we want to eliminate, but male power.*

Like Sheila, we are socialist feminists. But we believe that sexual difference *is* the problem, or at least a fundamental part of it. Does that mean that we are busy training for a final day of sexual Armageddon, when all 'biological male persons' will receive their just deserts (castration or annihilation, as we choose at the time)? No doubt every woman has had moments when such a vision seemed attractive, but what we have in mind is (to use Sheila's words) 'a more delicate matter altogether'.

Throughout her article Sheila assumes that sexual difference is a biological given, linked to reproduction. Clearly if it is defined in this way, it is hard to see how it can be changed. However, one of the most important breakthroughs in feminist theory occurred when women began to question this commonsense definition of sex, pushing past all the old assumptions about 'natural' womanhood and manhood to examine how deep the roots of women's oppression really lay. What was needed then, was a theory of gender itself, a new way of thinking about reproduction and sexuality. The search drew some of us towards structural anthropology and psychoanalysis. From a feminist reading of anthropology we learned that the social meaning of maleness and femaleness is constructed through kinship rules which prescribe patterns of sexual dominance and subordination. From psychoanalysis we learned how these kinship rules become inscribed on the unconscious psyche of the female child via the traumatic re-orientation of sexual desire within the Oedipal phase away from the mother and towards the father ('the law of the father'). The two arguments combined, as in Juliet Mitchell's highly influential *Psychoanalysis and Feminism*, provide a powerful account of the 'generation of a patriarchal system that must by definition oppress women'.

This account remains controversial within the women's movement, but it has greatly expanded our theoretical and political horizons. For if the mechanisms by which women's subordination are reproduced are also those which reproduce family structure and gendered individuals, then a revolution to eliminate such subordination would have to extend very widely indeed. It would need to be, as Juliet says, a 'cultural revolution' which not only eliminated social inequalities based on sexual difference, but transformed the meaning of sexuality itself. We would need to learn new ways of being women and men. It is this project, not the annihilation of 'biological male persons', which the theory of patriarchy points towards.

Constructing a theory of patriarchal relations is hazardous, not least because it analyses gender in terms wholly different from those of class. But without a theory of gender relations, any attempt to 'marry' the concepts of sex and class will simply do for theories of sex what marriage usually does for women: dissolve them into the stronger side of the partnership. It was precisely because a Marxist theory of class conflict, however elaborated, could not answer all our questions about sexual conflict that we tried to develop an alternative. If we need to keep the two areas of analysis apart for a time, so be it. Theories are not made all at once.

However, Sheila's own anxiety about this theoretical dualism conceals a greater anxiety about the whole attempt to construct a theory of sexual antagonism. She seems to view any such theory as an iron grid of abstractions placed over the flow of direct experience; and, as an alternative, she appeals to history to answer questions about female subordination which the 'fixed' and 'rigid' categories of theory cannot answer.

As feminist historians, we share Sheila's desire for more research into women's lives and experience. But this is no substitute for a theory of women's oppression. History only answers questions which are put to it: without a framework for these questions we shall founder in a welter of dissociated and contradictory 'facts'. Nor can women's own testimony about their relations with men be taken as unproblematic.

Women have dwelt within their oppression at all times, but it is only occasionally that some have become sharply aware of it. Our analysis of women's consciousness must (as Sheila says) explain the periods of quiescence, as well as the times of anger. Simply recording how women behaved or what they said cannot give us this analysis, any more than recording what workers do gives us a theory of class: it is the underlying reality which must be examined.

Finally, Sheila is unhappy with the concept of patriarchy because it seems to discount all the good things which happen between men and women. She reminds us that women love men, that men need women, and that both sexes often find real support in each other, especially in moments of class confrontation – all true (at least of heterosexual women). But does all this loving and needing and solidarising prove there is no general structure of sexual antagonism, only bad times and good times? Does it mean that loving men is unproblematic for women, something to be gratefully accepted rather than critically investigated? Surely not. Learning to love men sexually is a social process, not a natural one, and in a patriarchal society it involves at least as much pain as joy, as much struggle as mutual support. Again, it is the analysis of kinship rules and unconscious mental life – not the study of biology – which helps us to understand how this channelling of desire towards reproductive heterosexuality occurs, and also what some of its costs have been: not only in terms of the systematic repression of homosexual love and lovers in most cultures, but also in terms of 'normal' feminine sexuality. Did not Freud help us to understand that in learning to love men we learn also to subordinate ourselves to them? The ropes which bind women are the hardest to cut, because they are woven with so many of our own desires.

The concept of patriarchy points to a strategy which will eliminate not men, but masculinity, and transform the whole web of psycho-social relations in which masculinity and femininity are formed. It is a position from which we can begin to reclaim for political change precisely those areas of life which are usually deemed biological or natural. It allows us to confront not only the day-to-day social practices through which men exercise power over women, but also mechanisms through which patterns of authority and submission become part of the sexed personality itself – 'the father in our heads', so to speak. It has helped us to think about sexual division – which cannot be understood simply as a by-product of economic class relations or of biology, but which has an independent dynamic that will only be overcome by an independent feminist politics. Finally, it has allowed us to look past our immediate experiences as women to the processes underlying and shaping that experience. For like class, sexual antagonism is not something which can be understood simply by living it: it needs to be analysed with concepts forged for that purpose. The theories which have developed around 'patriarchy' have been the first systematic attempts to provide them.

Further Reading
* Sheila Rowbotham, 'The Trouble With Patriarchy', *New Statesman*, 21 December, 1979.

As our text indicates, we regard Juliet Mitchell's *Psychoanalysis and Feminism*, Harmondsworth, 1975 – a feminist reading of Freud – as a fundamental contribution to the issue of this debate. *Patriarchy Papers*, London, 1976, contains some of the most accessible British contributions to the discussion. We would also refer readers to 'The Unhappy Marriage of Marxism and Feminism: Towards a More Progressive Union', by Heidi I. Hartmann, *Capital and Class*, Summer 1979. As well as the articles cited by Sheila we would recommend – though they are not written from our position – Kate Millett, *Sexual Politics*, London, 1980: and Shulamith Firestone, *The Dialectics of Sex*, London 1979. Firestone gives a biological reading of social-sexual relations without resorting to a theory of patriarchy.

First published in *New Statesman*, December 1979. Thanks to Rosalind Delmar for her excellent advice on the first draft; and to Gareth Stedman Jones, Maureen Mackintosh, Carole Furnivall and Jane Caplan.

1979

FEMINIST HISTORY

The presence of feminist historians on the *History Workshop Journal* requires some explanation. For us, our feminism, our socialism, and our history are inextricably connected, each shaping the others. But women's history is not an inevitable extension either of social or of socialist history. It is well known that women receive little or no attention in traditional history writing, but even among radical and socialist historians they are all too often mentioned as an afterthought, if at all, tagged on rather than present in their own right. As recently as 1971, when the suggestion was made at a History Workshop session that people working on women's issues should meet later in the day, there was a roar of laughter. We know that women's history still has to be argued for.

Labour and social history up to now have shared with 'political' history an anti-feminist definition, and although there is of course much to be learnt from and valued in their contributions there is also much ground to be reworked. The separation of work and home, the identification of woman with the private world of the home, and the ideology which subordinates both women and domestic life, are all features of capitalism which are invisible and unquestioned within labour history. The working class has generally meant working men; women are the wives, mothers and daughters of working men. Domestic life is treated as a static unchanging backcloth to the world of real historical activity; unpaid domestic labour is absent and women's waged work is confined to a paragraph or two under 'unskilled labour' or 'factory work and the industrial revolution'. In political history the suffragettes do occasionally receive a chapter of their own, but otherwise as in labour history women are peripheral, both to production and to class struggle.

Insofar as the male definition of labour history has been the result of too narrow a focus on work and trade unions, social history can provide a useful and sometimes creative corrective. More and more areas of life outside the workshop, factory or trade society are being pulled into 'history', and women are one obviously neglected area to be salvaged and explored. Most social history books nowadays boast sections on the family and the position of women, along with religion, education, popular culture and so on. But they are still tagged on, not integrated into the overall understanding of a society or even of its parts. Social history like labour history takes for granted sexual divisions at work, in the home, or in political and cultural life. The sexual division of labour disappears in discussion of men and women's different 'roles'; domestic life is studied in a vacuum; popular culture is represented by working men's clubs, self-help organizations, or football, and the absence of women is scarcely noted let alone investigated or explained. As with most orthodox history, empirical material is used to document and describe the appearance of the world and not to explore its fundamental order. Even when capitalism and the capitalist mode of production have been placed under critical historical scrutiny, divisions other than those between capital and labour have either been ignored or have been dismissed as secondary. The result has been not only the neglect of women but also the impoverishment of socialist history.

Sexual divisions are being questioned now because of the women's liberation movement, and it is through investigating the problems which feminism has raised that we can expect the most useful women's history to emerge. One priority of feminism is necessarily the history of women, but the purpose is not simply to slot women in wherever they have been left out. Feminist history demands much more than the token recognition of women. For women are *workers* too, both waged and unwaged; and capitalism is as dependent on its 'unskilled' sweated labour force as on its skilled engineers. It is as important for an understanding of the development of capitalism to examine changes in how workers themselves were produced and maintained, as to know about the production of goods: feminism not only demands a history of the family but also seeks to explain why women's work as the reproducers of labour power, and their servicing of labour power in the home, has remained invisible for so long. By bringing women into the foreground of historical enquiry our knowledge of production, of working class politics and culture, of class struggle, of the welfare state, will be transformed. Men and women *do* inhabit different worlds, with boundaries which have been defined (and from time to time re-arranged) for them by the capitalist mode of production as it has made use of and strengthened the sexual division of labour and patriarchal authority. It is relationships like that between the two worlds, between the sexual division of labour and class struggle, home and work, or the private sector and the public, the social relationships between men and women, which form the substance of feminist history, and will enrich all socialist history.

In issue one the articles most influenced by feminism are Tim Mason's *Women in Nazi Germany* and Jeffrey Weeks' *Sins and Diseases*, neither of them exclusively about women. *Women in Nazi Germany* deals with women's productive work and with national socialist policies towards women, marriage, the family and reproduction. It tells us as much about the nature of fascism as about the situation of women. Jeffrey Weeks' account of his work in progress raises the question of social attitudes towards sexuality, homosexuality in particular, and indicates some of the ways in which they may be linked to wider political and economic change.

In future issues we hope not only to publish articles about and written and researched by women, but also to contribute to the development of feminist history in the broader sense. We want to examine the sexual division of labour in different historical contexts, under capitalist and other modes of production. A reappraisal of family history will be another priority because this has so often been the only place for historical mention of women. Family history, in British historiography at least, is usually confined to the period 1760–1840, and concerns the alleged disruptive effects on the 'pre-industrial' family of women's factory work. Even here the interest of the subject for academic history is often only tangential: Ivy Pinchbeck's classic *Women Workers and the Industrial Revolution* (1930) if admitted to undergraduate reading lists may get there only to supply ammunition on the 'optimist' side in the standard of living debate. Nor has socialist history dealt much better with the question. Taking the lead from Engels' otherwise remarkable *Condition of the Working Class in 1844*, most socialist historians have assumed that the entry of women into the factories was one of the disastrous consequences of industrial capitalism, without further investigating the grounds for Engels' statements, or the real experience of women in production. Engels later modified his own position by advocating the necessity of women's participation in production, but still the fact that most women had always been producers is ignored, and so the problem falsely posed. Much recent family history has emphasized demographic research; it has utilized sociological categories to describe changing relations within the family and the outside world. Socialist history on the other hand tends to pose a too simple one-to-one relationship between the family and the economy. Feminism clearly has different questions to ask, and some of its findings we hope to publish in future issues of the journal.

We are arguing for a political perspective in historical research and writing, a suggestion which must disturb every academic vigilant in pursuit of the 'value-free'. But we announce our perspective and our values, thus showing greater respect for the critical faculties of our readers, and perhaps greater self-awareness than the unguarded vigilants. It is only by seeking and recognizing political relevance in history that we can bring it more directly into the battle of ideas – history is too important to be left just to the professional historians.

History Workshop Journal, Issue 1, Autumn 1976

NOTES

INTRODUCTION

1. The Berwick Street Film Collective, *Nightcleaners*, 1977, The Other Cinema; Laura Mulvey and Peter Wollen, *Riddles of the Sphinx*, 1976, The Other Cinema; Mary Kelly, Margaret Harrison, *Women's Work in a South London Factory*, installation ICA 1974, are feminist documents in other media from the same political moment which trace these thoughts differently. Catherine Hall's Introduction, *White, Male and Middle Class, Explorations in Feminism and History*, Polity Press, Oxford, 1992, pp. 1–40.
2. 'The attempt to attain knowledge of the past is also a journey into the world of the dead', Carlo Ginzberg, *Ecstasies, Deciphering the Witches' Sabbath*, 1991, Penguin, p. 24.
3. Sheila Rowbotham, *The Past is Before Us; Feminism in Action Since the 1960s*, Pandora Press, London, 1989.
4. 'Good enough mothering': Donald Winnicott's concept was deepened by his study of the effects of evacuation on children during the Second World War. It refers to the capacity of the mother, and the child's environment to respond to the child's needs for continuity, reliability and the containment of illusion. Adam Phillips gives a lucid and compelling account of the concept's emergence and development and remarks too on its reassuring quality, *Winnicott*, Fontana Modern Masters, 1988, ch. 3 and p. 86. 'Never Again' 'captures the motivating impulse of the first half-dozen years after the war – never again would there be war; never again would the British people be housed in slums, living off a meagre diet thanks to low wages or no wages at all; never again would mass unemployment blight the lives of millions; never again would natural abilities remain dormant in the absence of educational stimulus.' Introduction, Peter Hennessy, *Never Again*, Penguin, 1991, p. 2.
5. The idea of marriages chilled by six years' separation came to me from seeing Julian Mitchell's play, *Falling Over England*, Amber Lane Press, Oxford, 1994, at the Greenwich theatre in June 1994. The action takes place in 1945, '56 and today. 'This Feminism' (1964), D. W. Winnicott, *Home is Where We Start From: Essays by a Psychoanalyst*, compiled and edited by Clare Winnicott, Ray Shepherd, Madeleine Davis, Pelican 1986, pp. 183–94

emphasizes the phallic 'swank' in feminism in a suggestive essay that is sometimes an uncomfortable read.

6. Sarah Benton, 'Slow death of the political generation', *Guardian*, 3.1.94. p. 16.

7. For example, 'We recognize that the dichotomy of despotism and free society has been essential to the self-awareness of Western societies', Introduction, (ed.) Luisa Passerini, *Memory and Totalitarianism*, International Yearbook of Oral History and Life Stories, vol. 1, Oxford University Press, p. 5.

8. The heroines of Doris Lessing's *The Golden Notebook*, (1962), a precursor of feminism for many of my generation, are in and out of the Communist Party and psychotherapy. They are also new women – 'have women ever lived like this before?' Molly asks Anna, in search of 'real men'.

9. Gareth Stedman Jones, 'The Historiography of Nineteenth Century Britain', *History Today* October 1991; David Cannadine, 'The Present and the Past in the Industrial Revolution 1880–1980', *Past and Present* 103, 1984; Ivy Pinchbeck, *Women Workers and the Industrial Revolution 1750–1850*, Frank Cass, 1969, p. 313.

10. The significance of women's waged work in the industrial revolution is once again a contentious issue as economic and demographic historians have reinterpreted the latter (focusing on indices of slow productivity and rising real incomes) while ignoring the former. Maxine Berg and Pat Hudson, 'Rehabilitating the Industrial Revolution', *Economic History Review*, XLV, 1992, Maxine Berg, 'What Difference did Women's Work Make to the Industrial Revolution?', *History Workshop Journal*, Issue 35, Spring 1993, pp. 22–44. I nevertheless found E. A. Wrigley's lucid reappraisal of the temporality and determinations of the industrial revolution *Continuity, Chance and Change*, Cambridge University Press, 1988, not incompatible with Berg's and Hudson's analysis.

11. Two invaluable studies of London's casual labour markets which critically discuss Mayhew and the relationship between women's and men's labour markets: Gareth Stedman Jones, *Outcast London, A Study in the Relationship between Classes in Victorian Society*, The Clarendon Press, Oxford, 1971, Part One; Jerry White, *The Worst Street in North London, Campbell Bunk, Islington Between the Wars*, RKP, 1986, ch. 2.

12. Nancy Osterud, 'Gender Divisions and the Organization of Work in the Leicester Hosiery Industry', ed. Angela John, *Unequal Opportunities, Women's Employment in England, 1800–1918*, Blackwell, Oxford, 1986, pp. 45–70, discusses these themes, filling them out with empirical detail.

13. See below p. 8. This was (still is) a childhood belief.

14. 'It has not been possible to demonstrate . . . that the human intellect has a particularly fine flair for the truth or that the human mind shows any special inclinations for recognizing the truth. We have rather found, on the contrary, that our intellect very easily goes astray without any warning, and that nothing is more easily believed by us than what, without reference to the truth, comes to meet our wishful illusions'. S. Freud, 'Moses and Monotheism: Three Essays', (1939 (1934–38)), *Standard Edition of the Complete Psychological Works of Sigmund Freud*, translated and edited by James Strachey, vol. XXIII, p. 129. (Hereafter *SE*.)

15. Julia Kristeva, 'Women's Time', translated Alice Jardine, Harry Blake, *Signs*,

Journal of Women in Culture and Society, Autumn 1981, vol. 7, no. 1, pp. 13–35.

16. From a letter in the handwritten collection in the Fawcett Library.
17. See p. 102 below.
18. S. Alexander, Anna Davin, Eve Hostettler, 'Labouring Women', *History Workshop Journal*, Issue 8, Autumn 1979, pp. 174–82.
19. Linda Colley, *Britons: Forging the Nation, 1707–1837*, Yale University Press, 1992, Peter Henessy, *Never Again*, Penguin 1991.
20. 'Girls on Top in Jobs Market', Victor Keegan, *Guardian*, April 9 1994.
21. Beatrix Campbell pointed this out at a conference on Contemporary Psychoanalysis and Contemporary Sexualities, June 1993.
22. Juliet Mitchell, 'Relections on Twenty Years On', eds. J. Mitchell and Ann Oakley, *What is Feminism*? Basil Blackwell, Oxford, 1986.
23. Carolyn Steedman, *Landscape for a Good Woman, Two Women's Lives*, Virago, 1986.
24. Rosalind Delmar, 'What is Feminism?', eds. Juliet Mitchell, Ann Oakley, *What is Feminism?*, op. cit. pp 24–25.
25. The novels which prefigured the Women's Liberation Movement describe mental breakdown: Penelope Mortimer's *The Pumpkin Eater*, 1962, Margaret Drabble's *The Garrick Year*, 1966, Sylvia Plath's *The Bell Jar*, 1963, Doris Lessing's *The Golden Notebook*, 1962.
26. Laura Mulvey points out the rejection of the body in feminist politics of the '70s, *Visual and Other Pleasures*, Macmillan, 1989, p. xii.
27. Juliet Mitchell, *Psychoanalysis and Feminism*, Allen Lane, 1974, Introduction p. xvi.
28. Joan Wallach Scott, *Gender and the Politics of History*, Columbia University Press, New York, 1988 has been the most influential historian in this field. Denise Riley, *Am I That Name, Feminism and the Category of Woman in History*, Macmillan, Basingstoke, 1989.
29. Perhaps a reason why I always emphasize the individualism of feminism. For a different memory Catherine Hall, *White, Male and Middle Class*, op. cit., p. 18.
30. Joan Scott, *Gender and the Politics of History*, op. cit., p. 2; Lyndal Roper, Introduction, *Oedipus and the Devil*, op. cit., pp. 14–15. give different accounts of gender.
31. Keith Thomas, 'The Double Standard', *Journal of the History of Ideas*, 1956 is a notable exception.
32. 'Analysis Terminable and Interminable' (1937) *SE*, vol. XXII, pp. 250–253.
33. General Sir Michael Rose interviewed on R4's *Today* 11.4.94. about the Serbian shelling said 'we have to distinguish between the rhetoric and what is actually happening'.

WOMEN'S WORK IN NINETEENTH-CENTURY LONDON: A STUDY OF THE YEARS 1820–60s

1. For a statement of the purpose and need for a feminist history, see Anna Davin, 'Women and History', in Michelene Wandor (ed.), *The Body Politic*, Stage 1, 1972.
2. Among many contemporary accounts of the breakdown of the family, see Leon Faucher, *Manchester in 1844*, Frank Cass, 1969, pp. 47–8; Frederick

Engels, 'The Condition of the Working Class in England', *Marx and Engels on Britain*, Moscow, 1962, pp. 162–3, 174–82; for Marx's view of the material effects of modern industry on the family, see *Capital*, Dona Torr (ed.), vol. 1, Allen & Unwin, 1971, pp. 495–6.

3. W. E. Houghton, *The Victorian Frame of Mind*, Princeton, 1957, is a useful introduction to Victorian mentalities.

4. Lord Shaftesbury's speech to the House of Commons, 7 June 1842, is cited in Ivy Pinchbeck, *Women Workers and the Industrial Revolution, 1750–1850*, Frank Cass, 1969, p. 267.

5. For example, John Simon, *Report on the Sanitary Condition of the City of London 1849–50*, p. 86:

> It is no uncommon thing, in a room of twelve foot square or less, to find three or four families *styed* together (perhaps with infectious diseases among them) filling the same space day and night – men, women and children, in the promiscuous intimacy of cattle. Of these inmates, it is mainly superfluous to observe, that in all offices of nature they are gregarious and public, that every instinct of personal or sexual decency is stifled, that every nakedness of life is uncovered.

6. The Children's Employment Commission, Parliamentary Papers (PP), 1843, XIII, p. 175. Mrs Austin, *Two Lectures on Girls' Schools, and on the Training of Working Women*, 1857, p. 12. Hannah More (education), Elizabeth Fry (prisons), Mary Carpenter (Ragged Schools), Louisa Twining (workhouses), Octavia Hill (housing and charity reform) all advocated 'industrial training' in the form of housework and needlework for their 'fallen' sisters. These women opened up social work as an appropriate activity for middle-class women. Mrs Jameson's lecture, 'The Communion of Labour', 1855, was the most influential expression of the sentiments embodied in such activities. The contiguity between evangelicalism, philanthropy and early feminism have, since I wrote this essay (1974), been studied: Anne Summers, 'A Home from Home – Women's Philanthropic Work in the Nineteenth Century', in Sandra Burman (ed.), *Fit Work for Women*, Croom Helm, 1979; and F. K. Prochaska, *Women and Philanthropy in 19th Century England*, Clarendon Press, Oxford, 1981.

7. Charles Dickens, *Bleak House*, Household Edn, n.d., p. 56.

8. 1851 Census, vol. 3, PP, 1852–3, LXXXVIII, table 2, p.8. Edward Higgs, 'Women, Occupations and Work in the Nineteenth Century Censuses', *History Workshop Journal*, no. 23, Spring 1987, pp. 59–80, is now indispensable to any historian of women's work.

9. For seasonality and irregularity in the London trades in the nineteenth century, see Gareth Stedman Jones, *Outcast London*, Oxford University Press, 1971, chs. 1–5; H. Mayhew, *London Labour and London Poor*, 4 vols., Dover Publications, New York, 1968, vol. 2 (1861), pp. 297–323. On p. 322, Mayhew wrote,

> I am led to believe there is considerable truth in the statement lately put forward by the working classes, that only one third of the operatives of this country are fully employed, while another third are partially employed, and the remaining third wholly unemployed.

But on the whole political economists spoke of seasonal, irregular, casual or under- rather than un-employment until the 1880s.

10. The preface to the 1841 Census for example stated that:

the number of women about 20 years of age, without any occupation returned, consists generally of unmarried women living with their parents, and of the wives of professional men or shopkeepers, living upon the earnings, but not considered as carrying on the occupation of their husbands. (PP, 1844, XXVII, p.9.)

But see E. Higgs, op. cit., for changing Census classifications. Alice Clark, *Working Life of Women in the Seventeenth Century*, Frank Cass, 1968, chs. 2, 5. Dorothy George, *London Life in the Eighteenth Century*, Kegan Paul, 1930, ch. 4. I. Pinchbeck, op. cit., ch. 12. Clara Collett, 'The Trades of East London Connected with Poverty', in Charles Booth (ed.), *Life and Labour of the People of London*, 17 vols., 1902, 1st series, vol. 4, *Poverty*, p. 249.

11. E. Thompson and E. Yeo, *The Unknown Mayhew*, Pelican, 1973, p. 394. See footnote 78.

12. H. Mayhew, op. cit., vol. 3, p. 344; and see vol. 2, p. 162, for one of Mayhew's sceptical commentaries on the accuracy of the 1841 Census:
    I am informed by persons in the trade that the 'females' here mentioned as chimney-sweepers, and scavengers, and nightmen, must be such daughters of sweeps and nightmen as have succeeded to their businesses, for no women work at such trades; excepting perhaps, in the management and care of the soot, in assisting to empty and fill the bags.(!)
    Also vol. 1, p. 4 for the lack of coster-mongers in the Census.

13. E. Thompson and E. Yeo, op. cit., p. 407.

14. H. Mayhew, op. cit., vol. 3, p. 221:
    (operatives) consist . . . of two distinct classes, that is to say of society and non-society men, or, in the language of political economy, of those whose wages are regulated by custom and those whose earnings are determined through competition . . . As a general rule I may remark that I find the society men of every trade comprise about one tenth of the whole . . . if the non-society men are neither so skilful nor well-conducted as the others, at least they are quite as important a body from the fact that they constitute the main portion of the trade.
    See E. Thompson and E. Yeo, op. cit., pp. 218–19, 409–10; Iorweth Prothero, 'Chartism in London', *Past and Present*, no. 44, 1969; and E. Thompson, *The Making of the English Working Class*, Pelican, 1968, p. 277.

15. Charles Kingsley, *Cheap Clothes and Nasty*, edn. 1850, pp. 510–13.

16. H. Mayhew, op. cit., vol. 2, p. 155. Mudlarks are
    compelled, in order to obtain the articles they seek, to wade sometimes up to their middle through the mud left on the shore by the retiring tide . . .
    They may be seen of all ages from mere childhood to positive decrepitude, crawling among the barges at the various wharfs along the river . . .
    mudlarks collect whatever they happen to find, such as coal, bits of old iron, rope, bones, and copper nails . . . They sell to the poor.

17. Humphrey House, *The Dickens World*, Oxford University Press, 1961, p. 146. H. J. Dyos, *Victorian Suburb, A Study of the Growth of Camberwell*, Leicester University Press, 1961, chs. 2, 3.

18. Charles Dickens, 'The Streets-Morning', *Sketches by Boz*, Household Edn. n.d. p. 22.

19. Charles Dickens, *Our Mutual Friend*, Household Edn, p. 17.

20. Hector Gavin, *Sanitary Ramblings in Bethnal Green*, 1848, p. 11. See also Dr

Mitchell's *Report on Handloom Weaving*, PP, 1840, XXIII, p. 239, for a description of housing in Bethnal Green.

21. Charles Dickens, *The Old Curiosity Shop*, Household Edn, n.d. p. 35.
22. Edwin Chadwick, *Report on the Sanitary Conditions of the Labouring Population of Great Britain*, 1842, p. 166.
23. *The Population Returns of 1831*, 1832, p. 14. These figures refer to the City within and without the walls. For a full account of London's industrial development in this period, P. G. Hall, *Industries of London since 1861*, Hutchinson, 1962, ch. 2.
24. See also K. Marx, op. cit., p. 674:

    Every unprejudiced observer sees that the greater the centralisation of the means of production, the greater is the corresponding heaping together of the labourers, within a given space; that therefore the swifter capitalistic accumulation, the more miserable are the dwellings of the working people. 'Improvements' of towns, accompanying the increase of wealth, by the demolition of badly built quarters, the erection of palaces for banks, warehouses &c, drive away the poor into even worse and more crowded hiding places.

25. 'Report of the Statistical Society on the Dwellings in Church Lane, St Giles's,' *Journal of the Statistical Society of London*, vol. xi, 1848, p. 18.
26. This estimate was constructed from R. Price-Williams, 'The Population of London 1801–1881', *Journal of the Royal Statistical Society of London*, 1885, no. 48, pp. 349–432.
27. Eric Hobsbawm, 'The 19th Century Labour Market', in Centre for Urban Studies (ed.), *London, Aspects of Change*, 1961, p. 9.
28. Apx to Fifth Annual Report of the Registrar-General of Births, Deaths and Marriages, PP, 1843, XXI, p. 283.
29. J. Hollingshead, *Ragged London in 1861*, 1861, p. 143.
30. E. Thompson and E. Yeo, op. cit., p. 122.
31. Charles Dickens, *The Old Curiosity Shop*, Household edn., n.d., p. 57.
32. Derek Hudson (ed.), *Munby, Man of Two Worlds*, J. Murray, 1972, p. 99.
33. D. George, op. cit., p. 170.
34. 'Report of an Investigation into the State of the Poorer Classes of St George's in the East', *Journal of the Statistical Society of London*, August 1848, p. 203. Of the women's occupations only one polisher, one yeast maker, and one coal wharf keeper fall outside the conventional category of 'women's work'.
35. Eric Hobsbawm's 'Introduction', Karl Marx, *Pre-Capitalist Economic Formations*, translated by Jack Cohen, 1964 edn, Lawrence and Wishart, p. 9.
36. Handicraft guilds excluded division of labour within the workshop by their refusal to sell labour power as a commodity to the merchant capitalist. See K. Marx, *Capital*, vol. 1, op. cit., pp. 352–3.
37. ibid., p. 341. 'The collective labourer, formed by the combination of a number of detail labourers, is the machinery specially characteristic of the manufacturing period.'
38. ibid., pp. 342–3.
39. A. Clark, op. cit., especially pp. 154–61.
40. K. Marx, op. cit., p. 646. Veronica Brechey's essay on female wage labour in 'Capitalist Production', ch. 2 of *Unequal Work*, Verso, 1987, further elucidates this analysis.

41. See P. Laslett, *The World We Have Lost*, Methuen, 1971, ch. 1; A. Clark, op. cit., p. 156, for women and marriage. Spinning for example, women's most important industrial work in the manufacturing period was ideal 'employment for odd minutes and the mechanical character of its movements which made no great tax on eye or brain, rendered it the most adaptable of all domestic arts to the necessities of the mother'. ibid., p. 9.

42. K. Marx, op. cit., p. 419. He was wrong of course, about the equalization of labour forces!

43. Select Committee on Handloom Weavers, PP., 1834, X, q. 4359.

44. Raphael Samuel, 'The Workshop of the World: Steam Power and Hand Technology in Mid-Victorian Britain', *History Workshop Journal*, Issue 3, Spring 1977, pp. 6–73, gives a definitive account of the continuing power of hand-labour in industrial production.

45. G. Stedman Jones, op. cit., ch. 4; Arthur Redford, *Labour Migration in England, 1800–50*, Manchester University Press, 1964, pp. 48–9, 137–9. In times of good trade, for instance in the Spitalfields silk industry, whole families were employed, and

> from the metropolis, the demand for labour goes into the country. All the old weavers are employed with their wives and families; agricultural labourers are engaged on every side, and everyone is urged to do all he can. Blemishes for which at other times a deduction from the wages would have been claimed, are now overlooked. Carts are sent round to the villages and hamlets, with the work, for the weavers, that time may not be lost in going to the warehouse to carry home or take out work. PP, 1841, X, p. 18.

46. Under- or un-employment was one of the features of the industrial reserve army of labour, since the demand for labour-power followed the fluctuations of the trade cycle. See K. Marx, op. cit., ch. 25, section 3. In those trades which had not been transformed by the factory system and machinery, lengthening of the working day and the reduction of wages below subsistence were the only means of increasing the productiveness of labour and hence surplus value. See ibid., pp. 302–3, 475, 484, 658–9.

47. H. Mayhew, op. cit., vol. 2, p. 312.

48. ibid., p. 314.

49. An analysis of the role of women in these struggles is to be found in Barbara Taylor, *Eve and the New Jerusalem*, Virago, 1983, ch. 4.

50. Statistical Society Journal, op. cit., p. 203.

51. K. Marx, op. cit., p. 179.

> The distinction between skilled and unskilled labour rests in part on pure illusion, or, to say the least, on distinctions which have long since ceased to be real, and that survive only by virtue of a traditional convention; in part on the helpless condition of some groups of the working class, a condition that prevents them from exacting equally with the rest the value of their labour power.

For women's exclusion from skilled men's unions see Barbara Drake, *Women in Trade Unions*, Labour Research Dept and Allen & Unwin, 1920, chs. 1–3.

52. E. Thompson and E. Yeo, op. cit., pp. 518–9.

53. House of Lords Sessional Papers, 1854–5, vol. 5, p. 27.

54. E. Thompson and E. Yeo, op. cit., p. 525.

55. (Apx) Reports and Evidence, Children's Employment Commission, PP, 1843, XIV, ff. 29, 204.
56. E. Thompson and E. Yeo, op. cit., p. 528.
57. C. Dickens, 'Shops and Their Tenants' *Sketches by Boz*, Household Edn, ch. III, p. 28.
58. I. Pinchbeck, op. cit., p. 290.
59. H. Mayhew, op. cit., vol. 1, p. 363.
60. E. Thompson and E. Yeo, op. cit., p. 363.
61. ibid., p. 452.
62. PP, 1843, XIV, op. cit., ff. 242–3.
63. J. Grant, *Lights and Shadows of London Life*, vol. 1, 1842, p. 196.
64. PP, 1843, XIV, ff. 241–2, and following quotes from same source.
65. G. Dodds, *Days at the Factory*, 1843, pp. 370–71, and following quotes from same source.
66. E. Thompson and E. Yeo, op. cit., p. 534 and following quotes.
67. J. R. MacDonald, *Women in the Printing Trades*, 1904, chs. 1 and 2.
    Summarizing the reasons why women replaced men, MacDonald wrote:
    The advantages of the woman worker are:
    1. That she will accept low wages; she usually works for about half the men's wages.
    2. That she is not a member of a Union, and is, therefore, more amenable to the will of the employer as the absolute rule of the workshop.
    3. That she is a steady worker (much emphasis must not be placed upon this, as the contrary is also alleged), and nimble at mechanical processes, such as folding and collecting sheets.
    4. That she will do odd jobs which lead to nothing.
    Her disadvantages are:
    1. That she has less technical skill than a man, and is not so useful all round.
    2. That she has less strength at work and has more broken time owing to bad health and, especially should she be married, domestic duties, and that her output is not so great as that of a man.
    3. That she is more liable to leave work just when she is getting most useful; or, expressing this in a general way, that there are more changes in a crowd of women workers than in a crowd of men workers.
    4. That employers object to mixed departments.
68. G. Dodds, op. cit., p. 139, and following quotes from the same source.
69. Dr Mitchell, 1840, op. cit., p. 271.
70. *Household Words*, 1852, vol. V, pp. 152–5; Children's Employment Commission, op. cit., pp. 252–56.
71. 'Transfer Your Custom', London, 1857, p. 16.
72. C. Booth (ed.), op. cit., vol. 4, p. 299. Clara Collett wrote of women workers, 'the position of the married woman is what her husband makes it, whereas her industrial condition may depend largely upon her position and occupation before marriage' ibid., p. 298, and see ibid. for married women's lack of freedom of movement.
73. H. Mayhew, op. cit., vol. 1, p.151.
74. PP, 1843, XIV, op. cit., f. 298.
75. H. Mayhew, op. cit., vol. 1, p. 466.

76. ibid., p. 39 and pp. 483, 172 the following quotes.
77. *The City Mission Magazine*, vol. 10, 1836, p. 127.
78. H. Mayhew, op. cit., vol. 3, p. 307.
79. H. Mayhew, vol. 1, pp. 463–4. Kensal Green was apparently 'the paradise of laundresses', Mary Bayley, *Mended Homes and What Repaired Them*, 1861.
80. 'Transfer Your Custom', op. cit., 1857, p. 22.
81. H. Mayhew, op. cit., vol. 1, p. 496.
82. ibid., vol. 1, p. 439.
83. I have filled out Mayhew's list. ibid., vol. 2, p. 457, and for the Irish women, vol. 1, p. 88.
84. ibid., vol. 1, pp. 43–4.
85. ibid., vol. 1, pp. 385–6.
86. Mayhew allowed working people to describe their own lives, buttressing their conversation with information from trade unions, parliamentary papers and so on. By the poor, he meant 'all those persons whose incomings are insufficient for the satisfaction of their wants'. By allowing the poor to define poverty themselves he was unique among Victorian investigators. However he did promote the notion that women and children should be the economic dependants of their menfolk, as a solution to the 'superfluity' of casual labour. England was producing sufficient wealth to support all her population, he argued, but not enough employment. Women should therefore return to the house. This underlying assumption led him to concentrate on men's casual labour rather than women's. See E. Thompson and E. Yeo, op. cit.; their introductory essays describe and assess Mayhew's methods of work.
87. E. Thompson and E. Yeo, op. cit., p. 463.
88. ibid., p. 139.
89. Appendix to *Report on Condition of Hand-Loom Weavers*, PP, 1840, XXIV, p. 77.
90. E. Thompson and E. Yeo, op. cit., pp. 142–3.
91. 'Transfer Your Custom', op. cit., p. 11.
92. E. Thompson and E. Yeo, op. cit., pp. 525–6.
93. According to the vestry-clerk of the Stepney Union, in a letter to the Poor Law Commissioners:
    The Commissioners are probably aware that the indoor female paupers within this and the neighbouring unions, for many years past, have been principally employed in needlework, such as shirtmaking or slopwork, which is almost the only kind of employment open generally to females out of doors within this district, in which there are no manufactories employing female labour. To this resource they are almost invariably driven whenever deprived of husbands or of parents. PP, 1843, XIV, op. cit., p. 124.
94. E. Thompson and E. Yeo, op. cit., p. 159.
95. PP, 1843, XIV, op. cit., f. 270.
96. H. Mayhew, op. cit., vol. 1, p. 45.
97. ibid., p. 372.
98. ibid., pp. 464–5.
99. PP, 1840, XXIII, op. cit., p. 270. According to the 'Investigation into the Poorer Classes of St George's in the East', op. cit., p. 198, the children observed by the Society were 'apparently very healthy' and sent as early as

possible to school, 'though sometimes into little, filthy, smokey, dame schools'; others were 'clean and fairly ventilated, and kept by persons with habits of order and propriety'.

100. H. Mayhew, op. cit., vol. 1, pp. 462–3.
101. ibid., vol. 3, p. 410.
102. Mins. of Evidence, Select Committee on Police of the Metropolis, PP, 1828, vol. 6, p. 31.

'BRINGING WOMEN INTO LINE WITH MEN': THE WOMEN'S TRADE UNION LEAGUE: 1874–1921

This paper was first given to a History Staff seminar at the University of California, Santa Cruz in February 1983, and to a Labour History School at Ruskin College on 'Women, work and trade unionism since the Industrial Revolution' in September 1983.

1. Sidney and Beatrice Webb, *The History of Trade Unionism* (1894), printed by the authors for the Movement, 1919, p. ix; p. 428 for the list of trades with heavy density of members; *Industrial Democracy* (1897), Longmans Green, London, 1920. See also their *Problems of Modern Industry*, Longmans Green, London, 1902. Beatrice Webb, *My Apprenticeship*, Longmans Green, London, 1926, ch. 7, 'My Apprenticeship', gives an account of the origins of this project; Beatrice Webb, *Our Partnership*, eds. Barbara Drake, Margaret I. Cole, Longmans Green, London, 1947, ch. 2 describes its execution.
2. Webbs, *History*, pp. 336–7. The name of the League was changed to Women's Trade Union League in 1891. I refer to the League throughout.
3. 'The facts that women have a lower standard of comfort than men, that they seldom have to support a family, and that they are often partially maintained from other sources, all render them, as a class, the most dangerous enemies of the artisan's Standard of Life', Webbs, *Industrial Democracy*, p. 497. and pp. 495–507.
4. Barbara Drake, *Women In Trade Unions*, Labour Research and George Allen & Unwin, London 1920, p. 9 for the 1870s estimate. H. A. Clegg, Alan Fox, A. F. Thompson, *A History of British Trade Unions since 1889*, vol. 1 1889–1910, Clarendon Press, London, 1977 edn. pp. 469, 467. The eight million men excludes professional workers, domestic workers and the armed forces. Barbara Drake, a Fabian, is still *the* indispensable study of women and trade unions. See also Sheila Lewenhak, *Women and Trade Unions*, Ernest Benn, London, 1977, ch. 5; Sarah Boston, *Women Workers and the Trade Unions*, Davis-Poynter, London, 1980, ch. 2. Lewenhak and Boston have slightly different emphases. Lewenhak argues for a feminist presence in the Trade Union Movement; Boston believes that the lack of a socialist perspective held women's trade unions back.
5. Webbs, *History*, p. 23.
6. A. Aspinall, *The Early English Trade Unions, Documents from the Home Office Papers in the Public Record Office*, Batchworth Press, London, 1948, Introduction; E. C. Tufnell, *The Character, Object and Effects of Trades Unions with some Remarks on the Laws concerning them*, 1834; George Howells, *The Conflicts of Capital and Labour*, London, 1878, second edn.

1890. The first edition of the Webbs' *History* included 14 pages of bibliographies, details of which are included with their papers at the London School of Economics Library. See also the bibliographical note at the end of *Industrial Democracy*.

7. For the political context of these Acts, E. P. Thompson, *The Making of the English Working Class*, Penguin, 1964, Part One.

8. Webbs' *History*, pp. 96–109. The Webbs recognized a kindred spirit in Place, a follower of Jeremy Bentham and James Mill, whose 'ideal may be summed up as political Democracy with industrial liberty' and who believed in freedom of contract between workman and employer. Place had researched trade disputes throughout Britain since 1814; he worked through the newspaper the *Gorgon* from 1818. Undismayed by public hostility and some trades union suspicion, he gathered information 'Knowing that with an English public the strength of his cause would lie, not in any abstract reasoning or appeal to natural rights, but in an enumeration of actual cases of injustice'. The workmen he said 'were not easily managed . . . Taxes, machinery, laws against combinations, the will of the masters, the conduct of magistrates – these were the fundamental causes of all their sorrows and privations . . . I had to discuss everything with them most carefully', etc. The employers, according to the Webbs, believed higher wages would reduce profits; parliamentarians believed higher wages would increase prices.

9. Political economy, the legislature and employers, continued to be divided on the effects of trades unions after 1825. In the 1830s the Oxford Professor of Political Economy, Nassau Senior, compiled a report recommending draconian legislative repression of them on the grounds of conspiracy; it was never published. Both Sir Robert Peel, Tory Prime Minister till 1830, and Lord Melbourne, Whig Prime Minister from 1830, regarded unions as a 'difficulty and danger' to the nation. This division of opinion continued until the 1860s at least, Webbs' *History*, pp. 138–141. E. C. Tufnell, *The Character, Object and Effects of Trades Unions*, 1834, for an eloquent argument against trade unions.

10. Webbs, *The History of Trade Unionism*, p. 291. This chapter is the Webbs at their best.

11. Webbs, *History*, p. 240; on pp. 178–9 the Webbs argue that this new leadership imbibed 'middle-class ideas'.

12. Webbs, *Trade Union History*, chs 4 and 5; p. 272 for a summary of Harrison's report to the 1867–9 Royal Commission on Trade Unions.

13. Webbs, *History*, p. 93 for the conditions of the 'class-war' which has characterized the nineteenth century. E. C. Tufnell's acute but hostile history (note 6) had argued that unions formed in opposition to factories and machinery; consequently manufacturers either moved their factories, or introduced labour from the agricultural districts, p. 59, and throughout.

14. Howell, *The Conflicts of Capital and Labour*, op. cit. p. 147; Ben Tillett, 'Trade Unions for Women', *Women's Trade Union Review*, 23 Oct. 1896, p. 8. Unions were formed among non-craftsmen in the building trades, transport, mining and agriculture as well as textiles, for example. For the most effective critical qualification of the Webbs, G. D. H. Cole, 'Some Notes on British Trade Unionism in the Third Quarter of the Nineteenth Century', ed. E. M.

Carus-Wilson, *Essays in Economic History*, vol. 111, Edward Arnold, London, 1962, pp. 202–220.

15. *Industrial Democracy*, pp. 495–507, p. 698, the Webbs distinguish also between the Standard Rate of the African and the Jew. See also S. Webb, 'Women's Wages', *Problems of Modern Industry*, pp. 46–81, in which he argues that women have something to sell other than their labour; and Mrs Sidney (Beatrice) Webb, 'The Wages of Men and Women, Should They be Equal?', The Fabian Society, London, 1919, first published as the Minority Report of the War Cabinet Committee on Women in Industry, PP, 1919, vol. 31, pp 254–341, in which she argues for the 'Occupational or Standard Rates' (p. 254), and no discrimination on account of sex, creed or race.

16. Webbs, *History*, p. 296.

17. Webbs, *Industrial Democracy*, p. 460 for trades with a tradition of patrimony. Keith McClelland, 'Time to Work, Time to Live; Some Aspects of Work and the Re-formation of Class in Britain, 1850–1880', Patrick Joyce, ed., *The Historical Meanings of Work*, Cambridge University Press, 1987, p. 194. McClelland gives a valuable discussion of 'independence' pp. 180–209, especially part 3. Arthur Scargill evoked the miners' patrimony during the strike of 1984–5.

18. Meanwhile the Webbs' sinister solution to the weaklings and degenerates produced by the 'parasitic' trades, was to recommend Labour Colonies to prevent degeneration spreading, *Industrial Democracy*, pp 784–789.

19. Webbs, *Industrial Democracy*, pp. 495–498.

20. The first Trades Union Congress met in Manchester in 1868 and annually since 1871, G. D. H. Cole, 'Some Notes on British Trade Unions', p. 214.

21. E. Sylvia Pankhurst, *The Suffragette Movement, An Intimate Account of Persons and Ideals* (1931), Virago, 1977, p. 47.

22. WPPL, 3rd Annual Report, 1877, p. 9.

23. Lady Dilke's trade union notebook, in the Trade Union Congress Library, quoted in Barbara Askwith, (see note 33 below) 1969, p. 194.

24. Goldman, *Emma Paterson*, p. 124. Emma Paterson comes alive in her speeches and writings in the League literature in the British Library; some in the Tuckwell Collection at the Library of the Trades Union Congress, available on microfiche. Barbara Drake, *Women in Trade Unions*, manages to be both detailed and analytical in its history of the League; see also the obituary 'Emma A. Paterson', *Englishwoman's Review*, Dec. 15, 1886, pp 540–543; and Emilia F. S. Dilke, 'Benefit and Trades Unions for Women', *Fortnightly Review*, n.s. vol. 45, Jan–June 1889, pp. 852–856. The latter says she was dismissed from her post as secretary to the Society for the Promotion of Women's Suffrage: 'The ladies have complimented me on my zeal,' she said, 'but they say my bodily presence is weak and my speech contemptible; so I must make room for one who can present them better.'

25. Beatrice Webb met Shipton at the TUC in 1889 where he was in opposition to the new unions, Norman and Jeanne Mackenzie, eds, 'Glitter Around and Darkness Within', *The Diary of Beatrice Webb, volume one, 1892–1905*, Virago and the London School of Economics and Political Science, 1982, p. 291.

26. Beatrice Webb, *My Apprenticeship*, pp. 142–151, suggests that the 'impulse of self-subordinating service' passed in mid-century from God to Man, and gives as its antecedents the American War of Independence, the French Revolution,

the Utilitarians and Robert Owen's life and work. With her contemporaries she learnt her Comtism, from the writings of G. H. Lewes, John Stuart Mill and Frederic Harrison the champion of Trade Unions. *Autobiography of John Stuart Mill*, with a Preface by John Jacob Coss, Columbia University Press, 1960, p. 149 criticizes Comte's elevation of philosophers as a source of despotic political authority. Royden Harrison, 'Professor Beesly and the Working-Class Movement', eds. Asa Briggs and John Saville, *Essays in Labour History*, Macmillan, London, 1967, pp. 205–241 outlines the relationship between the Positivists and the English trade union movement and argues convincingly that their work and thought represented a break with Liberalism.

27. Frederic Harrison, *Fortnightly Review*, 1865, vol. 1, May–Aug, p. 10. Beatrice Webb gives an attractive portrait of the Frederic Harrisons in *My Apprenticeship*, pp. 144–5; and p. 149 for a summary of his lecture, 'Live for others', the essence of Comteism, or the religion of humanity.

28. Paterson's friend and colleague in the WTUL, Miss Jeanette Wilkinson, had a similar working life and political formation. Born in 1842, the daughter of a London warehouseman who earned her living as an upholsteress from seventeen years, she studied to become a teacher at the Birkbeck Institute (walking there and back every evening from Peckham), worked briefly as a school teacher in the East End, till ill-health forced her to stop. She was secretary to the Vigilance Society, organizing secretary and lecturer for the Bristol and West of England Suffrage Society, organizer for the National Society for Women's Suffrage. An advocate of political representation and education for the poor from whom she herself came, she joined the Liberal Association in the mid-1880s. At the time of her death in 1886, she had succeeded (against serious opposition) in securing a resolution in favour of women's suffrage at the Trades Union Congress in 1885, where she was a regular and respected delegate of the Upholstresses Society. She had also made herself an expert on the Irish question and advocate of Home Rule. Obituary by Eliza Orme, *Englishwoman's Review*, Sept. 15, 1886, pp. 385–391. See also Gertrude Tuckwell, *Constance Smith*, London, 1931, a copy of which is in the Tuckwell Collection of the TUC Library, and Tuckwell's own unpublished ms. in the Tuckwell Collection.

29. Obituary 'Emma A. Paterson', *Englishwoman's Review*, Dec. 15, 1886, pp. 540–543; 'Thomas Paterson' by his wife, B. T. Hall, *Our Sixty Years*, published by The Working Men's Club and Institute Union, 1922, pp. 316–321. Thomas Paterson's book, *New Methods of Mental Science*, 1886, the product of 15 years' labour was published by his wife posthumously.

30. Goldman, *Emma Paterson*, p. 118, she was quoting from *The Times*. The Royal Commission on Labour, 5th and Final Report, Part 1, 1894, vol. 35, para 263, quoting the Board of Trade figures said that women's wages, in the second half of the nineteenth century, like men's have 'steadily increased with the growing wealth of the country, though not equally in all occupations'; para 267 discusses the 'exceptionally low' wages of women in sweated and home-working trades. Interesting to compare the League's analysis with the Fabian Women's below pp. 153–5, 165–7.

31. Goldman, *Emma Paterson*, p. 118.

32. *Women's Union Journal*, (WUJ) vol. 1, no. 4, May 31, 1876, p. 18.

33. The League created a spectacle of working women. The half-starved, roughly-

clothed, wan-faced working woman appears again and again in the *WUJ* and *Women's Trade Union Review* (WTUR) as she did at meetings and on public demonstrations. She was held up to rouse both the Christian and humanist conscience among the wealthy classes, and the respectable working men. See Barbara Askwith, *Lady Dilke, A Biography*, Chatto and Windus, London, 1969, p. 191; Sylvia Pankhurst, *The Suffragette Movement*, p. 125 on the power of poverty to rouse pity.

34. *Industrial Remuneration Conference, The Report of the Proceedings and Papers*, read in Prince's Hall, Piccadilly, under the Presidency of Sir Charles W. Dilke, January 1885, Cassell, London, p. 5; the gulf between wealth and want is a quote from Frederic Harrison, positivist advocate of trade unions, *Industrial Remuneration Conference*, p. x. Sir Charles Dilke was MP for Chelsea and heading for political glory when a sexual scandal rocked his career. He married Emilia Dilke (formerly Emilia F. S. Pattison) President of the League from the late 1880s until her death in 1904. He was MP for the Forest of Dean from 1892. B. Webb wrote in *My Apprenticeship* p. 150, that social concern was due neither to intellectual curiosity nor to philanthropy but to 'a panic fear of the newly enfranchised democracy'.

35. Industrial Remuneration Conference, *Report*, p. 203, for the list of causes of low wages, and throughout. Mr B. Jones, of the Co-operative Wholesale Society, for example, said his mother was a weaver and she had had to 'turn out more work in a given time than they did before that (10 hours 1844) Act came into operation', pp. 67–8.

36. *WUJ*, no. 120, vol. XI, Jan. 1886, p. 3.

37. For example, Emilia F. S. Dilke, 'Benefit Societies and Trades Unions for Women', *Fortnightly Review*, n.s. vol. 45, Jan–June 1889, p. 6.

38. Harriet Martineau, 'Female Industry', *The Edinburgh Review*, April 1859, No. CCXXII, pp 293–336, and Mrs Anna Jameson, 'The Communion of Labour: A Second Lecture on the Social Employments of Women', Longman, Brown and Green, London, 1856. Lee Holcombe, *Victorian Ladies at Work; Middle Class Working Women in England and Wales, 1850–1914*, David and Charles, Newton Abbot, 1973, pp. 6–7.

39. For example, Jessie Boucherett, 'How to Provide for Superfluous Women', ed. Josephine Butler, *Women's Work and Women's Culture*, Macmillan, 1869, pp. 27–48.

40. Teresa Olcott, 'Dead Centre: The Women's Trade Union Movement in London, 1874–1914', *The London Journal*, vol. 2, No. 1, May 1976, pp. 33–50 should be read with Drake, *Women in Trade Unions*, chs. 1–4. Drake, p. 13 for the League's model constitution, Mary Agnes Hamilton, *Women at Work, A Brief Introduction to Trade Unionism for Women*, The Labour Book Service, London, 1941, p. 53 for the first League Unions.

41. In the 1880s Emilia Dilke counted twelve in London, 'Benefit Societies and Trades Unions for Women', p. 852.

42. Royal Commission Labour, 5th and Final Report Part 1 (Cd. 7421), PP, 1894 vol. 35, p. 96, para 284.

43. Unions of unskilled men were only beginning to sustain organization in the 1890s. Recession in trade could wipe them out. Eric Hobsbawm, 'General Labour Unions in Britain 1889–1914' (1949), *Labouring Men*, Weidenfeld, 1968 edn., pp. 179–203. An interesting account of women's trades unions in Liverpool,

Linda Grant, 'Women's Work and Trade Unionism in Liverpool, 1890–1914', *North West Labour History Society Bulletin*, no. 7, 1980–81, pp 65–84.

44. Gertrude Tuckwell, unpublished ms., *Autobiography*, p. 129, for example.
45. Emma Paterson had wanted to set up a general union of women in 1874. One was set up in Bristol and survived for 20 years. Beatrice Webb referred to it as the 'Bishops' Wives', 'All the Good Things of Life', Webb Diary, vol. 2, p. 82.
46. Barbara Drake, *Women In Trade Unions*, p. 30; Evelyn March-Phillips, 'The Progress of Women's Trade-Unions', *Fortnightly Review*, n.s. vol. 54, 1893, pp. 93–4 for women in different sorts of unions; B. L. Hutchins, *Women in Modern Industry*, (1915), E. P. Publishing, Wakefield, 1978, chs. 4, 4a.
47. Census Returns 1881

milliners and dressmakers	358,000
cotton, flax, lace	355,000
shirtmakers and seamstresses	82,000
mixed materials, textile	60,000
tailoresses	53,000
silk	37,000
shoe and bootmaking	36,000
straw manufacture	30,000
hosiery	22,000
earthenware	18,000
glove making	13,000
bookbinding	11,000
furniture (upholstery and french polishing)	10,000
nail manufacture	9,000
hat manufacture (not straw)	9,000
box making	9,000
tobacco and cigars	9,000
paper manufacture	8,000
agriculture	65,000
domestic service	1,545,000

There are 53 industries employing from 1,000 to 8,000 female workers, and a large number below 1,000. *Industrial Remuneration Conference*, pp. 206–7.

48. Beatrice (Potter) Webb, *WTUR*, no. 6, July 15, 1892, p. 11, sweated conditions included in any combination an 'unusually low rate of wages, excessive hours of labour, and insanitary workplaces'. See also, ed. Clementina Black, *Married Women's Work* (1915), Virago 1983; Jenny Morris, 'The Characteristics of Sweating', ed. Angela V. John, *Unequal Opportunities, Women's Employment in England 1800–1914*, Basil Blackwell, Oxford, 1986, pp. 95–121. See essays by Joanna Bornat and Deborah Thom in the same volume for discussion of the themes of this essay. See also note 15 for wages.
49. Drake, *Trade Unions*, p. 40 for women hat-trimmers' resistance to a union set up for them by the men in their trade.
50. *WTUR*, no. 50, July 1903, p. 5, Mrs Marland-Brodie's report; Mary Macarthur, 'Trade Unions', ed. Edith Morley, *Woman in Industry from Seven Points of View*, 1908, pp 63–83. Harriet Martineau's 'Female Industry', the most influential essay on women's employment, argued that the increase in female industry in the previous fifty years was the result of the rise of the

middle class, shopping and marketing; that women's low wages drove them into charity, insane asylums or vice; that though 'every girl has an innate longing . . . for the household arts' and the household arts are 'the proper foundation of all others' nevertheless every girl in a manufacturing town should be given 'the clear understanding that she has to choose between being an earner of money in a way which precludes her being a housewife, or being qualified for a housewife, at the expense of some of her power of earning', pp. 294, 308, 316 and 324 respectively.

51. *WUJ*, vol. 1, no. 9, Oct. 31st, 1876, p. 59.
52. Ellen Mappen, 'New Introduction', ed. Clementina Black, *Married Women's Work*, being the report of an enquiry undertaken by the Women's Industrial Council (1915), Virago, 1983, p. ii. C. Black was a novelist, Fabian and friend of Eleanor Marx.
53. Drake, *Women in Trade Unions*, p. 27. Dilke, a close friend of Paterson was very different. She always carried *Confessions* of St Augustine with her, and read the *Imitation of Christ* every day; she was never without a maid and manservant (though she would not let a maid do her hair); attractive and exquisitely dressed she secured the loyalty of her fellow workers in the League. Askwith, *Emilia Dilke*; Gertrude Tuckwell, *Autobiography*, p. 20. Tuckwell was her niece, secretary to the League from the 1890s.
54. 66,000 out of 67,500 laundresses were in favour of the extension of the Factory and Workshop Bill of 1891, Drake, *Women in Trade Unions*, pp. 27–8. Drake attributes the League's change of heart to the influence of Sir Charles Dilke who was an enthusiast for Bismarck's Germany.
55. Dilke, 'The Industrial Position of Women', p. 3.
56. See for example, Ada Nield Chew's review of ed. Mrs S. Webb's *The Case for the Factory Acts*, *WTUR*, no. 43, Oct. 1901, pp. 14–16.
57. Compare these opinions with Tom Mann and Ben Tillett, 'The New Trades Unionism', *Murray's Magazine*, June 1890, p. 5, who put unions before legislation: 'We are convinced that not until Parliament is an integral part of the workers [world] . . . shall we be able to effect any reform by its means'.
58. Jessie Boucherett was among the feminists maintaining their opposition to legislation. E. J. Boucherett, 'The Fall in Women's Wages', *Englishwoman's Review*, n.s., no. CCXXXVII, April 15, 1898, pp. 73–81.
59. In the 1870s, for example from the *WTUR*, mule-spinners, printers, chainmakers, engineers, tailors, boot and shoes, potteries, and hosiery were among those trades where men were threatened with the replacement of women on some processes.
60. Some historians do point out that men's resistance or hostility to female labour in their trade made organizing them difficult when the crunch came which for many trades was the 1890s: Margaret Stewart and Leslie Hunter, *The Needle is Threaded*, Heinemann, 1964, p. 58; W. H. Warburton, *The History of Trade Union Organization in the North Staffordshire Potteries*, Allen & Unwin, 1931, pp. 40, 50.
61. *WTUR*, 15 1894, p. 9. See the London tailor on the same theme p. 25 above.
62. *WTUR*, 17 April, 1895, p. 19. Mrs Marland was a young blowing card room operator.
63. *WTUR*, 16 Jan. 1895, p. 5.
64. *WTUR*, no. 27 Oct 1897, pp. 6–7.

65. *WTUR*, 16 Jan 1895, pp. 3–5.

66. Drake, *Women in Trade Unions*, ch. 3. The 1890s were years of inter-union conflict between 'old' and 'new' unionism; and intensified organized employers' opposition to unions, H. A. Clegg, Alan Fox, A. F. Thompson, *A History of British Trade Unions since 1889*, vol. 1, 1889–1910 (1964), Clarendon Press, Oxford, 1977 edn. p. 96, and all ch. 2, ch. 4. This excellent book contains one page on the WTUL – 'middle-class women'.

67. Clementina Black left the League with others to form the Women's Trade Union Association, an organization to unionize the women in the east London trades. The WTUA became the Women's Industrial Council, see note 53 above.

68. *WTUR*, no. 6, July 1892, pp. 14–16. Drake, *Women in Trade Unions*, p. 30. Grace Oakshott, 'Women's Work in the Cigar Trade', *Economic Journal*, vol. 10, 1900, pp. 502–72 for a more optimistic account of the conditions in the trade, the distinctions between women and men's work, the gradual replacement of men by women and the effects on wages. Women's wages for the same work were 25 per cent lower than men's in the factories, women were also less valuable, she asserts. Women were 'addicted to marriage'; late in the mornings 'because the baby is ill, or because Monday is washing-day and Saturday cleaning-day'; women are 'hampered by their own idiosyncrasies: don't work steadily', they 'laugh and chat'. A girl summed it up thus: 'You work quicker . . . according to whether you want the money or not . . . Married women often work quick, men always do, and the men's work is better. They have families to keep, but we like to lark a bit.' The *Economic Journal* is a useful source for articles on women's work and its value in the 1890s and 1900s. See also the *Women's Industrial Council*'s reports on women's trades, Ellen Mappen, *Helping Women at Work, The Women's Industrial Council, 1889–1914*, Hutchinson, London, 1985, pp. 83–4.

69. *WTUR*, no. 4, Jan. 1892, p. 1.

70. Drake, *Women in Trade Unions*, p. 21. Royal Commission Labour, 5th and Final Report, Part 1, PP, vol. 35, 1894, p. 93, para 276.

71. *Women's Union Journal*, no. 2, March 1876, p. 1.

72. Drake, *Women in Trade Unions*, p. 41.

73. Drake, *Women in Trade Unions*, pp. 41–3; see also, Webb Trade Union Collection, Women's Labour, Coll E, Section A, XLVII, Library of London School of Economics and Political Science, evidence from Mrs Aldridge, of Manchester Trades Council and from Sarah Dickinson about hindrances of men's unions.

74. Letter to *Freewoman*, April, 1912, in ed. Doris Chew, *Ada Nield Chew*, Virago, 1982, pp. 237–8.

75. Mary Macarthur in ed. E. Morley, *Women in Industry*, op. cit., p. 74.

76. This had the approval of Barbara Drake, *Women in Trade Unions*, p. 119. Equal pay was approved every year at the TUC until the 1960s, pushed by white collar unions after 1908.

77. Linda Grant, 'Women's Work and Trade Unionism in Liverpool', p. 76 shows how minimum rates were in fact always differential.

78. Margaret Bondfield, *A Life's Work*, Hutchinson, London, 1948, p. 37.

79. In a note on method the Webbs point to the suitability of the woman for personal observation because of the woman's capacity for 'passive

observation' and her ability to become what she is studying. *Industrial Democracy*, pp. xxvii.
80. B. Webb, *Diary*, vol. 2, pp. 52–54.

WOMEN'S FACTORY WORK IN WESTERN EUROPE

1. ILO, *Equality of Opportunity and Treatment for Women Workers*, Geneva, 1974, p. 77.
2. Robert Gubber, 'Characteristics of Supply and Demand for Women Workers on the Labour Market', in *The Employment of Women* (Final Report of Regional Trade Union Seminar), OECD, Paris, 1970, p. 106.
3. F. Guéland Léridon, General Report, in *The Employment of Women*, p. 27.
4. Department of Employment, Manpower Paper No. 12, *Women and Work: Overseas Practice*, 1975, p. 2.
5. OECD, *The Role of Women in the Economy*, 1975, p. 51.
6. ibid., pp. 47–8.
7. The Employment of Women, 1970, op. cit.
8. ILO, op. cit., p. 1.
9. *Department of Employment Gazette*, April 1978.
10. John Stuart Mill, *The Subjection of Women* (1869) Everyman ed. no. 825, 1965, p. 233 and throughout, offers the classical statement of this argument which has its origins in eighteenth-century feminist polemic.
11. Viola Klein, *Britain's Married Women Workers*, Routledge & Kegan Paul, (1965); 1968 edn, p. 14.
12. F. W. Taylor, *The Principles of Scientific Management*, New York and London, 1911, p. 15.
13. Harry Braverman, *Labour and Monopoly Capital*, Monthly Review Press, 1975.
14. Barbara Drake, *Women in the Engineering Trades*, Trade Union Series no. 3, Fabian Research Dept and Allen & Unwin, 1917, ch. 1, for the story of dilution.
15. Miriam Glucksmann, *Women Assemble, Women Workers and the New Industries in Inter-War Britain*, Routledge, 1990, now tells this story anew. Her starting point was, like Marianne Herzog, her own work on the assembly line; Ruth Cavendish, *Women on the Line*, Routledge, Kegan Paul, 1982.
16. Board of Trade Evidence to the Barlow Commission, pp. 1939–40, Vol. 4, para 87.
17. Henry Fuss, *Unemployment and Employment among Women*, ILO, Geneva, 1936, p. 31.
18. Department of Employment Manpower Paper No. 9, *Women and Work: A Statistical Survey*, 1974, p. 22.
19. Jenny Hurstfield, 'Sex Inequalities and Pay', among the excellent papers exploring women's work and its human implications in local and international dimensions in WSU, *Women and the Economy*, a report of a Conference, Polytechnic of North London, 1988. The feminization of work has continued apace in Britain through the 1990s, enabled by the micro-chip, the free reign of the market, the destruction of manufacture, the abolition of the wages boards and so on. The return of high male unemployment in the 1980s and '90s has moved the focus of liberal anxiety from women's inequality to the

poverty of the family, provoking waves of moral panic around the single parent, and inadequately parented children in particular. A valuable summary of the psychological and economic costs of this economic restructuring is Victor Keegan's 'Girls on top in job market', *Guardian*, 9 April 1994.

20. See this volume p. 267.
21. Cynthia Cockburn, *Brothers, Male Dominance and Technological Change*, Pluto Press, 1983, with considerable skill unravels these processes in The Print. Her *Women, Trade Unions and Political Parties*, Fabian Research Series, no. 349, 1987, discusses women's relations with men in the unions.
22. The term 'piecework' is used loosely throughout industry and designates many different methods of payment by results. Often methods of pay are so complicated that it is difficult for the wage-earner to follow them. The widespread method for women workers in British light engineering is a basic rate with piece-rates above that. I could obtain no information about methods of payment prevalent in the engineering industry in the Federal Republic from the German labour attaché. Indeed the Embassy could give me no information at all about the conditions of women workers.
23. Quoted in the *Sunday Times*, 2 July 1978.
24. Miriam Glucksmann, unpublished manuscript, 1978.
25. Ruth Cavendish, 'On the Line', *Red Rag*, no. 11, pp. 4–6.
26. Diane Gold, *Leeds Tailoring Workers*, unpublished manuscript.

WOMEN, CLASS AND SEXUAL DIFFERENCE IN THE 1830s AND '40s

Raphael Samuel's provocative criticism and enthusiasm helped me in the writing of this essay. Gareth Stedman Jones and Barbara Taylor have been both critical and encouraging. Special thanks to Tony Wailey and Kate Shuckburgh.

1. John Knox; Robert Gittings (ed.), *Letters of John Keats*, Oxford University Press, 1982 edn, letter to J. H. Reynolds, 21.9.1817, p. 21. Barbara Drake, *Women in The Engineering Trade*, Trade Union Series no. 3, Fabian Research Dept and Allen & Unwin, 1917, p. 109.
2. Michelene Wandor (ed.), *Once a Feminist, Stories of a Generation*, Virago, 1990, gives fuller background through interviews.
3. Shulamith Firestone, *The Dialectics of Sex*, 1971. Kate Millett, *Sexual Politics*, Bantam Books, New York, 1970. For a survey of feminist theories of patriarchy, see Veronica Beechey, 'On Patriarchy', *Feminist Review*, no. 3, 1979, pp. 66–83. For a disagreement among feminist historians, see Sheila Rowbotham, Sally Alexander, Barbara Taylor, 'Debate on Patriarchy', in Raphael Samuel (ed.), *People's History and Socialist Theory*, Routledge, Kegan Paul, 1983.
4. For an account of the LNA's campaign, see Judith R. Walkowitz, *Prostitution and Victorian Society, Women, Class and the State*, Cambridge University Press, 1980, Part II. For its effects among women and the Women's Movement, Ray Strachey, *The Cause, A Short History of the Women's Movement in Great Britain* (1928), Virago, 1978, pp. 196–8.
5. Eleanor Rathbone, *Milestones*, Presidential Adresses, Liverpool, 1929, p. 28.
6. Histories of the suffrage movement pursue a fairly straightforward narrative of

the achievement of women's suffrage. The more comprehensive histories focus on the intellectual components of feminist thought, and the class composition of the feminists. There is a general consensus: the former derives from Protestant individualism, Enlightenment thought and philanthropy; and the feminists were overwhelmingly middle class (e.g. Richard Evans, *The Feminists*, 1977; Olive Banks, *Faces of Feminism*, Oxford, 1981). Feminism's middle-class character has led to its neglect by socialist historians. A valuable exception is Juliet Mitchell. 'Women and Equality', in J. Mitchell and A. Oakley (eds.), *The Rights and Wrongs of Women*, Pelican, 1976, pp. 379–99. No recent histories of British feminism have surpassed two classic studies: Ray Strachey's *The Cause* and Sylvia Pankhurst's *The Suffragette Movement: An Intimate Account of Persons and Ideals* (1931), both reprinted by Virago. Written by protagonists in the Cause, both view the struggle as a study in human progress. Ray Strachey, a liberal/socialist, gives a brief but comprehensive survey of the Women's Movement from the mid-nineteenth century to the 1920s. Despite Sylvia Pankhurst's tendency to shape her narrative around the achievements of her family (beginning with her father), *The Suffragette Movement* is nevertheless a mine of information on the early radical, socialist and labour movements, is full of fascinating thumb-nail portraits and packed with analysis. The reader is swept along by the messianic vision of the author, the elements of idealism, sacrifice and martyrdom that characterized the 'Cause'. (See also note 9.)

7. Gareth Stedman Jones, Introduction to *Languages of Class*, Cambridge University Press, 1984, critically assesses the ubiquity of vocabulary of class in English history and politics.

8. Keith Thomas, 'Women and the Civil War Sects', *Past and Present*, no. 13, 1958, pp. 42–57, Christopher Hill, *The World Turned Upside Down*, Temple Smith, 1972, ch. 15.

9. Among recent histories of feminism before the Second World War, Barbara Taylor, *Eve and the New Jerusalem*, Virago, 1983; Jane Rendall (ed.), *Equal or Different, Women's Politics 1800–1914*, Blackwell, Oxford, 1987; Barbara Caine, *Victorian Feminists*, Oxford University Press, 1992; Les Garner, *Stepping Stones to Women's Liberty, Feminist Ideas in the Women's Suffrage Movement 1900–1918*, Heinemann Education, 1984; Brian Harrison, *Prudent Revolutionaries, Portraits of British Feminists between the Wars*, Clarendon Press, Oxford, 1987; Johanna Alberti, *Beyond Suffrage, Feminism in War and Peace 1914–1928*, Macmillan, 1989; Denise Riley, *'Am I That Name?' Feminism and the Category of 'Women' in History*, Macmillan, 1988; Martin Pugh, *Women and the Women's Movement in Britain 1914–59*, Macmillan, 1992.

10. For a recent example of that 'stretching', Ellen Ross, 'Survival Networks: Women's Neighbourhood Sharing in London before World War One', *History Workshop Journal*, issue 15, Spring 1983, pp. 4–28. As I write this, E. Ross, *Love and Toil*, Cambridge University Press, is reaching the bookshops.

11. Karl Marx, 'Preface to a Contribution to the Critique of Political Economy', Marx and Engels, *Selected Works*, Lawrence & Wishart, 1970, pp. 180–85, is the most succinct statement.

12. V. I. Lenin, *What is to be Done*, (1902). Selected Works, vol 1, Lawrence & Wishart, 1947.

13. E. P. Thompson, Preface to *The Making of the English Working Class*, Pelican, 1968 ed.
14. Michèle Barrett, *The Politics of Truth*, Polity, 1992, is a valuable discussion of ideology and its provenance.
15. I thought of deleting Mao. But this is how many Marxists and feminists read him in Britain (and Western Europe) in the 1970s.
16. Juliet Mitchell, Introduction, *Psychoanalysis and Feminism*, Allen Lane, 1974, p. xv.
17. Juliet Mitchell's Introduction in J. Mitchell and J. Rose (eds.), *Feminine Sexuality, Jacques Lacan and the Ecole Freudienne*, Macmillan, 1983, p. 5.
18. Juliet Mitchell's and Jacqueline Rose's introductions to *Feminine Sexuality* are lucid accounts of Lacan's project. J. Mitchell's *Psychoanalysis and Feminism*, Parts 1 and 2, give a careful reading of Freud's account of the acquisition of femininity. The most useful essay on phantasy is Jean Laplanche and J-B Pontalis, 'Fantasy and the Origins of Sexuality', *International Journal of Psychoanalysis*, vol. 49, 1968, Part 1, pp. 1–17. Sigmund Freud, *Femininity* (1933), *Standard Edition*, vol. XXII, pp. 112–35, though controversial among feminists, is still – for me – both riveting and convincing. For aspects of that controversy, Elizabeth Wilson, 'Psychoanalysis: Psychic Law and Order', *Feminist Review*, no. 8, Summer 1981, pp. 63–78, and J. Rose, 'Femininity and Its Discontents', *Feminist Review*, no. 14, Summer 1983, pp. 5–21.
19. The use I make of Lacan's Freud, and the significance of language in the production of meaning and the construction of the subject are my own responsibility. Useful essays are Jacques Lacan, 'The Function and Field of Speech and Language in Psychoanalysis', and 'The Agency of the Letter in the Unconscious or Reason Since Freud', *Ecrits*, Tavistock, 1977, pp. 30–113, 146–78. E. Benveniste, *Problems in General Linguistics*, University of Miami, Florida, 1971.
20. This paragraph was cut from the first publication.
21. I am only speaking of the *public* political speech of these movements. While these do not and cannot convey less accessible forms of popular consciousness, many of which transmitted through oral traditions, myth, ritual, etc. have been lost or forgotten, public political discourse nevertheless indicates some incidents of popular identification. Dorothy Thompson's essay, 'Women in Nineteenth Century Radical Politics', in J. Mitchell and A. Oakley, (eds), op. cit., pp. 112–38, has shaped discussion around women's participation in working-class movements in the first half of the nineteenth century. Lin Shaw's 'Women in Working Class Politics in Norwich', paper given to the Feminist History Group, London, December 1979, covered forms and content of working-class politics in detail and related their decline to the changing local political and industrial structure of Norwich in the second half of the nineteenth century.
22. See for example the many reports on the Handloom Weavers and industrial populations in the 1830s and '40s. And in particular, Report and Minutes of Evidence of the Select Committee on the State of the Woollen Manufacture in England, Parliamentary Papers (PP), 1806, III, and Report from the Select Committee to examine Petitions from Handloom Weavers, PP, 1834, X.
23. R. G. Kirby, A. E. Musson, *The Voice of the People, John Doherty, 1798–1854*, Manchester, 1975, p. 73. Neil J. Smelser's *Social Change in the*

Industrial Revolution, Routledge, Kegan Paul 1959, is often criticized by historians for its dense methodology, mechanistic model of change, and specific inaccuracies. The central hypothesis, however, that operatives grew restless as kinship ties were severed in the reorganization of the labour process is suggestive in the context of this essay. Jane Humphries in 'Class Struggle and the Persistence of the Working-Class Family', *Cambridge Journal of Economics*, 1977, 1, pp. 241–58, and 'Protective Legislation, the Capitalist State and Working Class Men: The Case of the 1842 Mines Regulation Act', *Feminist Review*, no. 19, Spring 1982, argues that the resilience of the working-class family stems in part from men's defence of 'an institution which affects their standard of living, class cohesion and ability to wage the class struggle'.

24. Thomas Hodgskin, *Labour Defended Against the Claims of Capital*, 1825, reprinted 1922, pp. 31, 48, 50.

25. Lin Shaw op. cit. describes the Norwich weaver's political economy (drawn from Hodgskin) as including the demand for a wage to support a wife and three children. Adam Smith, *The Wealth of Nations* (1776), Chicago edn, 1976, pp. 76–7, suggests 'the husband wife together' must earn sufficient to raise four children, on the expectation that two will die, but implies that the woman's wage will only have to support herself. Smith's political economy was approved by radical working men; it was the infusion of Malthusianism into political economy that provoked hostility. For a discussion of the 'family wage' in the transition from manufacture to modern industry see Sally Alexander, *Women's Work in Nineteenth-Century London*, above pp. 3–56. For women's exclusion from skill and workmen's organizations, Ivy Pinchbeck, *Women Workers and the Industrial Revolution, 1750–1850*, Frank Cass 1969, pp. 126–7; for examples of women weaving with husbands, fathers, etc., A. P. Wadsworth and J. De Lacy Mann, *The Cotton Trade and Industrial Lancashire, 1600–1780*, Manchester, 1965, pp. 332, 336. For women in the early textile unions, ibid., ch. 18; H. A. Turner, *Trade Union Growth Structure and Policy*, 1962, Parts II, III and IV. For the masculine language and character of the early Trade Unions, A. Aspinall, *The Early English Trade Unions*, The Batchworth Press 1949, throughout.

26. F. Engels, *The Condition of the Working Class in 1844*, in K. Marx and F. Engels, *On Britain*, Moscow, 1962, pp. 177–9.

27. For example, the skilled tailor speaking to Henry Mayhew quoted in S. Alexander, *Women's Work in Nineteenth-Century London*, p. 25.

28. Michael Ignatieff, 'Marxism and classical political economy' in R. Samuel (ed.), *People's History and Socialist Theory*, Routledge, Kegan Paul, 1981, pp. 344–52, describes the similar narrowing of preoccupations as political economy became an economic science in the mid-nineteenth century.

29. 'Address of the Female Political Union of Newcastle upon Tyne to their Fellow Countrywomen', in D. Thompson (ed.), *The Early Chartists*, Macmillan 1971, p. 130.

30. Richard Pilling's Defence, from F. O'Connor (ed.), *Trail of Fergus O'Connor and 58 other Chartists on a Charge of Seditious Conspiracy at Lancaster*, 1843. I'm grateful to Eileen Yeo for this reference.

31. Address of the Female Union, D. Thompson, *The Chartists*, pp. 214–16, discusses Pilling's sophisticated use of political argument and economic

analysis in his famous defence speech. He was found not guilty. For a fuller discussion of the political language of Chartism, Gareth Stedman Jones, 'The Language of Chartism', James Epstein and D. Thompson (eds.), *The Chartist Experience*, Macmillan 1982, pp. 38–58. The wording of the 1838 Charter is worth quoting in full:

> Among the suggestions we received for improving this Charter, is one for embracing women among the possession of the franchise. Against this reasonable proposition we have no just arguments to adduce, but only to express our fears of entertaining it, lest the false estimate man entertains of this half of the human family may cause his ignorance and prejudice to be enlisted to retard the progress of his own freedom. And therefore, we deem it far better to lay down just principles, and look forward to the rational improvement of society, than to entertain propositions which may retard the measure we wish to promote. (*Address of the Working Men's Association to the Radical Reformers of Great Britain and Ireland*, 1838, p. 9.)

Whether the false estimate is attributed to their fellow working men, or their representatives in Parliament is not clear.

32. D. Thompson, 'Women in Nineteenth Century Radical Politics', p. 131. Cecil Driver, *Tory Radical, The Life of Richard Oastler*, Oxford, 1946, p. 408.

33. Extract from R. J. Richardson, 'The Rights of Woman', in D. Thompson, *The Early Chartists*, pp. 115–36.

34. Cecil Driver, *Tory Radical, The Life of Richard Oastler*, Oxford, 1946, p. 434, but see whole of ch. 32 for Oastler's Tory democracy.

35. Barbara Taylor, 'Lords of Creation', *New Statesman*, 7 March 1980, pp. 361–2, and G. Stedman Jones, 'Utopian Socialism Reconsidered', unpub. ms. 1979, B. Taylor, *Eve and the New Jerusalem*, ch. 2 for a discussion of Owenite ideas on the position of women.

36. Mins. of Evidence, Select Committee on Combinations of Workmen, PP, 1838, VIII, p. 263, R. G. Kirby, A. E. Musson, op. cit., p. 299, and passim. The Keats quote above (p. 122) is from *Letters*, op. cit., p. 21.

37. Angela John, *By the Sweat of their Brow, Women Workers at Victorian Coal Mines*, Routledge, Kegan Paul, 1981, p. 57. Those for and against the Factory Acts did not divide along party lines. By the 1840s there was universal agreement that female labour should be protected; the argument in Parliament was how best that intervention should be made. Samuel Kydd (pseud. Alfred), *The History of the Factory Movement*, 1857, is the most interesting discussion of contemporary political opinion as it divided between those who interpreted the laws of nature and revelations with benevolence (e.g. pp. 117, 118 and 208) and those who feared the dangers of intervening in the freedom of labour, and all opinion in between (esp. ch. 15).

38. Intentions are blurred, but whereas the working men delegates from the factory districts celebrated their victory in 1847 with the following resolution:

> That we are deeply thankful to Almighty God for the success which has on all occasions attended our efforts in this sacred cause, and especially for the final result of all our labours, by which the working classes are now put in possession of their long-sought-for-measure – the Ten Hours Bill

their friends in parliament reaffirmed their hopes that the increased leisure won would be used for 'mental and moral improvement' and especially that the female factory operatives would promote and improve their 'domestic habits'. Philip Grant, (ed.), *The Ten Hours Advocate*, for the Lancashire Short-Time Committee, 1846–7, pp. 300–301.

39. Ethel Snowden, *The Feminist Movement*, Collins, n.d. (1911), p. 258.

EQUAL OR DIFFERENT: THE EMERGENCE OF THE VICTORIAN WOMEN'S MOVEMENT

1. Sophia, *Woman Not Inferior to a Man* (1739), Brentham Press, 1975 edn. p. 10.
2. 'Sophia', p. 33. Both Mary Wollstonecraft in *A Vindication of the Rights of Woman* (1792), Everyman edn no. 825, 1965 pp. 20–22, and Virginia Woolf in *Three Guineas* (1938), Penguin, 1977, pp. 23–6, mock men for their attachment to uniforms and display.
3. M. Wollstonecraft, op. cit., p. 11 on men's tyranny, their 'forcing' of women into domestic duty and family; and the analogy with slavery.
4. Ray Strachey, *The Cause, A Short History of the Women's Movement in Great Britain* (1928), Virago, 1978, chs. 4, 5, 6. Jane Rendall, '"A Moral Engine"? Feminism, Liberalism and the *English Woman's Journal*', in Jane Rendall, (ed.), *Equal or Different, Women's Politics 1800–1914*, Blackwell, Oxford, 1987, pp. 112–38.
5. *English Woman's Journal*, vol. 4, no. 19, February 1860, p. 59.
6. *English Woman's Journal*, op. cit., pp. 19, 60.
7. Letter in the Fawcett Library autograph collection.
8. John Vincent, *The Formation of the British Liberal Party, 1857–1868*, Harvester, 1976.
9. For Mill's contribution to feminism see 'Introduction', Alice S. Rossi (ed.), J. S. Mill, Harriet Taylor Mill, *Essays on Sex Equality*, University of Chicago Press, London, 1970; Barbara Caine, *Victorian Feminists*, Oxford University Press, 1992, ch. 2.
10. Judith R. Walkowitz, *Prostitution and Victorian Society, Women, Class and the State*, Cambridge University Press, 1980, chs. 5, 6. Josephine Butler, *Personal Reminiscences of a Great Crusade*, 1910, pp. 45, 54.
11. R. Strachey, op. cit., ch. 18; Sylvia Pankhurst, *The Suffragette Movement, An Intimate Account of Persons and Ideals* (1931), Virago, 1977, p. 250 and throughout from Part 5.
12. A. V. John, *By the Sweat of their Brow*, Routledge & Kegan Paul, 1983; B. L. Hutchins and A. Harrison, *A History of Factory Legislation*, P. S. King, 1911.
13. R. Strachey, op. cit.; George Gissing, *The Odd Women* (1893), Virago, 1980, gives a fictional account of these women.
14. Olive Schreiner, *Woman and Labour* (1908), Virago, 1978, was an inspirational essay for feminists and others well into the twentieth century.

THE FABIAN WOMEN'S GROUP: 1908–52

1. Anna Davin, 'Imperialism and Motherhood', *History Workshop Journal*, issue 5, Spring 1978. This essay was written and first published as the Introduction to Maud Pember Reeves, *Round About A Pound A Week* (1913), Virago, 1978.

2. Charles Booth (ed.), *Life and Labour of the People of London*, 17 vols. 1902; Seebohm Rowntree, *Poverty, A Study of Town Life*, 1901.

3. John Burns, quoted in A. Davin, op. cit., p. 28. John Burns' socialism, a practical alternative to Fabian elitism, was founded on anger at his mother's poverty, voracious reading and a working life in London which began at ten years old in a candle factory. He was the beloved only son of a widow, an Aberdeen woman who washed clothes for a West End clientele, Dona Torr, *Tom Mann and His Times*, vol. 1 (1856–1890), Lawrence and Wishart, 1956, pp. 184–5. The Webbs blew hot and cold on him as a comrade and colleague, Norman and Jeanne Mackenzie (eds.), *The Diary of Beatrice Webb*, vol. 3 (1905–1924), *The Power to Alter Things*, Virago and the London School of Economics, 1984, pp. 24, 79.

4. Carolyn Steedman, *Childhood, Culture and Class in Britain, Margaret Macmillan, 1860–1931*, Virago, 1990, ch. 4.

5. Working-class women's lack of leisure became a theme of Labour women's feminism in the 1920s and 1930s: Margery Spring-Rice, *Working Class Wives, Their Health and Conditions* (1939), Virago, 1981, p. 200, and ch. 5.

6. M. P. Reeves, op. cit., p. 146.

7. Beatrice Webb, *My Apprenticeship*, Longman, 1926, p. 178. Her diaries (note 3), and autobiographies amplify Fabian politics and their context. Barbara Caine, 'Beatrice Webb and The Woman Question', *History Workshop Journal*, issue 14, Autumn 1982, pp. 23–43, is a valuable study.

8. Ray Strachey, *The Cause, A Short History of the Women's Movement in Great Britain* (1928), Virago, 1978, p. 8; Florence Nightingale's 'Cassandra', appendix to *The Cause*, is worth reading in full. Denise Riley, '*Am I That Name?' Feminism and the Category of 'Women' in History*, Macmillan, 1988, ch. 3, argues that women became identified with the social in the nineteenth century. Stephen Yeo, 'The Religion of Socialism', *History Workshop Journal*, issue 4, 1978.

9. *Fabian News*, vol. xix, no. 12, November 1908, p. 92. The Fabian Archive is in Nuffield College Library.

10. M. P. Reeves, op. cit., p. 226.

11. Fabian Women's Group, *Three Years' Work*, 1912, n.d. reprinted in S. Alexander (ed.), *Women's Fabian Tracts*, Routledge, 1988, p. 145. In 1912 the Fabian Society included 849 women among its 2,664 members.

12. Interview with Amber Blanco White, August 1978. *Times* obituary of Amber Blanco White, 6 January 1982.

13. The second was Edith Morley (ed.), *Women Workers in Seven Professions*, 1914; the professions were: teaching, medicine, nursing, sanitary inspection, civil service, clerks and secretaries, and acting.

14. *Fabian Women's Group*, op. cit., S. Alexander (ed.), op. cit. p. 147.

15. Christine Collette, *For Labour and For Women; The Women's Labour League, 1906–1918*, Manchester University Press, 1989; Mary Agnes Hamilton, *Women at Work; a Brief Introduction to Trade Unionism for Women*, The Labour Book Service, London, 1941, ch. 4.

16. Margaret Llewellyn Davies (ed.), *Maternity, Letters from Working Women* (1915), Virago, 1978.

17. *Fabian News*, vol. xxv, no. 6, p. 42.

18. Mabel Atkinson, 'The Economic Foundations of the Women's Movement', *Fabian Tract* no. 175, p. 15, reprinted in S. Alexander (ed.), op. cit., p. 270.
19. *Fabian News*, vol. xxi, no. 3, February 1910, p. 37.
20. For the unionization of women workers before the First World War, Barbara Drake, *Women in Trade Unions*, Labour Research Dept and Allen & Unwin, 1920, ch. 4; for unions among skilled and educated women workers, Mary Macarthur, 'Trade Unions', *Women in Industry from Seven Points of View*, 1908, op. cit., p. 76.
21. Interview with Amber Blanco White, August 1978. There was a cousin or brother, Fabian, who lived with them. I don't know where he went to university. Amber Blanco White told me that once when punished for kicking a football into a glass window by having his pocket money stopped he asked the workmen who came to mend it whether they were being paid trade union wages, 'and he wept bitterly to hear the good news that they were. He could imagine his pocket-money disappearing.' (ibid.) I was also told that her mother 'had not a hint of scandal about her', unlike herself, Jane Lewis, 'Intimate Relations between Men and Women: The case of H. G. Wells and Amber Pember Reeves', *History Workshop Journal*, issue 37, Summer 1994.
22. Ellen Smith, on behalf of the EC of the FWG, 'Wage Earning Women and their Dependants', 1912, found that 85 per cent of the 2,870 women who responded to their questionnaire were self-supporting and nearly 50 per cent of those were responsible or partially responsible for the maintenance of others. 4.8 million women in England and Wales were in paid employment. This was one of the most widely quoted surveys. Sidney Webb, 'The War, Women and Unemployment', in S. Alexander (ed.), op. cit., p. 287, found that the average wage of the woman worker before the First World War was 10s 7d (about 50p).
23. A Davin, op. cit., pp. 19–22.
24. M. G. Fawcett, 'The Emancipation of Women', *Fortnightly Review*, n.s., vol. 50, November 1891, pp. 673–85.

FABIAN SOCIALISM AND THE 'SEX-RELATION'

1. For the birth of the Fabian Society, Norman and Jeanne Mackenzie *The First Fabians*, Quartet, 1979; *Socialism and English Politics, 1884–1918*, Cambridge University Press, 1962, ch. 1. See also Havelock Ellis, *My Life*, Houghton Mifflin, Boston 1939, pp. 199–203. This essay first appeared as the Introduction to *Women's Fabian Tracts*, Routledge, 1988.
2. Beatrice Webb, *My Apprenticeship*, Longman, 1926, p. 57.
3. G. Bernard Shaw, 'The Fabian Society: its early history', Fabian Society, Tract no. 41, 1892, p. 30.
4. H. Ellis, op. cit., p. 203.
5. B. Webb, op. cit., pp. 177–8.
6. Norman and Jeanne Mackenzie (eds.), *The Diary of Beatrice Webb*, vol. 1, 1873–92, *Glitter Around and Darkness Within*, Virago, 1982, p. 115.
7. Norman and Jeanne Mackenzie, *The First Fabians*, op. cit., p. 115. Stephen Yeo, 'The Religion of Socialism', *History Workshop Journal*, issue 4, 1978.
8. G. Bernard Shaw, op. cit., *passim*. The Venturists in Mrs Humphry Ward's *Marcella* (1894), Virago, 1984, are based on the Fabians.

9. Interview with Amber Blanco White (née Reeves), summer 1978.

10. Peter Clarke, *Liberals and Social Democrats*, Cambridge University Press, 1978, p. 34.

11. The Fabians extended David Ricardo's theory of rent to explain the genesis of both surplus value and political and cultural inequality. Differential rents on land, capital, and brains were the cause of social injustice.

12. Ruth Cavendish Bentinck, 'The point of honour', Fabian Society, Tract no. 151, 1910, S. Alexander (ed.), *Women's Fabian Tracts*, Routledge, 1988, p. 129. B. Webb, op. cit., p. 178, no section of manual workers, she wrote, was secreting socialism!.

13. Norman and Jeanne Mackenzie, *The First Fabians*, op. cit., p. 185. The Mackenzies describe Kate Conway: 'The daughter of a Congregational minister and a graduate in classics from Newnham College, [she] was the kind of New Woman who was becoming familiar in socialist circles, fusing religion, social justice, and female emancipation into an emotional euphoria of the kind that Webb distrusted.'

14. Beatrice Webb, *Our Partnership*, Longman, 1948, p. 107.

15. The tracts by Beatrice Webb (no. 67) and Maud Pember Reeves, (no. 162) are reprinted in S. Alexander (ed.), op. cit. Barbara Drake *Women in Trade Unions*, Labour Research Dept and Allen & Unwin, 1920. Alice Clark, *Working Life of Women in the Seventeenth Century* (1919), Frank Cass, 1968. See also Beatrice Webb's minority *Report* from the War Cabinet committee on women in industry, 1919, vol. 31, and B. L. Hutchins, *Women in Modern Industry* (1915), E. P. Publishing, West Yorkshire 1978.

16. E.J. Hobsbawm, 'The Fabians reconsidered', in *Labouring Men*, Weidenfeld, 1964. See also pp. 155–6 above.

17. B. Webb, *My Apprenticeship*, op. cit., p. 43.

18. Jane Marcus (ed.), *The Young Rebecca: Writings of Rebecca West, 1911–1917*, Virago, 1983, p. 5.

19. Fabian Women's Group, 'Three years' work, 1908–1911', Fabian Society, in S. Alexander (ed.), op. cit., p. 154. See also the Minutes of the FWG vol. 1.

20. ibid., p. 153.

21. Beatrice Webb, 'Women and the Factory Acts', Fabian Society, tract no. 67, 1896, in ibid., p. 29.

22. Sidney Webb, 'Women's wages', in Sidney and Beatrice Webb, *Problems of Modern Industry*, Longman, 1902, pp. 78–9.

23. Emma Brooke and others, 'A summary of six papers and discussions upon the disabilities of women as workers', Fabian Society, 1909, in S. Alexander (ed) op. cit., p. 108.

24. M. A., 'The economic foundations of the women's movement', Fabian Society, tract no. 175, in ibid., 1914, pp. 273–4.

25. ibid., p. 280.

26. *The Diary of Beatrice Webb*, vol. 1, op. cit. p. 160.

27. *The Diary of Beatrice Webb*, vol. 3, op. cit., '*The Power to Alter Things*', 1905–24. H. G. Wells's *Ann Veronica* (1909) was based on his vision of Amber and the love affair; *The New Machiavelli*, Odham's Press, 1910, included an account of his quarrel with the Fabians and a very convincing satire of the Webbs.

28. Margaret Cole, *Growing up to Revolution*, Longman, 1949, pp. 43–5.

29. B. Webb, *Our Partnership*, op. cit., p. 360.
30. H. G. Wells, *The New Machiavelli*, op. cit., p. 16.
31. G. Bernard Shaw, *The Quintessence of Ibsenism*, Walter Scott, 1891, pp. 31–44.

WOMEN'S VOICES IN THE SPANISH CIVIL WAR

1. Margot Heinemann, 'Remembering 1936', *Women's Review*, October 1986.
2. Bill Alexander, *British Volunteers for Liberty*, Lawrence & Wishart, 1983, ch. 2; Hywel Francis, *Miners Against Fascism, Wales and the Spanish Civil War*, 1984, ch. 2; Jim Fyrth, *The Signal Was Spain, the Aid Spain Movement in Britain*, Lawrence & Wishart, 1986, Parts 1 and 2; Joe Jacobs, *Out of the Ghetto*, Lawrence & Wishart, 1978, ch. 10.
3. See also Claudia Koonz, *Mothers in the Fatherland, Women, the Family and Nazi Politics*, Methuen, 1988; Luisa Passerini, *Fascism in Popular Memory, The Cultural Experience of the Turin Working Class*, translated by Robert Lumley and Jude Bloomfield, Cambridge University Press, 1987. Maria-Antonetta Macciocchi, 'Female Sexuality in Fascist Ideology', *Feminist Review*, no. 1, 1979.
4. Sheila Grant Duff, *The Parting of the Waves, A Personal Account of the Thirties*, Unwin, 1984, p. 148; *Voices*, op. cit., p. 268 and *passim*. for quotes below.
5. For a brief account of the anti-war movement in Britain in the 1930s, see Noreen Branson and Margot Heinemann, *Britain in the 1930s*, Weidenfeld and Nicholson, 1971, ch. 19. On women's involvement see C. Bussy and M. Tims, *Pioneers for Peace*, Virago, 1965; Sybil Oldfield, *Spinsters of this Parish, The Life and Times of E. M. Mayor and Mary Sheepshanks*, Allen & Unwin, 1984, ch. 13; Vera Brittain, *Testament of Experience* (1957), Virago, 1979, *passim*. Leah Manning *A Life, for Education*, Gollancz, 1970, ch. X. For individual views of socialism and fascism see Harold Laski and John Strachey in *I Believe*, Allen & Unwin, 1940. Fyrth, *The Signal Was Spain*, op. cit., argues that the Aid Spain movement awakened understanding of fascism and appeasement and brought politics to the level of actions at which anyone could take part (p. 309). A. J. P. Taylor argues that the Spain question 'transcended politics in the ordinary sense . . . (it) provided for the generation of the thirties the emotional experience of their lifetime', and that what men believed was more important than what was happening: *English History 1914–1945*, Pelican, 1983, pp. 484–7.
6. Communists argued for a 'People's Front' of all anti-fascists from conservatives to left Socialists. The Labour Party in Britain would not co-operate with Communists (nor with Liberals). They had not forgotten the 'class against class' phase of the Communist International which had designated them 'social fascists' until the International's volte face in 1935. For a socialist account of the Independent Labour Party's outline of popular front politics see Fenner Brockway, *Workers' Front*, 1938. For a left-Labour view see G. D. H. Cole, *The People's Front*, Gollancz, 1937. See also Jim Fyrth (ed.), *Britain, Fascism and the Popular Front*, Lawrence & Wishart, 1985.
7. Autobiography of Storm Jameson, *Journey from the North* (1969), 1984, vol. 1, p. 316.

8. Winifred Sandford, 'Caring Through Cruel Times', *Women's Review*, April 1987.
9. *Voices*, op. cit., p. 346. Grant Duff, op. cit., p. 148
10. Gerald Brenan, *The Spanish Labyrinth*, Cambridge University Press, 1943.
11. Ronald Fraser, *Blood of Spain, The Experience of the Civil War, 1936–1939*, Penguin edn., 1981, pp. 431–3.
12. B. Alexander, op. cit., p. 208.
13. Wendy Mulford, *This Narrow Place, Sylvia Townsend Warner and Valentine Ackland, Life, Letters and Politics, 1930–1951*, Pandora, 1988, p. 88.
14. Kay Ekervall, 'Telling Myself', *Women's Review*, May 1987.
15. R. Fraser, op. cit., p. 289.
16. Jill Liddington, *The Life and Times of a Respectable Rebel, Selina Cooper, 1864–1946*, 1984, ch. 22.
17. S. Jameson, op. cit., Part 2: V. Brittain, op. cit., and Paul Berry and Alan Bishop, *Testament of a Generation, The Journalism of Vera Brittain and Winifred Holby* (eds.), Virago, 1985, p. 228.
18. I am thinking in particular of George Orwell, *Homage to Catalonia*, John Summerfield, *Volunteer in Spain*, 1936, James Pettifer, (ed.), *Cockburn in Spain*, 1986, parts of which read like adventure stories.

BECOMING A WOMAN IN LONDON IN THE 1920s AND '30s

Thanks to Catherine Hall and Gareth Stedman Jones.

1. J. B. Priestley, *English Journey*, Heinemann, Gollancz, 1934, p. 401; George Orwell, *The Road to Wigan Pier*, Gollancz, 1937, p. 76.
2. Significantly, Priestley wrote the screenplay for the 1934 Gracie Fields' film, *Sing As We Go*, in which as an unemployed Lancashire millworker Gracie succeeds in reversing the fortunes of both her boss and her workmates. She sets off for Blackpool, metaphor for the bits of the new, cheap, democratic England that Priestley liked: the north, shades of music-hall and English landladies, devoted to immediate fantastic and sensual pleasures, the product of industrial democracy, not the USA.
3. Rebecca West, *Family Memories*, Virago, 1987, p. 15.
4. G. D. H. and M. I. Cole, *The Condition of Britain*, Gollancz, 1937, p. 25; Sidney Pollard, *The Development of the British Economy 1914–1967*, Edward Arnold edn., 1973, ch. 5; Keith Middlemas, *Politics in Industrial Society: The Experience of the British System since 1911*, André Deutsch, 1979, p. 17, which describes the 'middle-class' growth . . . and derelict north'; John Stevenson, *Social Conditions in Britain between the Wars*, Penguin, 1977, p. 39, asks which mattered more in the 1930s, one million unemployed or one million cars?
5. Mary Agnès Hamilton, 'Changes in social life', in Ray Strachey (ed.), *Our Freedom and its Results, by Five Women*, Hogarth Press, 1936, pp. 234–9. See also Winifred Holtby, *Women* (1934) John Lane, The Bodley Head, 1941, introduction.
6. Ellen Wilkinson, *The Town That Was Murdered: The Life-Story of Jarrow*, Gollancz, 1939, pp. 262–3.

7. John Sommerfield, *May Day* (1936), Lawrence & Wishart, 1984, p. 4. p. 30; Max Cohen, *I Was One of the Unemployed*, Gollancz, 1945, p. 40.

8. Priestley's anti-feminism is relatively benign, Orwell's is more virulent. He scarcely writes of a woman except to reduce her to physical or mental caricature. Women of the middle class are especially despised in his documentary and fiction alike for being strike-breakers and materialists. See, for instance, *Keep the Aspidistra Flying* (1936), Penguin, 1963, p. 122, where the anti-hero Gordon argues sourly: 'it's the women who really believe in the money-code. The men obey it; they have to, but they don't believe in it. It's the women who keep it going. The women and their Putney villas and their fur coats and their babies and their aspidistras.' John Sommerfield's heroes echo these sentiments, op. cit., pp. 12, 24, 27, etc.

9. For further discussion of these themes, see 'Women, class and sexual difference in the 1830s and 1840s', pp. 97–126 above.

10. H. Llewellyn Smith, *The New Survey of London Life and Labour* (*NSL* hereafter), vol. 1, P. S. King, 1930, ch. 1.

11. Feminists in the 1920s and 1930s campaigned for equal pay, endowment of motherhood, birth control, custody of children, education and training for women, peace, housing, and health.

12. See, for example, Mary Wollstonecraft, *A Vindication of the Rights of Woman* (1972), Everyman edn. no. 825, 1965 pp. 37, 67–8. For women's addiction to romance in the 1930s, Q. D. Leavis, *Fiction and the Reading Public*, Chatto and Windus, 1965, pp. 27, 54–60.

13. Doris M. Bailey, *Children of the Green*, Stepney Books, 1981, p. 121. Only the 'really respectable' moved from Drury Lane to Becontree, according to Celia Wilmot, second interview, p. 1. The Ministry of Labour memo to the Barlow Royal Commission on the Geographical Distribution of the Industrial Population, *Minutes of Evidence*, 1937–9, p. 251, confirmed that the 'better type of person' from the slum areas was rehoused in the 1930s by the LCC.

14. Census, *General Report*, 1931, p. 111. For London, *NSL*, vol. 11, 1931, p. 19, and vol. 8, 1934, p. 34; Barlow, *Report*, 1939–40, IV, pp. 88–9. For the concentration of new industries in London, ibid., pp. 37–40; and Board of Trade's evidence, Barlow, *Minutes of Evidence*, BS/22/48, p. 50. See also note 16 below. The most recent study of women's work in this period is Miriam Glucksmann, 'In a class of their own', *Feminist Review*, no. 24, Autumn 1986, and *Women Assemble, Women Workers and the New Industries in Inter-War Britain*, Routledge, 1990.

15. Mrs Murphy (electrical engineering), p. 9; L. Van Duren (women's clothing), first interview, p. 19; Miss Tugwell (office), Women's Co-operative Guild interview, p. 6; Mrs Payne (leather), second interview, p. 1. In 1919 the War Cabinet Committee Report on *Women in Industry* found that women 'have habitually been paid at lower rates than men for equivalent work, on the pretence that women are a class apart, with no family obligations, smaller needs, less capacity, and a lower level of intelligence': 1919, vol. 31, p. 254.

16. Between 1932 and 1937 five-sixths of Great Britain's new factories were built in Greater London, and one-third of the extensions to existing ones. They were built on the outer ring of London, in the east, north-east, and west, where land, transport, and power were relatively cheap, and close to consumers and to supplies of unskilled and 'adaptable' labour, especially females and

juveniles. See, for instance, Barlow, *Report*, pp. 46, 88–9, 166–7. Employers' evidence to Barlow reiterated the search for flexible supplies of semi-skilled machine-minders and process workers, away from the organized labour of the north of England, and the preference for female and juvenile labour: Barlow, *Minutes of Evidence*, pp. 491–504, and memo from Nr Noel Hobbs, Chairman, Slough Estates Ltd, pp. 336–49.

In 1931 approximately 1.4 million women over 14 years were occupied in industry (compared with 1.1 million in 1921) in Greater London (and 2.7 million men out of a total population of 8.2 million). These included (to nearest thousand): 20,000 in chemicals, etc.; 64,000 in metals, jewellery, etc. (45,000 in 1921); 167,000 in clothing (137,000 in 1921); 67,000 in food, drink, tobacco; 59,000 in papermaking, stationery, etc.; 36,000 in other manufacturing industries; 263,000 in commerce and finance (213,000 in 1921); 98,000 in public administration and defence; 86,000 in professions (65,000 in 1921); 21,000 in entertainment and sport; 448,000 in personal service (334,000 in 1921): Census, *Industry Tables*, 1931, table C, p. 730.

17. I have interviewed twenty-one women, most more than once, and in five cases several times. I have drawn on interviews from other sources, oral histories, and autobiographies (of men as well as women). All my subjects except one were born in the first twenty years of this century, were brought up in London (except for the domestic servants, one of whom came from South Wales, the other from the Isle of Wight), and worked through the 1920s and 1930s, having left school at 14.

18. Rose Gamble, *Chelsea Child*, Aeriel Books, BBC, 1979, p. 122; the following pages are drawn from her autobiography.

19. Leonore Davidoff, 'Mastered for Life: servant and wife in Victorian and Edwardian England', in A. Sutcliffe, P. Thane (eds.), *Essays in Social History*, Oxford, 1986; and 'Class and gender in Victorian Society: the diaries of Arthur J. Munby and Hannah Cullwick', in J. L. Newton, M. Ryan, and J. Walkowitz (eds.), *Sex and Class in Women's History*, 1983, discuss these issues further.

20. Mrs Payne first interview, p. 1. In fact, people travelled long distances to work. Workers were bussed to new factories in the west from East London, for instance, in the 1930s: Barlow, *Minutes of Evidence*, p. 174.

21. Lily Van Duren, first interview, p. 3. Almost everyone I interviewed mentioned the reluctance of London girls to become domestic servants. They came from Wales, Scotland, the rural districts, and unemployed towns, I was told, and the girls were very homesick. 'I did my share of crying,' said Miss Sutton, WCG interview , p. 1. Homesickness becomes 'hysteria', said Ellen Wilkinson op. cit., p. 268. Munitions had led the exodus of girls in London away from service.

22. Jane Smith, second interview, p. 2.

23. Celia Wilmot, first interview, p. 11.

24. Formal apprenticeships for girls were non-existent. Dressmaking, millinery, tailoring, embroidery, and some large shops offered to pay girls a low wage while they 'learned' the trade: Ray Strachey, *Careers and Openings for Women*, Faber & Faber, 1935, pp. 98–9. She lists 150 technical schools for girls provided by the LCC, pp. 99–100. Dressmaking, for example, put girls

through a four-year 'learnership' in factory or workshop: *NSL*, vol. 2, p. 13. *NSL*, vol. 5, p. 15, adds bookbinding to the list above.

25. Lily Van Duren, first interview, pp. 2, 3, 7. In 1926 the factory inspectors found that most women learned their skill by watching: *Annual Report of the Chief Inspector of Factories and Workshops*, 1927, vol. 9, p. 63.
26. Jane Smith, first interview, pp. 9–15.
27. ibid., p. 15.
28. ibid., p. 15. (The Tailors and Garment Workers' Union absorbed the handicraft union, the Tailors and Tailoresses, in 1932.)
29. ibid., pp. 16, 19.
30. C. Wilmot, first interview, p. 23.
31. Mrs Payne, first interview, p. 1; Mrs Murphy pp. 6–7. Employers wanted their workers young; they were easier to train: S. R. Dennison, *The Location of Industry and the Depressed Areas*, Oxford University Press, 1939, p. 78.
32. May Jones, first interview, p. 3.
33. Jerry White argued in a recent seminar (June 1988) that women were the 'vectors of change' in London in the inter-war years; and see his *Campbell Bunk, the Worst Street in North London*, History Workshop Series, Routledge, Kegan Paul, 1986.
34. Mary Welch, leather worker, *Working Lives*, vol. 1, 1905–45, *A People's Autobiography of Hackney*, Centreprise, n.d., p. 52; May Jones, first interview, p. 3.
35. See note 11 above.
36. Barlow, *Minutes of Evidence*, Ministry of Labour memo, p. 322, stated that in central London employment exchanges (City, Gt Marlborough Street, and Westminster) there were 9.5 vacancies for each boy, and 33.3 for each girl.
37. R. Gamble, op. cit., pp. 186, 122.
38. ibid., p. 61.
39. Jeffrey Richards, *The Age of the Dream Palace*, Routledge, Kegan Paul, 1984, pp. 208–10, 224, 323–4, where he argues that English films of the 1930s perpetuate ruling-class hegemony and the political consensus and conservatism of that decade. Cynthia L. White, *Women's Magazines, 1693–1968*, Michael Joseph, 1970, ch. 8, traces the uneven relationship between class identities and aspirations, new affluence, and domestic consumerism.
40. Robert Murphy, 'Fantasy worlds: British cinema between the wars', *Screen*, vol. 26, no. 1, January–February 1985, pp. 10–20, points out that cinema needed its mass appeal to rake in the profits, so it combined with the plebeian entertainments of showmanship and variety in the 1930s to secure them. Interestingly, Elizabeth Bowen, in *The Death of the Heart* (1938), has her elegant, upper-middle-class hero and heroines transform into 'workers' when they visit the cinema in London in the 1930s, Penguin edn, 1984, p. 43.
41. For my understanding of fantasy, I draw on J. Laplanche and J. B. Pontalis, 'Fantasy and the origins of sexuality', *International Journal of Psycho-Analysis*, vol. 49, 1968, Part 1. See also Elizabeth Cowie, 'Fantasia', *m/f*, no. 9, 1984, pp. 71–104, for a reading of some of the connections between femininity, fantasy, and film.
42. May Jones, first interview, pp. 8, 13.
43. Margery Spring Rice, *Working Class Wives*, (1939), Virago edn 1981, ch. 5.
44. May Jones, first interview, p. 10.

45. R. Gamble, op. cit., p. 48; Beatrice Webb, *My Apprenticeship*, Longman, 1926, p. 43.

46. D. M. Bailey, op. cit., p. 18. See also Ellen Ross, ' "Fierce questions and taunts" ', in D. Feldman, G. Stedman Jones eds., *Metropolis: London*, Routledge, 1989, for violence within marriage in late-nineteenth-century London.

47. Mrs Murphy, first interview, p. 4. Frances Partridge, the daughter of an architect, discovered that one pair of shoes cost her 45s (£2.25) in 1918): *Memories*, Gollancz, 1981, p. 58.

48. May Jones, first interview, p. 61; C. L. White, op. cit., p. 114: only 20 per cent of women wore lipstick in 1930.

49. Vera Brittain, *Testament of Youth* (1933), Gollancz, 1948, p. 304.

50. Jane Smith, first interview, p. 19.

51. May Jones, second interview, p. 7; third interview, p. 5.

52. May Jones, second and third interviews, *passim*.

53. May Jones, first interview, p. 16; R. Gamble, op. cit., p. 11. For a woman waiting, see, for example, Doris Knight, *Millfields Memories*, Centreprise, 1976, p. 8.

54. May Jones, third interview, p. 3; Angela Rodaway, *A London Childhood* (1960), Virago, 1985, p. 52; Marie Carmichael Stopes, *Married Love, A New Contribution to the Solution of Sex Difficulties*, Puttnam's, 1918, broke the silence according to herself, and this is confirmed by Robert Roberts, *The Classic Slum: Salford Life in the First Quarter of the Century*, Penguin, 1973, pp. 231–2.

55. Jean Moremont, in Jean McCrindle and Sheila Rowbotham (eds.), *Dutiful Daughters*, Penguin, 1977, p. 149. Diana Gittins, *Fair Sex, Family Size and Structure, 1900–39*, Hutchinson, 1982, argues that women altered family size according to changing socio-economic circumstances, in particular their work outside the home and their degree of knowledge concerning sexuality and birth control; see esp. pp. 19, 25, chs. 5, 6. Eva M. Hubback, *The Population of Britain*, Penguin, 1947, ch. 4, argues that higher standard of living and aspiration reduced the birth rate.

56. Celia Wilmot, first interview, p. 22.

57. A. Rodaway, op. cit., p. 82; Margaret Cole, *Growing Up in a Revolution*, Longman, 1949, p. 22, one of the many who wanted to be a boy.

58. May Jones, second interview, p. 15. For women's cinema attendance, *NSL*, vol. 9, p. 40. Memoirs reveal that men too dressed up, but drink, gambling, boxing, and the possibility of sex with a woman rather than romance were their (sometimes transgressive) pleasures.

59. Violet Boulton, second interview, p. 10. Marie Lloyd sang about London, love, drink, and husbands and wives; she was like her audiences; for a description of her, Storm Jameson, *No Time Like the Present*, Cassell 1933, pp. 73–4. Jessie Matthews, the second most popular English music-hall star in the 1930s (Gracie Fields was the first) was also closer to London than Hollywood.

60. Ann Mitchell, in conversation; Celia Wilmot, fourth interview, p. 2.

61. Raphael Samuel (ed.), *East End Underworld: Chapters in the Life of Arthur Harding*, Routledge, Kegan Paul, History Workshop Series, 1981, p. 237.

62. May Jones, first interview, p. 8.

63. Celia Wilmot, first interview, p. 22.
64. George Orwell, *Road to Wigan Pier*, Gollancz, 1937, p. 90.
65. May Jones, first interview, p. 4; second interview, p. 15.
66. R. Gamble, op. cit., p. 33.

FEMINIST HISTORY AND PSYCHOANALYSIS

Thanks to Jacqueline Rose.

1. Michelene Wandor (ed.), *Once a Feminist, Stories of a Generation*, Virago, 1990.
2. Sheila Rowbotham, *Hidden from History*, Random House edn., 1973, p. xxx, 'we have to dig deeper than conscious systems of ideas. Our very sexual responses and ways of relating are not removed from society or history', for example.
3. Cora Kaplan, 'Wild Nights', *Sea-Changes, Culture and Feminism*, Verso, 1986.
4. Olwen Hufton and Joan Scott, 'Survey Articles Women in History: No. 1 Early Modern Europe'; 'No. 2 Women in History, The Modern Period', *Past and Present*, November, 1983. For an earlier generation of feminist history, Joan Thirsk's Foreword, in Mary Prior (ed.), *Women in English Society 1500–1800*, Methuen 1985. Jane Rendall, 'Women's History, Feminist History, Gender History in Britain', in Karen Offen, Jane Rendall and Ruth Roach Patterson (eds.), *Writing Women's History: International Perspectives*, Macmillan, 1991.
5. Sigmund Freud, Two Encyclopaedia Articles in James Strachey (ed.), *Psychoanalysis*, 1923, see *Standard Edition*, vol. XVIII, 1981, p. 235, and ibid., vol. II. pp. 21–47.
6. Jacqueline Rose, 'Femininity and its Discontents', *Sexuality in the Field of Vision*, Verso, 1986.
7. Juliet Mitchell, 'Introduction', in Juliet Mitchell and Jacqueline Rose (eds.), *Feminine Sexuality, Jacques Lacan and the Ecole Freudienne*, Macmillan, 1983.
8. For an English radical feminist history, see London Feminist History Group, *The Sexual Dynamics of History, Men's Power, Women's Resistance*, Pluto Press, 1983.
9. Jane Lewis, 'The Debate on Sex and Class', *New Left Review*, no. 149, January/February 1985.
10. C. Kaplan, 'Language and Gender' in op. cit.
11. Luisa Passerini, *Fascism in Popular Memory, The Cultural Experience of the Turin Working Class*, translated by Robert Lumley and Jude Bloomfield, Cambridge University Press, 1987; Sally Alexander, 'Women, Class and Sexual Difference, some reflections on the writing of a feminist history', *History Workshop Journal*, issue 17, Spring 1984 (above pp. 92–125.); Alex Owen, *The Darkened Room, Women, Power and Spiritualism in late Victorian England*, Virago, 1989.
12. Carolyn Steedman, *Landscape for a Good Woman, A Story of Two Lives*, Virago, 1986.
13. Peter Gay, *Freud, for Historians*, Oxford University Press, 1985; 'General Introduction', *The Bourgeois Experience, Victoria to Freud*, vol. 1, 'Education

of the Senses', Oxford University Press, Oxford and New York, 1984, p. 8. In this and vol. 2, 'The Tender Passion', Gay recovers Victorian bourgeois love and passion from contemporary prurience and condescension, and finds them to be less about hypocrisy and private perversion, than shaped by anxieties about change and innovation. See also Timothy Ashplant, 'Psychoanalysis and Historical Writing', *History Workshop Journal*, issue 26, Autumn 1988.

14. Maria-Antonetta Macciocchi, 'Female Sexuality in Fascist Ideology', *Feminist Review*, no. 1, 1979.

15. Claudia Koonz, *Mothers in the Fatherland, Women, the Family and Nazi Politics*, Methuen 1988, pp. 405, 413, xx.

16. Klaus Theweleit, *Male Fantasies*, 2 vols, Polity, Cambridge, 1987, 1989, see particularly 'Introduction', vol. 1, p. xvi.

17. Joan Wallach Scott, *Gender and the Politics of History*, Columbia University Press, 1988.

18. Denise Riley, *'Am I that name?'; Feminism and the Category of 'Women' in History*, Macmillan, 1988, p. 6. Mary Wollstonecraft, *A Vindication of the Rights of Woman* (1792), Everyman edn no. 825, 1965, p. 109.

19. The French historians, the Annales, in their first generation at least, were unrepentant about the omission of the unconscious. Michel de Certau, *The Writing of History*, Columbia University Press, New York, 1988, translated by Tom Conley, ch. 1, espouses a history that acknowledges the unconscious of myth, allegory and ritual.

20. Julia Kristeva, 'Women's Time', *Signs*, vol. 7, no. 1, Autumn 1981, translated by Alice Jardine and Harry Blake. Maxine Berg, 'Women's work, mechanisation and the early phases of industrialisation in England', in Patrick Joyce (ed.), *The Historical Meanings of Work*, Polity, Cambridge, 1987, employs circular and cyclical notion of time in her study of industrialization. See too, Tamara Harevan, *Family Time and Industrial Time*, Cambridge University Press, 1982.

MEMORY, GENERATION AND HISTORY

This essay is for Catherine Hall.

1. Jacqueline Rose, *The Haunting of Sylvia Plath*, Virago, 1991, p. 222. I had forgotten Rose's exact formulation which, in defending Plath's use of the holocaust, revisits the debates about the holocaust, guilt, silence and metaphor: 'What the poem ("Little Fugue") seems to narrate is at once the historical engendering of personal time and the psychic engendering of history.'

2. Joyce MacDougall, *Theatres of the Mind: Illusion and Truth on the Psychoanalytic Stage*, Free Association Books, 1986, pp. 12, 14, stresses the psychic recognition of generational difference; p. 20 the imprint of the several parents of each sex; p. 117 unconscious scenario of the oedipal couple and so on throughout.

3. Herbert Morrison, for example, son of a London policeman and one of the architects of municipal socialism in London, and Home Secretary in Clement Attlee's first government, mentions decency twice in two sentences and often throughout *An Autobiography*, Oldhams Press, 1960, p. 24. Morrison tells us

that all political parties have now accepted what the Labour Party first understood: 'the thoughtful, responsible attitude of the modern adult in the United Kingdom, irrespective of class, age or occupation', p. 244. But Robert Skidelsky, 'The Reception of the Keynesian Revolution', in Milo Keynes (ed.), *Essays on J. M. Keynes*, Cambridge University Press, 1975, pp. 89–107, refers to the politics of 'decency and consensus' developed by Baldwin and Macdonald in the 1920s in response to the imminence or possibility of revolution.

4. This is not strictly true. The first exception who comes to mind is George Orwell who reminded the English insistently through the 1930s and 1940s that their standard of living depended on the empire, that anti-semitism was rife in English life and letters, and that the English liberal intelligentsia were myopic and self-satisfied: 'Anti-Semitism in Britain' (1945), 'Wells, Hitler and the World State' (1941), *Collected Essays*, Mercury 1966, for example.

5. The phrase is borrowed from Geoffrey Nowell-Smith, 'On history and the cinema', *Screen*, vol. 31, no. 2, Summer 1990, p. 169, in which he talks about the unknown history of the cinema and outlines the historicity of modern subjectivities.

6. Some recent reworkings include: Terence Davies' film, *Distant Voices, Still Lives*, 1989; Stephen Humphrey's, BBC2 series *The Eighties*; Jean McCrindle and Sheila Rowbotham (eds.), *Dutiful Daughters*, Penguin, 1977. Generations are difficult to distinguish from each other if phantasy and identifications are the criteria.

7. William Beveridge, *Plan for Social Security*, 1942. Lord Beveridge, *Power and Influence, An Autobiography*, Hodder and Stoughton, 1953, ch. 14.

8. Adam Phillips, *Winnicott*, Fontana Modern Masters, 1988, p. 37, and Eric Raynor, *The Independent Mind In Psychoanalysis*, Free Association Books, 1990, p. 255. Denise Riley, *War in the Nursery*, Virago, 1984, ch. 4, for the popularization of Winnicott's thought and work in the 1940s and 1950s. Winnicott claimed in 1950 that from twenty-five years' practice he had about 20,000 case-histories: 'Some Thoughts on the Meaning of the Word Democracy', *Home is Where We Start From, Essays by a Psychoanalyst* (1950), compiled and edited by Clare Winnicott, Ray Shepherd, Madeleine Davis, Penguin, 1986, p. 247.

9. I'm compressing here of course; but read Paul Fussell, *The Great War and Modern Memory*, Oxford University Press, 1977, ch. 1 for both death and loss of innocence; Robert Wohl, *The Generation of 1914*, Weidenfeld & Nicholson, 1980, Virginia Woolf, *A Room of One's Own* (1928), Granada, 1984, p. 16.

10. Liz Heron (ed.), *Truth, Dare or Promise, Growing Up in the 1950s*, Virago, 1985.

11. Paul Foot and Nigel Fountain offer acerbic portraits of the reformers and revolutionaries respectively of the generation of 1956–68 in David Widgery (ed.), *The Left in Britain 1956–68*, Penguin, 1976, pp. 225–7, 421–3. Michelene Wandor (ed.), *Once a Feminist, Stories of a Generation*, Virago, 1990.

12. Charles Booth (ed.), *Life and Labour of the People of London*, 17 vols., 1902. Beatrice and Sidney Webb, *Industrial Democracy*, 1920 edn, Longman, pp. 766–84 for their discovery of the National Minimum. George Dangerfield,

The Strange Death of Liberal England (1935), Paladin, 1970, ch. 2. The Pilgrim Trust, *Men without Work, A Report made to the Pilgrim Trust*, Cambridge University Press, 1938. William H. B. Beveridge, *Pillars of Security*, Allen & Unwin, 1943. Paul Addison, *The Road to '45*, Quartet Books, 1977 ch. 5, for war radicalism. Jane Lewis, *The Politics of Motherhood, Child and Maternal Welfare in England 1900–1939*, Croom Helm, 1980. Richard and Kathleen Titmuss, *Parent's Revolt, A Study of the Declining Birth-Rate in Acquisitive Societies*, Secker and Warburg, 1942.

13. Jennie Lee, *My Life with Nye*, Penguin, 1980, p. 187 attributes the disagreement between Hugh Dalton and Nye Bevan in 1949, over the optimum number of lavatories in a council house, to their different class backgrounds.

14. Brian Harrison, *Prudent Revolutionaries, Portraits of British Feminists between the Wars*, Clarendon Press, Oxford, 1987, throughout.

15. ibid., p. 131. I am compressing complex processes in the formation of the citizen here. For an excellent account of Morrison's Strategy for Labour in London between the wars, and its victorious if brief achievement in 1945, Tom Jeffery, 'The Surburban Nation: Politics and Class in Lewisham', in D. Feldman, G. Stedman Jones (eds.), *Metropolis · London: Histories and Representations since 1800*, Routledge, 1989, pp. 189–216.

16. Alison Light, *Forever England, Femininity, Literature and Conservatism Between the Wars*, Routledge, 1991, and Carol Dyehouse, *Feminism and the Family in England, 1880–1939*, Basil Blackwell, 1989, offer respectively literary and feminist visions of the family and domestic life between the wars.

17. Neil Kinnock's Labour Party did some useful rethinking on family policy. For example Patricia Hewitt, *About Time, The Revolution in Work and Family Life*, Rivers Oram Press, 1993.

18. A. Light, op. cit., Introduction, pp. 14–19, imaginatively explores conservatism.

19. Raymond Williams elaborates this concept and its changing meanings in *Politics and Letters, Interviews with New Left Review*, NLB and Verso, 1979, pp. 158–74. What begins as a notion of something in excess of material life, which is expressed in conventions and forms, belongs to a generation and had a 'wider possession' than that of the writers whose work might reveal it, becomes, in his later thinking, the manifestation of disturbance, of whatever cannot be explained.

20. Carolyn Steedman, 'Raymond Williams and History', Raymond Williams' Memorial Lecture, Summer 1993.

21. See 'Women, Class and Sexual Difference', above pp. 97–125.

22. Cora Kaplan, 'Language and Patriarchy', *Sea-Changes, Culture and Feminism*, Verso, 1986, gives a valuable discussion of femininity and metonymy in women's poetry.

23. V. Woolf, op. cit., pp. 72–3.

24. Jessica Benjamin, 'The Omnipotent Mother: Phantasy and Reality'; Conference on Contemporary Psychoanalysis, Contemporary Sexualities, held at the Institute of Romance Studies, Senate House London, June 1993. See her *The Bonds of Love, Psychoanalysis, Feminism and the Problem of Domination*, Virago, 1990, ch. 1, for the mother/child relationship. Mary

Kelly, *Post-Partum Document*, RKP, 1983, is a unique visual and verbal exploration of the maternal relation.

25. Carolyn Steedman, *Landscape for a Good Woman, A Story of Two Lives*, Virago, 1986 has achieved this.

26. Alessandro Portelli, 'The Peculiarities of Oral History', *History Workshop Journal*, issue 12, pp. 96–107.

27. Karl Figlio, 'Oral History and the Unconscious', *History Workshop Journal*, issue 26, Autumn 1988, pp. 120–32.

28. Virginia Woolf, Introduction, in Margaret Llewelyn Davies (ed.), *Life as We Have Known It* (1931), Virago, 1977.

29. Lily Van Duren, second interview, 14 October 1980. I have used Lily's first name throughout because she is remembering herself as a child. For an interesting if slightly agonized discussion of the ethics (is the historian's use of testimony a form of dispossession?) and effects (will the interview be used to advance the academic's career, or challenge the cultural symbolic?) of life history and interview recording and use, Gillian Elinor, 'Stolen or Given: An Issue in Oral History', *Oral History*, vol. 20, no. 1, Spring 1992. Paul Thompson, 'Oral History and the Historian', *History Today*, June 1983, writes about the origins of all history in the oral tradition and the changing meanings of oral history and deals with some of its critics.

30. Immigrants often settled with or near relatives. About one half of the 120,000 East European Jews who came to Britain between 1880 and 1914 settled in London. Charles Booth described their presence in the East End in the 1880s as like the 'slow rising of a flood, family follows family, street after street is occupied', David Feldman, 'The Importance of being English, Jewish immigration and the decay of liberal England', in D. Feldman, G. Stedman Jones (eds.), op. cit. See also the importance of the extended family in migration patterns in Europe, Isabelle Bertaux-Wiame, 'The Life History Approach to the Study of Internal Migration', *Oral History*, vol. 7, no. 1, 1979, p. 29. Immigrants to London from other parts of the UK usually came in search of work, and settled near their work: John Marriott, *The Culture of Labourism, The East End Between the Wars*, Edinburgh University Press, 1991, p. 19.

31. Lily Van Duren, second interview, p. 1.

32. Jewish Women in London Group, *Generations of Memories, Voices of Jewish Women*, Women's Press, 1984, p. 10, remark on the way in which we tell and retell our life-stories to ourselves before we tell them to others.

33. ibid., Introduction. Ron Grele, 'Listen to Their Voices, Two Case studies in the Interpretation of Oral History Interviews', *Envelopes of Sound, The Art of Oral History* (1975) second edn, Precedent Publishing, Chicago, 1985, pp. 212–41, discusses the visions of history and myth in the life history.

34. Lily Van Duren, first interview, throughout.

35. Paul Willis, *Learning to Labour*, Saxon House Farnborough, 1977.

36. Luisa Passerini, *Fascism in Popular Memory, The Cultural Experience of the Turin Working Class*, translated by Robert Lumley and Jude Bloomfield, Cambridge University Press, 1987, ch. 1, pp. 21–2; see also what she says about laughter and violence p. 69.

37. Julia Kristeva, 'Women's Time', *Signs*, vol. 7, no. 1, Autumn 1981, translated

by Alice Jardine and Harry Blake, distinguishes between two concepts of time in Western modernism.

38. See 'Women's Voices from the Spanish Civil War', this vol. pp. 171–81.

39. See 'Becoming A Woman', this vol. pp. 203–7. *Left Review*, for instance, in its first issues encouraged working-class writing, but as Annabel Williams-Ellis put it in 'Not So Easy', *Left Review*, issue 1, October 1934, p. 40, it avoids words 'which have been dulled of sensation and provoke nausea, like home, flag, mother'.

40. Vera Brittain, *Women's Work in Modern England*, Noel Douglas, 1928, pp. 30–32, describes the need for training in domestic service, and the centres for housecraft which trained about 440,000 girls in the mid-1920s.

41. L. Smith, *New Survey of London Life and Labour*, P. S. King and Son, vol. 2, *Industry*, 1931, vol. 1, *Forty Years of Change*, 1930, chs. 4 and 5.

42. Sarah Boston, *Women Workers and the Trade Unions*, Davis-Poynter, 1980, ch. 6.

43. Jewish Women in London Group, op. cit., pp. 13–14; William Fishman, *East End Jewish Radicals*, Duckworth, 1975.

44. Lily Van Duren, first interview, pp. 16, 17.

45. Second Interview, p. 9.

46. Rose Lowe, *Liz, The Story of Two Girls Growing up in Hoxton Between the Wars*, Rose Lowe, 1982.

47. As I edit this for publication I am reading Lyndal Roper's exhilarating insistence on the body in history in her introduction to *Oedipus and the Devil, Witchcraft, Sexuality and Religion in Early Modern Europe*, Routledge, 1994.

48. Rose Lowe, op. cit., p. 12.

49. Isabelle Bertaux-Wiame, op. cit., p. 29.

50. Liz, op. cit., p. 12.

51. In a note 'The Psychogenesis of A Case of Homosexuality in a Woman', Freud, *Standard Edition*, vol. XXVIII, p. 162, reflects on the associations between death, pregnancy and birth conveyed by the words 'to fall' pregnant, Liz, op. cit., pp. 20, 25–6.

52. Ann Scott James, 'The Welfare State and Mothers', *Picture Post*, no. 13, 1943, urges for a drive against domestic drudgery and for economic and social provision for mothers, given the two million fewer children under fourteen years than during the First World War. Women must be encouraged to have children, she argued. The following month women wrote in explaining why they weren't. D. Riley, op. cit., puts this issue in context. Liz, op. cit., p. 34.

53. Rose Lowe, *Liz*, op. cit., p. 34.

54. I'm deliberately making an analogy between spirit possession and inherited memories.

55. The *New Survey of London Life and Labour* found that the percentage of the total population of the County of London born in London increased consistently between 1881 and 1921: from 63 per cent to 70 per cent. The percentage born in other parts of the United Kingdom decreased proportionally: from 34.4 per cent to 25 per cent. The percentage born abroad rose from 2.7 per cent to 4. 3 per cent peaking in 1911 at 4.7 per cent. The majority of the latter were Jews fleeing the pogroms (see note 30). L. Smith, op. cit., vol. 1, p. 68.

56. Brian Harrison notes the prominence of Jews in early twentieth-century British feminism, op. cit., pp. 274–5; their presence in Communism is well-known;

women's experience is subdued in the memory and history of Jewish radicalism however.

57. Margot Oxford (ed.), *Myself When Young*, Frederick Muller, Plymouth, 1938, p. 411.
58. Marie Carmichael Stopes, *Married Love, A New Contribution to the Solution of Sex Difficulties*, preface by Jessie Murray, London, Puttnam's (1918), 18th edn, 1926, the mysticism is in the combined alchemy of the soul and the body's chemistry. Leonore Eyles, *The Woman in the Little House*, Grant Richards, 1922, p. 15. The phrase 'woman's most important occupation' was feminist speech in among other organizations, the National Union for Equal Citizenship in the 1920s.
59. D. W. Winnicott, 'The Mother's Contribution to Society' (1957), in op. cit., pp. 123–7 and see also 'Some Thoughts on the Meaning of the Word Democracy' (1950), ibid., pp. 238–59.
60. John Maynard Keynes, *Essays in Persuasion*; Macmillan, 1931.

FEMINISM: HISTORY: REPETITION

1. 'Remembering, Repeating and Working-Through (Further Recommendations on the Technique of Psycho-analysis 11)' (1914) *Standard Edition*, vol. XII, pp. 145–56. This was a short talk given at the Institute of Contemporary Arts in May 1993, for a conference: History as Repetition, The History of Repetition – What's New?, convened by Homi K. Bhabha.
2. Freud, 'The Unconscious' (1915), *Standard Edition*, vol. XIV, p. 177, Freud asks whether there are unconscious instinctual impulses, emotions and feelings, and suggests that only the ideas attached to feelings can enter consciousness, otherwise we can know nothing of the instinctual drive or feeling. In 'Why War?', *Standard Edition*, vol. XXII, pp. 211, 212, he speaks about science as myth. For a historian's impatience with the myths of identity in politics, Eric Hobsbawm, 'The New Threat to History', *The New York Review of Books*, 16 December 1993, pp. 62–4.
3. The term New World Order was coined in the media to indicate the post-1989 fall of the Berlin Wall. I use it as unsatisfactory short-hand. The conflicts in Bosnia and the countries of former Yugoslavia have been described as repetitions of ancient ethnic rivalries in the daily news.
4. This phrase itself is a repetition: 'the God that Failed'; Gareth Stedman Jones, 'Faith in History', *History Workshop Journal*, issue 30, Autumn 1990, pp. 63–7, speaks about the faith at the basis of all belief.
5. Richard Rorty, *Contingency, Irony, and Solidarity*, Cambridge University Press, 1989, pp. 30–34.
6. Jacqueline Rose, *Why War, Psychoanalysis, Politics and the Return to Melanie Klein*, Blackwell, 1993, includes brilliant essays on, among other things, the location of violence.
7. Rosalind Delmar, for a discussion of the wider context, 'The Uses of Psychoanalysis in the Women's Liberation Movement' unpublished paper, 1992.
8. Adam Phillips, 'Psychoanalysis and Idolatry', *On Kissing, Tickling and Being Bored, Psychoanalytic Essays on the Unexamined Life*, Faber and Faber,

1993, p. 122, suggests, in a fascinating discussion of belief, that Freud's 'project was the destruction of idolatry'.

9. Mary Kelly, *The History Shrew*, Magazine of the London Women's Liberation Workshop, London, 1970.

10. F. Engels, *Origins of the Family, Private Property, and the State* (1888); Mary Wollstonecraft, *A Vindication of the Rights of Woman* (1792), Everyman edn no. 825, 1965. Julia Kristeva, 'Woman's Time', *Signs*, vol. 7, no. 1. Autumn 1981.

11. 'Heterosexual imperative' was a term coined by Rosalind Delmar in the mid-1970s. For Lenin on the woman question, Clara Zetkin, *Conversations with Lenin*, Lawrence and Wishart.

12. Barbara Taylor, *Eve and the New Jersualem*, Virago, 1983, ch. 8.

13. An oral history of the WLM in London was begun in the early 1980s, never finished and is held at the Feminist Library in London.

14. Beatrix Campbell, *The Independent*, 28 April 1993, 'The New World Order and Intimate Warfare', quoting David Owen and the UN representatives in Bosnia who found themselves unable to raise the question of the soldiers' rape of women 'What is there to be said?'

15. Laura Mulvey and Peter Wollen's *Riddles of the Sphinx*, 1976, The Other Cinema, for instance, asked whether a politics of the unconscious was possible. Julia Kristeva, insofar as she has intervened in feminist debate, implies such a politics, in, for example, op. cit.

16. K. Marx, the Eighteenth Brumaire of Louis Bonaparte, *Karl Marx and Frederick Engels, Selected Works*, vol. 1, Lawrence and Wishart, 1962, p. 247; Francis Fukuyama first published his essay *The End of History*, in the USA in 1989; for an interesting interrogation of this, Perry Anderson, 'The Ends of History', *A Zone of Engagement*, Verso, 1992.

Index